VEDIC METAPHYSICS

The Author
Jagadguru Śaṅkarācārya
Śrī Bhāratī Kṛṣṇa Tīrtha Mahārāja
(1884—1960)

Vedic Metaphysics

JAGADGURU ŚAṄKARĀCĀRYA

ŚRĪ ŚRĪ BHĀRATĪ KṚṢṆA TĪRTHAJĪ MAHĀRĀJA

MOTILAL BANARSIDASS PUBLISHERS
PRIVATE LIMITED • DELHI

Reprint: Delhi, 1983, 1999, 2008
First Edition: Delhi, 1978

ISBN: 978-81-208-1092-1

MOTILAL BANARSIDASS
41 U.A. Bungalow Road, Jawahar Nagar, Delhi 110 007
8 Mahalaxmi Chamber, 22 Bhulabhai Desai Road, Mumbai 400 026
236, 9th Main III Block, Jayanagar, Bangalore 560 011
203 Royapettah High Road, Mylapore, Chennai 600 004
Sanas Plaza, 1302 Baji Rao Road, Pune 411 002
8 Camac Street, Kolkata 700 017
Ashok Rajpath, Patna 800 004
Chowk, Varanasi 221 001

Printed in India
BY JAINENDRA PRAKASH JAIN AT SHRI JAINENDRA PRESS,
A-45 NARAINA, PHASE-I, NEW DELHI 110 028
AND PUBLISHED BY NARENDRA PRAKASH JAIN FOR
MOTILAL BANARSIDASS PUBLISHERS PRIVATE LIMITED,
BUNGALOW ROAD, DELHI 110 007

PREFACE

Knowledge of identity of the essence of man and the essence of universe, the nature and attributes of this Supreme Entity and the way to It's realisation constitutes by far the greatest discovery of mankind. The Vedas epitomize the highest expression of the body of knowledge that grew out of the vision and experience of this spiritual truth. Great souls from time to time have recaptured that supreme state of bliss, treading on the various paths indicated by the ancient sages and have reflected in turn the light of their experience for the benefit of mankind.

In the nature of things, however, this light is obfuscated in more or less measure in various times and climes due to the prevailing ignorance and impurities of the social psyche, though the vast span of the cosmic evolution appears to assist ultimately in its increasing manifestation. There is, however, no dispeller of darkness other than light and for all ills that beset mankind the spiritual values contain the best cure.

The advance of science and technology in recent times brought about a revolution in man's life and thought. For a spell it appeared as though it would bathe the mankind in elysian bliss and plenty. But, the dream did not come true. No doubt, the scientific and industrial revolution did multiply the material powers and possessions of the society as a whole but it also released in its wake too many cross-currents of cravings, strife, exploitation, misery and confounding and erosion of values. As a result, the humanity is divided today between a few people suffering from the ennui of affluence and the remaining vast majority suffering the pangs of destitution. The cycle of life has become too swift and complex. Man is whirled around by inner cravings and outer compulsions, scarcely aware of any sense of identity, belonging or purpose in life.

Democracy and socialism, humanism and communitarianism, self-actualization and synergy are all correctives to the state of chaos, conflict and distress, attempted by the modern mind in the various domains of life. Being based on concepts like freedom, dignity and development of man, love and harmony, in the ultimate analysis, they are only faint echoes of the eternal spiritual quest. The spiritual values hold, thus, the key to all means and measures calculated to achieve true and lasting peace, progress, prosperity and happiness for the individual as well as society.

On the consummation of spiritual sādhanā 'all else will be added unto you' is inspiring enough. But, what is more, even the smallest sincere endeavour in this direction has the strange alchemy of bringing forth instantaneously immense benefic mutations in the relationships of man with himself, man with the world around, and man with the Divinity. The techniques of spiritual unfolding propounded by the Vedānta — the crest of the Vedic knowledge — bring about an integration and efflorescence of the human personality most conducive to releasing puissant forces of creativity, synthesis, peace, harmony and bliss.

Vedic metaphysics is, therefore, a treasure of eternal relevance — all the more useful to the contemporary society. And who could unravel its mysteries to the modern mind better than Jagadguru Shankaracharya Shri Bharati Krishna Tirtha delivering lectures in America? The Jagadguru commanded the rare combination of ancient spiritual wisdom and latest scientific thought. Not only had he mastered the entire Vedic lore, he was an M.A. in eight modern subjects and spoke fluently about a dozen languages (including several foreign ones). Neither was he content with mere intellectual cogitations. He had undergone a profound and rigorous sādhanā culminating in direct spiritual realisation.

The lectures reproduced in this book contain the mellowed fruits of the Jagadguru's ripe wisdom delivered almost at the close of his earthly sojourn and they were addressed to groups that can be easily taken as representative of the most advanced modern society. Expounding though the loftiest secrets, they are couched in a language so simple and lucid as to be easily comperhensible to even the totally uninitiated.

Here is, therefore, the spiritual elixir in its pristine purity and yet with the freshest aroma. Those who chance upon it are fortunate; those who receive it with faith and reverence will be blessed, and those who drink it deep will be freed.

S. I. Tripathi
Organising Secretary,
Shree Vishwa Punarnirmana Sangha

January, 1978

CONTENTS

Shri Daya Mata
President, Yogoda Satsanga Society of India
(Self-Realization Fellowship)

THE WORLD PEACE MISSION OF HIS HOLINESS ŚRĪ JAGADGURU ŚAṄKARĀCĀRYA BHĀRATĪ KṚṢṆA TĪRTHA OF GOVARDHANA MATH, PURI, INDIA

by

Sri Sri Daya Mata

President, Self-Realization Fellowship, Los Angeles

It has been said that man cannot fully understand the principles of truth expressed in the scriptures until he sees them manifested in the life of an enlightened teacher. Such a teacher was His Holiness, Śrī Jagadguru Śaṅkarācārya of Puri.

His Holiness, the late Jagadguru ("World Teacher") Śrī Śaṅkarācārya Bhāratī Kṛṣṇa Tīrtha was the ecclesiastical head of the Govardhana Monastery in Puri and was the apostolic successor of the first Śaṅkarācārya (ninth century; India's greatest Philosopher).

His Holiness was founder-president of the World Reconstruction Association (Vishwa Punarnirmana Sangha), Nagpur, whose aim is the furtherance of world peace and universal brotherhood, an ideal dear to the heart of my own Guru, Sri Sri Paramahansa Yogananda. When His Holiness, the Jagadguru arrived at our International Headquarters in Los Angeles, California in 1958, it was with a special sense of awe and respect that I greeted him. For he was 82 years of age, and he was a living example of the highest principles taught in the scriptures of India.

It was the first time in the history of the thousand-year old monastic Śaṅkarācārya Order that one of its leaders had visited the West. His Holiness was a saintly personage of vast learning, and a gifted speaker. He was also an outstanding mathematician.

As a sage, His Holiness felt profoundly that a great spiritual awakening is vital and urgent in order to preserve world peace. By "spiritual awakening", the Śaṅkarācārya meant the

Self-realization of every human being, each according to his chosen path or religion.

Self-Realization Fellowship (Yogoda Satsanga Society of India) was chosen by His Holiness as his official sponsor in the United States. An itinerary was drawn up, and His Holiness delivered addresses at many universities, several of which bestowed on him honorary doctorate degrees. He travelled from coast to coast to speak at centers of learning in America, among them the University of California, Stanford University, California Institute of Technology, Washington and Lee University, Rutgers University, and the United States Naval Academy. The Jagadguru also spoke on radio and television programs, and before numerous religious, cultural, and educational groups. He had received 150 invitations to speak, and in the relatively brief span of his visit, this frail-bodied, yet spiritually vital soul, fulfilled more than fifty engagements. Millions heard his talks on radio and television. Always his speech centered on Truth; on the Goal of life, and the furtherance of world peace and universal brotherhood.

The Jagadguru's activities were widely reported by the press. *Newsweek* wrote in April 1958 : "Last week, His Holiness had just arrived in New York on the second leg of his three-month lecture tour of the U.S., which began in February. He started in Los Angeles at the headquarters of his sponsor, Self-Realization Fellowship, a society that professes a combination of Eastern and Western thought. Moving East, the Jagadguru has so far made 36 public appearances. Perhaps the most spectacular occurred at Washington and Lee University, Lexington, Virginia, where he engaged in debate on religion and peace with the distinguished historian, Arnold Toynbee . . . the non-violent Hindu insisted that peace with honor was something worth fighting for.

"As he sat erect in his wing chair, the Holy Man spoke about tenets of the Śaṅkarācārya Order (his vows forbid him to talk about himself): 'We believe in the oneness and solidarity of the whole universe.' What about the conflict of religious ideas ? 'The principles and ideas of all religions are the same. Historical accidents have produced differences in attitudes and superficial beliefs; that is all."

It was with a sad heart that I bade farewell to His Holiness. However, it was not long before I found myself in his presence again, this time in India. It was in May of 1959 in Calcutta. During this period he came to our Yogoda Math and Yogoda Ashram in Dakshineswar and in Baranagar. We had many interesting discussions, but what was most enjoyable was just sitting quietly in his presence.

From His Holiness emanated the peace of a man of God. He exemplified the virtues written about in the great scriptures of East and West. He was truly a universal man. Yet, he was humble; the words of Sri Sri Paramahansa Yogananda better describe what I felt about the Jagadguru : "Humbleness is a fertile valley of consciousness where the rain of God's wisdom falls fruitfully. Humbleness is a manifestation of an understanding heart and sets an example of greatness for others to follow."

MY BELOVED GURUDEVA

Very few persons can there be amongst the cultured people of India who have not heard about His Holiness Jagadguru Śaṅkarācārya Śrī Bhāratī Kṛṣṇa Tīrthajī Mahārāj, the magnificent and divine personality that gracefully adorned the famous Govardhan Mutt, Puri, his vast and versatile learning, his spiritual and educational attainments, his wonderful research achievements in the field of Vedic Mathematics and his consecration of all these qualifications towards the service of humanity as such.

Birth

His Holiness, better known among his disciples by the beloved name 'Jagadguruji', 'Gurudeva' or simply 'Guruji' was born of highly learned and pious parents in March, 1884. His father, late Shri P. Narasinha Shastri, was then a Tahsildar at Tinnevelly, (now Tirunelveli in the state of Tamilnadu, India) who later retired as a Deputy Collector. His uncle, late Shri Chandrashekhara Shastri, was the Principal of the Maharaja's College, Vizianagaram and his great-grand-father Shri C. Ranganatha Shastri was a judge of the Madras High Court.

Early days

Guruji, known as Venkatramana in his pre-sanyas days, was an exceptionally brilliant student and invariably won the first place in all the subjects in all the classes throughout his educational career. During his school days, he was a student of National College, Tiruchirapalli, Church Missionary Society College, Tirunelveli and Hindu College, Tirunelveli. He passed his Matriculation examination from the Madras University in January, 1899 topping the list as usual.

He was extraordinarily proficient in Sanskrit and oratory and on account of this he was awarded the title of 'Saraswati' by the Madras Sanskrit Association in July 1899, when he was still in his 16th year. At this stage a profound impression was left on him by his Sanskrit Guru, Shri Vedam Venkataraya

Shastri, whom Guruji always remembered with deepest love, reverence and gratitude, with tears in his eyes.

After winning the highest place in the B.A. examination, Shri Venkatramana Saraswati appeared for the M.A. examination of American College of Sciences, Rochester, New York from Bombay centre in 1903; and in 1904 at the age of twenty passed the M.A. examination in further subjects simultaneously securing the highest honours in all, which is perhaps an all-world record of academic brilliance. His subjects included Sanskrit, Philosophy, English, Mathematics, History and Science.

As a student, Venkatramana was marked for his splendid brilliance, superb retentive memory and ever-insatiable curiosity. He would deluge his teachers with myriads of piercing questions which made them uneasy and forced them frequently to make a frank confession of ignorance on their part. In this respect, he was considered to be a terribly mischievous student.

Even in his university days Venkatramana Saraswati had started contributing learned articles on Religion, Philosophy, Sociology, History, Politics, Literature, etc., to W.T. Stead's "Review of Reviews" and later also worked as its Indian representative. He was specially interested in all the branches of modern Science. In fact, study of the latest researches and discoveries in modern Science continued to be Guruji's hobby till his very last days.

Participation in National Movement

Venkatramana Saraswati started his public life under the guidance of Gopal Krishna Gokhle in 1905 in connection with the National Education Movement and the South African Indian issue. He had acquired an endless fund of learning and his desire to learn ever more was still unquenchable and, the urge for selfless service of humanity swayed his heart. Yet the deepest attraction that Venkatramana Saraswati felt was towards the study and practice of that science of sciences — the holy and ancient Indian spiritual science of Adhyātma Vidyā. In 1908, therefore he proceeded to the Śṛṅgeri Maṭh in Mysore to lay himself at the feet of the renowned Jagadguru

Śaṅkarācārya Śrī Saccidānanda Śivābhinava Nṛsimha Bhāratī Swāmī.

But he had not stayed there long, before he had to assume the post of the first Principal of the newly started National College at Rajamundry under a pressing call of duty from the nationalist leaders. Prof. Venkatramana Saraswati continued there for three years, but in 1911 he could not resist his burning desire for spiritual knowledge, practice and attainment and, therefore, tearing himself off suddenly from the said college he went back to Śrī Saccidānanda Śivābhinava Nrsimha Bhāratī Swāmī at Śṛṅgerī.

Sādhanā at Śṛṅgerī

The next eight years he spent in the profoundest study of the most advanced Vedānta Philosophy and practice of Brahma Sādhanā. During these days Prof. Venkatramana used to study Vedānta at the feet of Śrī Śivābhinava Nṛsimha Bhāratī Swāmī, teach Sanskrit and Philosophy in schools there, and practise the highest and most vigorous Yoga Sādhanā in the nearby forests. In the solitude of the forests of Śṛṅgerī, Guruji discovered the hidden meaning of the Gaṇita-sūtras, a Pariśiṣṭa of Atharvaveda. Occasionally, he was also invited by several institutions to deliver lectures on Philosophy. For example, he delivered a series of sixteen lectures on Śaṅkarācārya's Philosophy at Shankara Institute of Philosophy at Amalner and similar lectures at several other places like Poona, Bombay etc.

Sanyāsa

After several years of the most advanced studies, deepest meditation and the highest spiritual attainment, Prof. Venkatramana Saraswati was initiated into the holy order of Sanyāsa at Banaras (Varanasi) by His Holiness Jagadguru Śaṅkarācārya Śrī Trivikrama Tīrthajī Mahārāj of Śāradāpītha on the 14th July 1919 and on this occasion he was given the new name, Swāmī Bhāratī Kṛṣṇa Tīrtha.

This was the starting point of an effulgent manifestation of Swāmiji's real greatness. Immediately after initiation into sanyās, Guruji started touring India from corner to corner and delivering lectures on Sanātana Dharma and by his scintillating intellectual brilliance, powerful oratory, magnetic personality, sincerity of purpose, purity of thought, and loftiness of character he took the entire intellectual and religious class of the nation by storm. Within two years of his initiation into the holy order, he was, owing to his unique suitability, picked up for being installed as Śaṅkarācārya on the pontifical throne of Śāradāpītha, Dwāraka and accordingly on 27th Feb. 1921, he was so installed with all the formal ceremonies despite all his reluctance and even active resistance.

Participation in Congress movement and Khilāfat Conference

Even as a sanyāsī, Guruji continued to participate in the national movement. He attended the Nagpur Session of the Congress in 1920 and took active part in its deliberations. He also attended the meetings of the All India Muslim League, and the All India Khilāfat Conference. Very few people perhaps know, that Guruji was prosecuted along with Ali Brothers for taking part in the Khilāfat movement. How much was Guruji respected by the leaders of the Khilāfat movement can be judged from the fact that at the trial when the British Magistrate did not offer a seat to Guruji, the Ali Brothers spread their gowns for him to sit on.

Politics and Dharma

Guruji was also prosecuted and actually sentenced to one year's rigorous imprisonment for preaching 'sedition' against the British Raj by the Distt. Magistrate of Monghyr. Answering the charges in that trial Guruji said, "According to all religions, 'Dharma' is as illimitable in its jurisdiction as the Lord Almighty Himself. Or, in other words it pervades and permeates every activity and department of life from our birth to our death. Thus politics too comes under the 'Raja Dharma' portion of the religious literature of all religions .... And as the Jagadguru i.e. as the Ecclesiastical Head of Sacerdotal Hinduism, we have necessarily to expound Dharma in all its manifold and multifarious aspects and ramifications, to the fervent seekers after Truth and lovers of Dharma; and we have no choice left to us at all in the matter."

Religious basis of Hindu-Muslim Unity

According to Guruji there is nothing inherent in Hinduism or Islam which would tend to militate against Hindu-Muslim unity of a permanent character. In Guruji's view "a correct knowledge of and faithful adhesion to one's own religion, hand in hand with the rendering of sympathetic assistance to people of other faiths in similar studies of and fidelity to their own Dharma, is all that is necessary", for the undisturbed continuance of Hindu-Muslim unity. Such a unity "does not mean a relaxation on either part towards his own faith". Guruji says, "Just as we would condemn a Brahmin for indifference towards his Sandhyā-vandana etc., so too do we forbid a Muslim from being lax or indifferent towards the performance of his 'Namāz'. Unswerving allegiance to one's own Dharma plus cordial cooperation with others in the performance of their 'Dharma', is the secret of unity underlying diversity, which alone, we with our doctrine of 'Swadharma' for all, can possibly approve of and which alone can, in addition, help us to speedily attain Swaraj and worldly prosperity" (From an interview taken at the time of Khilāfat movement).

Jagadguru Śaṅkarācārya Śrī Madhusūdana Ṭīrtha of Govardhan Maṭh, Puri, was greatly impressed by Guruji and when the former was in failing health he requested Guruji to succeed him on the Govardhana Math gaddī. Guruji continued to resist his importunate requests for a long time; but, at last, when Śrī Madhusūdana Tīrtha's health took a serious turn in 1925, he virtually forced Guruji to accept the Govardhana Maṭh gaddī. Accordingly Guruji installed Śrī Swarūpānandajī on the Śāradāpītha gaddī and himself assumed the duties of the ecclesiastical and pontifical head of Govardhana Maṭh, Puri.

In the capacity of Jagadguru Śaṅkarācārya of Govardhana Maṭh, Puri, he continued to disseminate the holy spiritual teachings of Sanātana Dharma in their pristine purity all over the world the rest of his life for 35 years. Month after month and year after year he spent in teaching and preaching, talking and lecturing, discussing and convincing millions of people all over the country. He took upon himself the colossal task of the renaissance of Indian culture, spread of Sanātana Dharma, revival of the highest human and moral values and enkindling of the loftiest spiritual enlightenment throughout the world and he dedicated his whole life to this lofty and noble mission.

From his very early days Guruji was aware of the need for the right interpretation of Dharma which he defined as "the sum total of all the means necessary for speedily making and permanently keeping all the people individually as well as collectively, superlatively. comfortable, prosperous, happy and joyous in all respects (including the physical, mental, intellectual, educational, economic, social, political, psychic, spiritual, etc., *ad infinitum*)". He was painfully aware of the escapism, of some from their duties under the garb of spirituality, and of the superficial modern educational varnish of the others, divorced from spiritual and moral standards. He therefore always laid great emphasis on the necessity of harmonising the 'spiritual' and the 'material' spheres of daily life. He also wanted to remove the false ideas, on the one hand, of those persons who thought that Dharma could be practised by exclusively individual spiritual Sādhanā coupled with mere honest bread-earning ignoring one's responsibility for rendering selfless service to society and, on the other hand, of those who thought that the Sādhanā could be complete by mere service of society even without learning or practising any spirituality oneself. He wanted a happy blending of both. He stood for the omnilateral and all-round progress simultaneously of both the individual and the society towards the speedy realisation of India's spiritual and cultural ideal — the lofty Vedāntic ideal of Pūrṇa (Perfection and Harmony all-round).

World Reconstruction Association

With these ideas agitating his mind for several decades he continued to carry on a laborious, elaborate, patient research, day and night, to evolve finally a splendid and perfect scheme for all-round reconstruction of first India and through it of the world. At this juncture, the great Yogi Saint, Śrī Aurobindo Ghosh, expressed his last wishes to Guruji to take over and shoulder the sacred but onerous responsibility of giving the spiritual-cum-nationalistic-cum-humanitarian lead to all the sincere Sādhakas seeking this path of Service. Urged by Śrī Aurobindo's wishes and requests of several other persons,

Guruji founded in 1953 at Nagpur an institution named Shri Vishwa Punarnirmana Sangha (World Reconstruction Association). The Administrative Board of the Sangha consisted of Guruji's disciples, devotees and admirers of his idealistic and spiritual ideas for humanitarian service, and included a number of High Court Judges, ministers, educationists, statesmen and other personages of the highest calibre in Indian public life. It was, however, after a long and incessant search that Guruji had found his General Secretary, Shri Chimanlal Trivedi, whom he called his Scipio Africanus, and who truly thought, worked, planned and dreamt unceasingly for the Sangha's welfare and progress. Although the Sangha could not function very effectively in the beginning on account of Guruji's failing health, various preoccupations and other unforeseen hurdles, after a few years it started disseminating Guruji's message and teachings, with Sri B. P. Sinha, the ex-Chief Justice of India, as its President, and Dr. C. D. Deshmukh, I.C.S., the ex-Finance Minister of India and ex-Chairman of the University Grants Commission, as its Vice-President.

American tour

With a view to promoting the cause of world peace and spreading the lofty Vedantic spiritual ideals even outside India, Guruji went on a tour to America in February, 1958, the first tour outside India by a Śaṅkarācārya in the history of the Order. The tour was sponsored by Self-Realisation Fellowship of Los Angeles, the Vedantic Society founded by Paramahamsa Yoganandaji in America. Guruji stayed there for about three months and during this period addressed rapt audiences in Colleges, Universities, Churches and other public institutions. He was also invited to give talks and mathematics demonstrations on television. In fact, he released an exceptionally powerful current of moral and spiritual enlightenment, peace and harmony throughout America during his tour which proved a phenomenal success comparable perhaps with that of Swami Vivekananda only. A request was also received by him from Dr. Hornaday, the Minister for Church of Religious Science, to open a Branch of Sri Vishwa Punarnirmana Sangha in America with a view to establishing one religion all over the world. This could not materialise at that time for certain reasons. On his way back Guruji gave some lectures in U.K. also and returned to India in May, 1958.

Mahāsamādhi

Guruji had been undergoing a terrific strain for more than five decades in devoting his body, mind, heart and soul to the cause of service to humanity, spread of spiritual enlightenment and revival of Vedantic ideals. This had already undermined his health, but still, Guruji never devoted any attention to his personal comforts. The excessive strain of the vast hurricane tour abroad affected his health severely, but he refused to take rest and incessantly continued to pursue his studies, talks, lectures and writings with unabated and youth-like vigour and enthusiasm. In fact it required great vigilance and heroic effort to prevent him from giving darśan, advice and talks to his devotees and disciples even when he could hardly speak on account of strain. As a result he fell seriously ill in November 1959 and, despite the best available treatment, shed off his mortal frame and attained Mahāsamādhi at Bombay on February 2nd 1960.

His greatness

From the very day of his assuming the throne of Jagadguru Śaṅkarācārya, Śrī Bhāratī Kṛṣṇa Tīrthajī had become the cynosure of all eyes. His winning personality, his charming innocence, his eager thirst for knowledge, his religious zeal, his earnest belief in the Shastras, his universal kindness, his retentive memory, all these attracted every living soul that came in contact with him. People flocked to him in crowds and waited at his doors for hours together just to get a glimpse of that divine countenance. It was nothing but the marvellous superhuman milk of kindness that flowed from his heart.

He was always perfectly impartial. Every one was equal in his eyes. He cared not for riches. He cared not for position. Nothing but Bhakti could attract people to him; rich or poor, high or low, everybody had to go through the portals of Bhakti to approach his august presence. Exhibiting his divinity, he loved as himself everyone that came to him. Every one who had even two minutes conversation with him went out with the full conviction that he was the object of some special love of His Holiness.

Of such a divine personality, it is impossible to draw a sketch. His activities were many-sided. To hear him was a pleasure. To see him was a privilege. To speak to him was a real blessing and to be granted a special interview — ah! that was the acme of happiness which the people coveted most in all earnestness. The magnetic force of his wonderful personality was such that one word, one smile, or even one look was quite enough to convert even the unrelenting sceptic into his most ardent and obedient disciple. He belonged to all, irrespective of caste or creed, and he was a real Jagadguru, a Guru to the whole world.

People of all nationalities, religions and climes, Brahmins and non-Brahmins, Hindus and Mohammedans, Parsis and Christians, Europeans and Americans, received equal treatment at the hands of His Holiness. That was the secret of the immense popularity of this great Mahātmā.

He was grand in his simplicity. People would give anything and everything to get his blessings and he would talk words of wisdom freely without fear or favour. He was most easily accessible to all. Thousands of people visited him and prayed for the relief of their miseries. He had a kind word to say to each, after attentively listening to his or her tale of woe, and then gave them some 'prasāda' which would cure their malady whether physical or mental. He would actually shed tears when he found people suffering and would pray to God to relieve their suffering.

He was mighty in his learning and voracious in his reading. A sharp intellect, a retentive memory and a keen zest went to mark him as the most distinguished scholar of his day. His leisure moments he would never spend in vain. He was always reading something or repeating some thing. There was no branch of knowledge which he did not know and that also 'shastraically'. He was equally learned in Chandasśāstra, Āyurveda and Jyotiṣa Śāstra. He was a poet of uncommon merit and wrote a number of poems in Sanskrit in praise of his Guru, gods and goddesses, with the charming flow of Bhakti so conspicuous in all his writings.

Above all, his Bhakti towards his Vidyā Guru was something beyond description. He would talk for days together about the greatness of his Vidyā Guru. He would be never tired of worshipping the Guru. His Guru also was equally attached to him and called our Swamiji as the son of the Goddess of Learning Herself, Śrī Śāradā. Every day he would first worship his Guru's sandals. His *Gurupādukā Stotra* clearly indicates the qualities he attributed to the sandals of his Guru.

Śrī Bhāratī Kṛṣṇa Tīrtha was a great Yogī and a Siddha of a very high order. Nothing was impossible for him. Above all he was a true Sanyāsin. He held the world but as a stage where every one had to play a part. In short, he was undoubtedly a very great Mahātmā but without any display of mysteries or occultism.

I have not been able to express here even one millionth part of what I feel and what he was. His spotless holiness, his deep piety, his endless wisdom, his child-like peacefulness, sportiveness and innocence, and his universal affection beggar all description. His Holiness has left us a noble example of simplest living and highest thinking. May all the world benefit by the example of a life, so nobly and so simply, so spiritually and so lovingly lived.

The humblest of his disciples,
MANJULA DEVI
Hon. General Secretary,
Sri Vishwa Punarnirmana Sangha.

NAGPUR

EXTRACT FROM SRF CENTER'S BULLETIN
No 23, Feb.-Apr. 1958

Dear Ones :

As most of you know, His Holiness Sri Jagadguru Śaṅkarācārya of Puri, India, has come to America to lecture at a number of universities and churches in this country. His topics include practical means for attaining world peace, and the essential unity of all religions. His tour is being sponsored by Self-Realization Fellowship. As seniormost leader of the 1,000-year-old monastic Order of Swamis, His Holiness is recognized by countless Hindus as the spiritual head of Hindu India. It is a blessing for the entire West that he has come to this part of the world.

Śrī Śaṅkarācārya might take exception to the statement that he has come to the West at all. When asked recently whether there was any possibility for East and West working harmoniously together, he replied : "'East' and 'West' are artificial conceptions." East is only east of whatever happens to be west of it. The world is globular. It cannot be divided, as it seemed to be when men thought of it as flat, into areas of east and west." To His Holiness, as to our own great Guru and to all other true saints, man's race, nationality, and religion are superficial and are not indicative of his true Self. Essentially all men are brothers under God — nay, more, we are all one for we are but manifestations of the one infinite Life and Consciousness.

His Holiness has addressed numerous gatherings in California, many of them overflow audiences. Listeners have been deeply inspired by his talks which have pleaded for greater international understanding and co-operation.

Śrī Śaṅkarācārya has declared that through years of study he has found literally thousands of passages where the Hindu scriptures and the Bible are in complete agreement with one another not only in fundamental issues but also in details. He hopes for the day when a deeper understanding will dissolve the false barriers of apparent differences between the various religions. The alternative to a sincere and wide-spread effort toward religious understanding, he says, is race extinction through ever-increasingly violent warfare.

While in Southern California, His Holiness is staying at the SRF Mother Center in Los Angeles. He will begin his trip East around mid-March. Details of his visit here and elsewhere will appear in March-April issue of *Self-Realization Magazine*.

THE PRESENT WORK

This book is a compilation of some of the lectures on Vedānta and allied topics, delivered by His Holiness late Śrī Jagadguru Śaṅkarācārya Swamī Śrī Bhāratī Kṛṣṇa Tīrthajī Mahārāja during his tour of the United States of America. As mentioned in the life sketch titled "My Beloved Gurudeva", Guruji (as His Holiness was lovingly known among his disciples and admirers) visited U.S.A. in 1958 at the invitation of Self Realization Fellowship, a society founded by Sri Sri Paramahansa Yogananda. He arrived in New York on February 4th accompanied by Shri C. M. Trivedi and his wife Shrimati Manjula Devi Trivedi who acted as Guruji's aides-de-camp. Guruji proceeded to the West Coast the same day arriving at the International Airport, Los Angeles at 10-17 a.m. He visited Los Angeles, San Fransisco, San Deigo and other nearby places and delivered lectures on various subjects but his main theme was world peace and the basic unity of all religions. He also gave enlightening discourses on spiritual inquiry, Vedānta and the three well known paths of God realization viz. Karma, Jñāna and Bhakti. Guruji received invitations and had planned to deliver lectures at Universities and Colleges all over U.S.A., but owing to certain unavoidable circumstances, most of the engagements had to be cancelled. Guruji left west coast on 22nd March for Washington D.C. On the east coast, Guruji delivered lectures at various Universities and institutions in Lexington, New Brunswick, Annapolis, New York and other places. He left U.S.A. on April 29, 1958 for India. Details of his lecture tour are given separately in Appendix II.

Transcripts of some of the lectures delivered by Guruji in America were received by the kind courtesy of the Self-Realization Fellowship of Los Angeles. The transcripts contained gaps in places where Guruji quoted any Sanskrit text. These quotations have been supplied keeping in view the context and the meaning of the quotation explained in the lecture. Misquotations, if any, should not be attributed to Guruji.

Those who have read other writings of Guruji would no doubt, recognize in these lectures his characteristic style and diction, which fact speaks volumes for the accuracy of transcription by the workers of the Self Realization Fellowship who painstakingly transcribed the lectures from tape recordings and shorthand notes. We express our heartfelt gratitude towards Sri Sri Daya Mata, the President of the S.R.F. and her devoted followers but for whose courtesy and kindness it would not have been possible to publish these lectures in India. We would be failing in our duty if we do not record our indebtedness to late Sri Chimanlal Maniklal Trivedi, the former general secretary of Shree Vishwa Punarnirmana Sangha, who persuaded Guruji to undertake the tour and single-handed made all the arrangements attending to the minutest detail of the tour. To him goes primarily the credit for affording us an opportunity of placing before the readers Guruji's ideas on world problems and his marvellous exposition of Advaita Vedānta in a simple language every one can understand.

World Peace

The lectures contain a fervent plea for world peace and unity of all people. Guruji is of the view that all religions are, in essence, the same, the differences being attributable to the needs of the communities among whom the religions were propounded by Masters. He concedes that people are bound to differ, but reminds us that difference in stand-points is no reason for picking up quarrels. The right way, according to Guruji is to consider matters from the standpoint of cool, calm, and dispassionate judgment without prejudices and prepossessions and with the sole purpose of discovering the truth and acting upto it. Analysing the broad historical trends in the lecture entitled 'World Peace', Guruji divides history into two periods; one during which the conflicts were based on differences in religious beliefs and the second, the modern period, in which the socio-economic concepts predominate. Whatever may be the genesis of the conflict, Guruji decries war as a means to solve it. War, says Guruji, never benefits anybody, not even the warmongers responsible for starting it. Guruji wants that all disputes should be solved by discussion between the disputants. But he does not advocate surrender on matters of principle. He does not advocate peace at any price. Human dignity, honour, truth and welfare of mankind cannot be sacrificed for securing peace. But Guruji has immense faith in the human nature and believes that given a sincere effort, all problems can be solved without recourse to war.

Spiritual Inquiry

Guruji considers intellectual freedom, and not unquestioning blind faith, as the starting point of spiritual quest. The Bṛhadāraṇyaka Upaniṣad gives the essential steps in a spiritual inquiry in these words "ātmā vā are draṣṭavyo śrotavyo mantavyo nididhyāsitavyaḥ" which Guruji in his lecture entitled "Spiritual Inquiry" puts in modern terms as (i) investigating carefully (ii) deciding correctly and then (iii) following faithfully. These steps are necessary for the intellectual satisfaction without which there can be no self-realization. In the course of the spiritual inquiry, a stage of absolute agnosticism or positive atheism may come, but Guruji says that if the inquiry is pursued further the inquirer will come back to theism of a much stronger kind, an unshakable faith in God, which Carlyle calls the "Everlasting Yea". Guruji supports his views from the Bible which also speaks of "faith born of understanding". But "realization of truth" is qualitatively a totally different thing from indirect intellectual conviction. Drawing his support from the Gītā, Guruji says that only a realised soul is fit to be approached for help in the spiritual quest, and not anyone who has only a bookish knowledge of the subject. The reader will find the reading of the lecture headed 'Spiritual Inquiry' a memorable experience.

Divine attributes of Soul

In the next lecture 'Light from Ancient India' Guruji analyses the basic desires of human beings and comes to the rather startling conclusion that all human beings share the same five basic objectives viz. the desire to exist for ever, the desire to know everything, the desire to have happiness unmixed with pain, the desire to be free, and the desire to dominate. These desires, in a realised form, are the attributes of God, who exists for ever, who is omniscient, who is joy incarnate, and who is himself unfettered but who controls everything. Is it just a chance that the soul also strives to achieve the same attributes? Is it not an indication that the soul and God are essentially of the same stuff, and are one in the ultimate analysis ? Continuing the theme a little further, Guruji deduces step by step, the inherent qualities of the soul and finds them to be identical with the aforesaid attributes of God. Guruji brings home this fundamental truth taught by Vedānta, with the aid of do-it-yourself metaphysics.

Karma

In the next lecture styled "Karma Yoga", Guruji first describes in modern terms, the three paths to God realisation viz., Karma-mārga, Jñāna-mārga and Bhakti-mārga. These very three paths are to be found in the Bible, followed in their actual lives by the Prophets of the Old Testament and the Apostles of the New Testament. Karma mārga, according to Guruji is the performance of duty with sincerity and purity of heart, leaving the fruits or the results of the performance of duty to God, which is also the teaching of Gītā and other Hindu scriptures.

True religion

Speaking of India's heritage of unity in diversity and of welcoming every religion to its soil Guruji, in his lecture entitled "India's Role in the Modern World" at Santa Monica College, dwells on his pet theme of essential unity of all religions. True religion cannot, according to Guruji, be inconsistent with the basic tenets of other religions. The seeming differences in the tenets of various religions are only outer differences, which have been introduced by the Masters to meet the needs of the societies in which the religions were propagated. Doing good to other human beings, is the essence of all religions.

Guruji's opinion of Americans

Some readers may perhaps be surprised to learn that Guruji did not consider Americans as materialistic. In his view (as expressed in the interview with Dr. Hornaday) the very genesis of America, right from Pilgrim Fathers and George

Washington to the present day, was against materialistic or purely selfish tendencies. Pursuit of material ends does not, in Guruji's view, stand in the way of spiritual progress. Guruji considers science and religion as complementary and not mutually exclusive as some people think. Indian tradition is to treat the science as part of and as aids to religious studies.

For the Indians living in U.S.A., Guruji has one message i.e. 'be true to the Indian tradition of considering the world as one's family'. In his address to the Indians at the S.R.F. India Hall, he calls upon them to strive for world peace and universal harmony.

As these lectures werè delivered at different places and to different audiences, there are bound to be some repetition of themes and arguments. In the lecture styled 'Practical methods of World Peace', Guruji draws our attention again to the basic unity of all religions and the futility of wars based on religious differences which are more apparent than real. He considers unity and solidarity of all human beings as a basic tenet of the religion of his conception.

In the T.V. interview styled 'Greet the People', Guruji answers questions on such varied topics as Hindu-Muslim problem, Women's place in Hindu Society, and true religion.

In the Hank Weaver T.V. show also he answers similar questions. He avoids questions of personal nature as is enjoined by the rules of the Order to which Guruji belonged.

Vedic Mathematics

In the demonstrations organised at the California Institute of Technology, Guruji gave an introduction to the basic mathematical operations derived from Vedic sūtras. A report of the demonstrations, and of Guruji's lecture preceding the demonstrations, appears in this compilation. For fuller treatment of the subject the reader is referred to Guruji's book *Vedic Mathematics*. But the lecture included here contains a detailed and lucid step-by-step explanation of the few mathematical operations covered in the demonstrations, which is easy to understand.

Three Paths

In the lecture styled "Karma and other paths of Yoga", Guruji describes the secret of the three paths of sādhanā viz. Karma, Bhakti and Jñāna and how they converge to one goal of self realisation.

Vedic Metaphysics

In his discourse styled 'Vedic Metaphysics and Advaita', Guruji brings Vedānta to the level of the common man. His conclusions are all in accordance with the scriptures and expositions of the Masters like Śaṅkara. One wonders at the lucidity of his treatment of so abstruse a subject as Advaita Vedānta. His elucidation of the concept of 'Mithyā' helps to dispel the misconception that Vedānta denies the world, and is negative in approach. In this lecture Guruji demonstrates that ordinary language is sometimes inadequate to depict the reality from the correct philosophical standpoint. Guruji maintains that Advaita or Monism is the only doctrine which is consistent with the belief in the existence of God and his being the Creator of the world. He holds that other religions also in essence teach Advaita Vedānta. This lecture gives the essential teachings of Advaita Vedānta in a nutshell and in a language the layman can understand. In answer to a question from one of the listeners Guruji explains how the concept of rebirth comes as a logical consequence of the belief in divine justice. From many standpoints this is one of the most important lectures in this compilation.

Bhakti

In the lecture styled 'Bhakti Yoga and Divine Mother' Guruji examines the pitfalls and difficulties of Karma Yoga and Jñāna Yoga and puts forward Bhakti Yoga as the infallible path to God for most of the people. He asks every one of us to take, like Arjuna, God as his guide, as the driver of his life's chariot. Absolute trust in him is the only thing that is required of us. Guruji also discusses the three degrees of dependence on God springing from devotee's capacity to fend for himself, exemplified by three maxims well known in Vedantic parlance. In this connection Guruji also examines the concept of God as mother, the three mother-goddesses of Hindu mythology, and how the concept of mother-goddess comes in as a natural extension of Bhakti Yoga.

Discussion with Toynbee

Dr. Arnold Toynbee, the noted British historian philosopher was a visiting lecturer at the Washington and Lee University, Lexington, Virginia during the spring semester. Dr. Paul Hayner, Assistant Professor of Philosophy at the University sponsored a discussion between Guruji and Dr. Toynbee, which was held on 26th March in the Lee Memorial Chapel. Excerpts from the discussion appeared in the May 1958 issue of the S.R.F. Magazine. A report of the discussion has appeared as an appendix in the Guruji's book called *Sanatana Dharma.* The discussion is included here as it serves to further elucidate Guruji's view on War and Peace and their limitations and other topics which have been touched upon only incidentally in other lectures.

Peace

In the last lecture included in this book Guruji describes his approach, which is essentially a spiritual one, to the problem of World Peace. Some ideas have, no doubt, been repeated, but the subject bears repetition and Guruji gives a new treatment to the problem in every lecture, which is an added attraction.

These lectures contain a message which is addressed not only to the western audience but through it, to the entire humanity.

ACKNOWLEDGEMENTS

I express my heartfelt gratitude to Sri Sri Daya Mata and her devoted followers in the Self Realisation Fellowship for making available to me the transcripts of Sri Gurudeva's lectures, but for which this work would have never seen the light of the day. Sri Sri Daya Mata has also very graciously sent for this publication an introductory message aglow with her reverence and admiration for Sri Gurudeva which reveals the depth of her vision, catholicity of her heart and purity of her soul.

I am deeply obliged to Shri S. P. Pande, Inspecting Assistant Commissioner of Income-tax, New Delhi, for having undertaken the laborious task of reviewing and editing the transcripts of these lectures, providing the original references in Sanskrit and compiling the Bibliography, Glossary and Index with great perseverence and devotion. Thanks are also due to Shri E.M. Nanu who took pains to type the entire text of the book.

Lastly, I am grateful to Shri J.P. Jain, Shri N.P. Jain and Shri M. Ramakrishna Shastri of Messrs Motilal Banarsidass whose efforts have made it possible to bring out the work in this beautiful form.

Smt. Manjula Devi

HOMAGE TO THE MASTER

These verses were recited by Smt. Manjula Trivedi at the commencement of all the lectures by His Holiness. The first verse is by the Paramaguru (the guru of His Holiness) Śrī Śivābhinava-Nṛsiṁha-Bhāratī, and the other three are by His Holiness himself. The Sanskrit compositions of His Holiness have been published by Bharatiya Vidya Bhavan, Bombay, under the title *Stotra-Bhāratī-Kaṇṭhahāra.*

OM

Ananta-samsāra-samudratāra-
naukāyitābhyām gurubhaktidābhyām,
Vairāgya-sāmrājyada-pūjanābhyām
namo namaḥ śrīgurupādukābhyām.

Obeisance again and again to the Guru's (Master's) sandals which are like a ship for crossing the ocean of the endless world and which give (the aspirant) devotion to the Guru and the worship of which (Sandals) bestows (on the devotee) the Empire of Renunciation.

Homapramukhyair jagati dvijādyāh
karmavrajair bhaktivibodhanābhyām,
Icchanti yat tat phaladāyikābhyām
namo namaḥ śrīgurupādukābhyām.

Obeisance again and again to the Guru's sandals, which enkindle devotion, and which bestow all that the twice-born and others, desire in the world from the performance of various actions like offering oblations (to gods) etc.

Hautrāgni-hotrāgni-haviṣya-hotṛ
homādi-sarvākṛtibhāsamānam,
Yad Brahma tad-bodha-vitāriṇībhyām
namo namaḥ śrīgurupādukābhyām.

Obeisance again and again to the Guru's sandals, which impart the knowledge of Brahman, manifesting itself in all shapes like the priestly fire (the priest himself), the sacrificial fire, the offering, the sacrificer, and the sacrifice.

Haṁsādimair āryaparamparāva-
taṁsāyitaih santatapūjitābhyām,
Saṁsārapāthonidhi-kumbhajābhyām
namo namaḥ śrīgurupādukābhyām.

Obeisance again and again to the Guru's sandals which have continuously been worshipped by the leading sages who have adorned the Aryan tradition, and which sandals are like Agastya for the oceanlike world.

I PURPOSE OF THE AMERICAN TOUR

Press Conference For His Holiness,
Jagadguru Śaṅkarācārya,
Mount-Washington, Februrary 6, 1958, 10 *A.M.*

Question. Speaking of tour, are you speaking primarily on self-realization or do you get off into the field of mathematics, which I understand you are interested in ?

His Holiness. I would be speaking on subjects of all kinds and types I'm interested in, and mathematics happens to be one of those subjects.

Q. Why did you decide to take such a trip to the United States at this time ?

H. H. I have felt that the world was in need of such a message,* especially at this time. And as one of the leading powers in the world at the present day, America has a great deal of responsibility.

Q. What do you believe your mission will do to advance the cause of peace ?

H. H. By going to the roots of the question, and examining the root causes that lead to individual clashes and international clashes, etc., I believe that this mission shall be successful in promoting the cause of peace and harmony by bringing to the people, and all concerned, a sense of unity and solidarity amongst themselves.

Q. We realize that you don't want to discuss political questions, but, would you make some comment on the hydrogen bomb? Do you think we should stop these tests of these bombs ?

H. H. (His Holiness, refusing to be drawn in this controversy, replied) Fundamental sense of unity and solidarity amongst the people should be most helpful in the cause of peace. It is from that standpoint that I have started on this tour. There is no conflict between individual and individual, nation and nation, and even between what they call the spiritual and temporal aspects of life and a harmonious and felicitous combination

*Also see answers to first three questions in Radio Interview.

of all the seemingly conflicting elements in life that is the most important truth to be realised.

Q. Your Holiness, while you are here, will you speak upon the great religious truths of India ? Will that be one of your subjects ?

H. H. This will be part of my subject. Consciousness of separateness, of inferiority, these are the obstacles to peace. And as a contribution towards the cause of world peace, I propose to speak in this tour about the fundamental religious truths which bring these obstacles to an end.

Q. What could be done, your Holiness, about this greater friendliness between India and the United States ?

H. H. Any factor that brings about greater friendliness between the two countries or advance them in that direction is desirable. And, I would like to be helpful in bringing about that kind of consummation.

Q. Do you believe that the world is progressing toward this universal peace ? Are we moving forward ?

H. H. I believe that there is no cause of hostility between one country and another, one nation and another. What makes misunderstanding is the confusion about the fundamental principles. If there is a proper understanding of the fundamental unity and solidarity of the universe, external factors of a superficial and unimportant character cannot cloud out our vision of the reality — the internal unity and solidarity underlying all the seeming differences.

Q. What would you suggest as a type of reconstruction the world could bring about for a more rapid peace in the world ? What type of reconstruction would you mention or suggest ?

H. H. One which will remove all misunderstandings and will promote world peace. Things which emphasize differences should be recognised as obstacles to the path, not merely of peace, but of truth. They are not the things that require the kind of attention and appreciation we are giving them. The reconstruction should be of such a character as to remove the root cause of the trouble. The unity underlying not merely all the diversity but all the infinite universe, that should receive proper attention, and that will be stressed in my lectures. It is necessary for reconstruction of the world to have peace and mutually cooperative goodwill.

Q. Do you believe the world needs such leaders as Mahatma Gandhi ? Will more men like him help the cause of peace ?

H. H. All people who develop towards realization of the fundamental unity are helpful, and the world needs more and more such people.

Q. Your Holiness, what is the contribution you feel India can make to the world in the cause of world peace and understanding ?

H. H. India is well fitted for this work for the simple reason that, in her tradition and cultural belief, this is the very principle that is inculcated. India ought to be, therefore, much more useful to others. Unity among differences is the theme of her cultural life.

Q. We know that in the West the Christians view other religions as less than theirs. What is the Hindu view of Christianity and of other religions ?

H. H. We believe in the fundamental unity of all religions. We have no quarrel with any religion, any sect, any denomination, any sub-sect, or any other such diverting factor. My one big quarrel is with quarrelling, and especially in the name of religion.

Q. Won't you tell us something about your own Order — Śaṅkarācārya Order ?

H. H. My own order is the one which promulgates, and propagates, and diffuses this kind of attitude toward the world.

Q. Would it be out of place here at this conference to ask you something of your views on mathematics ? Or would that require too much introductory talk ?

H. H. I would like to go into the details of the question later. In our culture, there is no undue stress laid on matters purely spiritual, or purely temporal. We regard life as one composite whole. And the purely spiritual and purely temporal are terms that express only parts of one unity. Culture that goes to uplift mankind is *ipso facto* a part of the Vedic studies, as we understand them. Mathematics, physics, chemistry, biology, and other subjects which are supposed to be purely material, temporal, are considered parts of the holy science. We start with that advantage. There is no conflict between religion and science. In fact, all sciences* are regarded as integral parts

*In the twelfth lecture, His Holiness, explains this further.

and inexorably intertwined with the spiritual life as such. Each according to his own capacity, inclination, etc., studies the subject which is most congenial to him. According to our scriptures superiority and inferiority in any respect whatsoever, including the spiritual and other aspects of life is not justified, even inferentially. Man cannot have such distinctions between religion and science. . As I have said, the two are inexorably intertwined. Matter is the medium through which the Spirit manifests Itself. We have no quarrel between what is called secular science on one hand and religion on the other. As I happen to have studied the Vedas from this standpoint, particularly their specialized mathematics, I give demonstrations that ought to show that spiritual and temporal life can go together and there is no irreconcilable antagonism between them.

Q. And you've discovered in the Vedas that they are not only ceremonial and poetic, but that they are very practical applications to man's daily life in all phases of it.

H. H. Oh, you do believe that ! Undue emphasis on the external side is harmful for our progress and development on the spiritual side. But, at the same time, the choice is left to the individual according to his inclination, capacity, etc.

Q. Then, could you give us some brief mention of the origin of your Order? It would be interesting to us.

H. H. For this purpose, we have to go back to the time when about 2,000 years ago people had fallen away from the way of life taught in the Upaniṣads, the Vedānta, as we call it. There was a gradual deviation from the Vedic path, the religious path. And in the name of external purity, ceremonialism, and things of that type, the essential unity within was forgotten. More and more emphasis was being laid on the secular or the material side, as we call it, but with a justifieation in the name of religion, by ignoring the spirit and insisting on the letter of the law (religious texts). And when that state of affairs continued for a long time, it was then, in order to restore India's religion to its pristine purity, we had a man, the Buddha, who re-emphasized the Spirit, and brought the people back the consciousness of their spiritual heritage. The idea that the Buddha was anti-Vedic is absolutely erroneous. He came to restore the Vedic religion to its original purity. And when the wave set him also passed away, and his followers did the same thing his predecessors had done, then we had Śrī Śaṅkarācārya, the first in this Order which I represent. He came to restore the Vedic religion, the Buddhistic religion, as it has been called. The idea that Śaṅkara threw out Buddhism, is also absolutely wrong. We regard the original Vedic texts, the Buddbi c teachings, and the Śaṅkara's own teachings, as practically the same. But people, looking at the question from a very short-sighted point of view, speak of the conflict between the Vedic religion and Buddha, and of the conflict between the Buddha and Śaṅkara. There was no such conflict at all.* The genesis of our Order was the restoration of the original Vedic faith and the real Buddhistic faith, which were practically the same. The Order gave the people a practical doctrine of peace, which was the doctrine of the Vedas, the Buddha, and Śaṅkara. This practical doctrine could be accepted by all without any difficulty. Between this and the teachings of the Buddha there was only a seeming conflict. Those who studied the teachings of the Buddha deeply and knew it, removed the causes of conflict, and the misunderstandings. At the time that I am speaking of, that is, the time of the decline of Bud-

*"The Śākyan mission was out 'not to destroy but to fulfil', to enlarge and enhance the accepted 'faith-in-God' of their day, not by asseverating or denying but by making it more vital. It was Brahmans who became the leading disciples". Mrs. Rhys Davids—*Mannual of Buddhism—p.* 194.

In an article published long ago, His Holiness wrote:—

"He (Śaṅkara) has been credited with the destruction of Buddhism or rather the exiling of it from India. This is not historically true. For, while we find his Sūtrabhāṣya (commentary on the Vedāntic aphorisms of Bādarāyaṇa) condemning the muddled philosophy of decadent Buddhism, we never find him speaking derogatorily of the Lord Buddha himself; nay, on the contrary, he actually described the latter in terms of the highest reverence as 'Yoginām cakravartī' (the greatest amongst yogis or ascetics). And the real historical truth of the matter is not that he killed or drove it out but only that, by honestly and categorically admitting the ethical and psychic beauties of Śrī Buddha's own teachings (while controverting and disproving the later Buddhists' distortions thereof) he made it unnecessary for the Buddhists to continue their separate existence (except as an integral part of Sanātani Orthodox Vedic Hinduism). It was thus a unique process, not of extermination but of reabsorption of the Buddhists into their own original fold".

dhism, the days of decadent nihil-Buddhism,* as they call it, Śaṅkara came and restored the Vedic faith, and by doing so, he restored the Buddhistic faith also, to its original purity.

Q. Sir, how is a person, say Śaṅkarācārya appointed ? In other words, someone in your position.

H. H. The normal position is that each Śaṅkarācārya nominates his own successor, because he is supposed to know best the qualifications of various qualified persons and select the best person possible for the succession. In case the Śaṅkarācārya passes away without appointing a successor, then, it is the duty and privilege of the righteously inclined persons all over the country, to gather together and select the best person available for the purpose according to the qualifications the original Śaṅkarācārya himself laid down. When they are in doubt, they refer to a separate textbook, which bears on the question. The qualifications and the functions are mentioned. Only a properly qualified person can be chosen. And even amongst the qualified persons, the best must be chosen. And in case through any kind of private intrigue a person has unworthily coveted the position, it rests with the righteously inclined persons to remove him and install a proper person in his place. Even that is specially mentioned in the text.†

Q. What is this text ?

H. H. Maṭhāmnāya, the law of succession with regard to the monasteries.

Q. Could you tell us something of the duties of a Śaṅkarācārya ?

H. H. He has to be a person who is qualified morally in every way, and has acquired learning in the various scriptures and a practical application thereof. And his function is to go about, preaching to the people, and setting his own example for the

*Nihil Buddhism is not to be equated with Śūnyavāda School of Buddhism. Perhaps His Holiness had in mind the (other three schools of Buddhism which have been called Vaināśikas by Śaṅkara in his commentary on Brahmasūtra (II-2-18 et seq.) and have been refuted extensively.

†Mahānuśāsana, has the following text:—

Uktalakṣaṇasampannah syāc cen matpīṭhabhāg bhavet,
Anyathārūḍhapīṭho (a) pi nigrahārho manīṣiṇām.

"If the incumbent is endowed with the above qualities, he is entitled to the headship of my monastery. Otherwise, even after his assumption of the headship, he deserves to be punished (expelled) by the wise people".

purpose, so that the ideal state as conceived by him, could be realized.

Q. Do the four Śaṅkarācāryas in the different parts of India, work together or does each take his own maṭh, his own hermitage, and part of India, and work there ?

H. H. There are four divisions, and I happen to be now, the senior-most of them. Generally there is united action. But, of course, so far as the law is concerned, it doesn't take into cognizance any kind of internal relationships of that type. Each (division) has its own independent constitution and its functions are carried on without interference from others. That's not the religion but civil law. But a sentiment of unity is there and actual cooperation is also there.

Q. After leaving America, do you plan on going to Europe, and carrying your message there ?

H.H. Well, I will visit as many places as I possibly can manage. The Americans however have some advantages which few others have. The Indian cultural mission that I represent, can most easily be accepted, assimilated by America's own natural trend; spiritual and intellectual trend.

Q. America is considered by many nations to be very materialistic, but do you feel that it is also spiritually deficient ?

H.H. That is a very superficial rating of character, spirituality, and so on. Even if we judge by external appearances, I don't believe, that any justification can be given for a statement like that. We believe that America represents necessary advancement in material and positive sciences. That is a reason for congratulations; that is no reason for condemnation at all. The very genesis of America as a State and the whole course of her history should refute that kind of imputation.

Commentator : I hope you carry this same message every where you go.

H.H. I will endeavour to do so. I've been doing it in India all the time. I've now come out of India to pursue the same policy, the same procedure.

The root cause of the misunderstanding that I mentioned is that people distinguish between the spiritual and the temporal and think that any attention to temporal matters is, *ipso facto* worldliness. That kind of wrong conception is there, and people who hide themselves under spiritual ceremonials, rituals of an external character, speak in these terms. I am a believer in all-round education and progress. Even the study of grammar, and prosody, and astronomy, are vital, integral parts of a Vedic education.* I cannot quarrel with a nation advancing on the scientific side. But a happy and harmonious blending of all the various aspects of nature should be there, instead of lop-sided progress of any type.

Q. Will Hindus have to have a kind of revision after the new laws are introduced by the (Indian) Government, such as re-marriage of the widows, and abolition of untouchability which was an inherent part of the Hindu religion. Would it have to undergo a revision, or the changes will automatically take place and be accepted ?

H.H. Here again I will dispel a misunderstanding. The idea that the Hindu religion supports this view or that view, with regard to marriages, etc., is wrong. People who have been giving this interpretation of an external character have been misrepresenting our texts and other religious literature. There is no question of the Hindu religion coming into the matter at all.

Q. But, as far as untouchability is concerned, it was there. I lived twelve years in India, and I just came back from there. And of course, the trend has changed, but there was such a thing like an untouchable, and there was no way for an untouchable to go himself, to do anything. So, I was asked this question yesterday. I couldn't answer it. It is just a government law or is it accepted by the Hindu religion ?

H.H. The word 'Hindu' is very comprehensive. Any person who declares himself a Hindu is entitled to the heritage, history and freedom of a Hindu. That's according to modern law. But where the question comes of the interpretation of the scriptures, it is not the decision of the authorities, or even conclusions founded in a lifetime study, but everyman's more or less enlightened personal opinion† of matter which decides the picture.

*The six Aṅgas (parts of) or aids to Vedic education are:—(1) Śikṣā (Pronunciation), (2) Jyotiṣa (Astronomy), (3) Chandas (Prosody), (4) Nirukta (Etymology & Lexicography), (5) Kalpa (Rules for ceremonial acts) and (6) Vyākaraṇa (Grammar).

†Manu says:—

Vedāḥ Smṛtiḥ sadācāraḥ svasya ca priyam ātmanaḥ,
Etat caturvidham prāhuḥ sākṣāt dharmasya lakṣaṇam.
Manu 2-12

And, therefore, the picture necessarily gets muddled in that way. Each case is to be considered individually on its merits. There is no sweeping rule. Time, place, and circumstances make tremendous differences. Circumstances that would be injurious to society, might very well be beneficial in another context. These are to be taken into account.

Q. What is your opinion ? Do you think the caste system is injurious to society in India ?

H.H. Well, as you see it, it is injurious in many respects. The caste system, as we understand it, is an attribute of what the materialists would call the science of Eugenics.

Q. Your Holiness, many books by western religious writers, and even scholars, in comparing Christianity and Judaism and western religions with Hinduism, make the prime distinction that Judaic and Christian religions speak of one God, whereas the Hindus talk of many Gods. I think it would be helpful to have a statement from you on the real Hindu viewpoint.

H.H. We do not believe in more than one God. We are not polytheists at all. Not merely do we believe in the oneness of God, we believe in the oneness and solidarity of the whole universe. We speak of different manifestations of the various forces in nature. And these are the deities, gods, and goddesses that we deal with in the Hindu religion.

Q. I often laughed because the westerners have angels and the Hindus have gods. If they changed the words around, they would have the same ideas.

H.H. The word 'angel' carries with it a sense of personality which the gods and goddesses of Hindus do not really have. There is something more in the shape of the forces of nature — goddesses, deities. They are not different gods and goddesses, but different manifestations of the same divine principle or the same nature. Whether you use the word god or nature, ultimately it comes to the same thing. One God overseeing an infinity of gods — no, that is not our position. We believe in one Essence, one Substance, one Principle, one Being, underlying an infinity of manifested shapes, and so on. I can give you the texts and the translations of those texts if you would

(i) Vedas, (ii) Smṛtis, (iii) normal conduct of good people and (iv) own conscience — These four are the criteria of Dharma.

like to read.* The position is really simple. We are believers not only in monotheism but something more, monocosmism, if you prefer a new word for the purpose.

Q. Do those who believe in the doctrine of karma resent western missionaries' efforts to change things in terms of hospitals and health clinics ? I understood that in Southeast Asia, the American policy of trying to cure people of eye diseases and various other ailments was resented by many people because they subscribed to the doctrine of karma, or reincarnation. Is this true ?

H.H. Wrong translations and misrepresentations are responsible for all such impressions. In the course of my discourses, I shall go into details of how very simple things have been misrepresented, and in such revolting manner. Regarding woman's position in society, as well as all the various questions on which there are differences of opinion, there has been presentation of Hinduism as being anti-social — I shall be going into details of these in the discourses and I'll be showing how there is absolute unity between aspirations of social progress of the East and the West. The conflicts that have taken place in the world are the result either of misunderstanding, or, in rare cases, of deliberate misrepresentation.

Commentator : Thank you, your Holiness.

*The following text in the Ṛgveda (I-164-46) conveys a similar idea—
Ekam sad Viprā bahudhā vadanti
Agnim Yamam Mātariśvānam āhuh.
Reality is one, seers speak of It as many — (They call It) Agni (Fire), Yama (Death) and Mātariśvan (Wind).
Another hymn (III-55) of Ṛgveda has the following refrain—
"Mahad devānām asuratvam ekam".
Great is the one lifeforce behind the (various) gods.

II INDIA'S MESSAGE OF PEACE

Radio Interview of Ruth Ashton with His Holiness, Jagadguru Śaṅkarācārya on Station KNX AM at 2.35 *on Thursday, February* 6, 1958. *Interview was recorded in the morning of the 6th, in the lobby of the Main Building at the Headquarters of the Self-Realization Fellowship,* 3880 *San Rafael Avenue, Los Angeles* 65, *California.*

Ruth Ashton : Well, in the realm of religion, which naturally encompasses all life, an historic event has taken place. For the first time, a spiritual head of Hindu India, His Holiness Jagadguru Śaṅkarācārya, has come to this country. His Holiness will deliver addresses at many universities from coast to coast. And this morning he kindly subjected himself to the rather confusing Western custom — a news conference. This reporter asked His Holiness the purpose of his trip to this country at this time.

His Holiness : I have come to lecture at this time for the simple purpose of carrying India's message of peace, unity and solidarity amongst all humanity.

R. A. And you came at this particular time, is that correct, because you feel peace is in jeopardy ?

H. H. Yes, because of world conditions relating to peace and war, it seemed to me that this time was most opportune, and also one in which there is great need for this kind of mission.

R. A. Your Holiness, what is your message to the American people ?

H. H. My message is the same one as I have already explained as the object of my coming here — the promotion of unity, harmony, and solidarity amongst all the peoples of the world.

R. A. There is a feeling at times that there are conflicts among some of the religions of the world; at least there are differences. It has been believed in the West, perhaps — or in some texts, at any rate — that Christianity and Judaism believe in one God, whereas Hindu religion subscribes to more than one God. Would you explain to us if there is any such difference ?

H. H. We are not polytheists in the sense that we believe in different gods — in a multiplicity of gods. On the contrary, we believe that there is a Unity underlying the whole universe — not merely a unity underlying the Trinity,* but unity underlying not multiplicity but infinity of things in the cosmic world around us. And the gods and goddesses which people speak of are manifestations in various forces of the universe of the same Reality. While Christianity and Judaism speak of one God, with tremendous differences coming up in the conceptions of that oneness, we believe in the oneness and the solidarity of the whole universe.† So that the charge of polytheism against us is absolutely due to a mistaken conception of the gods and goddesses described. The gods and goddesses described are merely forces of Nature. They are not personal gods and goddesses in any sense of the term.

R. A. You have come to the United States, Your Holiness, to deliver your message to the people here. Some people think of America as materialistic. Do you feel there is a spiritual sensitivity here ?

H. H. In our conception of things, the spiritual and the material sides of life are inextricably intertwined, and any attempt to divorce one from another is bound to be a failure in both directions. In the name of spirituality people talk in terms of contempt, or at least of indifference, toward material prosperity and things of that type. And there is a notion abroad that religion and science are fundamentally conflicting things. We, on the contrary, believe that every branch of science is an integral part of our Vedic lore. And from this standpoint, there would be no question of any country being condemned for its attention to material progress. That America is rooted to materialism and has no concern for her spirituality, is a completely and fundamentally erroneous idea altogether. My own view is that the origin of America, as a state, its historical course all through, will be sufficient to refute any such charge. On the other hand, we need more and more of a happy and

*Brahmā, Viṣṇu and Śiva.

†Advaita (Non-duality) or Monism. His Holiness also called it Monocosmism. (Press-conference)

felicitous blending of the spiritual and material sides. In fact, we do not believe that there is any antagonism between religion and science; and the more we can bring these together, the greater will be the chances for world peace and world progress all around.

R. A. Your Holiness, where else will you travel ? You are travelling in the United States now. To what other countries will you go with your message ?

H. H. Oh, I propose to go around to all the countries where there is the possibility of my doing so, with regard to local conditions and things of that type.

R. A. Do you plan, Your Holiness, to go to Russia at any time ?

H. H. I have not been to Russia, so far. I have no notion when the idea will materialize; but I hope for the day when I shall feel as much at home there as in other parts of the world, because so far as I am concerned the question is one of intrinsic merits, and there is no answer to a question like this from a mechanical standpoint. My attitude towards all is one of peace and good will, and therefore there can be no question of excluding Russia from my jurisdiction. But, as to whether I actually go there, whether the desire to see it materializes or not, will depend on the circumstances of the time.

R. A. That was the spiritual head of Hindu India, head of the Śaṅkarācārya Order, Jagadguru Śaṅkarācārya.

III WORLD PEACE

Lecture at Pepperdine College, February 7, 1958

Friends :

Strange and stirring, critical and epoch-making are these times, these transition times, in the history of the world in general, and of the United States of America, Russia and India, in particular, times during which our lots have been cast, times during which we feel various and incessant, termendous and seemingly interminable conflicts between two different idealogies, two different ideas, two different ideals, two different modes of life, two different lines of thinking, in fact, if one may say so, two different everythings. The position is rendered more critical by the fact that owing to international troubles of various types, we are apprehensive that the war drums may at any time begin to sound in our ears. And therefore, it is all the more necessary that we should pin our attention, our concentrated attention, on the subject, and do what we can as human beings interested in the welfare of humanity as such.§

It therefore behoves every thinking person amongst us to think over all the facts and factors of the situation, weigh the pros and cons, and come to conclusions calculated to lead us, as individuals, and also to lead us as society as such to the goal of happiness, peace, plenty, and joy, which is the heart's goal of us all.

Impartial inquiry

In starting on such an inquiry, we have to begin by clearing our minds of all prejudices and prepossessions absolutely and approach the question from the standpoint of seekers after truth. Those who will seek the truth, will find it, and act up to it. We have, in Sanskrit, a phrase containing three words, *Śrotavyo mantavyo nididhyāsitavyaḥ.** I render these words

§In 1958, when this lecture was delivered, the 'cold' war was at its peak. But these words have not lost their relevance even now.

*Bṛhadāraṇyaka Upaniṣad II-4-5.

into three phrases of two words each, a predicate and an adverb:—investigate carefully, decide correctly, and follow faithfully. The tendency of seeing matters from the stand-point of only the immediate consequences, and agitation, excitement, etc., on our part, can certainly be the straightest way possible to confused thinking, to distortion of vision, and to the warping of our judgment in matters of serious import. The right way is to view matters from the standpoint of cool, calm, and dispassionate judgment, without prejudices and prepossessions as I have said, and with a sole eye to the discovery of truth, in order to act up to it and thereby benefit not only the individual self but the whole of humanity as such.

Human conflict : historical approach

This question can be looked at from two different standpoints. In fact, from the standpoint of historical study, we may roughly divide the history of the world in respect of this particular question, into two periods, both of them tragic and pathetic in the extreme, and yet, as historical facts they have to be viewed dispassionately and calmly.

Age of religious conflicts

The first period was one in which, in the name of religion, wars were being fought from place to place. In this period we have the history of conflicts arising from what was supposed to be religious standpoint as people concerned fully and sincerely perhaps believed it to be. They went into a war which was to terminate with the extermination of one party by the other as a divinely appointed victor. No one was prepared to look towards another in peace and amity. That was the state of affairs in the first period of which I have been talking.

Now, in the name of religion, questions of tremendous differences arise, not between merely one religion and another as we might call in general terms, but also amongst Christianity, Judaism, Islam, etc., in the western world, and Hinduism, Buddhism, Jainism, and so on, in the eastern world. In all these matters, the differences are such that the diverse followers deem it their duty to fight to the finish and bring forward before the world their own particular religion, not merely as the best of all, but as the only one leading to heaven; all the others being straight paths to hell.

Identity of viewpoints impossible

Now, if we go into the question dispassionately, it will be obvious to all of us at the outset that no differences and no conflict of views in regard to doctrinal matters, in regard to theology, or philosophy, etc. could justify this kind of attitude of war to the finish. Even with regard to matters which are within the jurisdiction of our physical senses, the eyes, the ears, etc., it is impossible for us to agree. We're all mentally constituted in different ways. We have our own ideas with regard to beauty, with regard to harmony of sound, with regard to taste, with regard to touch, with regard to odour, etc. These are objects which we, according to our ordinary conceptions of things in life, regard as objective realities, realities about which there can be no question of any conflict at all. And yet, even with regard to these things, we find there is a tremendous difference owing to differences in taste, inclinations, capacities, etc. And therefore, the religious differences cannot justify waging of a big war which will determine not merely the fate of this or that country, but perhaps exterminate and wipe off from the history and from the map of the world followers of all religions.

With regard to the eye, the sense organ with which we see things, I will mention, by way of illustration, an incident in my own experience. A few years ago in India, on a certain day, a photographer came and took my photograph. And in order to be sure there was no mistake, a second photograph was also taken, the interval between the two being perhaps a minute or less than a minute. And yet, there was a slight difference in the facial expression, and when the negative was developed and the picture was presented before us, two devoted disciples of mine were found bitterly quarrelling with each other as to which was the better of the two. And this quarrel was with regard to a photograph about which, from the standpoint of objective reality, there should have been no difference of opinion at all.

This is the way we look at things. We love certain things for their shape, for their beauty, etc. and these are detested by people who have other conceptions of beauty. Ugliness and beauty are not things about which we can form one opinion, for tastes differ, capacities to appreciate differ, and there is difference all round. Similarly, with regard to sound. We hear the same sounds, but as to whether they are harmonious and melodious, there are tremendous differences of opinion. Here again, there can be no other explanation than that our ears are differently constituted. What is harmonious to me, what is melodious to me, may be just the opposite to another.

Similarly, with regard to taste, in respect of food, drink, etc., with regard to flavourings, with regard to touch. In all these matters, which are purely within the jurisdiction of our physical senses, and not beyond our sense ken, we find that human beings, on account of different internal constitutional peculiarities — you may call them temperamental idiosyncrasies if you like, but there they are — on account of them, there is tremendous difference of opinion. If even with regard to these matters, we cannot arrive at uniformity of opinion, and our conceptions differ, then much more therefore, does it logically follow, that with regard to matters beyond the physical senses, matters relating to the life after death with regard to other worlds, etc., we will have different opinions. It is impossible to conceive of the possibility of oneness of opinion, oneness of approach, oneness of attitude, and oneness of reaction in respect of matters which are beyond our physical senses, and which after all have to be decided on the basis of faith. Whatever justification or explanations are given in support of this or that view of the particular religions, one will, at last, say, "That is my faith, That is my belief." The last resort is to faith. All the intellectual capacity may be expended in trying to understand the reality beyond the possibility of controversy, beyond the possibility of discussion, etc., and yet one must admit that there is still a space left, perhaps only one little item of a very small character left, on which we have to take shelter under faith as the determining factor. So, my point is that we expect people to be of one opinion, to work together on the basis of uniformity of ideas and so forth. Now, that is a thing that is beyond possibility. And when we are talking from the standpoint of realism, and that too of practical material realism etc., as we are fond of doing these days, there's no getting away from the fact that the very idea, the very hope, the very conception, of oneness, of uniformity of opinion, is an illusion, of which every one of us will in due course find the necessity to be disillusioned.

So, from the standpoint of religion, there can be no justification for wars and things of that type. On matters which we can agree upon, we agree to agree. And on matters where disagreement is inevitable, we must agree to disagree, and that is how in life, there is no possibility of forcefully converting people from one religion to another.

As a matter of fact, there is another aspect of the question into which I do not propose to go in detail just now, but I will only mention it. Our own view, with regard to the various religions in the world is that there is no inherent conflict between one of them and any other. From time to time, different needs arise in society, and according to the needs, and the exigencies of each predicament, great saints and leaders of spirituality come into the world to place before the world what is necessary, what is beneficial, at the time. And quarrelling with regard to these tenets of the various religions can only be compared to quarrelling with a doctor who prescribes for a patient suffering from heart disease certain medicines, and prohibits salt, and in the case of a person suffering from diabetes, prescribes a different set of medicines and prohibits sugar. They may say "The two are irreconcilably antagonistic. The doctor prohibits sugar in this case, and allows salt, and in the case of another patient he does just the reverse. How inconsistent and stupid he is !" Now, the same kind of trouble comes here. From time to time, as the need arises, the deficiency has to be made good. Any excess has to be removed. Just as for the physical constitution of the physical body there are different prescriptions similarly with regard to the social constitution and its virtues and vices, there are different religious tenets. The great men, the saints and sages — we have different nomenclatures for the different individuals who founded the religions, come down for the benefit of humanity and to tell us what is necessary for us at that particular juncture in the history of the world.

Therefore, from this standpoint, there can be no justification for war. I may sum up my whole position with regard to the various religions of the world by saying, I have no quarrel with any religion, any denomination, any sect, any sub-sect, etc. My one big quarrel is with quarrelling, and that too, in the name of religion. Religion ought to be a unifying factor, but in actual historical experience, it proved to be the cause not merely of heart-burning but also of bloodshed and burning alive of human beings and so on.

This is with regard to wars fought in the name of religion. I need not go into details of the crusades, and the conflicts between the Protestants, and the Roman Catholics, in England, France, Spain, and so on. I am not going into these details because students of history know them and I feel sure that what I've been saying on the matter fits into the historical facts as we know them from the great text-books of history.

Age of economic conflicts

The second period, in which is included the transition period to the present time, is one in which the racial, national and other differences continue at bottom, as motivating factors of most of the conflicts. But at the same time, there is what I might call "evil with a curtain drawn over." People now talk in the name of economics. And that too is an important standpoint from which the question has to be considered and ought to be considered.

The Malthusian concept comes before us at this point, and we are told that while food production is increasing in arithmetical progression, population is increasing in geometrical progression, and therefore, the trouble arises initially because of economic crisis in various countries. And the only way in which one nation can survive is by going to war with others. The question comes up in that shape and that too is a shape which is quite ugly enough in our conscience and which at the same time under careful dispassionate study, is bound to be, to our conviction, absolutely irrational. We talk of practical realism and from the standpoint of practical realism we say that war on an economic basis is justified for the purpose of feeding the population that we are interested in, at the expense of those whom we are not interested in, and whom we can despoil. Well, that kind of feeling, that kind of approach to the question is one which is not clearly calculated to benefit anybody. Here again, I will not go into details of historical and other analyses. Students of history know of what is called the victory in which the victor suffers more than the vanquished.* Again and again,

*Pyrrhic Victory.

in recent history, in all these wars — we have in our own lifetime witnessed two — we find that while the vanquished has been perhaps absolutely rooted out altogether and finds it difficult to go on, and that is an accrued result of the external action to which that particular nation was subjected, the victor himself has serious consequences to suffer and to deplore and which he tries to set right if possible.

High cost and futility of War

So it is not the fault of prudence, not the fault of sensible correct thinking, but of the immediate excitement and agitation of the moment that is responsible for all the suffering that these wars entail on humanity. I do not know of even one country which desired war at any time. Even the warmongers as they are called, who felt it to be in their interest to have war in order that they might profit as individuals etc., did not keep up that attitude towards the end. So long as things favoured them in that way, they would have been in favour of the war. But the moment the favourable circumstances ceased, and the consequences began to assert themselves, even the warmongers who were responsible for the war, felt that there should be an end to the matter at that stage. That kind of position comes up and even those who have not suffered much and who have practically benefited by these wars to some extent over some period of time, well, even they are reduced to the position where they cannot keep up that attitude forever. They must cry halt, and say that far and no further.

We all seek peace quite hard and when we talk of peace we desire peace in which we hope to surpass the other camp, the other nations, etc. If however, we think over the matter with cool, calm and dispassionate judgment, I think even there we are bound to feel disillusioned with regard to preparations for war.

In all these wars that we have had to deal with in the immediate past and the future wars about which we are fearful, the loss to humanity is terrible. All people agree about that. And the scientists tell us again and again that the latest weapons of warfare that science has placed before us, have made the situation still more critical than ever and the seeker after peace will have to seek peace by absolutely renouncing the idea of war altogether.

The hopes of benefiting by war are more than counter-balanced by the fate that would overtake humanity and human civilization. It is not the western civilization or the eastern civilization or this or that culture, but the entire humanity as such which will be hurried out of this planet prematurely and with no justification for such an end. If people can sit together and think over matters, it is possible to adjust the differences in that way. The League of Nations after the first war, the United Nations now, and other such bodies, have been responsible for starting and keeping the ball rolling, with regard to the eschewing of war as a means of settling the international questions and things of that type. If we have the common sense to see the direction in which things are drifting we would see that we are ourselves endangering by what I would call criminal thoughtlessness the future of humanity itself as a whole. These are the thoughts to which I would like to draw your attention.

I do not suppose that there is any possibility of agreement on many questions of conflict. Ideologies are different. The great statesmen, the politicians, the economists, and other servants of society think for the society, and work for the society, and establish ideals for the common people to understand and follow. Well, it is the task of these people to bring about the necessary change in the world conditions.

Resources of the world should be used for reconstruction of society

If people realize that the millions and billions, and trillions and quadrillions of dollars spent on preparations for war could be utilized on positive and constructive processes for the reconstruction of society, I think the food problem too will by itself get automatically solved. If the scientists who are now preparing equipment for the destruction of enemies, etc., harness the energy and the financial resources of all countries in the world for the purpose of bringing about such a happy, desirable consummation, the interests of the world will be very well safeguarded and the scientists' work as scientists will be of utilitarian value and not merely of destructive purpose and consequence.

I have just said that if the disputants, or the parties to the controversy sit together and calmly discuss all matters and devise ways and methods for the re-establishment of society, for the re-establishment of the nations on a secure economic and other bases, their purpose will be served, and war will not be necessary.

Peace at all costs ?

The question may arise as to what should be done in case of absolute obstinacy and obtuse perversity where a person has made up his mind on the matter already and because of his closed mind has no intention to hear, let alone think of the various arguments from other parties concerned, and from humanity at large. Well, that too is a possibility we have to take into account. There is nothing impossible in the world. My own conviction is that positive attempts should be made for doing away with all these conflicts at least to the extent of preventing evil consequences to humanity itself from these conflicts. What can be done ought to be done. But if perversity and obstinacy come in the way and we are called upon to take a decision on such occasions, the question will naturally be put, "Should it be peace at any price ?" That's a question that we very often ask, when we talk of peace, the necessity of peace, and the methods of achieving peaceful solutions for the various problems involved. In all these various disputes, the question is asked, "Should there be peace at any price ?"

Well, I must candidly say, "No." Peace cannot be purchased at any price. And if purchased at the price of dignity, of honour, of truth, in disregard of the welfare of mankind, etc., that peace is not worth such a costly price. As a pacifist, I would grant that and that would be the end of the matter. That would mean that there is no possibility or chance of our salvaging any salvageable part of the world's culture, the world's civilization, and so on. If that extreme state is reached, it would be like the deluge which no individual as such can possibly prevent. We speak of mahāpralaya in our Indian scriptures. We have the descriptions of the deluge in the Bible and scriptures of other religions of the world. When that kind of cataclysm which engulfs the whole world comes upon us, well, we are helpless, and we look upon this as defeat, and nothing further.

Disagreement need not lead to war

But even then, I would not feel that we should contribute to it by any attitude of a pessimistic character, by any attitude which says the other man must be in the wrong and whatever I say is right. If we sit together and discuss matters we will often find that many great troubles have been automatically removed. And the few that are left over may be things that we have agreed to disagree upon. The arbitrament of war is not necessarily the one leap out. On the whole my own belief is that it is possible for humanity to develop rational thinking over matters, because even those whom we oppose for the welfare of humanity, for the dignity of human life, etc., even they have among themselves persons of intellectual calibre, even they have thinkers amongst them. Thinking is not the monopoly of any individual, or any nation. So far as we can learn from the pages of history, all countries have from time to time produced great men, leaders of thought, deep thinkers, etc., and have contributed towards the welfare of the world. There has never been a famine of leaders. All that is wanted is the inclination, the will to go on the path of peace and avoid, as far as may be humanly possible, the path of war.

These are the stray ideas that I have placed before you, out of a whole mass of considerations which I would, with more time and scope for it, desire to take into consideration. But, I think that in the short time at my disposal today, I have placed the whole gist of the subject in as condensed a form as possible without leaving anything to be misunderstood or any gap to be filled in the wrong way. In connection with this trip of mine to America at this time, I can only express my desire that the statesmen and the President of the nation, and the professors and students in colleges, etc., should all put their heads together for solving the problem from what I have called the positive and constructive standpoint; and not give way to despair beforehand. The idea that something is aboslutely beyond us, or is absolutely without any possibility of achievement, is not reasonable at all from my standpoint. At any rate, it must be regarded as premature.

Very often, our differences arise from incomplete understanding or positive misunderstanding. And for the achievement of world peace these misunderstandings must be removed by heart to heart conferences. And if that is done, I feel sure that there will be no difficulty at all.

Verbal misunderstanding

Well, very often as I have said, we discuss matters and we fail to arrive at satisfactory and peaceful solutions, for the simple reason that we use the same words with different meanings or we use different words for conveying the same meaning. All the time, perhaps we may be fighting for the same ideal and the same ultimate goal; but all the time we are fighting on account of misunderstandings of language only.

I remember, several years ago, in Bombay there was an occasion for me to speak on the subject of misunderstandings caused by mere use of different language for conveying the same idea. I gave the example of exactly opposite words being used by two different parties and meaning exactly the same thing while they were wrangling with each other and coming to blows on the subject under controversy. It was actually a bottle of wine which they were discussing. One said the bottle was half-full and the other said the bottle was half-empty and they quarrelled about it. Each one was right from his own standpoint. His angle of vision was different. One was thinking of the full bottle, and was complaining that it was half-empty. The other was thinking of the possibility of an absolutely empty bottle, and was satisfied that it was half-full. The pessimist and the optimist do not differ in their calculations as regards actual facts and figures, statistics, etc. They have the same view, the same appreciation of things around them. And yet, they fight. They fight because they use different terms to denote the same thing. There can be nothing more mutually antagonistic than full and empty. But half-full and half-empty mean the same thing. It required someone who was calmly thinking over the matter to come in and say, 'The pessimist and optimist both are justified, both are right, and both are wrong.' They are both right insofar as they assert that particular aspect which appears to them correct and both are wrong because each of them ignores the aspect which the other is interested in placing before him.

So, this kind of controversy very often takes place and we find at the end of a long argument, at the end of a long war, that what we fought for was not worth the cost we paid for it. And still worse, there was no justification for the fighting at all.

Let us not, by our hasty actions, by giving way to agitation and excitement, etc., help the forces which are anti-social, the forces which are for extermination, the absolute rooting out of all culture and civilization, in fact, of humanity itself from this globe of ours. I look to the United States, her people, especially the professors and the young generation who are now here as students, to take active part in this work, and to see that this educational and cultural work, which requires such a great deal of patient and calm thinking, and is at the same time replete with consequences of the utmost benefit to the humanity at large, is conserved and preserved and not allowed to go waste.

Indian tradition of religious coexistence

This is my message with which I conclude this first address of mine in America on the subject of War and Peace. I feel that India has a special mission in this direction—a special mission not merely because of India's position of detachment from active points of the dispute, but also because of her own traditional and historical background. I was talking of wars fought in the name of religion. Students of history will remember that when the Parsis, persecuted in their own native land, Iran, went in search of shelter and freedom to worship their God according to their conscience, they went in search of shelter here and there and everywhere and found none anywhere and at last came to the western coast of Bombay State* in the Republic of India. Rājā Yādava who was the ruler of that part of India at that time** came forward to help them. He not merely helped them to find accommodation and a living for themselves, but loaded them with material riches and prosperity of every kind. So even to the present day, in India, every year when the Parsis celebrate the new year, they begin all the proceedings, whatever they may be, with a tribute to the Rājā Yādava of those days who was responsible for making the Parsi community what it is in India today. And it is said, if I may introduce a personal element into it, that Rājā Yādava referred the question

*Now reorganised as Gujarat and Mahārāṣṭra states.

**Parsis first came to India in the beginning of the 8th century A.D. After spending some years in the island of Div they came to the mainland and settled in Sanjān in 735 A.D. Sanjān is 145 km. north of Bombay. "Kissā-i-Sanjān" a beautiful long poem in Persian, written in 1599 A.D. records the saga of the first Parsi settlers in India. It mentions the name of the Indian King as Jādi Rānā.

to the Śaṅkarācārya of those days and was given this advice: Treat the guest at the gate as the Indian law of hospitality lays it down. And Rājā Yādava followed that advice and the Parsi community remembers him ever since then.

Then again, with regard to Christianity itself, you will remember the historical fact that Christ's religion went into the west in the teeth of very bitter fighting. It was a fight to the finish. Each one saying to Christianity and Christianity saying to the others, "It is you or I that can survive. Both of us cannot live under the same sun." It was a fight to the finish. The Greek religion, the Roman religion, the Syrian, the Assyrian, the Babylonian, and other religions, which came in conflict with Christianity were wiped off the face of the earth.* At the present day, there is not a single person who can come forward and say that he is a follower of the Greek religion, the Roman religion, etc. It was hard for Christianity to be accepted into the western world. But in India, you have a gratifying picture. The first Christian colony, that was ever founded in any part of the world is the Christian community of South India. We have the historical precedents and we have the scriptures declaring that this is the line of conduct that will lead to the welfare of individuals as individuals and of society as such.

I feel therefore, that I am entitled from the standpoint of intrinsic merit on the one hand and of historical tradition on the other, to place this standpoint, this aspect, this view of the matter before you all and plead for, not blind acceptance, but for careful examination so that you may not miss the important aspects of the question. As I have said, contribute positively all that you possibly can for the achievement of world progress through world peace.

This is my appeal to you and to others whom I propose to address later on here or in other countries. This is the message of India, the message of the Vedas, the message of Hinduism which I happen in my own humble ability to represent at the present day. Thank you.

*By Syrian, Assyrian and Babylonian religions, His Holiness perhaps means the various forms of paganism prevalent in the eastern parts of the Roman Empire, before the spread of Christianity.

IV SPIRITUAL INQUIRY

A talk given to the monks of SRF, Mt. Washington, India Centre and Lake Shrine — with about four of the sisters present — at the home of Mrs. Glick — at five o'clock on the evening of February 8, 1958.

Sri Sri Dayā Mātā asked His Holiness to talk to them on how they should conduct themselves as they seek to serve God, trying always to keep Him in their thoughts.

His Holiness said:

All the difference between one kind of life and another lies in the approach. The details may differ, but the fundamental principle behind the whole attitude and the whole approach is the chief thing that matters; and if one is attuned, or self-adjusted in that way — in the right direction — the question of detail does not really matter.

So that means that you must have an outlook, an approach, and angle of vision which decides for you whether the life that you have chosen to lead is on the right lines or not. Now, this means that you wish to have in the first place the right idea of the relationship between what in technical, philosophical and theological terminology we speak of as God, the individual soul, and the universe.

Inquiry with open mind

This generation takes it for granted the existence of God. All theologians and philosophers, at any rate, are supposed to start with the fundamental idea that the existence of God must be taken for granted. In fact we have had in India some two or three years ago the annual conference of the Indian Philosophical Association at Poona. The association passed a resolution to the effect that no system, no scheme, no school or thought which did not take the existence of God for granted could be regarded as philosophical at all. And I remember feeling that even that was not right. Philosophy means the study of this very subject; and if we insist on taking something for granted, the level of the study reduces in the process. We begin with what one might call a closed mind. Although the study is in relation to a subject on which all agree, a subject about which there is really no controversy, yet, the fundamental principle of the study is investigation. That very fact should suffice for disallowing a resolution of that type. Anyhow, the resolution was passed unanimously. And as an ecclesiastical head of Hindu India, I felt that unfortunately I was the one person to protest against the resolution. I was not present at the conference, but when I heard about it I said that it was unphilosophical and unscientific. In the Upaniṣads, the Vedānta, we have the three steps of Sādhanā. Sādhanā means the necessary psychic, ethical and metaphysical and other progress by which we attain our goal, — the ultimate goal of humanity. What that goal should be is a matter for intellectual understanding. And if anyone has any doubt on the question itself there should be room for such a person to come forward with an exposition of his doubt and difficulty and have the doubt explained away and the difficulty removed.

Three steps of Sādhanā

There is a notion abroad that with regard to matters of religion there should be no questioning; it should be a matter of blind faith. In fact, those who oppose religion in the name of science in the Western world as well as in the Eastern, come forward with this great objection to the philosopher and the theologian — "Here is a thing which is not scientific at all." The scientific spirit of inquiry is one which takes all possible doubts and difficulties into account and provides for their being satisfactorily dealt with. Not exclusion by dogmatic assertion, but intellectual satisfaction is what is necessary. In the Upaniṣads we are told of three steps in the process — "*Śrotavyo, mantavyo, nididhyāsitavyaḥ*".* These are the three words from Vedānta. They mean, as I translate each one with an adverb and a predicate, '*śrotavyaḥ*'—investigate carefully, '*mantavyaḥ*'—decide correctly and '*nididhyāsitavyaḥ*'—follow faithfully. This is the threefold process; investigate carefully, decide correctly, and follow faithfully. So before one can decide correctly, there must be careful and correct investi-

*Bṛhadāraṇyaka Upaniṣad II-4-5.

gation. The mere fact that something is told and is imposed from above does not satisfy the intellectual inquirer. Even those who begin with blind faith to start with, because of associations, family traditions, their training and so forth, accept these doctrines on the basis of blind faith and carry on in that way for some time. But when the mind becomes capable of going into these things, and analysing them introspectively, and coming to conclusions, the mere fact that they were told so and that they believed something all the time, will not suffice to establish the particular doctrine as the correct philosophical and scientific doctrine. And that is why in the Upaniṣads, we have the three injunctions : Investigate carefully etc. This very idea has been explained to Arjuna by Bhagavān Śrī Kṛṣṇa in the Bhagavad Gītā itself. A parallel idea, in fact, the application of this passage from the Vedānta to the Bhagavad Gītā is found in this verse:—

"Tad viddhi praṇipātena paripraśnena sevayā."†

We begin with the investigation. There is no way of getting away from the point — namely of intellectual satisfaction. Even for the person who has absolutely blind faith in the words of the master, the parents and so on, and who follows things blindly, and when a doubt assails the mind, he suppresses it with his own intellectual power, even for such a person, if there is an initial satisfaction he would naturally feel gladder and happier about it.

Everlasting Nay and everlasting Yea

Carlyle, in his *Sartor Resartus*, speaks of the everlasting nay, and the everlasting yea. He speaks of the everlasting nay, because he says that at one time or another when you do the thinking for yourself and don't take the results of other people's thinking for granted, when that stage comes, it comes with a sudden burst like a furious hurricane. It may have a tendency to sweep you along, because you have taken things for granted and acted upon them and when you begin to think for yourself and act for yourself it will not do to say that someone said it, you believed it, and have acted up to it, and therefore consistently with the past you should continue to do the

†Gītā IV-34.

same in the future, although you are not satisfied. Well, that is a preposterous proposition from the standpoint of the philosophical or scientific inquirer. We are here as seekers after the truth. We have a beautiful text in the Sanskrit which goes absolutely against the idea of mere blind faith:

"Yuktiyuktam vaco grāhyam
bālādapi śukādapi,
Yuktihīnam vacas tyājyam
vṛddhādapi śukādapi."

Here is a pun on the word Śuka. On the one hand, śuka means a parrot. On the other hand, Śuka was the name of a great sage, a leader practically, of those who have gone through the process of Self-realization and who are in what you might call 'eternal divine illumination'. The text says :

"Yuktiyuktam vaco grāhyam
bālādapi śukādapi."

'What is consistent with right reasoning ought to be accepted even though it proceeds from a boy or even from a parrot."

"Yuktihīnam vacas tyājyam
vṛddhādapi śukādapi."

"And what is inconsistent with right reasoning ought to be rejected even though emanating from an old man, or even from the great sage Śukadeva himself."

Think for yourself

So we don't start with closed minds.* The scientist has no right to dub us cranks, superstitious people, intellectually lacking, and incapable of deciding things for ourselves, or to say that things have been decided for us ages and ages ago and we haven't got the capacity to think. If we look at the physical side of life from the standpoint of growth even there we will admit that although in infancy, when we are unable to care for ourselves, we have to depend on others to do all the thinking and providing for us. Yet a stage soon comes when we have to think out for ourselves, move and act for ourselves in all the various activities of life. The new-born child is absolutely

*Śaṅkara says (in his commentary on Brahma Sūtra, I-1-1) "...avicārya yat kiṁcid pratipadyamāno nihśreyasāt pratihanyeta anartham ceyāt...".
Anyone who adopts any view without full inquiry will miss his aim of beatitude and incur grievous loss. (Radhakrishnan on Brahma Sūtra).

helpless both physically and mentally. He is worse in that respect than the young ones of dogs, cats and so on. Within a short time they get into the stride; in just a few days they begin to move about and to go out and do things for themselves. Not so the human child. The human child is physically incapable of even asking for things to be done. He is helpless. The child cannot do anything for himself, that is bad enough. He can't even tell others what ails him and get his difficulties, his troubles, his sorrows, and his sufferings removed. The parents have to think out for themselves what might be ailing the child, and on the basis of that kind of inquiry decide the course of action necessary. The child knows no language except the language of crying. People now fight about their mother tongues. Nationalistic, linguistic, and other quarrels are to be found all over the world. And recently in India we have had divisions of provinces on a linguistic basis; and unfortunately there was a lot of bloodshed too. People talk about the mother tongue and fight about the mother tongue. So far as I am concerned, with my introspective self analysis, I say there is no question of different mother tongues for different people. There is only one mother tongue, the first tongue in which all children speak, and that tongue is the tongue of crying, nothing further. The heat troubles the child, cold troubles the child, well, the child weeps. It may be a disturbance in the stomach on account of indigestion; it may be hunger. Well, both these troubles are expressed in the same language, the crying. And the mother has to infer for herself what the trouble is and she does something to relieve the trouble. And sometimes she takes a wrong decision in this gamble — because an inference is after all an inference — and the mother may be wrong in the inference, so I call it a gamble; it's a lottery. You know in all lotteries there are more blanks than prizes, and it is really a lottery, perhaps the child has been unable to digest and assimilate the milk it has already taken, and the mother infers, not on the intrinsic merits of the particular case, but judging by the watch, by the mechanical standard, it is such and such time after she suckled the child, and therefore the child must be hungry. The child is suffering from colic on account of constipation; and the mother infers the child must be hungry and feeds him again and adds to the trouble. This kind of helplessness is the lot of the human child for a considerable period of time.

But when that period is passed, a stage soon comes when the child says, "I will do everything for myself. I will bathe myself; I will feed myself; why should I be fed by mother ?" That stage comes not on account of any kind of active thought out scheme of self assertion, independence and so forth. It comes naturally as the body grows, the mind grows, the capacity for thinking also grows. The child soon comes to the stage in which he can think, act, and do things for himself. And at that stage, the mother perhaps says, "You will spoil all your clothing if you feed yourself." But the child is not satisfied with that kind of objection. The growth is the chief thing there, and it is there instinctively. It is not an assertion of some right and so forth, the child doesn't know anything about rights and duties and all that. Nature automatically, asserts herself when the proper stage is reached. And parents who grudge the independence of the child in that way and want to go on fathering and mothering the child are obstacles in the way of its progress.

In reality, when that stage comes — well, they should encourage it; only looking on to see that the child does not hurt himself in the process. They can't catch hold of the child on both sides by the arms — the father on one side and the mother on the other — and drag him along in order to make him walk. The walking has to be done by the child, sitting up, walking, catching hold of a wall or a bedstead, or something, and moving along, and sometimes falling in the process. The parents will not say that because at the very beginning the child cannot walk without falling and hurting himself therefore they will not allow the child to walk. That would be most silly.

When it comes to bathing the child says "No , I will bathe myself." That kind of assertion comes not out of any kind of perversity or obtuseness, but because it is the natural law of God. And when that stage comes, as I have said, the parents have to look on, and see that in the falling there is no more falling than will be bearable for the time being. The child should not fall and break his head. The falling, by itself is a painful process, but it is an inevitable part of the growth. This is how you can study the question from the physical side. And even with regard to the mind, the intellect, and so forth, the same rule applies. A stage comes when the child is capable of doing things without being spoon-fed all the time or hand-led all the time.

Self-analysis

So that is why in his *Sartor Resartus* Carlyle says there is a time of the 'everlasting nay' as he calls it. I will explain this. "Does God exist"; "Is there such a thing as the soul ? If so, where did it come from ?" "Where is it going ?" All these questions are inevitable. Any attempt to silence these questions will be an act of intellectual tyranny and spiritual oppression, and nothing further. If our mind asks itself this question : "I am here as an individual. My present existence is undoubted. I feel; I want to know things; therefore I am. There is no doubt about it; but what am I ? Where did I come from ? Whither am I going ?" These questions are the same in every mind. There is one difference between the intellectual, the adept, the expert, the master, Jñānī, Yogī and so forth, and the man in the street who doesn't understand anything of philosophy at all, who is frightened at the mere mention of the name of metaphysics. The difference is that although both are being assailed by the same questions, so far as the answer is concerned, one goes on investigating and does not desist from the inquiry until he has arrived at a satisfactory solution of all the problems which are involved in the process of self-anyalysis, while the man in the street has no patience for it, and is always engaged with outward affairs and concerns of the world, or hasn't got the necessary intellectual capacity for the purpose, and therefore he stops short in the course of the inquiry. I have been told, and I have believed. But was I rightly told ? Was I right in believing ? This question comes up at the stage at which the physical helplessness and the mental helplessness have gone, and the mental capacity to think over matters and the physical capacity to do things for ourselves have developed. This is the process of the intellectual satisfaction that is necessary. The very first step is one of doubt, if not of positive negation. And this is what Carlyle calls "the everlasting nay."

But soon a time comes when, after careful investigation and study of the subject, with various experimentations, or self experience if necessary, you come back to what you started with on the basis of blind belief. Bishop Berkeley, the Irish philosopher, also said the same thing.

Everlasting Yea

Put philosophy and science to the test; pursue that direction, and you will, in the course of investigation reach a stage of absolute agnosticism, or worse still, atheism positive. But pursue the same spirit of inquiry further, and you will come back to theism of a much stronger and better and more virile type — a practical theism capable of enduring all kinds of attacks and influences on it. You will be a better theist than you ever were by virtue of blind faith. And that Carlyle calls the "everlasting yea." You start with the everlasting nay and then go on to the everlasting yea.

Faith born of understanding

Now, coming back to the Gītā passage:

"Tad viddhi praṇipātena paripraśnena sevayā,
Upadekṣyanti te jñānam jñāninastattvadarśinaḥ."*

With all humility, for humility alone behooves the seeker after truth, you start the investigation. And at the end of the process you come to conclusions which the others can help you to form — they can't dictate the conclusions to you. St. Paul, too, speaks of the faith that is born of understanding. Not blind faith, not mechanical faith, but faith that is the result of experience and understanding. The child who knows nothing about the responsibility of their parents, their financial difficulties, and how they manage to keep the pot boiling, goes on playing, centred in his play. But the moment hunger or thirst assails him, he runs to his mother. What is the process ? What should be the correct name for the intellectual process by which on feeling hungry or thirsty the child runs to the mother ? The faith that is born of previous experience. The child has had previous experience that whenever he is hungry or thirsty and can't even express his trouble to the parents, the parents look after these things. The mother has been doing all this. Denying herself food, sleep, and everything of a comfort, she sits by the bedside of the ailing child; she does things for him.

*Gtiā IV-34.

And with that experience, the child automatically (not by any lengthy process with dialectics of logic, induction and deduction and so forth, but instinctively on the basis of the previous understanding born of experience) goes to the mother and seeks the nourishment there.

And the next stage comes when not merely with regard to eating and drinking, but with regard to other matters also, whenever some trouble comes and the little child's mind is not sufficiently strong to grapple with the trouble, the child again thinks of the mother and the father. And that is the process which St. Paul describes as being faith that is born of understanding.

We all know, we realize in the early childhood that we are helpless; and we seek shelter where the shelter is to be found. And that is the result of the faith that is born of understanding.

You have all heard about Sir Isaac Newton, the humility with which he describes his investigations. When people were talking to him about the great and grand discoveries that he was making, his great reputation as a scientist, as a physicist, he said, very meekly and in the utmost humility, "I am like a child picking pebbles on the sea shore. There are thousands and thousands, millions and millions more of them to be picked up." So that is the spiritual basis of the scientific spirit, the spirit of inquiry, Jijñāsā.

Three Paths

In our Sanskrit literature, when dealing with what we call the Sādhanā, where we concentrate on processes of Self-realization through devotion etc., we have what we may put roughly into three phrases: Bhakti Mārga, Karma Mārga and Jñāna Mārga. Karma Mārga is the path of works; Bhakti Mārga is the one of devotion; and the third is the one where Jñāna, wisdom, or illumination predominates.

And in the Bible, too, you will find amongst the Master's own apostles, his own immediate disciples a slight difference in the trend, according to the intellectual and temperamental inclination, or the personal equation of each. St. Peter and St. James emphasized the path of works. St. John is always on the path of love, what we call the Bhakti Mārga or the Upāsanā Mārga. In fact, in one of the most brilliant contexts of St. John's 'Epistle'* we have this statement, "God is love." Not that God loves, or is the object of love but God is love — love itself. That is the highest definition of God as conceived of by St. John the Evangelist. And you have St. Paul who represents the path of knowledge or Jñāna, as we call it.

Path of Knowledge

Now in our Jñāna Kāṇḍa where various ideals and forces and Sādhanās, or means and instruments for physical, metaphysical, moral and spiritual progress and so forth are described, we are told of the goddess Sarasvatī. Sarasvatī is the goddess of learning. The Divine Mother is described in three different aspects: Durgā, Lakṣmī, and Sarasvatī; Durgā as the mother, Lakṣmī as the mother, and Sarasvatī also as the mother. Because these three together nourish and maintain, keep up and help in the progress of the child. The physical strength necessary for grappling with physical troubles, with physical enemies and so forth, is symbolized by the eighteen-armed Durgā, that we worship during the Durgā Pūjā festival in October and November each year. You have seen the picture of the eighteen-armed mother that we have in the Pūjā. Then there is Lakṣmī, the goddess of wealth. Wealth is necessary for carrying out all the various activities in life. Not any kind of slavery to wealth, but making good use of the wealth. Wealth in various ways — wealth of kingdom, wealth from the agricultural and other income of the land, and so forth. There are various kinds of wealth, and all of these are represented by the goddess Mahālakṣmī. And then we come to the goddess of learning, intellect, education, culture, and so on; that is Mahāsarasvatī. In the description that we get of Sarasvatī, the goddess, or the presiding deity of learning, there is always a book in the hand of the goddess. We are told that the book in the picture in Sarasvatī's hand symbolizes the ocean or the mass of knowledge, or wisdom contained within the goddess of learning. The process of learning can never end. We have to continue as students all the time.

*He that loveth not, knoweth not of God; for God is love. (The First Epistle General of John — IV-8) (Also see IV-16. Ibid.)

"Tad viddhi praṇipātena
paripraśnena sevayā,
Upadekṣyanti te jñānam
jñāninastattvadarśinah."*

Always with humility, hear, learn from those who have had the necessary experience in these matters, who have gone through the mill all the time, who know where the difficulties come, and who can sympathetically agree to help you. Those who have not had this kind of experience will probably laugh at us. They will think that we are cranks and that it is an intellectual obsession which might be regarded as a form of insanity. That kind of attitude the outside world has with regard to the seeker after truth. But only those persons have this attitude who have not been through the mill themselves.

"Irks care the cropfull bird;
Frets doubt the maw-crammed beast."

That is from Robert Browning's "Rabbi Ben Ezra". Well, persons who are satisfied with the filling of the stomach from time to time and have no further interest in any kind of intellectual activity, they may be satisfied with that kind of attitude, that kind of approach. But for those who have passed through this very process that we are now passing through and can understand and sympathise with us, "jñāninas tattvadarśinaḥ," they feel, because they can feel; they have passed through the mill themselves. And therefore, they will be helpful to us. And that is the first step. We go to the Guru.

Who is Guru ?

And who is the Guru ? The word guru also is full of spiritual and practical meaning and significance. Guru; two syllables are there. *Gu* means ignorance, and *ru* means destroyer. Guru means "ignorance-destroyer"; or the destroyer of ignorance. And, as you know, in the outer world, light alone can dispel darkness. So is the case with regard to the inner world, the mental world, the world full of doubts and difficulties in a new path altogether. There too, light alone can dispel darkness. Darkness was never removed by abusing it, or by hurling instruments of destruction at it, howitzer guns

*Gītā IV-34.

and cannons, and all sorts of things. Light alone can dispel darkness of ignorance. So, in a corner which is full of darkness and despair, you have the guru coming in with the light. And with his light he dispels the darkness, and that is why he is called the guru or gurudeva. The word deva means the bright ones, the illumined ones, the devatās, gods and goddesses, that we speak of in Hindu Religion. They speak of angels in the Christian theology, but our conception of the devatās is of a less mechanical kind, but more helpful to us from the standpoint of the aspirant who is on the ladder of spirituality, of psychic progress and so forth.

The spirit of inquiry

And then the process of investigation is described by Śrī Kṛṣṇa in the Bhagavad Gītā—"Tad viddhi praṇipātena paripraśnena sevayā" by inquiry, by asking questions. Not merely 'praśnena' by inquiring, by asking, but 'paripraśnena' by inquiring from every possible standpoint. If in respect of any proposition every thing is all right theoretically, but on the side of practical economics, there is a difficulty; we cannot brush aside that difficulty and belittle it by saying it is not worth attending to. The person who is in pain knows it. Any and every person in pain regards that particular pain to be worst pain in the world. The person with a tooth-ache will say there is nothing so bad as tooth-ache in the world. The person with a stomach-ache will say that all other aches can be borne, but there is nothing so painful as stomach-ache. The person with a head-ache will say that his ailment is the worst in the world and requires the greatest attention. Now it's not a question of which pain is greater and which is not. The question is what are you feeling ? That which you feel but are unable to bear, causes you all the suffering. And if I, being in a position of health and strength and financial and other prosperity, tell you not to mind ill health and weakness and poverty and so on, that would be an easy-chair attitude towards the problem. Well, the person who comes to us for advice will feel repelled by this and will not seek further advice from us. It's a very unpsychological method of dealing with the trouble. We have to take all possible troubles into account and deal with them, and see them removed. So Bhagavān says in the Bhagavad Gītā—

"Upadekṣyanti te jñānam
jñāninas tattvadarśinaḥ."

first of all investigate carefully — and of course the investigation will have to be with the help of those who have gone on before us, who have passed through all this and who can help us. But we don't accept everything with blind faith. Pariprasnena — We put questions with all humility no doubt. The spirit of inquiry prompts us. And there is freedom to ask questions. Any silencing of a question can only be a silencing of the question from the lips; the question is not silenced in the heart. Any attempt at forcible silencing, by oppressive tyrannical use of power or authority of the elder, of the superior towards the younger person, the inferiors as he dubs them in his superiority complex, will not solve the problem, will not remove the difficulty, but will only worsen things by producing a feeling of embitterment, a feeling that you are inhuman, you are not thinking of the suffering that the other person is enduring. We generally take it for granted that any unbelief, any kind of disposition to question is something perverse, is something to be cut out from the very outset. That is a very wrong process. So long as the difficulty is there, steps will have to be taken for removal of the difficulty. That should be our attitude towards those who come to us for help. So there is no question of banning the inquiry. On the other hand, the teacher, the real master encourages the spirit of inquiry. Because unless we know what ails the patient, we cannot prescribe. A diagnosis is necessary. And in this case, self-diagnosis will help us. Sometimes the patient may have wrong notions and delusions about what really is the trouble. But we have to hear the patient also. Even in cases of absolute insanity, patient's description of his trouble will help us to ascertain the real trouble. So there is no curbing, no quelling, no resenting of the spirit of inquiry on the part of the pupil. And you will find that this textual attitude, the academical doctrine, is actually followed by Śrī Kṛṣṇa in his own practice, in the Bhagavad Gītā for example. At the end of the discourse, the eighteen chapters of the Bhagavad Gītā, Śrī Kṛṣṇa does not say, "I have explained all these things to you. Act according to my instructions." In fact, Arjuna originally asked for orders.

"Kārpaṇyadoṣopahatasvabhāvaḥ
pṛcchāmi tvām dharma saṁmūḍhacetāḥ,
Yacchreyaḥ syānniścitam brūhi tan me
śiṣyas te 'ham śādhi mām tvām prapannam."*

"I haven't got the capacity now in my present intellectual position — the necessary capacity for understanding what is good and what is injurious to myself. Think for me; decide for me; and issue your commands to me. I am here to obey orders. I am a disciple, and a disciplined disciple. I will obey orders. I throw myself at your feet. You are the ultimate, the highest shelter that I can think of. Issue your orders to me." But Bhagavān does not issue orders. On the contrary, you have the eighteen chapters of the Bhgavad Gītā in which Bhagavān goes into the question from every conceivable standpoint.

"Eṣā te' bhihitā sāṅkhye
buddhiryoge tvimām śṛṇu."†

"Now what I have told you is from the standpoint of Sāṅkhya, that is the Jñānakāṇḍa. Now hear what I have to say with regard to the Yoga path." And then, one after another, all possible standpoints are taken up, and even the atheistic standpoint of the naturalist taken care of.** "If you believe that there is no spirit behind anything at all, that it is all mechanical, lifeless, inert nature, and that things are going on mechanically in that way, in which the lightning and thunder and so forth are there, the rains from time to time according to the seasons are there, and you have no voice in the matter, you were never consulted with regard to the framing of the laws governing the universe; these rules, these regulations came into existence and began to be applied ages and ages, eons and eons ago with no help from you by way of consultation and so forth. And they are there, and you are to follow them mechanically." No, that's not the

*Gītā II-7.

†Gītā II-39.

**Perhaps His Holiness had the following verse of Gītā in view:—
Asatyamapratiṣṭham te jagadāhuranīśvaram,
Aparasparasambhūtam kimanyatkāmahaitukam. —Gītā XVI-8.

"They (the materialists) say that the world is false and without any basis (of ultimate reality) and is without God. It is born of meeting of sexes and has no purpose except pleasure."

spirit at all. There is an intelligent power behind all this. Even with regard to madness of the worst type, you will find doctors treating lunatics telling you that there is a method behind the madness. It is up to the doctor to find out that method; how that madness works, and how it should be removed. So, even the naturalist attitude, the attitude of the atheistical or the agnostical frame of mind, even that is taken into account. And from that standpoint, too, the question is tackled and dealt with by Bhagavān. And at the end of the whole discourse when we have heard from every standpoint, Bhagavān is not found saying, "Well, I have given you more than enough explanation of what I think is the right path. Now follow my orders". No. No question of orders again.

Iti te jñānamākhyātam
guhyād guhyataram mayā
Vimṛśyaitad aśeṣeṇa
yathecchasi tathā kuru.*

"I have told you everything; you are now in a position where you can understand things for yourself; and now, as the result of understanding what I have told you, do what you think is the right thing." That liberty is still given even in that last stage. And then the question is asked, "Has the trouble in your mind, the perplexity, the difficulty, the sadness that you were suffering from, been removed by what I have told you ? Or do you require any further exposition of things ?" There is the helpful master coming in even at that stage.

Intellectual satisfaction

But Arjuna has reached the stage in which he is fully satisfied. Intellectual satisfaction is there, and he says—

Naṣṭo mohaḥ smṛtir labdhā
tvatprasādānmayācyuta,
Sthito' smi gatasandehaḥ
kariṣye vacanam tava.**

That is at the end of the Bhagavad Gītā, "All my doubts and difficulties and perplexities are gone. I shall now perform my duty." He rises to perform his duty thereafter. He does

* Gītā XVIII—63.
**Gītā XVIII—73.

not say, "My doubts and difficulties continue, but because I am bound to obey tyrannical orders I am obeying them, grudgingly, weeping inside and smiling outside." That kind of thing is not there.

So the whole question comes up in that way from the standpoint of intellectual satisfaction. Even the person who has a strong element of blind faith in his blood, even he will rejoice when something which was difficult for him to understand has been made intelligible to him. I have always been a school master. It was open to me to go into various walks of life. There were those who wanted me to go in for the life of a barrister, a lawyer. There were those who wanted me to become an engineer. Others suggested that I should become a doctor. There were various paths which were open to me and for which I was eligible on account of academical qualifications and so forth. But somehow from my childhood, well, the school master, the pedagogue was in the blood. And I have always been an educationist, and to the present moment I am a school master. And as a school master, I have always felt that the cries of the little children, the troubles of the little children are more agonizing and excruciating and torturing than anything that bigger people with greater responsibility in life can think of as sufferings. Finding a child unable to understand something that I am explaining, well, the face shows that the child has not been able to follow. The child is perplexed. That perplexed face of the child, well, hurts me. It has always done so, and it still does. And when I explain the thing over again to the child and the little boy or little girl at the school understands, the smile that comes on the face, is a tremendous compensation for the trouble taken in explaining things once again. The attitude of the person who says, "Well, you cannot understand this; you are not fit for this class. How did you pass your entrance examination ? Go back to the High School." That kind of attitude is not helpful at all, and is unworthy of a teacher. I very often feel that any discouragement of the spirit of inquiry on the part of the student by the teacher is a criminal sin against the progress of the child. It is a sin against the progress of the child's soul. That has always been my feeling. On other sides of life you have people who are really dealers and who call themselves leaders. Similarly in the educational field, I think of such people as fit to be described as cheaters who call themselves teachers. So-called leaders are really dealers, and so-called teachers are really cheaters.

Only a realised soul can be the Guru

So the question comes up in that way, and it has to be tackled in that way. The intellectual satisfaction has to be found. And if you find there are obstacles in the way, you naturally don't feel satisfied. Of course you are compelled to bear things; and yield to the inevitable, bowing down before what you are unable to cure. It is the application of the English proverb "What one cannot cure one must endure." The enduring is not voluntarily done; or willingly done. There is no happiness. The inquiry is necessary. The spirit of inquiry should be there, 'paripraśnena'. And there too, the expression used 'jñāninas tattvadarśinaḥ' is very significant. You are told to approach the master, but who is the master ? One who has acquired academical or theoretical qualifications as regards doctrine, dogma and so forth ? No. The text does not say "tattvavidaḥ" "Those who *know* the right doctrine." That's not the wording: It says "tattvadarśinaḥ." "Those who have realized, who have visualized, and who go on enjoying from moment to moment the realized Self within".* That is the master who will be helpful even with regard to those things which the master has not passed through. He has the sympathetic conception by which he can put himself, inside of the skins of those who inquire, take a sympathetic attitude and give help. There are things which I have not passed through, but which I can imagine and I can give advice to others. But that spirit is not there at all, if the master has an attitude of snubbing and resenting the spirit of inquiry. Well, "I open my mouth and let no dogs bark"—that is from Shakespeare. That kind of thing is not helpful at all. The spirit of inquiry has to be encouraged; and unless the spirit of inquiry is satisfactorily dealt with by proper reaction from this side

*"....na ca jñāninas tattvadarśinaḥ iti smṛtiḥ parokṣaniścayavatas tadabhyasanaśīlasya pratipādikā darśanaśabdena sākṣātkārasya eva rūpādidarśanasya iva abhidhānāt.—Citsukhi-IV.

"Here the scripture (Gītā) does not refer to a person who has only indirectly convinced himself about the Reality. The use of the word "darśinaḥ" denotes direct perception (realisation) like seeing objects with eyes".

(master's side), we don t do justice to the individual soul that has come before us. There are different levels and gradations on the rungs of the spiritual ladder. And the part of the person who has reached a higher rung is naturally to be helpful to those who are still below. This idea of above and below should not lead to any feeling of superiority complex. Superiority complex on the one hand, automatically means creation of inferiority complex on the other. And the two together are sufficient to extinguish the whole candle altogether. The relationship is that of the student and the expounder — I don't speak of the master, the teacher, the orderer and so forth — I speak even of the teacher as your co-thinker, who thinks aloud. When I speak to my students, I am thinking aloud, and giving the pupil an opportunity of picking holes if necessary. Very often it so happens that people who have attained a high position in a certain line have forgotten, or have ignored something of importance, and reached the wrong conclusion. And a little child, unable to understand puts a question which starts the master athinking, and is responsible perhaps for a complete reversal of the conclusion which the master reached in the earlier stage. The master thanks the pupil, and says, "This pupil was responsible for my getting over this difficulty, and for such and such intellectual, moral, psychic, and spiritual satisfaction as I now feel." So we say the pupil is the master's master. Difficulties which the master never thought of are placed before him by the different students; and therefore he gets a better scope for his own thinking, for his own elevation. It's a mutual process and that is why I say the pupil and the teacher are co-thinkers. We think aloud. There is no need to assume that we are infallible, that we have reached beyond the stage of taking advice from others. The closed mind is always objectionable because it warps our judgment, it distorts our vision. It's injurious in every way not merely to those who come to us for help, but even for our own progress.

Scientific attitude towards religion

Well, this would be the kind of preamble, what I might call prolegomenon, with which to start the study of any subject whatsoever. And that is a scientific attitude. The scientists cannot now come and complain that it is all dogmatic assertion, it is all blind belief, it is this and that. We welcome the scientific attitude. To say that philosophy is unscientific — is a disgrace and an insult to philosophy. If as a theologian, as a philosopher, I fight shy of scientific questions, I admit beforehand that I have no right reasons to adduce for the position I take except on the score of authority. But even then the question arises: Supposing I take it for granted that what a certain person in authority has dictated is the right thing and ought to be followed, well, there are others who will feel differently on the matter. Why should not their authority be equally accepted ? If you are going to make a sweeping proposition like that — not a generalization, but a universalization — that what has been said must be accepted, well, this must be equally acceptable to others also. And if people with their different views come and each insists on his view being adopted and acted up to by all, that would mean terrible confusion. The whole thing gets into a mess. And there is no possibility of satisfaction at all. And when the intellectual satisfaction is not there, there is no peace. You may do things, you may do them grudgingly, you may do them unwillingly, but there is no peace of mind, there is no happiness. No system deserves to be called a philosophy unless it caters for the peace of mind, for the harmony inside, for the happiness and joy within. "The peace that passeth all understanding,"* that is how St. Paul describes it, ineffable peace. This is the relationship between the philosophical and scientific attitude.

Harmony between science and religion

When people talk to you about the antagonism between the philosopher and the theologian on the one side, and the scientist on the other, well, they are going against the fundamental truth. The law of nature, or the divine law Ṛtam as we call it, should be one, is bound to be one. It is inconceivable that the rules and regulations made by God for my benefit and ordered for me to follow should come into conflict with the rules and regulations which we find in nature around us. In the pages of nature and in the pages of the revealed texts there can be no conflict at all. If at any time we feel that there is a conflict, well we may be sure

*Philippians IV-7.

that either we have misread our scriptures or misunderstood the nature around us or blundered in both. We cannot possibly have understood both aright and yet found unreconcilable antagonism between the two.

When people talk of rationalism, I say I am a rationalist. When people talk of science, I say I am a scientist, I am with you. There is no quarrel at all; there cannot be a quarrel. The methods may be different, the paths may be different; and yet when you reach the goal, it must be the same. You may go from here by train, by air plane, by bullock cart, or by any other kind of conveyance but when you reach New York it is the same New York reached by whatever conveyance. Similarly the ultimate truth is one and the same though it is reached by philosophical inquiry on one hand, and scientific inquiry on the other. There cannot be thus any kind of conflict, any kind of discord in the name of religion and science, and much less therefore in the name of one religion and another, That is still more preposterous. If two such things which are supposed to be absolutely unrelated to each other as religion and science are not merely reconcilable but have their own natural, inherent, internal harmony and concord; much more therefore it would stand to reason that different religions cannot be mutually conflicting. There again you may have misunderstood this or that or both; you cannot have understood both aright and found an antagonism of an unreconcilable character. And still worse is the conflict between sub-sects of the same religion like Protestants and Roman Catholics. There are sub-sects, sub-sub-sects, sub-sub-sub-sects carried to an infinity of terms, and Subdivisions — vertical, horizontal, crosswise, all sorts of divisions. People have their loyalty to these sects and not to the truth. That is where the trouble starts. We start with closed minds, with prejudices and presuppositions. Clearing our minds of all "Can'ts", preconceived notions, *a priori* notions, we sit down to the task of studying things, not in order to find what we would like to find there — that would be dishonest — but to actually find out what is there and to abide by it, to benefit by it. That's the process of harmony. We call it Śānti in Sanskrit. Śānti, śānti, śānti*—

*Before and after the study or recitation of the Vedas a Śānti-pāṭha (or invocation to peace) is recited. At the end of the invocation the word

Peace. There can be no forced peace. The peace must come from the heart. And if that peace is not from the heart, well, it means you are only lying down for a rest after fighting and will resume the fighting as soon as you are able to stand up again and fight. That's what's going on in the world; in the political and military field. It is an interval, an interregnum. It is not the end of the troubles of the past.

Universal harmony

But we should attune ourselves to this frame of mind of harmony and concord, not merely amongst countries and countries, religions and religions, but worlds and worlds together. The astronomer speaks of other worlds than ours, he talks of the sun, the moon, Mars, and other planets and stars. Even with those other worlds and beings there, if any, we should be in a spirit of being in tune with the Infinite. *In Tune With The Infinite* is the name of a famous book by Ralph Waldo Trine. There should be no kind of discord between one thing and another. They are all parts of the same. And even the seeming differences have an underlying unity. We talk of the seed of a tree. A small seed contains within itself all the various developments which come on later when the seed gets the necessary soil, necessary manure, the necessary ploughing and the necessary rain or other water as needed from time to time. So many things come out of it, which the sight of the seed could never have caused you to imagine, or even to dream about; the seed, or the root, the stalk, the stem, the branches, the leaves, the flowers, the fruits. They are different in position, in colour, in shape, and even in physical qualities, and therapeutical value, and so forth. The flower may have the effect of producing diarrhoea; while the fruit may stop it. All kinds of things are there as integral parts of the same unit, in spite of, and along with, and

Śānti (peace) is pronounced thrice. Śankara explains its significance as follows: Om śāntiḥ śāntiḥ śāntir iti trir vacanam ādhyātmikādhi bhautikādhidaivikānām vidyā-prāptyupasargāṇām prasamārtham.
(Commentary on Taittiriya Upaniṣad I-1-1)

"Repetition of the word śānti thrice is for removal of spiritual, natural and supernatural hindrances to self-realisation".

probably by virtue of the particular thing that you are speaking of as being in conflict. Diversity, no doubt, in details; but unity underlying all the diversity of the infinity in the universe.

Similarly with regard to the physical body, we have the various portions in the body. None under natural circumstances performs the functions of the other. A person who has gone blind, makes use of his feet and his legs for functioning in the place of eyes. Things like that do happen, but that is out of sheer necessity caused by unnatural circumstances, by accidents, and so forth. In the normal state you have these various organs of the body functioning at their own levels, having different physical and other construction. All these differences are there, and yet there is the oneness behind them. They are the physical parts of the same human body. There is no internal quarrel at all. The feet do not say to the eyes, "Why should you be above, and why should I be below. I will strike work." Labour strikes and other sorts of strikes are very ordinary things now. If individual parts of the human body go on strike on account of such discontent, that would mean a complete paralyzing of physical activities of the body.

I was mentioning an example yesterday, to you (Śrī Dayāmātā), of the physical body-and occasional conflict, seemingly between the different parts of the body. Sometimes our own finger hurts our eye; our own teeth hurt our lips and our tongue. On any such occasion would any person come forward and say, "Well these fingers are innimical, they are injurious to my eyes; and therefore I will have the finger, cut off"? No one says that. Similarly with regard to the teeth, no one says that because the teeth have injured the lip or the tongue, he will call the dentist and get all the teeth pulled out. No one does that; because there is a realization — not on account of argumentation, but inherent, mechanical and automatic realization — that this whole body is one, in spite of all the diversities. We can extend this idea to others in society — when another person's finger hurts our eye, we should be able to say with regard to that finger, "Oh, that is also part of my own organism." If that stage can be reached, if we can extend our jurisdiction in that way, the jurisdiction with regard to internal oneness, well, conflicts will begin to disappear.

We start with the individual as an absolutely selfish, unthinking being, inconsiderate of the sorrows and joys of others. Then we go on expanding and extending our jurisdiction, as we call it. The child says "My mother,". The mother's interest is there. With the identification of interests of the mother, the father and the child, the family comes in that way. And then a small area, the county, the district, then the province, the state, the country. And then after that we come to international relations also. I say 'international' is not sufficient; "interuniversal" is necessary. We can go even to that extent. The whole thing is based on the relationship between God, the individual soul, and the universe. But before we can get to that unity, there must be the necessary philosophical and practical understanding of how that unity is really based upon physical truth. All that has been said so far only shows the desirability of it.

But everything that is desirable is not necessarily true. If this kind of oneness can be felt, actually experienced and put into action, that would no doubt mean so much greater peace and harmony in the world. And whatever is saved from destruction in the shape of dollars, in the shape of energy, in the shape of feelings and so forth, can be harnessed to positive and constructive processes for reconstruction of society on a better basis and for all round human progress. We find that we are wasting lots of money on these conflicts. The preparation for the conflicts, by the other side and the possibility, and the fear of the conflict makes you prepare for it on this side. And preparation on this side makes the other side prepare further and it goes on in that way. It becomes an endless thing, a vicious circle and there is no breaking of the deadlock. It is desirable to realise the essential unity behind all the diversity to break this deadlock. Well, the person then argues in this way: it is no doubt desirable, but is it true, is it correct? Merely because it is desirable, is it being imposed upon us as being the right thing, the true thing? The next question comes in that way.

I don't know about the time. I generally forget time (everyone laughs).

Unity based on truth

We have taken up this side of the question today. At another sitting, on another occasion, I may take up the other aspect, as to whether what is very desirable is true. That has to be answered also for the intellectual satisfaction of the inquirer, the seeker after truth — the seeker after truth with no other limitations whatsoever. If this truth comes into conflict with such and such considerations, will I subordinate the truth to those considerations? — No. It is not the right attitude. It may stand the strain of actual trial for some time; but it can't go on for ever in that way. You can't go on mending and bending for ever. People do it for some time in the hope that they will get over the difficulty for the time being. But they find after some time that each submission, each bending down has only led the other side to pitch up their claim a little higher still. That kind of thing takes place. And if that is the reaction, the natural result of our attitude of peaceful and helpful coordination and cooperation with others for the sake of world peace and world prosperity and so forth, well, such a peace is not worth purchasing at such a price. That kind of feeling comes. And therefore the truth part of it should also be investigated. The desirability is incontestable; and incontrovertible. The next question arises in this way: how shall we reconcile the historical truth, or what seems to be the actual state, with the thing desirable for the moment ? Is there a conflict ?

I think, at another sitting I shall be able to deal with the matter and show that there is no conflict there too. No internal conflict, no inherent conflict, and no conflict of an irreconcilable character. It's our own readjustment of our own frame of mind that is necessary. We have, speaking on the physical side, differences of vision. And the differences of vision require the use of different kinds of glasses with their different powers, and so forth. My eyes have been recently operated upon and I am now using high-powered glasses I was not using for reading and writing before that. Some months ago I was not doing it, and it's only a short while ago that these glasses, refracting lenses, became necessary and are being used. Why ? Because the eyes are not seeing properly; they are refracting. And the counter-refraction is necessary for removing the refraction. If we turn our minds into reflecting mirrors, and see the exact truth it will be found that it is all harmony, it is all concord. The music of the spheres, which the poet, and the saint speak of, is not imagination. It is absolute physical and historical verity; one of the eternal verities, in Carlyle's language. It is there.

But, as a matter of fact, the eyes that we have, are rarely reflecting mirrors; they are generally refracting lenses. And counter-refraction becomes necessary. Similar is the case with regard to the mental eye. We start with predispositions, with preconceived notions, with the result that when need arises, we see things distorted, not exactly as they are. So the necessity arises of counter-refraction. The refracting lenses with which we are born into the world come, according to our philosophy which I shall be going into later on, as a result of things relating to the past. There can be no tree without a seed causing it to come into existence — and without other sorts of causes also; soil, and monsoon, and manure, and all. Similarly here, there can be no effect without a cause. There can be no justification for a different effect without there being a different cause, and so on.

Cause and effect

If for example — to take a very homely illustration — a person wants to start a fruit garden of his own, he sows various kinds of seeds of various trees, but has not sown a particular seed — say a mango seed. And he finds when seeds begin to grow, to sprout out of the ground, there is a mango tree in his garden. He will not be justified in saying, "I never planted a mango seed, and no one of my friends did, so — in fact no seed was planted at all, and yet the tree has arisen." That would be illogical. Even from the standpoint of the most shallow thinker, the answer would be, "You may not be aware of having sown the seed, or any friend having sown the particular seed but the seed must have fallen into the soil, perhaps from the mouth of a passing bird, but the seed must have been there for the tree to grow." This is the law of cause and effect, inevitable cause and effect, which is a physical law, and is taken into account in dynamics. We talk of the resultant of two forces, or three forces, and so on. In physics, dynamics, and so forth, we talk of these things.

The discussion of the resultant of forces coming from the past takes me to another question with regard to rebirth, and the law of karma, and so on. I don't want to take up several questions at one time. We have a part of the first question still to be taken up. And this will come as part of the consideration over that other question, because it fits in there. As we are speaking of the truth, the exact historical and scientific position with regard to ourselves as individuals, with regard to the whole cosmos, as individuals and as members of society, it is necessary to consider such questions. These we will take up at another opportunity.

V LIGHT FROM ANCIENT INDIA

Hollywood Church of All Religions,
Sunday, February 9, 1958

Friends:

It is a matter of universal experience within the reach of every one of us that, in spite of all of the hundreds and thousands of differences that divide individuals from individuals, with regard to ideas, with regard to conduct, etc., the goal, the objective sought to be obtained by all, in spite of these differences, is one.

Universal Objective

It is not merely a matter of universal experience, but a matter of surprise on the one hand, and of pleasure on the other, that, in spite of all the differences, there is this unity of goal to start with. If we analyse our own feelings and sentiments, with regard to all the various activities that we go through in life, we find that all persons are motivated in their activities by the desire to enjoy happiness and to be free from sorrow and suffering.

If and when we go deeper into the subject, we shall be able to see what the various elements are that constitute happiness as we seek it, and what it is that we think of as misery, unhappiness, suffering, etc. Each individual has his own particular temperamental predilections, or idiosyncrasies, if you like to put it so. But in spite of these differences, the wonderful and the most gratifying thing is that we all wish to reach the same goal. And if we want to have light on that goal, well, there is no difficulty at all. Each one can address one's own mind and intellect and ask "What do you seek; what is it that you seek to avoid ?" And, the answer invariably comes without any kind of tutoring from any person, in the name of religion, philosophy, science, or economics, etc. Irrespective of all these considerations, the one answer is : "I seek to avoid unhappiness and I seek happiness." That is universal.

The capacity to bear suffering when it comes, is a different thing. Even the person who has enormous endurance, temperamentally and by training, does not seek suffering for its own sake. When the suffering is there, he is able to bear it. He has trained himself in such a manner that he is able to bear what others do not find it so easy to bear.

Well, the first thing that surprises one in this is that although conceptions differ as to the means of attaining happiness and avoiding all unhappiness, yet, the goal as I have been pointing out, is exactly the same for all. That should make our task easier. For, if people have not merely different ideas as regards methods and plans of work and means of achievement, etc., but if their goals are also different, the paths are bound to be different. And therefore, that means a tremendous complication. With minds differently constituted, as they are, as they were, and as they ever will be, so long as the world lasts, we're bound to have differences of opinion with regard to the means for the attainment of our one common goal. Much more therefore will be the difficulty before us in case the goals were also different. There is sufficient strife, and conflict, heart-burning, and even blood-shedding, and so on, because of differences, because of conflicts in various directions, from various quarters, and on various subjects. If to all this there should be added a further difference, the worst difference, namely, that the goals are different, then the position would be absolutely hopeless indeed. But, we begin by thankfully acknowledging that such is not the case.

We all seek happiness and seek to avoid unhappiness. So the goal is the same.

And then when we speak about the means of the attainment of the goal, all the differences arise. And even there, if we attune ourself in the right spirit, in the right direction, to the truth around us, if we clear our minds of all prejudices and prepossessions, if we are here as seekers after the truth, not merely in order to acquire the academical or theoretical knowledge of dogma and doctrine, etc., but in order to put it into practice and thereby raise ourselves on the one side, and raise others also within our sphere of influence on the other, sameness of approach is possible.

Spiritual light, the first creation of God

Speaking of the creation of the world by God as related in the first chapter of the first book of the Bible, Genesis,* the author tells us that the first creation was light. The sun, the moon, the

*Genesis I-3.

stars, and the other lights which we know of in the physical world around us, were yet to be created. The creation process begins by God saying, "Let there be Light, and there was Light." Carlyle, the famous sage-author, the sage of Chelsea in England, poses this question, "What is the kind of light that is referred to as the first creation ?" The sun, the moon, and the stars are to be created yet, and before that there was the creation to start with, of Light. God said, 'Let there be Light', and there was Light. The process begins in that way.

And, in answer to his own question which he poses before us and before other thinkers, Carlyle says, the only imaginable light could be the light of knowledge, the light of reason, the light of wisdom, the light of self-introspection.

Bhārata defined

And speaking on the subject, from the standpoint of "Self-Realization and Light from Ancient India," I wish to point out that the very name that we know India by, Bhārata, gives us the necessary clue, gives us the right direction, tells us the right trend, the standpoint from which we should look at matters, we should approach the subject. Bhārata, is the name. Bhā, means light, and knowledge, and rata means devoted, Bhārata, means devoted to light, as against darkness.* The definition itself starts in that way. We have this unique feature with regard to our Sanskrit literature, that the language, the rules of grammar, the diction, etc., necessitate the use of words for denoting objects in such a manner that the philosophy, the science, and the theology behind the whole thing is clear, not merely from the standpoint of an historian who wants to seek the truth of historical occurrences before him, and the nature of the world before him, etc., but also from the practical, realistic standpoint of the means to be adopted for achieving his purpose.

Bhārata, I do not know what Asia, Europe, and Africa mean, and why they were so named. With regard to America, I know that there was an Italian named Amerigo Vespucci, who was wrongly credited with discovering this western continent.

* "Bhā dīptiḥ. Bhāsi dīptau rataḥ Bhārataḥ".—
This is the derivation of the word Bhārata as given by His Holiness in another lecture.

And after Amerigo Vespucci—Vespucci, that is the Italian pronunciation — the country was named America. That gives us no hint at all as regards the character, the purpose, the trend, the ideal, the outlook, the angle of vision, etc. (of Americans).

But, with regard to India we have this. The rules of the language dictate that every object is to be named with a significance of its own. Significance, not merely explaining its present condition, its present meaning, exigencies, requirements, etc., but how the name should be justified by actual action.

Nathaniel Hawthorne, the American author, has placed before us this idea of a child being taught to have a great ideal and go on idealizing and trying to realize that ideal in actual practice, and the result of such a course of training is described as being, well, what you might call, merging into, or becoming one with that ideal, realizing it in due course.

If there are great ideals before us, they affect our lives. The examples, the surroundings, and all these, have their various influences on us from this standpoint and there is nothing like having great ideals before us. Bhārata means devoted, dedicated, consecrated, to the light, that means against darkness. Light alone dispels darkness. Darkness was never yet removed by abusing it, beating it with a stick, or shooting at it with bigger and worse instruments of destruction.

Well, similarly, on the intellectual plane, we have light alone, spiritual light alone, dispelling the darkness of ignorance.

So, Bhārata is not the name of a mere geographical entity placed in some corner of the world and having its own geographical, topographical, and other limitations. Bhārata stands for every individual soul that has this ideal of light, the dedication to the light, as against immersion in darkness. So we speak of the light that God's creation of the world began with, and we think of the Light that India claims to be its chief aspiration, its chief, its most important and most valued goal. Starting from that standpoint, we go on to the last portion of that very first chapter of Genesis with regard to creation.

The creation began with light, and the last to be created in the series was the human being, conscious and having various equipments of a kind denied to other parts of creation. The birds, the bees, the worms, the insects, they too are all sentient beings, but there is this tremendous difference between them and us. We have the capacity to think about our future, to plan ahead, to understand things philosophically and scientifically, and raise ourselves to that level, to that rung on the spiritual ladder which is our goal. The creation of man is described in this way, "God made man in his own image."*

Let us go into this question again as regards light.

Man in God's own image

What is the meaning of this passage ? What is the light that God created in the very beginning ? The Light, the internal light, the psychic, spiritual, physical, and so on. But with regard to man's being created in God's own image, well, we look around us and we see human beings of different types, in physical appearance, in mental calibre and outlook, and in various other ways, there are tremendous differences. And yet, the Genesis does not tell us in so many terms that a particular individual alone was created in this way. God created the first man Adam in His own image, and the others are of a different type, they come from a different kind of parentage, their genesis is different, etc. No. God created man in His own image. Man as such, humanity as such has been created in God's own image. What can it mean ?

Let us go into a little self-analysis.

The self-analysis should not be of a technical and difficult character which is beyond the capacity of ordinary thinking human beings. Anything in the nature of a tough and technical proposition, full of technical terminology, and requiring techniques difficult to understand and put into practice, would mean practical exclusion of most of mankind from all possibility of sharing in the pursuit of those aspirations. The text simply says, "God created man in His own image."* You may put the word man in capital letters and say the whole of humanity, mankind itself, as such, was created in God's own image. What can this mean ?

Study of metaphysics

I wish to go into the study of this subject, not from the standpoint of someone outside, but in the capacity of a teacher, a

*Genesis I-27.

person with experience, I wish to aid, as far as I possibly can, aspirants on the spiritual ladder who are thinking of these matters to look into the question from within themselves, not calling upon people on the basis of faith to accept this or that particular doctrine or dogma on pain of being consigned to eternal hell and brimstone, and fire, and things of that type, not by any kind of application of force, physical, intellectual, or otherwise but, by simple, clear understanding of the things, even though the things have always been labelled difficult. We find the great majority of persons at the present day around us telling us again and again that metaphysics is a very difficult subject. Well, I feel very sad when I hear people talking about philosophy, about metaphysics, about self-introspection, self-analysis, self-realization, etc., as being difficult.

People will come and tell you that they avoid metaphysics. "Meta-physics, oh, that is for great souls. That is not for the ordinary man in the street. We are far below that kind of level. It is beyond us. There is no chance of our realizing a thing like that." That is the kind of attitude that many people present to the study of philosophy.

I feel sad over this because this is just the opposite of what it ought to be. In fact, according to my conception of the subject which I hope I shall presently convince you is the right one, philosophy should be the easiest of all and the most natural and the most thoroughly assimilable of all subjects. With regard to other subjects, whatever they may be, you will have this to start with, namely, that things are told to you and you are asked to get them by heart and remember them.

Let us for example take the study of history, physics, chemistry, and other subjects. They say these are practical subjects; they are realistic subjects; and therefore, easier for people to go into. But as for philosophy, oh, that is beyond us. It's too big for us. We can't have such lofty ambitions. It must be years, thousands and thousands of them, before we can become eligible for the study of metaphysics. That is how people tell you of their mental reaction to the proposal for the study of philosophy on the basis of self-analysis, retrospection, introspection, and so on.

Now, let us take, for example, the case of history. The text book or the teacher in the high school tell you, that William the Conqueror invaded England in the year 1066 A.D. You take it from the author, you get it by rote, well, to put it bluntly, you cram it. And then, you have to remember it. That's all there is to it. There's nothing further, no method by which you can know whether 1066 A.D. is the correct date or not. Why it should have been 1066 and not 4932, there's no reason whatsoever. Whether it really happened or not, even that may be doubtful. Sometimes, on points of controversy, where there have been religious persecutions, and so on, we have the Protestant version, and Roman Catholic version, of the troubles between the two in England, France, Spain, and so on. The historians give different accounts of the same incident. They give different details altogether. And, you do not even know how much of it is historical, how much is merely an attempt to prop up things that are otherwise indefensible. That kind of thing is always there. Take any date, any particular incident whatsoever, the same thing happens. Is there any reason why the Battle of Bosworth Field was fought in 1485 and not in 1493? No reason at all. It happened so. I tell you so; accept it and state it in the examination, otherwise well, you'll fail. That is the punishment, there's nothing further. There is no method by which I can say, "I'm convinced that this is right and this is wrong." In fact, there are no data available for the purpose at all, and the subject is one that is really absolutely external and beyond us, dependent on memory and nothing else, whatsoever.

Similar is the case with regard to geography, with so many transformations taking place from time to time, with regards to boundaries of states, kingdoms, and so on. How inefficient is the method by which we try to assimilate these facts in ourselves. States have gone out of existence. Names that we knew in our childhood, Bohemia, and so on, few people recognize now. Changes have taken place from time to time and what you studied probably at school by cramming it with tears, well, you find that that has gone out of date and there is no further applicability of it. It becomes wrong at the present day. The countries are differently named. You have no clue whatsoever from anything within yourself, within reach of you, within your jurisdiction, by which you can say, "this is the correct answer".

But philosophy, what is philosophy?

Immediate evidence

When we talk of philosophy, we talk of the individual soul, the internal soul, the soul within ourselves. We understand our own feelings. We don't need any aid, any kind of assistance from others as to what we desire. If a person has a different view from ours, we say, that may be his view of the matter, it may be his psychology, his mentality in the matter, it is not mine. So you have got material for saying what is the nature of things within yourself, how you are constituted, what is really within you, well, you don't need help from others for describing your desires. In fact, all other people including your own parents, have to get description from you as to what ails you, what you need, and so on. There is nothing which you can learn from outside in that way. Everything is within. "The Kingdom of God is within you."* Christ's own teaching is to that effect. Everything is inside. And it is not so very deep, so very subtle as to be beyond ordinary man's understanding. In very simple terms you can answer the question for yourself. "What is your internal composition? What is your constitution ? What is the characteristic, or the set of characteristics, which distinguish you from other creation ? Is there any or isn't ?" All these questions can be answered from within. And how ?

Well, I don't propose to say anything which will be difficult for the hearers to follow, for any of you to follow or which will be beyond your experience and therefore has to be accepted on the basis of faith, because I have said it or some other person has said it. You can put to your own self the question, "O, heart, what is it that you desire ?" I am going into this kind of self-analysis from what I call the internal standpoint, and not from subjective reasoning, not on the basis of evidence from outside. Evidence may be false, evidence may be tainted in various ways, but this is the evidence coming from inside, first-hand evidence. In the law courts too, they insist that any evidence which is not within one's own experience, is not admissible. Primary evidence or direct evidence is the only one acceptable and if you say anything from hearsay, they at once turn it down and say, well, it cannot be put on record because it is not within your experience. You cannot know anything about it yourself, you heard about it. Hearsay evidence, indirect evidence, or secondary evidence, is no evidence at all. That's what the judges, the magistrates tell you.

*St. Luke XVII-21.

Here I'm putting before you a process of ratiocination by which you can find things out for yourself.

Instinctive aspirations : desire to live

The first question that we raise is, "what is it that you want ?" Well, the natural, instinctive desire of all beings, you'll admit, is an instinct what the biological expert will call, an instinctive instinct for self-preservation, for continual existence. All persons have that natural desire. There may be special circumstances on account of which a person wishes to commit suicide. But, that is on account of certain particular circumstances which he will certainly like to remedy but finds powerless to affect in the least. But when the question comes, as to what you yourself desire, and without the force of external circumstances compelling you into the opposite direction, what is your own primary desire ? And the answer is: the desire to live eternally, to have continuity of existence. A person is very badly ill, the doctor is sent for. The doctor comes and examines the patient and says, "It is a critical condition, but the patient will survive it. I will prescribe the necessary treatment for it. He will live, there's no fear of immediate death. But, he'll be very weak, he cannot see, he cannot hear, he cannot eat and assimilate his food properly, he will not be able to do anything at all. He will simply live on." And everyone, including the patient, his relations, his friends and well-wishers, everyone says, well, it does not matter how and with what incapacity, physical and otherwise, he lives. Let him live, that is all. And if you ask the patient in that condition, "what is it that you will do by continuing to live". In answer to the question he does not say what he will do by living or what is the purpose of his desiring to live. The answer is simply what the instinctive desire within dictates.

And even in those extreme cases in which a person has become very old and decrepit and unable to do anything at all, even then the desire to live persists. There are other considerations coming up on account of which, well, the patient himself says, or some other person says, let us put an end to this suffering, and so on. But, the desire to live, the biological self-preservation instinct, that is there all the time. That is natural. You need not be told by any person that you wish to live.

When a person who does not know how to swim, it may be a

little boy, or a child, is thrown into a flood, his limbs naturally begin to struggle. He is powerless to resist the torrential flood, and he goes under. That's a different thing altogether. But what is the desire ? What is the instinctive reaction to anything which will produce death ? Resistance to it, that is the natural thing. Unwillingness for it, that is the natural instinctive thing. So that is the first thing we start with.

Desire to know

In the next place, ask yourself the second question : "Suppose some deity grants you the boon of eternal existence. Are you satisfied with it ? Is there anything further that you require ?" At the time when there was the apprehension of immediate death, the patient and others said, "It's quite enough if the life continues, no matter how, in whatever condition." But once that danger is passed, that apprehension ceases to trouble the patient, he says, "I wish to see a little, I wish to hear a little, I wish to do this, I wish to do that." That is the natural instinctive desire. Once the continual existence is there, the second step comes in this way. And what is the meaning of his desiring to see, desiring to hear, and so on. It is a form of knowledge. What is seeing ? Knowledge of shapes. What is hearing ? Knowledge of sounds. What is smelling ? Knowledge of odours. There are five senses with which we sense the things in the outside world. The desire to have these senses working as satisfactorily as they possibly can, is the second natural desire.

Desire to be happy

Now, are you satisfied even with that ? Suppose you get both these boons from somebody; eternal existence and the capacity to see, hear, and so on, are you satisfied ? The next answer comes, again from the heart, from inside. I am not trying to impose anything upon you from outside. Your hearts tell you the answer.

Well, the things that I see and the things that I hear and so on are all of two different kinds: pleasant experiences and painful experiences. Both are there.

All sights are not pleasant. Some of them are painful, ugly, agonizing to look at. Similarly with regard to sound. Some sounds please the ear. Even a little child turns his ear to harmonious music coming from somewhere. The animals do so. They like it. And if it is a noise, people feel irritated by it. Similarly, with regard to smell, with regard to taste, with regard to touch. There are painful sensations and pleasant sensations, and as between these two, we say let us have all the pleasant sensations and none of the painful ones.

The desire for happiness or pleasure or joy and the distaste, the unwillingness for the other variety, is instinctive. And if you ask any person "How much of happiness do you want ? What proportion of happiness do you want ?" Well, the answer will be, "What a fool you are. There is no question of proportion at all, I want absolute unmixed happiness, unlimited joy." That's what all of us want.

Let us take a concrete example:

Suppose a person who is otherwise quite healthy and well and strong, has, in the right side, not the whole right side, in the right hand not the whole right hand, in the fingers not all the fingers, in one finger, not in the whole finger, only just below the nail, a small thorn, which gives pain. Well, he is uneasy. He is not able to relish the food that he takes. He does not like to gossip with his friends as he always did. He is unwilling not merely to talk but even to hear, and so long as that pain is there, so long as it is not removed, he is uneasy. He pines for something. And what is that ? The removal of pain which is there all the time.

And if a person with his rule of three, simple proportion arithmetic, comes and says to the sufferer, "Have a sense of proportion. Out of 108 parts of the body, 107 are in good health and strength; there is only one part out of 108, that is causing pain. Well, smile 107 parts and weep one part. The patient will say, "I'm unable to bear the pain, something must be done immediately." Relief from pain is wanted immediately. We do not want unhappiness at all. We seek happiness all the time; and happiness, unmixed, unadulterated, pure, complete. And if any adjective is needed to describe the kind of thing, you will say, 'Complete', 'perfect.' No other adjective is possible. If any qualifying adjective which limits down the quality, quantity, the extent, jurisdiction, the duration, etc., of happiness, it is unwelcome. We don't want it. That's the third thing. Now we take up the fourth.

We have all three: eternal existence, knowledge of all things around, and also pleasant as against painful experiences. Is that sufficient ? No.

Desire to be free

If all these things that we enjoy are there at our own command, we are masters of the situation. We can do what we like with them. And the joys that we enjoy are ours because we have mastery over them. We have absolute control over them. Well, that is acceptable. But, if the joy itself comes through the grace of somebody, we have to try and flatter that somebody and if that flattered person is satisfied, well and good. Otherwise, there will be trouble. Then we say at once, well, that kind of thing is not pleasant at all. All the joys that we want, all the sweet things that we want in life are available but, if they are at our own disposal, at our own free will and pleasure, we like it. Otherwise, it becomes irksome.

Manu, the great law-giver in our Indian scriptures, defines happiness and misery in terms of independence and dependence—

Sarvam paravaśam duḥkham,
sarvam ātmavaśam sukham,
Etad vidyāt samāsena
lakṣaṇam sukhaduḥkhayoḥ.*

Anything and everything that is under our own control about which we are independent means happiness, and anything in which there is dependence upon others, means suffering. The seed of misery is there, and that is no happiness at all. You will find people in good positions in life abandoning those positions in favour of something less. You ask them "What is this ? You are earning 500 dollars ? Now, you've come down to 400 dollars ? And the answer is, "Oh, that was a life of perpetual slavery, I couldn't have my own way, 400 dollars with independence are much better than 500 dollars or even 5000 dollars or 50,000 dollars with dependence." The desire for independence is also there.

Desire to dominate

And does that close the whole question ? No. There is a fifth

*Manusmṛti IV-160.

"Everything dependent on others is suffering and everything under own control is happiness. One should know this to be, in short, the criterion of happiness and suffering."

thing, another thing which from the standpoint of mere logical consistency seems to be absurd, and yet it is there all the time, naturally within ourselves.

We are not satisfied with saying "I wish to be independent, I don't wish to be controlled by the wishes of others, I wish to follow my own path." We would go further and say "Others should follow my path. Others should go according to my wishes." Even a little child, inexperienced in ways of the world wants to guide his experienced parents as to what should be done and what should not be done. This is the fifth thing that also comes up.

Now consider the question from the standpoint of the internal test, the internal experience. In any of these matters, well, it was not the American war of independence, or James Russell Lowell saying, 'they are slaves so they are not in the right' that gave us the ideas of independence and slavery. We did not learn the rules of liberty from Milton's essays on liberty or John Stuart Mills' or other authors' writings on liberty. It is instinctive. You go and try to catch a mouse running from you. Well, the mouse has not got a house of its own much better than ours, doesn't have provision for food and so on independent from ours. And yet, it does not wish to come into dependence and stay within our hands. It prefers its own liberty and follows its own path.

A father who comes and complains that his son is disobedient, may be asked, "Why do you wish him to follow, to obey you ?" And the answer is, "He is my son and I'm entitled to his respect, reverence, and obedience." And suppose the man's father is alive and he is asked, "What is your attitude toward your father ?" And then he says, "Oh, Father doesn't understand." We wish to have, not obedience, politeness doesn't allow that word, but agreement and so on, even from our parents. The desire is there.

These are the five things which are the five instinctive aspirations of man.

With regard to other matters in the world, when someone wants a thing, you ask, "Why does he want it ?" A person comes and asks you for money. You question him, "Why do you want money. What will you do with it ? What's the purpose ?" And he gives the answer. "I want to purchase my own land and property. I want to build a house. I want to marry. I want to do this, I want to do that."

The desired thing is not wanted for its own sake, but as a means to something else. But with regard to these five things, there is no question of any purpose behind them, on account of which you desire to live, on account of which you desire to see, hear, and so on, on account of which you desire pleasure and not pain. Why you desire independence ? It is instinctive. It is natural. We're not led by books. We're not led by others. Little children do it of themselves, and even mice, and parrots, and even worms and insects, have that feeling.

These are the five instinctive desires in all of us. I call this self-analysis in which we don't want the author to tell us 1485 or 1066 or 1922. These things are not needed from others. We know them from our own examination of our own hearts. These are the things that we desire.

Now, along side of this picture, place before yourself the descriptions given in all these systems of thought, all theologies, all philosophies, etc. They describe them as the attributes of God. What are the attributes of God ?

Attributes of God

In our Sanskrit, we say, (Sat, Cit, Ānanda) eternal existence, unbounded absolute illumination, perfect knowledge, and then, absolute bliss, without any admixture of pain, sorrow, and the like. Svātantrya and Prabhutva, absolute independence and absolute suzerainty. These are the five things that are described in all the text books as the attributes of Divinity.

And as human beings, what is it that we are seeking to achieve ? In all our efforts it is one or another of these desires, a combination of two, three, four, or all the five that can be held responsible for the various activities. When you call the doctor it is perhaps to save a life. That is in accordance with the first desire, eternal existence. Well, the doctor tells us that life is not in danger, though on the contrary, there's pain and suffering. Even that we don't want and we want the help of the doctor for remedying the pain. So there again, any and every activity of ours, is motivated by one or more of these desires. When people fight with each other, there again, you will find either the fourth or the fifth desire as the motivating factor. Either being dependent on others and unwilling to continue in that kind of dependence, we wish to throw off the yoke and assert our independence, or fifthly, although we're quite independent in all matters, we are not satisfied with that, and we want to rule over other persons also. So all these things come up.

These are our own aspirations and the realized aspirations are the attributes of God.

So the next question naturally will be what is the relationship between the two ? The answer to this also doesn't require any great metaphysical thinking or help from books and saints, and so on. Again, the same process of introspection and self-analysis will suffice for the purpose.

Man desires to attain the attributes of God

What are the characteristics of the individual soul ? What am I ? Man, with a soul, whom the first book of Genesis in the old testament of the Bible describes at the very time of creation, as having been created in the image of God himself. What is this individual soul of ours ? What does it constitute ? What does this contain ? What is there within it ? What does it mean ? What is the connotation of the individual soul ? If you go into the analysis you will find a still more pleasant and beautiful thing. We have come to the position in which we find that there are five desires of ours, which are instinctive, which nothing can get over. And we seek correctly or wrongly, by right methods, or wrong methods, successfully or unsuccessfully, to achieve these aspirations of ours. And there, as against this picture, we are told, that these are the very attributes of God. Being human beings, we seek oneness with the Divinity. And that would really mean having been created in the image of God.

After consideration of the constituent elements that are the attributes of God on the one hand, and also the objects of our own aspirations on the other, when we come to that next stage, we find externally that in the midst of life, we are in death. We wish to know things, and there are hundreds and thousands of things which we wish to know but can never hope to know. In fact, we do not know what is going to take place tomorrow or this very evening and so on. That is what makes us still more sad. We want joy all the time, without even the least admixture of pain, and we have one sorrow or another all the time. Even those who are rich, rolling in wealth and plenty, have their own sorrows, their own anxieties, their own fears and troubles. We all have these things.

We want absolute independence and we are dependent on thousands of persons and things for every thing that we could possibly have in life. We want to rule over all and what do we actually experience. We have the sad experience that not others but our own kin, our own brothers and sisters, nay, our own children, do not agree with us, do not follow our wishes, and there is constant friction on account of that.

So it looks as if all the five attributes that we find as things desired by us are the things which we do not have, and these are the things which are Divine in character and in composition.* At the first sight this is what seems to be the actual position, but, let us go a little deeper. Without great metaphysics about it, without great technical and other exposition necessary for it, we will find that this assessment of our position is wrong. Our appreciation of our internal condition, being subject to death, ignorance, sorrow, dependence, and so on, is not the right assessment at all.

We are now thinking of the internal characteristics of the soul, the individual soul. What are the internal characteristics ?

Let us first define what we mean by internal characteristics. Very often we blunder because we don't define our terms to start with. If we have a right conception as to what we exactly mean by each word that we use, there is no possibility of confusion. Very often we don't do that. The other day, in my first discourse in the college over there (Pepperdine), I mentioned, both in jest and in earnest, the case of two people who were fighting about a bottle, one man saying it's only half-full, and the other man saying it's half-empty. Half-empty and half-full, mean the same thing, though the words are different. The same thing is here. We use certain terms without understanding what we mean by them. Coming to the question again, what are the properties, or the characteristics of the individual soul ?

In physics and chemistry, we speak of properties of solids, liquids, gases, properties of sulphuric acid, of hydrogen, of nitrogen, carbon dioxide, and so on. What do we mean by properties ? Properties are qualities and characteristics which are inherent in the thing and cannot be separated therefrom. And

*Naro Nārāyaṇo bubhūṣati—"Man wants to become God".

if it is possible to separate one attribute, you will say it is a passing attribute of the moment, not a property of it. You write on the blackboard with a piece of chalk,well, that white chalk is not part of the blackboard at all. It is not an inherent property. It's a passing thing of the moment. Similarly here we talk of the internal qualities, the characteristics, the properties of the soul, the individual soul. I am not talking of the Almighty God, I'm talking of the individual soul just now. With regard to the individual soul, we at once say, well, such and such are the properties of the individual soul and such are the characteristics of Divinity and the attempt to go over from this present starting station of ours to that destination, would be an impossibility, physically beyond the possibility of achievement or of conception. That is what we generally say. But let us go into the matter and see what are the properties ? What do we mean by properties ?

Take the example of water. We say, "Here is a glass of hot water." Where did the heat come from ? Is it a passing thing of the moment ? The answer is: it is not an internal property at all. It comes from a passing cause of the moment, an external cause. The rays of the sun, fire underneath, etc., will account for the heat. The question "Why is this water hot?" can be asked, and is asked, and there always is an answer to it. The very question "why ?" shows that it has left its own natural property and needs an explanation, and the explanation is always forthcoming.

Similar is the case with regard to gilt, imitation gold, electrical gold, chemical gold and imitations. By splendid chemical processes, you made brass look like burnished gold, but that burnished gold color will not last. It goes off. It has come from outside, like the heat in the hot water, which even though you try to preserve it by means of thermal flasks and so on, it will go on decreasing and decreasing, until it goes off altogether.

That is how one can distinguish the passing quality from the permanent attribute.* That which is permanent, and inherent, whether it is really a chemical or a physical property will reassert itself. When you heat water, or when you boil it, you do not drive away the cold, or when you cool it you do not

*The permanent attribute is called 'lakṣaṇa' and the passing quality 'upalakṣaṇa'.

drive in the cold. The cold will reassert itself in due course, expelling the foreign raider from outside. This is the distinction between inherent properties and what we call passing attributes of the moment. The contact with something distrubs the actual position, and even suppresses the inherent property for the time being and puts you into the delusion that that property has gone. But it does not go. It reasserts itself.

Now let us take the question of man's attribute in respect of joy and sorrow. People assume that joy is the divine attribute and man is not entitled to it. Man, even when he does enjoy it, gets to love it. in proportion to his admiration. Robert Burns, the Scottish poet, has written a mystic poem. The name of it is, "Man was made to mourn." Man was created for the purpose of mourning. There is always sorrow. And Shakespeare has said, "Uneasy lies the head that wears the crown."

Now, with regard to this question of joy and of sorrow, let us see, which is the inherent quality and which is the passing attribute ?

Joy, not sorrow inherent quality of soul

When you see a person, he may be an elderly person, or he may be a boy, coming along weeping, you will at once ask him "Why ? What is the matter ?" The very question "Why ?" shows that there must be some reason for it of the passing moment. The very question "why ?" proves that sorrow is not an internal or inherent attribute, and that it is, an external attribute from passing causes from outside. And there always is a reply, there is an answer, "I've got a stomachache", "so and so died". "Such a thing happened", "Someone hit me." Some explanation or another is always there for the sorrow. What needs an explanation is not an inherent property but is something momentary from outside. We can indefinitely and infinitely pursue this inquiry and all questions will be answered by this one simple process of internal testing.

Now let us take the question up from another standpoint.

All sorrow is external, and joy is the internal nature, not of God that's a different matter altogether, of the individual soul. The second, or the complementary part of it, that is, sorrow is momentary also holds true. Just as the heat of the hot water diminishes gradually and goes away altogether, the sorrow caused by something or the other of the moment, too goes on decreasing. It is not so poignant later on as it was at the very first onslaught. It goes on decreasing, and a time soon comes when the person whom you were mourning twenty-four hours a day is forgotten altogether. With regard to fire, you will notice that when the fire is gone, the heat is gone. But when the heat of the hot water is gone, you don't say the water is gone. The heat has gone but the water is still there. The departure, the going away of the heat, that does not affect the existence of the water as water. With regard to the fire, if you were asked to go and see if the fire is there. And you say: the heat is gone, the fire has gone. That is a relationship between the property and the possessor of the property. The two are never separated permanently. But sorrow is not the real property of soul. It is a momentary attribute which wears away with time. Whatever may be the depth of your sorrow in the beginning, as time goes on, your real nature (of joy) asserts itself, and you recover your balance and you go about doing things. A time comes when the sorrow has completely passed out, except as a faint recollection of the past. That's all that remains there.

Life, not death, inherent characteristics of soul

We will extend this analysis to the first point, the one in regard to eternal life. We talk of death as being an inherent property of the individual soul. People ask you, did I live before I came into birth ? Shall I continue to live after I die ? These questions are asked. Everyone asks these questions of himself, and asks others, and there again the same method of internal analysis will suffice. You hear about the death of some person. At once, you ask "What happened ?" Your question "Why ?" shows that death is not the nature, or the internal characteristic of the soul. That is something caused by an external cause of the moment. What is the meaning of that ? We wrongly imagine that death ends everything. It does not. And this applies with regard to all things.

Even when an elderly person dies, you want to know the cause of the death. You inquire, "why ?" "What happened at once ?" Cholera, TB, plague, a motor accident or a cobra bite, something or the other is always there. In those cases where no such cause is perceptible, the doctor says, "He must have had heart disease." Why that "must" if death was a natural property, the inherent property. There should be no question about what could have happened in that way.

And then sometimes, we suspect that there is murder, by poisoning, etc. A post mortem examination takes place. If death were normal, if that were an inherent property, no post mortem should take place at all. There would be no such necessity. But as a matter of fact, we see that there is this kind of experience all the time. The cause (of death) is wanted.

Suppose you hear of the birth of a child to a next-door neighbour, and you meet that neighbour in the club, or in some meeting, somewhere later on in the evening, and you ask the friend, how is the child getting on ? And the father says, "Well, it's gone." "What was the matter ?" The answer is given "Convulsions descended," or some explanation. But suppose, on the contrary, the man says, well, the boy is getting on fine. No one asks why does he continue to live. Unlike as you ask "why, what happened to cause the death ?" no one asks why there was continuance of life. Continuance of life is natural, it needs no explanation. Eternal existence.

Take this same question from the standpoint of mere physical science. Even there you will find the same answer coming. Standpoints may differ and we may look at the same question from different angles of vision. But, in every case, the conclusion will be the same, the result will be the same. The scientist talks of uncreatability of matter, indestructability of matter, conservation of energy, and so on. Well, what do these terms mean ? There is a chair, a cot, a table, a desk, and so on before you. You say the carpenter made it. Did he bring into existence what was not in existence before ? He took the God-made wood from the God-made forest and put it into different positions, into different shapes, and gave a different name. There is only a change of shape, a change of place, and a change of name. Nothing which was not in existence before has come into existence. Nothing which is in existence can go out of existence. It's a very simple physical law that every physicist recognizes. There's only change of combination taking place. And for example, you release hydrogen when you put zinc and sulphuric acid together. There is only a change of combinations, and nothing further. You take money from the bank and put it into the box. Well, the sum total is the same. You spend it somewhere; the sum-total is still the same. Only the place has changed. The shape has changed. The name has changed. There is no new existence of the thing which was not in existence before.

In the second chapter of the Bhagavad Gītā, this grand law of physics is put in very simple terms—

Nāsato vidyate bhāvo
nābhāvo vidyate sataḥ.*

That which exists cannot go out of existence; that which does not exist cannot come into existence. All that we find is difference of manifestation, difference of place, difference of shape, and difference of name, and so on. Eternal existence is assured. There's no question of anything vanishing. If you say you will burn up the cot altogether, and you burn up the cot, the cot's shape, and even the wood perhaps is destroyed. But, in some other shape now, ashes, charcoal, and things of that type, the matter exists. The whole thing goes on in that way.

When a person comes and asks me, "Was I or was I not before I was born ?" Well, I say that physical science is sufficient to give the answer to this question. No philosophy is necessary. "Do you exist now ?" "Of course I do." "Very good. If so, you existed in the past because nothing not in the past can come into existence now. You exist now. Nothing which is now in existence can go out of existence." It's not a big philosophy for philosophers to wrangle over. A little child knows it. A boy places five cents in a certain corner, a nook, a hiding place, and goes out for play, and he returns to find, not five but, only one. What's his question ? "Where have my other four cents gone ?" Where have they gone ? He does not take it for granted that things can go out of existence and vanish in that way. If instead of five cents there he finds ten. "Where did these five come from ?" The question is there. There is eternal existence. Even the little boy knows it. We are grown up people, wise in our experience and wisdom. What do we do if a ten dollar note is missing ? We don't say it must have vanished because it is possible for things to vanish. We say "Find the thief." "Examine the bedding and other things of the servants, and hand them over to the police." Why do we do all these things ? Because we

*Gitā II-16.

are assured, we are instinctively certain, not by study, nor by any kind of argument, but instinctively certain that things do not come into existence, things do not go out of existence of themselves.

This is the kind of method by which, if we try to analyse things for ourselves, we shall be able to find that the constitution of the individual soul is the same as we have been aspiring to obtain. We can go into further and further details of the subject. I've given an inkling into the kind of introspective analysis with which, with no help from outside, where all the experience is from inside, you decide for yourself the right philosophy on the matter. And that is where the self-realization comes in. We realize the Self, not as all sorts of odd things gathered together in a confused medley of words, but, as realisation of the truth that in all there is the same Divinity within, man having been made in the image of God.

We can take text after text from our scriptures, from the scriptures of various religions in the world. It will be found that everywhere the teaching is the same. The language is different, the manner of presentation is different. And all of them depend upon the capacity of the reader, the student, the aspirant for understanding and his acting up to the teaching in question.

On another occasion, I shall seek the opportunity of going into further details of this very subject as regards the attributes of Divinity, as regards our own present conditions, about which we feel hopeless, about which we are so desperate, thinking that nothing good can come out of it, it's a matter of sorrow all the time, etc. We can go into these questions from the standpoint of internal analysis and you will find that self-realization means the realization of God within. In our textbooks, Vedānta texts* a splendid illustration is given with regard to how we have to shape our own destiny by merely bringing into manifestation the divinity which is instinctively within us.

The example is given of how a marble statue is made. You go to the artist with a piece of stone, or marble, and ask him if he can make for you a statue of Christ or the Virgin Mary or Queen Elizabeth, or any other person. And at once the artist says, "What a fool you are. All the existing shapes, all the conceivable shapes are there in the stone already. All that I do is to strike

*See Appendix I for Sanskrit texts conveying ideas discussed here.

off, to chisel off those external coverings which hide from my gaze the particular shape which I wish to materialize." Nothing is put into the stone in order to put it into a certain particular shape.

There is divinity within ourselves. Christ said the Kingdom of God is within us. There's nothing difficult about it. You find Christ saying "I and my Father are one."* And also, on a very important occasion, and in answer to a very serious question, when he calls himself the son of God, and people present protest against it, we know your father, your mother, and your uncle and your aunt, and your sisters and brothers, you call yourself the son of God! And the answer is, "Have not your forefathers said unto you, ye are gods ?" It is the most convincing and instructive passage. The whole thing is there.

How is it that in spite of this internal constitution of ours containing the divinity within, eternal existence, complete knowledge, absolute joy, absolute independence, and oneness with God Himself, we are not actually experiencing it ? Why are these troubles that we are actually going through, and what is the way in which we can avoid these troubles and realize, continually and perpetually experience, oneness with Divinity ?

Yesterday, at a small discourse that we had in my quarters there, I was speaking of this. The whole question is, how to find out the method to experience the reality ? Nothing has to be put newly into it, everything is there already. But lots of things have been allowed to come over and encrust, corrupt the divinity within. And all that is necessary is to make arrangements for giving scope for that divinity to manifest itself, to come out into actual action and benefit thereby from moment to moment. The very word education; which you constantly use in your thoughts gives us the necessary clue. Education does not mean putting anything inside, it means drawing out what is there already. That's the meaning of the word education.** If education was to be a process of putting things in, well, it should be called injection, not education.

*St. John X-30.

**Education is derived from 'Educare' (Latin) meaning 'to educe', 'to draw out'.

Removal of obstacles to knowledge, is self-realization

We believe that by education, by right training, environs, etc., we should be able to eliminate those things which stand in the way of self-realization. And after that is done, no positive action is necessary. It's like saying, after the clouds have departed, well, there's nothing necessary for seeing the sun, the sun is automatically seen again. When the clouds pass away, all the obstruction passes away. A new sun has not been brought into existence. The same old sun is there, and will continue to be there. All that we have to do is to remove what hides the sun from the view. The sun is physically at a great distance. So in that example there will be great difficulty. But here, with regard to our own inner constitution, it is within our own mind. The obstacles which stand in the way the encrustments, have to be removed, and by dedicated effort, by concentrated processes, of a practical character, we can achieve success in the realization of the divinity within ourselves and that is self-realization.

And self-realization, along with the word fellowship is a wonderful combination. Not merely with regard to our own individual self, but with regard to every individual self, the same attributes are there, the same emotions, the same aspirations, and the same joys and sorrows, and therefore, it should not be difficult for us to understand others and to arrange world affairs in such a manner as to produce concord and remove all the discord that we find in actual existence, in our experience.

All that I wish to do to-day for the time being — it's already very, very late — is to close this part of the discourse by simply calling your attention to the fact that the goal of our ambitions or aspirations is divinity itself. That is, the experience of the divinity, which is within, and is not being experienced. That's all that is necessary. And in order to attain that self-realization process and not in conflict with others, but in concord, by means of fellowship we promote not merely world peace, but world prosperity, world joy, all the time. May God the Divinity within, help us to achieve that object of ours, bring about that consummation by which we help not merely ourselves but help humanity. We are instruments in the hands of Providence. Self-realization, is the means of attainment of the goal of absolute peace. Christ was known as the prince of peace. St. Paul speaks of the peace that passeth all understanding. And we, in our scriptures.

speak of shanti, shanti, shanti, peace, peace, peace, all the time. Peace, harmony, joy, these are the attributes we seek, and we pray to God for the realization of this composition of ourselves within. I don't call it chemical composition, I don't call it psychological or structural composition, I call it divine composition within the human body. And thereby, fulfil the purpose of existence; not merely fulfil the existence, but also help others to influence themselves in that way, and to find the purpose of their existence and to be instruments of achieving world prosperity all around.

VI KARMA YOGA

Discourse at Methodist Community Church, Westwood, February 9, 1958

Friends:

It is a matter of universal experience that the quest and the efforts of all human beings in various directions, are all directed towards the attainment of happiness. Our conceptions of happiness may vary, our conceptions with regard to means for the attainment of the end in view, the goal we are after, may differ, and there may be all sorts of differences of physical capacity, intellectual calibre, moral strength and other qualifications and qualities which are of use to us in obtaining success in the world's affairs. But, there can be no question about the fact, no doubt possible at all, as regards the goal of all, that is, the avoiding of all that means unhappiness to us, and the obtaining of happiness in all directions. Physical happiness in the shape of health, strength, and so on? Yes. Intellectual? Yes. Political, social, economic, and so on, in all the various departments of life? Well, to all these questions the answer is "Yes." No one says I want to be perfectly healthy in the physical body and insane along therewith. No one says I wish to have high intellectual capacity for understanding and assimilating things of the most recondite and technical character, and I want to have a crippled body incapable of shouldering any burden whatsoever. All of us are for the attainment of happiness and with no qualifying attributes with regard to the direction, the subject matter, and so forth.

In the Vedantic language of the Upaniṣads,* what we're after

*The idea of God as the 'Perfect' is expressed in the following:—
Pūrṇamadaḥ purṇamidam, pūrṇāt pūrṇamudacyate.
Pūrṇasya pūrṇamādāya, pūrṇamevāvaśiṣyate.
(Bṛhadāraṇyaka Upaniṣad V-1-1).

That (God) is Perfect, this (the universe) is perfect. The perfect comes from the Perfect. The perfect merges into the Perfect, and the latter alone remains (as the Ultimate Reality).

Pūrṇa according to Śaṅkara, means "na kutaścid vyāvṛttam", not limited in any direction, in any manner. (see his commentary on the above).

is perfection, Pūrṇatā, perfection all around. And if anyone wants to put in an adjective, it can not be of restricting character, restricting the jurisdiction of the object in view. It should be Sampūrṇatā complete all-around perfect perfection. That is what everyone would naturally desire to have. Whether we have the necessary means for achieving our purpose, whether such qualities as we are endowed with suffice for the purpose, are different matters. That the quest is for the attainment of happiness, that the goal is the attainment of happiness, there can be no doubt.

So all the differences arise with regard merely to the means for the attainment and the retention of that happiness. Attaining happiness is a sufficiently difficult problem for us, and to retain it after attaining it, is an additional thing. We have all our own moments of anxiety, trouble, and sorrow, with regard to our failures. We find that by our own efforts, we have unconsciously spoiled our own cause. In attaining the happiness that we thought, we sometimes see that by our own fault we have done things which have removed even what little chance of happiness we had before, we have lessened our situation by our own foolish or thoughtless action or inaction, as the case may be.

So the whole question revolves around the means for the attainment of our goal.

Three paths

And as regards means, there are three paths which have been laid down by the ancients in the scriptures of the various religions and which thinkers of an independent calibre have also accepted as the threefold path. The threefold path is what we are after.

These three paths are :—the Karma Mārga, the Bhakti Mārga, and the Jñāna Mārga, as we call them in Sanskrit. The path of work, then the path of devotion, reverence, love, faith, and so on, that is the second path. And the third path is the path of absolute illumination where the person rises above, and transcends all possibility of being subject to or being susceptible to joys and sorrows. He is called a saint or a sage and is at a much higher level than the ordinary run of humanity. He has reached a rung on the spiritual ladder for which very few people would think of competing with him.

The question naturally arises in the next place as to how each an individual should make use of the three paths. Separately, or jointly. And here, all the controversies in the name of religion start, because as human beings, we are constituted differently. We comprise several different and sometimes even conflicting elements within ourselves. A harmonizing of the whole constitution, with the various parts fitting in together, and not producing any kind of conflict or internal trouble, this is what is wanted. And generally it is found that on account of things which we can't account for, as consequences of actions done in this very world, there are what you may call different starting points for different individual souls.

Why the difference in paths

We don't start with zero as the starting point, with absolutely nothing to our credit, with nothing, so to say, as reserve in the bank. We start with some capital. We all start as individual human beings with tendencies, with trends, with inclinations, with tastes, and with capacities and potentialities of a different character. And therefore, the start becomes different.

If we were all made of the same constituents, if we were all endowed with the same kind of qualities, the same trends, the same inclinations, the same idiosyncracies, etc., from the very outset, the question would be easier to solve because it would admit of only one answer in all cases. But, there are all sorts of permutations, and combinations, of factors, sub-factors, and so forth, to be taken into account. That is how the problem becomes complex, and complexity is added to various other complications which are the consequences of occurrences of the present day. We start with an initial starting point of a different character. And afterwards, we find that circumstances around us also have their own part to play. They have their own contribution to make to the resultant of all the various forces concerned in the question.

Now then, the difficulty being of this nature, we have to make up our minds as to what exactly suits each one's individual case best. There is no mechanical rule which can apply to everybody automatically. Each case has to be taken on its own intrinsic merits. Allowances have to be made, things have to be discounted on account of certain circumstances of a special nature in each particular case. And then if that is done, there is no possibility of an un-successful end to the quest. We are not machines. To think of us as machinery which can all come under the same rule with some hard and fast standard, would be absurd.

Even with regard to machines, we find very often that they have an individuality of their own. We don't speak of them as individual personalities, the word personal seems to be out of place when we talk of machines. But, as a matter of fact, in our actual experience we find that individual objects of machinery do have their own individuality, so to say.

Much more individual therefore, is a human being with an intellect capable of reflecting upon the pros and cons of each situation, weighing things, and coming to conclusions calculated to insure happiness and to avoid misery. For a human being it is therefore all the more necessary that there should be a greater and deeper psychological study of the various factors involved in his particular case.

We find however that the Masters, the founders of religions, were not affected by any particular temperamental equation, etc., and therefore, all the three paths find ready, easy, and equal acceptance in the words of the Masters themselves.

In Hinduism, in the Vedic Sanātana Dharma, as we call it, the eternal verities are described. We have what we have called the Karmamārga, or the Karma-yoga, the Bhakti-mārga, or the Bhakti-Yoga, Jñāna-Mārga, or Jñāna-Yoga. Well, corresponding technical terms may not be in constant use in Christian theology, but the three are represented among the Christian theologians, the Christian evangelists, etc., from the very beginning.

Christianity and the three paths

We have for example Christ himself dealing with all the three paths. Christ is the Master, the Saviour whom the evangelists learnt from, and whose message they carried into the world. But the evangelists were persons who had their own predilections, their own individual personal equations, so to say, and that added a different shade to their teachings also.

We find for example Jesus Christ saying again and again, "By their works ye shall know them." You shall judge the character, the capacity, the future, salvation or otherwise of the individual by the kind of work they have been doing. That is the Karma-

Yoga, the path of works. And we find St. Peter and St. James representing that school of thought. That school of thought not in the sense that the others can be abandoned, but in the sense that this is the predominating factor so far as their mental composition goes. With regard to physical body, all the various elements needed for the nourishment will have to be supplied. The fuel which is consumed by what chemists call katabolism is of manifold and multifarious character. There's no doubt about that. But as regards composition, the internal proportion of elements, there are tremendous differences between body and body. A doctor who is prescribing for a diabetes patient suggests a sugarless diet. Another doctor prescribing for a heart patient, recommends a saltless diet. Now, both salt and sugar are inherent integral parts of the diet that we take. But it may happen in a particular case that there has been an excess of a particular thing, over what its proper proportion should be. And there may be another case in which something is in deficit. And both these situations, both these predicaments have to be taken into the reckoning and tackled with. Where there is an excess, the doctor prescribes a slowing down of the process, not increasing what is already in excess, diminishing it as far as possible, and in some cases, prohibiting it altogether.

And similarly, with regard to what is insufficient, the doctor suggests such medicines, and tonics etc., that will help to restore the balance, to supply the deficiency. Now, you will not say that the two doctors belong to two different religions and that they should fight with one another because one is of this denomination and the other is of that denomination and there can never be peace between the two.

Each individual case has to be examined and adjudicated on its own intrinsic merits. That is what we do in the outer physical life with regard to treatment of physical maladies, heart disease, diabetes, and various other things.

Similarly, on the mental, the intellectual, the psychic, the spiritual side, individuals are not of the same constitution, the same composition. There are differences. All the basic elements are there but not in the proper proportion, and therefore, necessary adjustment has to be made. And when that comes up, you find that the individual trend, or tendency, or personal equation has a great deal to account for the path prescribed for him.

I was just saying that St. Peter and St. James were representatives of the school of works, not because of any particular superiority in this particular path, but because they found in their actual experience that the persons to whom they were preaching, to whom they were carrying the message of the Lord for the attainment of salvation, had a certain tendency, a certain peculiar trend containing excesses on the one side and deficiencies on the other and they had tackled the situation accordingly. Not that St. James and St. Peter were against the path of love, the path of devotion, or the path of knowledge, but they found that the people amongst whom they were called upon to work, there were these differences, and these differences were of what you might call a communal character, not of this individual or that individual but of a mass of individuals gathered together and presenting, manifesting the same tendencies in one direction or another.

Then you have St. John, the evangelist. Not John the Baptist, who was the precursor of the Lord. St. John the evangelist emphasized the path of love. Again and again, you find him talking in terms which remind the Indian student of the Bible of his own bhakti-mārga, the path of devotion, of reverence, of faith, of absolute self-surrender to the Lord, and so on. In fact, you find St. John going so far as to say, "God is love."*Now this does not mean that he rejects the path of works and the path of illumination, or self-conquest, where a person transcends all ordinary human passions, etc.

In the third place, you have St. Paul. St. Paul was originally known as Paul (Saul) of Tarsus. And he became notorious as a persecutor of the small Christian Community which had come into existence soon after the crucifixion of the Lord. And, gradually, it so happened that after his persecution had done a lot of harm, and brought a lot of suffering to the people, there was a miracle of miracles. He was converted to the same faith and he became from the standpoint of oratory, from the standpoint of epistle writing, and so forth, the greatest propagandist preacher of Christianity. He became the greatest apostle of them all.

St. John was the favourite disciple of Christ, we are told. And he emphasized the path of love. In St. James and St. Peter you have representatives of the karma-mārga. Not that they preferred

*First Epistle General of St. John IV-8, 16.

the one to the other two, etc., but because the requirements, the exigencies of the situation were such that in each particular case, the thing that was emphasized was most emphatically needed by the people themselves.

So, there is no question of any hostility between one path and another, no question of irreconcilable differences and antagonisms of any type, but only of the psychological needs, the psychological, moral, metaphysical, spiritual needs of the individual being taken into consideration like the doctor prescribing for each patient what would best meet the requirements of his case.

Purity of heart essential

Now, in our times, we find a tendency of disregarding what you might call the karma-yoga path, the path of works. Generally, people talk in very easy and cheap terms, as regards purity of heart, devotion, reverence and love. "If these are all right, how does it matter what we do in this or that particular respect?" That's the kind of question which you are asked from day to day. When we are dealing with the path of karma, or the path indicated by the law of works, the questioner, the inquirer gets up and says, "These are all matters of detail. They are not essential. What is necessary is purity of heart."

Now, the objection is correct as far as this goes. It's perfectly right. We have in the scriptures of all the various religions of the world passages with tremendous fire, denouncing the people who were intent on the external ritual and ceremonial of various types, but who absolutely lacked in sincerity, and purity of heart. Take the Old Testament, the last portion of the Old Testament, dealing with the prophecies of Isaiah, Jeremiah, Ezekiel, Daniel, the four major prophets and Hosea, Joel, Amos, Obadiah, Jonah, Micah, Nahum, Habakkuk, Zephaniah, Haggai, Zechariah, Malachi, the twelve minor prophets of Israel. You will find that they denounced the performance of various kinds of sacrifices and other rites according to the Mosaic law, not because they objected to the obedience to the Mosaic law but because everything was being done for mere show, for pomp and pageantry, for getting applause from people, for self-praise, and for nothing else. There was a lot of hypocrisy about it. People broke the spirit of law at every step while hugging the letter of the law to their breasts. That kind of thing had become too common and you find the prophets condemning it in strong terms.

And similarly, in the history of the various other religions, from time to time we have descriptions of people leading a life of an external intensity of religious character. I don't call it religious, but religiose character, formal paraphernalia type, pomp and pageantry type of religion, for mere show and ostentation, and nothing within the heart. Well, that kind of thing is denounced.

We find it denounced in the Bhagavad Gītā also.* Such persons are impostors, they are cheats, and should not be relied on, or followed. On the contrary, we should carefully prevent ourselves from going along that path, from being misled by those who ought to be leaders in the right direction. If the leaders themselves, the so-called leaders, the self styled leaders themselves become misleaders, well, the fate of that particular community, that society becomes most deplorable. Therefore you find in the above portions of the Old Testament, and in similar parallel passages of the New Testament also, in the Lord's own words, denunciations of the Pharisees, the Sadducees, and so on, who showed a great deal of religiosity, but had no religion in their hearts. From these passages, people come to the conclusion that the law, or the path of works, is of no importance, and they come and say that sincerity of heart only is the thing absolutely required. It is essential. It is fundamental. I grant that. Every person, belonging to any and every sect of any and every religion must necessarily concede that. Sincerity is absolutely necessary and without sincerity all the pomp and paraphernalia, the pageantry and the show of religiosity will be absolutely useless.

The human master who does not know, who cannot probe into the hearts of people, may be pleased by external show, but, the omniscient, omnipotent, all-pervading, all-permeating Lord of the Universe, who looks into the hearts of men and knows the contents of their hearts, cannot be cheated by any kind of show.

*In Gītā II-42, 43, 44, Lord Kṛṣṇa denounces, those who in flowery language speak about Vedic rituals and indulge in earthly pleasures.

In Chapter XVII of Gītā the Lord denounces and relegates to second rank, all deeds done for show only.

Also see Gītā XVII-28.

That the sincerity of heart is the essential thing, the love and devotion is the essential thing and should be the predominant consideration, is no matter of doubt. People of all religions, all sects, all sub-sects must agree on this point. There is no difficulty at all. But, that does not end the whole thing.

There is a purpose, a necessary purpose, an essential and important purpose, an indispensable purpose for which the path of karma, the law of works is also laid down. And that is to help the aspirant forward on his path.

You may say that you are perfectly sincere.

Natural laws do not depend on the state of mind

Well, let us take an example. Take it for granted that the case of a certain person is one of that type. He is perfectly sincere. Would you therefore, on the physical side, claim that whatever he does, does not matter because he is perfectly sincere. Science comes and tells us that nature punishes ignorant blunderer as severely and as relentlessly as she punishes deliberate sinner. Suppose you put your hands into the fire, not knowing that it will burn your fingers. Well, because of your sincere ignorance of the law pertaining to the subject, does the fire cease to burn ? Not at all. Sincerity of heart, and correctness of conduct are different altogether and people have been confusing and muddling up matters in this way.

Let us take for example the case of electricity.

When the scientists made great and rapid strides in their discoveries with regard to the application of electricity for various useful and necessary purposes in the world, they, with a great sense of superiority complex, began to talk about their having subjugated, dominated, conquered, and defeated nature. Nature has become our humble maid-servant at the present day. With modern discoveries and inventions, the scientists have achieved a lot by which they claimed to have conquered, subjugated nature and made her man's willing slave and servant and so on. Within a short time, this pride, this superiority complex tumbles down, crashes. And when does that happen ? It happens when there is the first experience by a scientist of an electric shock. This very electricity which we describe as maid-servant, because it serves us in so many ways, in the shape of light, in the shape of sound, in the shape of heat, and so forth, kills us. Now, certainly that is not the function, it is not the proper characteristic or quality of an obedient maid-servant of our own.

What does the scientist do then ? He starts his investigations again. He experiments, he investigates and he tries to find out not why this takes place or why that takes place. There's no question of why at all. The question is simply as regards what takes place. What is the law governing the universe ?

The laws, the rules and regulations governing the universe came into existence not millions but aeons and aeons of years before we were born. Our vote was not taken on the matter at all. Without any consultation with us on Democratic or Republican lines, whatever party you particularly belong to, the rules came into existence, and they have been in existence, and they will continue to be in existence until eternity.

Well, the scientists experiment, they investigate, and they find out that the electrocution takes place when you are standing on the floor and handling the leaking electricity, but not when you are on wood, a wooden stool, bench, etc. Well, you add this knowledge to the stock of knowledge you already possess and then you obey the law already existing in the universe.

It will not do to say that there is perfect purity of heart and therefore nothing else matters. Also material are the means that we adopt for the purpose of attaining happiness. You may call it happiness here and salvation hereafter. A person who calls himself a naturalist, agnostic, or atheist, or something of that type, does not believe in future worlds and future existences, etc. Even he, well, for that matter all persons, will have to recognize that there is the law of cause and effect. And that law of cause and effect has in many cases what you might call an objective existence of its own, an objective application of its own.

Where subjective matters are concerned, the purity of heart and the sincerity will suffice for the purpose. For example, a case of murder comes before a magistrate, or a judge, for decision. It's found that the accused had deliberately committed a cold-blooded murder, planned, premeditated, and taken all necessary precautions in every way, and yet somehow he was detected. Well, he has to be tried and the magistrate finds that the man is guilty of the grossest, the most cold-blooded premeditated murder, and of a most violent and most virulent and a most exceedingly well, disgusting character, with many kinds of details adding to the poignancy of the suffering caused even to the news reader. Well, that is one kind of case before the magistrate.

Another case comes up in which not on account of any premeditation, not on account of any hatred from long ago, but on account of a sudden passion on the spur of the moment, a person forgets himself, becomes practically insane, and commits a murder. Here the judge does not say that the two murders are of the same kind. He considers and gives his verdict. The jury give their verdict. They say, it was culpable homicide. It was homicide. It was culpable. It was a crime, punishable according to the law, but culpable homicide not amounting to murder. That's the second example.

And then you have the third variety in which a person in sheer self-defence attacks the attacker and saves himself. And this is not a cold-blooded murder, not a culpable homicide not amounting to murder, but justifiable murder in self-defence. You have these varieties where the intention comes into account. But, so far as the physical, the mechanical, the external result is concerned, the death was the same in all three cases. It was not less, three-fourths death or half-death in the case of the culpable homicide, or only one fourth-death in the case of self-defence. The death has taken place of a certain person and in awarding punishment, the court takes into account not merely the external physical facts, but also the intention. The sincerity and purity of heart, these are the corresponding terms we use in our religious and other such contexts, while in criminal law the intention is taken into account.

But there are lots of other things in the world in which the intention does not count at all as regard the result. Whatever the intention may have been, the result is there. The electrocution and things of that type are examples of this kind. Therefore, it will not do for us to say that we are absolutely safe from all evil or injurious consequences because we have done something with sincerity and purity of heart. The intrinsic merits of the means adopted should also be taken into account because they have the tendency — there is an inevitable natural law by which that tendency is to be there — of producing their own effect from a purely mechanical angle. That too has to be taken into account.

And similarly with regard to the path of wisdom, or the path of illumination. A person who has transcended all distinctions, and has no partialities, no hatreds, no prejudices and no prepossessions, and therefore, has no particular interest in this thing or that thing, may be regarded as being above the law. That is an aspect of the matter which comes before us in regard to theological dialectics, or discussions of religious character. That again is an overdoing of the process.

It's not at all true that in such cases, there is no question of personal inclination at all. And yet, whether the personal inciination is there or not, the consequences to society have to be taken into account. We are dealing with society and not with the individual. The individual in the forest, absolutely by himself in solitude may be above the law. In fact, there is no question of the law coming at all, because there is no second person with whom he can come into conflict. But when we are together in society, as members of a body, a community, even the things that we do with all purity of heart and with no bad intentions whatsoever, may affect the surroundings and cause trouble to the society. And in such cases, it will be the duty of those who are the custodians of the law, who are responsible for the preservation of health, of wealth, etc., and the interest of the nation, the community, and so forth, to see that even the person of that type is not allowed to do anything which may be calculated to do injury to the community, to the society, and so on.

Karma

These are all necessary factors no doubt, but according to the time, place, circumstances, etc., various other factors have to be taken into account also. The law of works operates there, and the Lord himself says, "As thou shalt sow, thou shalt reap." The law of cause and effect is there in the physical world around us.

A person wants to plant a fruit garden for himself. He sows various kinds of seeds, orange and this and that, a number of things, but no mango seed. And he is not aware of anyone having sown a mango seed. But afterwards, when the various seeds begin to sprout forth into trees ultimately he finds a mango tree in the garden. Well, he will not say, he will not be justified in saying that he never planted a mango seed, and no one else did it, and therefore, the tree came into existence without any seed. That would be a false statement from the purely physical or the mechanical standpoint. That would be wrong. Well, all that anyone could say under the circumstances would be, "I never knowingly planted such a seed, and no friend or other person did it, but all the same possibly from the mouth of a flying bird above which went along the seed fell. Not merely was the seed there, but proper manuring, proper ploughing and other things were there. The necessary water at different times in the shape of rainfall or otherwise came into the picture, and the result is the mango tree which you see before you."

That is the law, the law of karma as we call it, the law of cause and effect. "As thou shalt sow, thou shalt reap." We have the Master himself giving us the necessary guidance, of course, in what we call sūtra form,* in the shape of aphorisms, not elaborate and detailed discussions, but laying down what you might call mathematical formulae at the end of the whole mathematical working.

The Master gives to his disciples the instruction they need in short, pithy sentences which cover the whole ground. And afterwards, the evangelists and the commentators, expound the principles, give illustrations, and go into a great deal of technical, logical, philosophical, and other expositions of the matter. They show how this was necessary and why a particular word is to be found there, and what the removal of that particular word might mean by way of damaging the whole sense. All these things are the work of the commentators, the evangelists, the expounders, the explainers, and they are needed. You will remember that in its long history, Christianity had to face tremendous opposition from all the then existing military powers. The Roman empire itself was there with its full political and military might. And there were other empires, kingdoms, which all strenuously opposed the onward progress, the onward march of Christianity in the western world. None welcomed Christianity. And among the evangelists who carried the message into the world, into the western world, there was, until St. Paul actually

*Alpākṣaramasandigdham sāravad viśvatomukham,
Astobham anavadyam ca sūtram sūtravido viduḥ.

According to Viṣṇudharmottara Purāṇa, 'Sūtra' has fewest letters (words) but is unambiguous. It contains the essence of the matter and is versatile. It is unobstructing and faultless.

came into the picture later on, none of towering intellectual, academical, and other qualifications. They were poor fishermen whom the Lord had taken up and made his disciples. He had taught them and they had the full power of the Spirit; the Spirit within was the great strength, the treasure-trove behind them. With that and with no external circumstances to aid them, no military power, no political power, no wealth behind them, they went ahead and almost every one of them suffered the same fate as the master, so far as the physical side went. The Master was crucified. St. Peter, St. James, St. John, St. Paul, they all had to undergo the same fate.

Well, what was the result of it? The fight was a fight to the finish. Each of the existing religions of those days said to Christianity, and Christianity had to say to them, "Either you survive, or I, there is no place for both of us underneath the same sun, on the same earth." That was the position. And the result of it was that all those religions, the Greek, the Roman, the Assyrian, the Syrian, the Babylonian, the Carthaginian, and other religions of the world were exterminated. In that fight to the finish, they exterminated themselves, and went out of the history and the map of the world, so much so that in the present day, you cannot find a single person coming forward to say "I am of the Greek religion or the Roman religion", and so forth.

And what was the power on the side of Christianity? The faith, the spirit that the evangelists had. In spite of all sufferings and sorrows, they went on relentlessly, ceaselessly, undauntedly, carrying on their mission, facing all the suffering that they were subjected to, and thinking it their privilege to be of service to the Lord in that way too. In that extreme manner, they did it.

And what was the Master himself?

The Master was one whom they had looked upon as the founder of a new Kingdom. The Jews of those days were looking for the Messiah, and Christ was supposed to be the person who was to install the Hebrew race on the highest pedestal. They were looking forward to that kind of consummation. But what they actually experienced was something of a most humiliating character. The founder of the new world, whom they looked forward to as their saviour, wore the crown of thorns and bore the cross of shame. No one can suggest that under such circumstances, there was any kind of facility which the evangelists could have made use of. They had every possible disadvantage and handicap that could possibly be conceived of. And yet, they went and conquered. They were representatives of the same human race as we are. They had their own sufferings, their own weaknesses, and other things from time to time as the whole narrative itself describes. And in spite of all these, they could rise above the circumstances around them, because they had the necessary spirit, the spirit of the seeker after truth, who seeks the truth to find it and to put it into practice.

This is the lesson of Karma Yoga in which we perform our duties with sincerity, with purity of heart, and with all the necessary qualities of the highest, the most moral and spiritual character. At the same time we are responsible for the actions which we perform, the consequences of which we reap in the births to come, perhaps amongst other peoples, other times and other climes also. With this sense of responsibility, if we tackle the performance of our duties, the future will be assured.

This is called the law of karma, or karma-yoga of the Bhagavad Gītā and other scriptures. Perform the duty and leave the result in the hands of the All-Knowing who will not take sides, who will not be a partisan, who tempers justice with mercy, and who is the best judge imaginable, under any circumstances. That is the attitude, the frame of mind, with which we look into this question and regulate our lives accordingly.

I conclude with a word of prayer to the All-Mighty to give all assembled here the strength to understand and to practise the principle which I have tried, in my own humble way, to expound to you in the few minutes at my disposal.

Questions and Answers following the discourse :

Q. Why did Lord Kṛṣṇa advise Arjuna to fight. Was it because that was his duty at that point ?

H.H. Yes, because it was his duty, which he had to perform, irrespective of gain and loss, victory and defeat, and other considerations of that type, or whether the duty, is painful or pleasant. That was the actual advice given. And Arjuna fought in the performance of his duty.

Q. Why was this his duty ?

H.H. As the protector of the people from the tyranny of tyrants and oppressors, that was his duty. If by peaceable methods, that could be done so much the better. I was speaking in another place the other day that we are pacifists; we want peace. But when we talk of peace, it is not peace at any price. Peace at the price of honour, diginity, truth, and so on, is not worth purchasing at such a price. There is a limit. If there is perversity, obstinacy, and so on, of that kind, of that type which is symbolized in the Mahâbhârata, in the Bhagavad Gītā context, well, all that could be done was to say most reluctantly, "War is unavoidable. In the performance of duty, I have to fight."

Q. Did the law of cause and effect work in the case of the crucifixion of Christ ?

H.H. Those who crucified him suffered the consequences. That's the law of karma.

Q. Was Christ crucified because of his own behaviour or was he crucified because of the behaviour of others ? How did the law of cause and effect work here ? Was his behaviour the cause of his death ?

H.H. This is a different question altogether. I've not gone into that subject today at all. I have been speaking of the responsibility involved in actions and of the consequences of that responsibility which have to be borne by the individual. As regards the problem of Evil, how bad things do occur, that's a different question altogether, and I have not dealt with it at all. The question is a very interesting and a very necessary question no doubt, but it doesn't arise out of today's discourse. It can be the subject matter of another discourse.*

*Jesus signified himself as a ransom for the sins of many. With his divine powers, Christ could never have been subjected to death by crucifixion if he had not willingly co-operated with the subtle cosmic law of cause and effect. He thus took on himself the consequences of others' Karma, especially that of his disciples. In this manner they were highly purified and made fit to receive the omnipresent consciousness or Holy Ghost that later descended upon them.

--Ch. XXI "*Autobiography of a Yogi*" by Paramahansa Yogananda.

VII INDIA'S ROLE IN THE MODERN WORLD

Discourse a Santa Monica College,
February 11, 1958

These are transitional times of the utmost strain and stress from various directions in the history of whole world and especially of the United States of America, Russia, India, and other countries which figure prominently in the history of the modern world. It behoves every thinking person to consider carefully all the facts and factors of the situation, weigh the pros and cons correctly, and arrive at conclusions calculated to lead us on, both as individuals and as members of society, to the highest possible reaches of welfare and prosperity all round. Peace is the heart's desire of every normal person under normal conditions, and unless something comes up to upset the balance, we naturally feel desirous of leading quiet, peaceful lives of happiness and of joy all around.

Now, we have around us in the world a situation which is full of apprehensions, a situation which causes anxiety to all thinking persons concerned with the welfare of world. Under these conditions, and under these circumstances, the questions before us become more difficult than ever because of complications from various different directions which exert an undesirable influence and very often serve to distort our jundgment and warp our vision.

Now, under these circumstances, I have felt it my duty to go from place to place, and place before the thinkers, students, and all persons concerned, the exact need of the times, the real character of the exigencies and requirements all the world over, and if there be avoidable misery, the ways of avoiding such misery. Of course, with regard to those things which are unavoidable, which are beyond the sphere of our jurisdiction, well, we can only attempt but not hope for much success. Where world cataclysms take place, well, things are taken out of our hands altogether, and man, in spite of all his superiority complex, his conception of himself as the crown of creation, and so forth, finds himself powerless and looks on helplessly when the work of destruction is going on around him.

But if there is avoidable misery, if by steps that we can concertedly think over and adopt, we can avoid such misery, it would be criminal folly, criminal negligence, criminal inactivity on our part not to do our utmost and best in this direction. From this standpoint, I have, on behalf of India, a special mission, a special message, to deliver to the world.

India's heritage

From times immemorial, India has had a heritage of her own. Her response is not conditioned by limitations of present day matters, but is based absolutely on the intrinsic merits of each matter as it arises before us.

Now, the most saddening of all reflections is that under circumstances of the present inflammatory character, there is apprehension as regards what may begin to happen tomorrow. The war drums may any time sound in our ears, with pretty short notice or no notice at all. Under such circumstances, it behoves us all to do everything in our power to see if matters are manageable, and if they are manageable, try and do our best to manage them. In India, we have had, I don't say any unique or special superiority and things of that type, but somehow from centuries, perhaps myriads of years past, a tradition, not merely a bookish tradition which is to be found in the theoretical, dogmatic doctrinal side of the scriptures, but a living tradition in actual practical life, from day to day, a tradition which helps us in the desired direction. And, I therefore believe that it is the duty of all of us to see how we can benefit by this tradition, both on the theoretical aspect and from the standpoint of practical realism.

There is a general notion abroad that religion is a bone of contention between people and people. Differences of races, of religions, of communities, of denominations, of sects, and even of sub-sects and sub-sub-sects there are, which have been causing friction in the past history of the world. Wars fought in the name of religion have been plentiful and one feels very sad when he finds that religion, which ought to be a uniting force, has in our actual experience and as reported in the records of the past, acted in the opposite direction altogether.

It is my contention, which I hope I shall be able to convince all of you is the right one, that I have no need for any kind of quarreling with any religion whatsoever. I have been an humble student of the scriptures of various religions in the world, not from the standpoint of the critic, not from the standpoint of a person who seeks to pick holes, but from the standpoint of one who wishes to go into the heart of religion as presented to us by the saints, the sages, and the seers of the past, not merely by way of acquiring literary wisdom but also of realising it in actual practice. We have, so far as other religions are concerned, a starting handicap, a starting disadvantage that somehow or the other, rightly or wrongly, so far as I am concerned wrongly, but so far as the general student of religion and culture is concerned rightly or wrongly, there is a notion that religious differences are responsible for inevitable fighting, fighting not merely in the sense of heart-burning, but even in the sense of bloodshed and the burning of human beings alive, and so on. Crusades fought in the name of religion, then the mutual burnings of Roman Catholics, Protestants, and so on, in England, France, Spain, and other countries, and various other incidents have been reported to us in the pages of history, and described differently by different authors because of their alignment with this side or that side. Party affinities, sectarian affinities, and so forth, came in to complicate a state of affairs already complex enough for us. There is a feeling that there are differences of a fundamental character, differences which cannot be got over, which we can never possibly surmount by any amount of human wisdom and therefore we must bow down to the inevitable and face necessarily the existence of such a state of affairs.

And this is the proposition with which people start. They take it for granted that conflict is inevitable between religion and religion and therefore quarrels in the name of religion are justified.

As I have been saying, religion ought to be a force of uniting people who are disunited. We have Christ, the Master, Lord, and Saviour, accepted by many people, a great majority of the people in the western world. We hear him hailed, described as the prince of peace. In our scriptures here in India, in the Vedānta, we have Śāntiḥ, Śāntiḥ, Śāntiḥ, peace, peace, and peace again, and nothing but peace. This is the cry of the human soul tossed here, there and all around on account of the circumstances and agitations, into various kinds of sufferings and sorrows which are of an avoidable or irremedial character. Through the vedantic scriptures, we are told that religion ought to unite; it should not disunite. In contrast, the pages of history go to show that religion, or at least what was conceived of as religion, was responsible for many a blood-shed in the history of the western world.

Now, my position is simply this, that this position was one not really of a rightly reasoned character. Persons who have been talking in the name of inevitable conflicts, irreconcilable antagonism between two religions, etc., will generally be found to have been fanatically partisan, with one-sided equipment only.* And with that particular knowledge alone as their equipment, being ignorant of the views of the other side, having no data for purposes of comparison and contrast, and jumping to conclusions, such people justified themselves in their own minds by the little evidence before them, the few data before them. But their attitude is certainly not at all justifiable from the standpoint of a person of broad and wide outlook, and who seeks the truth and has no axe of his own to grind.

In all these religious fights, we find a predominating factor, that is the sincerity of the person who goes into the war. He goes there as a sincere partisan, but in spite of all his sincerity, the partisanship is there, and that partisanship is due to ignorance of the standpoint of the other side altogether and due to fanatical bigoted stress of a most virulent character on the

* Compare Māṇḍūkya Kārikā III-17 of Gauḍapāda, the grand-preceptor of Śaṅkara.

Svasiddhānta-vyavasthāsu
dvaitino niścitā dṛḍham,
Parasparam virudhyante
tairayaṁ na virudhyate.

The dualists (or pluralists), rooted in their respective dogmas, quarrel with each other. But Vedānta has no quarrel with them. (Vedānta reconciles their stand points into a single monistic philosophy like various limbs coexisting harmoniously in one body.)

standpoint of the one side he is conversant with, and has experience of, and about which he can say something.

Uniformity of views impossible

Now, if and when we go to the root of the question, the thing seems to be most ridiculous from the standpoint of elementary ratiocination. Any person who thinks on the question from an impartial standpoint, as a seeker after truth, will be forced to admit that uniformity of opinion, uniformity of belief, uniformity of faith is an impossibility in matters religious. That is the first thing which we have to start with. That stares us in the face.

We have the objective real world around us, perceptible through our five senses, things which have shape, sound, smell, touch. and taste. We have five corresponding sense organs with which we feel these things. We experience the world in this way as the object of vision, as the object of sound, as the object of smell, and taste, and touch. There is a particular part of the physical constitution which is calculated to give us the knowledge of these five things around us. We call them in Sanskrit—tanmātras.

Now, when we have got all these five sense organs and the capacity through them of sensing the things around us, one may take it for granted, one may feel justified in supposing that the things around us have an objective reality and that there can be no dispute about these objects. But, unfortunately, as a matter of fact, we find that although the same kinds of five sensory organs are there in all the individual bodies, there is a tremendous difference as regards the actual experience.

Let us take for example the case of a beautiful picture in an art gallery, an exhibition, and so forth. There is a certain picture which not a layman of doubtful artistic knowledge, but the highest, the most renowned of artists, comes and describes as a splendid picture, a beautiful work of art. Another person of the same calibre with the same kind of status as an artist, an equal authority on the subject, comes and says it is all rubbish. Splendid is the description on the one side and rubbish is the description on the other. And that too from experts. When experts differ, what shall the man in the street do in such a case? Similarly, with regard to music. What is most harmonious and melodious to me, is hateful to another and vice versa. The same thing is there with regard to taste, with regard to touch, and with regard to smell.

So even with regard to these things which are purely material as we call them, there is a tremendous difference of opinion, because of the special personal idiosyncracies of the individual. The personal equation counts. The eyes with which we see things, are not reflecting mirrors, they are really refracting lenses. There is greater refraction in one, less in another and so on, but the refraction is there.

We start with backgrounds, historical backgrounds, not of our own lifetime, but coming from centuries and generations past, inherited through the blood and so on. We start with prejudices and prepossessions and the consequence is, that our vision is distorted. And when the vision is distorted, the judgment is bound to go wrong.

We can see for ourselves that there can be no unanimity of opinion with regard to goodness or badness, with regard to beauty or ugliness, with regard to objective things around us.

Now proceeding further, it will be clear that much more therefore will be the differences, uniformity being impossible, with regard to matters beyond the reach of our physical senses. If, with regard to the objects of the senses, we are in this predicament, much worse is the predicament with regard to those things which are not within the jurisdiction of our physical senses. Things relating to life after death, after-life worlds, existences, etc., must necessarily be subject matters for a great deal of difference of opinion. And if and when we analyse the position of any person who believes in a certain religion, or a sub-sect most intimately connected with himself, we will find in the ultimate analysis that there is at least at the very end an element, a substratum of pure personal faith, which he can describe only as, "That is what I believe in the matter."

We can go on discussing with all our intellectuality, with all our powers, logical and psychological, we can bring to bear on the subject any and every kind of mental, intellectual, and other equipment that we have, and at the very end, the philosopher, the theologian, the scientist too, will have to say, "Well, that is my belief."

From the same state of things around, different people infer differently. The inferences are, after all, inferences, in the nature of a gamble, nothing more. And when I talk of gambling, I need not remind you that there are more blanks than prizes, more errors than right solutions. Things are beyond us because the element of faith comes in. Absolute scientific certainty, or mathematical certainty is much more, therefore, out of the question.

We have, for example, in courts of law, criminal cases adjudicated on by different judges, not different judges of different levels in different courts, a lower court and an appeal court and so on, but the same bench of two judges or more. They have the same evidence, documentary and oral, hear the same arguments, follow the same textbooks of law with regard to civil procedure, criminal procedure, and so on, and honestly come to different conclusions and give different judgments.

When this is the case with regard to matters of inference, it naturally follows that with regard to things which are not of the objective, material world around us, there must be enormous individual differences of opinion. The very idea with which we start is wrong, when we say this is the right thing and all others are wrong and therefore all must follow our path otherwise we'll do our utmost to coerce them to follow our path. We cannot look to uniformity of opinion in any matter whatsoever and especially with regard to matters pertaining to the non-material or the supra-material or the after-death world and so forth.

This is a point of view which has been taken into account very closely in the scriptures of India. In the other religions too, the same thing is there as I study them. I have been a very humble and inquisitive inquirer in my study of the Bible and other scriptures of various religions in the world, and I have been fully convinced again and again that the teachings are not merely basically and fundamentally the same, but, still more, even with regard to details, there is a tremendous parallelism between them, almost as if two persons sitting at the same table, were citing in two different languages the same thing which had been placed before them. One translating from the original into English, and the other from the original into Greek, Latin, Sanskrit, Tamil, French, German, or Caucasian, and so on. There is that intense parallelism with which I have been not merely astounded but enormously gratified because that shows us the way to peace.

Adhikāribheda

Differences there are. But these differences are generally found to be, as ordinary circumstances of our own lifetime here are, the inevitable consequences of different historical backgrounds and so forth. Something of the moment, something of a passing character, something of merely local character, is responsible for some kind of injunction or some kind of admonition or prohibition and so forth found in the scriptures. But, even there our scriptures take the view that these differences based upon historical considerations, consequent on historical conditions, and necessitated by historical background of different character, should not be treated as differences of opinion at all, and should not lead to conflict. On the other hand, they should be looked upon as the different needs of different individuals and different communities at different times. And the example given in the scriptures, in the Vedic literature that we have, is a very instructive one, and is very easy to understand and to apply in all these affairs where there are tremendous differences 'adhikārī-bheda' as we call them. The differences are, under natural conditions, reduced to natural causes of a passing character.

For example, take the case of two doctors, one who has to treat a diabetic patient and another who has got to treat a case of heart disease. The doctor who is treating the diabetic patient, prohibits sugar; the other doctor prohibits salt. Now, the two different cases being of different types, the treatments required are different, the medicines are different, and the diets are also different, and therefore, the difference is inevitable. But, there is nothing fundamentally, basically in conflict between the two. You will not say that as the two doctors belong to two different religions, they can never agree, and they must fight. Suppose a specialist on diabetes writing on the subject, says, that in a particular combination, concatenation of circumstances, it is necessary to avoid sugar and other such things altogether, and the other doctor, in his book, tells us how salt is injurious in cases of heart disease, and therefore should be absolutely avoided.

Well, we'll, say, "There is no question of a conflict between the two, they are not representatives of different types of thought, two different schools, two different religions, and so forth. The differences are due to the differences in the condition of the patient, the exigencies and requirements of the patients, and nothing else."

Religions are not hostile

This kind of attitude is explained in the following :

Dharmam yo bādhate dharmo
na sa dharmaḥ kudharma tat,
Avirodhī tu yo dharmaḥ
sa dharma iti niścayaḥ.

That religion, that faith, that sect, which comes into conflict with another is not true religion; it is a parody of religion. That's how the text begins. And the second part, the counterpart, the complementary part says, that religion which not merely exists alongside of another, but in actual cooperation, not merely sympathy, but active coordination and cooperation with other religions, is the essence of true religion.

We talk at the present day, of spiritual fellowship, religious cooperation, religious toleration, and so on. Well, from the state in which we were continually fighting, this rise to the level of religious toleration is a matter for congratulation, for self-felicitation. But, even that phrase, "religious toleration," is something obnoxious to us from our standpoint. What is it that you tolerate? You tolerate what is evil. You tolerate what you condemn as being wicked, and you say, "I tolerate it." You've cultivated a temperamental position of sufficient power of endurance to bear things around you, like heat and cold and so on. Similarly, praise and censure make no difference to you. You have come to that stage and you tolerate things. You bear, you endure them.

But, the very word 'tolerate' suggests the condemnation before hand of the thing in itself as something evil. Well, we don't talk of toleration. We talk of oneness, not mere mechanical unity, but solidarity from within. According to the needs of the situation, in each case, according to the exigencies of the case, the doctors have to give their prescriptions, change the diet, permit today something that was prohibited yesterday, saying that the restriction is no longer necessary. This kind of thing is there. And as regards other religions, for example, in the Bhagavad Gītā, we have :

> Ye (a) pyanya devatābhaktā
> yajañte śraddhayānvitāḥ,
> Te (a) pi māmeva Kaunteya
> yajantyavidhipūrvakam.*

"Even those who believe in and worship other deities, with sincerity of heart, they do worship Me." That is a clear expression there. You will not find such an actual declaration in so many categorical terms of this type in other literatures. But, even there, it is my contention that the attitude is the same. I will presently show how it is so. Even when there is no such declaration to this effect in so many categorical terms, the meaning is the same. The teachers, the masters who founded and expounded these various religions were one in their views as regards what religion really meant.

Purity of heart

We may take Lord Jesus Christ's words on the subject. When questions of self-realization or God-realization come up, people will tell you that attainment of that state of intellectual, spiritual, and high perfection is possible only through purity of heart. Our texts say that realization, visualization, is possible only through purity of heart. And we find Christ himself saying. "Blessed are the pure in heart for they shall see God.† The idea is the same.

Right knowledge

Volumes have been written in great detail dealing with the means for emancipation, emancipation from all bondage, not merely external bondage like political, economic etc., but internal bondage, that is, slavery to our own senses, and so forth.

* Gītā IX-23.
† St. Matthew V-8.

In all these books, we are told again and again that right knowledge, practical not merely dogmatic doctrinal or academical but realistic and practical which is applicable and which is actually applied to every aspect of life from day to day, from moment to moment, is the equipment, the means, the instrument by which man can emancipate himself.

And, in St. John's gospel (VIII-32), we have Christ giving the same idea in his own language, "Ye shall know the truth and the truth shall make you free." Knowledge of the truth. And that knowledge is defined not as mere theoretical knowledge, what is to be found only in bookshelves and so forth or in the memory by mechanical repitition, or by cramming. That is not described as knowledge. Knowledge is that that which is in the nature of actual realization and practical, realistic application to everyday conduct in life. That is described by our scriptures as the mode for emancipation, and here, we have the same thing coming up, "Know the truth and the truth shall make you free." "Know," includes knowledge and practice.

Attitude towards other religions and towards agnostics and atheists

"Śrotavyo mantavyo nididhyāsitavyaḥ"*

Investigate carefully, decide correctly, and follow faithfully with purity of heart."

Now, when the text is placed before us :

Ye (a)pyanyadevatābhaktā
yajante śraddhayānvitāḥ,
Te (a)pi māmeva Kaunteya
yajantyavidhipūrvakam.†

—even those who worship other deities really worship Me, if they are sincere, if there is purity of heart. That's what the text says. Now a question will arise. Those who are worshippers of other deities have been given this assurance that if with purity of heart they are pursuing the game, well, there is nothing for them to fear. They're worshipping the same deity, the all-pervading, all-

* Bṛhadāraṇyaka Upaniṣad II-4-5.
† Gītā IX-23.

permeating, all-knowing, all-potent, almighty Lord of the Universe. Well, what about atheists, what about agnostics? What about those who do not believe in any deity at all? Well, will they be consigned to eternal hell ? And the answer is given in the same Bhagavad Gītā, another part, a subsequent portion, subsequent to, and consequent on this previous portion. And that portion says:

"Ye tvakṣaram anirdeśyam
avyaktam paryupāsate,
Sarvatragam acintyam ca
kūṭastham acalam dhruvam.
Sanniyamyendriyagrāmam
sarvatra samabuddhayaḥ,
Te prāpnuvanti māmeva
sarvabhūtahite ratāh.†

Even an atheist, or an agnostic, even a person who not merely doubts the existence of God, but denies the possibility of any such existence, even he is not condemned to eternal hell if with sincerity of heart, he seeks to do good, to be benefactor, and if he thinks over the joys and sorrows of people around him, and as a humanitarian he has benevolence of heart which shows itself in actual practice in his incessant and strenuous activities for the uplift of humanity.* And in this very context, we have Vyāsa stating :

Definition of merit and sin

Ślokārdhena pravakṣyāmi yaduktam grantha-koṭibhiḥ,
Paropakāraḥ puṇyāya pāpāya parapīḍanam.**

† "Those who continuously meditate on the Reality as imperishable, undefinable, unmanifested, omnipresent, unthinkable, unchanging immobile, and constant, and restraining their senses, and being even-minded, devote themselves to the welfare of all beings, they reach Me (God)." Gītā XII-3,4.

* Also see:
Api cet sudurācāro
bhajate mām ananyabhāk,
Sādhureva sa mantavyaḥ
samyag vyavasito hi saḥ. (Gītā IX-30)

"If a man of vile conduct, follows me with exclusive devotion, he should be considered as a righteous man for he is on the right lines."

** Mahābhārata.

I give you the gist of millions and millions of scriptures, and that is, "Merit is philanthropy, benevolence, doing good to others, and sin is doing harm to others unjustly and out of partiality on account of self-seeking of various kinds and so on." This is the definition given of merit and of sin. This is the line that we have here put definitely before us.

Now let us take the inference which I mentioned with regard to the teachings of other great Masters, founders of religion, propaganders, expounders of religion and so forth in other places in other context and so on.

We have for example, a beautiful passage in the Bible. I don't want to go into details and give too many quotations because the time is very short. We have Christ himself saying, "Not all that come to me and say Lord, Lord" will have salvation.* A person who comes in that way is taken as an example. Not only one particular person but a number of persons coming under that category, are taken into account and described. God will say unto them, "Depart from here; I don't want you here; I came to you hungry, you did not feed me; I came to you thirsty; you gave me no drink; I came to you in this and that kind of suffering, and you did nothing to relieve the suffering. Depart." And they will ask, "When Lord, did you come to us hungry and we refused to feed you? When did you come thirsty and we refused to give you drink? And when did you come to us in suffering and we refused to mitigate the sorrow and the suffering ?" And the answer will be, "Because you did not do this to any man, to any human or other sentient being, therefore you did not do it to me." And there will be others who were not regarded as followers or devotees of the Lord and they hear that their names have been entered on the top of the list of candidates eligible for salvation. They are themselves surprised at this. And the Lord will say to them, "I came to you hungry, and you fed me; I came to you thirsty, you gave me drink; I came in such and such suffering, you relieved my suffering. Therefore, you are here." And then, they too will ask, "When Lord, did you come and when did we

* See St. Matthew VII-21.

serve you in this way." And the answer is, "Because you did this to the least of my creation, therefore, you did it to me."†

Fundamental religion

The teaching is clear. We do not have to go into any great philosophical and technical recondite discussion on the subject. The religion of humanity is the fundamental religion which is the core of all religions. The other things are only manifestations, various kinds of activities, and we need collateral help from this or from that sādhanā, as we call it, help, and nothing else. The fundamental point is this : humanity for its own sake, doing anything and everything humanly possible for the relief of suffering, for doing good to the world, is the essence of religion. A person who does good, who seeks the welfare of others, and who seeks to do good, and actually does good, cannot come to an evil end* whether he believes in me or not, that is what Śrī Kṛṣṇa says in the Gītā. The religion of humanity is the religion. That is the common factor, not the greatest common factor, but the only common factor for all religions.

Anything which calls itself technically religion, which is officially called a religion, and which lacks in the elementary and fundamental conception of true religion, is no religion, but a parody of religion. It's a mockery of religion, and all the fighting that we have in the name of religion is the consequence of that kind of wrong conception about what religion really means.

This has been put before us in so many terms, clearly again and again. With regard to people of other religions, the attitude is not of the passive "don't disturb." The texts go further and preach an active cooperation, and help to them. On all matters on which we can agree to work, we agree. And on those matters on which differences of opinion are unavoidable, where owing to differences of constitution, mental, intellectual, and so

† See St. Matthew XXV-32 to 46.

* Nahi kalyāṇakṛt kaścit
durgatim tāta gacchati. (Gita VI-40)

forth, we are differently placed. and on account of the differences of refraction in the lenses as I have called them, there is inevitable difference of vision, we agree to disagree. We disagree on those points on which disagreement is unavoidable, and in other things, we work together for the welfare of the common man.

All religions welcomed in India

This is the practical message of the Indian history. This is the precept, but what about the actual practice ? We have a grand tradition in that way. That tradition is one in which religions from other countries came into India one after another. Take up the history of any of these religions, you will find one and one thing only, that India has always welcomed people from other religions, from other countries, from other races, and so forth, and has not merely given them shelter, but given them every possible cooperation, coordination, and help. At the first onset when something new came, there may have been surprise, there may have been an aberration, a deviation from the usual path, but, after a little reflection and thinking over the matter, the Indian, the Vedic devotee satisfied himself on the matter as regards his duty and treated the stranger at the gate with the hospitality enjoined by the Hindu Dharma-śāstra.

We have for example the Parsees. The Parsees were persecuted in their own oriental native land, Iran, on account of their religious beliefs. And seeking a safe place where they could go on with their worship in their own way according to their conscience, they went from place to place in Asia and in Europe; and found no shelter anywhere. They came at last to the Western coast of India, to Gujarat province, in the Bombay presidency, where one Rājā Yādava was ruling. Things were reported to him; "Hundreds of shiploads of foreigners have come in, strange in dress, strange in appearance, strange in language, strange in everything." And Rājā Yādava was not sure what his duty was under the circumstances. He then applied for advice and guidance to the then Śaṅkarācārya who was camping nearby. And the then Śaṅkarācārya told him, "They are strangers at the gate. In spite of all their differences, their strange ways and customs and manners and so on that you are talking about, they should be treated as guests. Receive them with hospitality that one only beholds in India. That is what has to be done." And Rājā Yādava did it. He encouraged them, he housed them, he sheltered them, he gave all necessary facilities, not merely facilities, but advantages of a unique type, so much so that at the present day, the Parsees on New Year's day, in their celebrations, or whatever urgent matters they may have to dispose of, always begin with a resolution of thanks to the memory of Rājā Yādava who was responsible for what they are in India today.

Similar has been the attitude of Indians towards Christianity. Let us look into the history of Christianity, very briefly, in its onward march towards the West.

Struggles of early Christianity

When people talking about the East and the West, indulge in the luxury of untruth and pass disparaging remarks about orientals in general, they forget that Christ the Lord, the Master, and the Saviour whom they profess to believe in, was himself an oriental. He was not an occidental. And his religion spread from Palestine and Judea towards the West. At every step, Christianity had to fight its way into the western world. The whole strength, military and otherwise, of the Roman empire was pitted against the Christians. And religion after religion rose to fight them. It was a fight to the finish. They all said to Christianity, and Christianity had to say to them, "Either you survive or I; both of us cannot survive under the same sun." That kind of opposition was there, And the result was that all those religions were wiped out, exterminated from the face of the earth But tremendous sacrifices had to be made before Christianity could hope to live. St. Paul, St. James, St. John, St. Peter, all had to follow the same path that the Master had. They were crucified, beheaded, and so on. It was a tremendous fight. And the people who carried on the fight there, went on in spite of all obstacles and when Constantine became a convert, when St. Paul's influence, oratorical, and epistilic, and so forth, had its own impression and Constantine became a Christian, things changed for Christianity. And

Christianity found it easy afterwards to disperse into the western world.

India's attitude

But what about India ? The very first colony of Christians in the whole world was the colony which St. Thomas, one of the evangelists of Christ, brought to India. The then sovereign of Calicut welcomed the Christians there, housed them, and so on, and at the present day, they are considered to be the most prosperous and also, at the same time, the most intellectual amongst the Christian communities all over India.

This has been our attitude, not merely in theory, but in actual historical practice. One may ask, "What about Islam? Were there not continuous and bitter fights?" Well, it is true. There were fights, and bitter fights. But the fights were not on the score of religion.

The followers of Islam came to India not as religionists seeking shelter and safety in a strange land amongst new surroundings and so forth; but as political and military conquerors. And they were resisted. That had nothing to do with religion at all. In modern India, there is a tendency to talk of religion; 'Islam in danger', this thing in danger, and that thing in danger, when all the time it is a matter of a few more posts in government offices, of manipulations, for office of power, or of communal representation, and things of that type and nothing more. Again and again, we have had this experience there.

So, under the present day world conditions, which are of a most threatening, most saddening, most tragic and pathetic character, I feel that the voice of India should be heard. She should exert to make herself heard. And with regard to the United States, I have felt that by virtue of her military position her political position, and her financial position, she has opportunities and consequently responsibilities which are above those of any other country in the world. Having these facilities, having these advantages, and the consequent responsibility as I have called it, the United States, I thought, would be the first place for me to make the sphere of my active work: the propagation of world prosperity through world peace.

This is India's contribution. This was India's contribution to world peace in the past. And if India is true to herself, this should be and I hope, will be the attitude, the actual contribution of India to the promotion of all causes of a positive and constructive character which are beneficial to nations at large.

If all the billions and trillions and quadrillions that we spend for military and other equipment can be used for work of positive and uplifting character, of a nation-building character and so forth, humanity will be benefited to that extent. Any voice however feeble, any attempt however feeble, to bring about this consummation is to be welcomed.

And this is the message, this is the mission, on which I have come. I look to leaders of thought here in America and especially the professors and the students in the colleges, students who are the hopes for the future generation. We are already "back-numbers" or out of date. We will be called upon soon to retire not merely from this or from that position, but from the world itself.* All that we can hope for is that the future generations will be nurtured on right lines, and will learn to cooperate with others in bringing about an era of peace and plenty. That would be the return of Christ to the world.

It was a cynic that said, but to some extent he was telling the truth when he said, "There was only one Christian ever and that Christian died on the Cross."

But, if we could gather together for the purpose of bringing about the realisation of the ultimate objective of peace and joy for all, that would be not a crucifixion of Christ but a rewelcoming of Christ into the religious world from the practical standpoint.

I will therefore conclude by appealing again to all the leaders of thought, to the men in authority, and especially to the students and to those who guide the students, to gird their loins and apply themselves to this great task. This is my prayer. I hope that there will be a quick response which would in practice show itself in the avoidance of blood-curdling wars, resulting

* His Holiness had a premonition of his impending departure from this world. Soon after his return from America, His Holiness fell ill. He attained mahāsamādhi on 2-2-1960.

in the wastage of human life, human property, and other things which can be much more usefully employed. It will be an honour, a dignity, a glory for us to have been able to depart from the kind of shameful and othrewise inhuman, if not fully at least partly inhuman or non-human kind of life that we are leading with our petty notions and jealousies and other things of that type detrimental to the human progress.

This is the mission I wish to place before you and call your earnest attention to it with the view to enlisting as much co-operation in all the directions as possible,

VIII VIEWS ON AMERICA, SCIENCE AND RELIGION

Broadcasts on Tuesday and Thursday evenings, February 11th & 13th at 10-30 p.m., over radio station KFI Los Angeles, sponsored by Church of Religious Science — "This Thing Called Life" — interviewed by Dr. Hornaday.

Dr. Hornaday. Your Holiness, on behalf of all America, we welcome you not only to this country, but indeed, to this programme which is heard around the world. Your Holiness, what do you hope to accomplish by your visit to the United States ?

His Holiness. I have always felt that all the religious conflicts and other clashes between country and country, religion and religion, community and community,.etc., are due to misunderstandings and are not of what might be called an inevitable character. The countries themselves, the races themselves, the religions themselves, are not irreconcilably hostile or antagonistic to one another. But, at the same time, in the course of long experience, in fact, five or six decades of experience as an ecclesiastical preacher of Hinduism, I always found that the misunderstandings are there, and as they are avoidable misunderstandings, it is the duty of all persons interested in the promotion of world harmony to do their utmost, and to contribute their best and highest, for the removal of such misunderstandings and for the promotion of peace, good will, and positive, active cooperation with one another. I am not content merely with the idea of peace in the sense of absence of hostility, absence of war, and so forth, but something more positive in the shape of coordination, cooperation all round. And I have felt latterly, with war-clouds threatening us on all sides and with our premonitions that the war-drums might begin to be heard at any moment, that the time was more than ripe, more than mature, for a visit to the United States and other countries all the world over for helping in the process of removal of misunderstandings and promotion of peace and amity, in the positive sense that I have mentioned, and not merely in the negative sense in which people talk of peace. And this purpose I hope to achieve through the cooperation of all concerned because there is no great demand made upon any person by way of sacrifice of principles and so forth. The peace and amity that I am talking of is inherent in the situation and there is no straining of, forcing of matters in the name of religion in order to achieve the promotion of peace. It fits in naturally and therefore no special effort is necessary from outside. Only a recognition of the misunderstandings and the sincere desire to remove those misunderstandings are what are necessary. I hope to achieve this purpose by my visit, and I felt that according to world conditions, this was very urgent and no time should be lost, no delay should be countenanced, and the work should start at once. And, as I felt that by virtue of her political, military, financial, and other positions, America, this American Republic has greater opportunities and consequently greater responsibilities in the matter, I should start with United States of America as the sphere of my activity in this direction.

Dr. H. Your Holiness, could you tell us what attitude does India have towards the United States from the standpoint of the people themselves ?

H.H. From the standpoint of the people of India, there is absolute cordiality. And, the people of India look forward to positive help and cooperation and even leadership in matters of this type, so that we may be assured of peace and goodwill prevailing all round and all the resources of the various countries being applied to positive and constructive purposes of nation-building character and not thrown away on meaningless wars which have no real justification on the intrinsic merits, but which are due to misunderstandings mostly.

Dr. H. Yes, I was very happy to hear you say that you were a preacher, and although we are here in a predominantly Christian nation, what special contribution do you feel Hinduism can make toward creating better world understanding ? As you are the leader of millions, I'm sure our listeners would like to hear of this contribution.

H.H. : Our position is that while other religions have been subject to the handicap that, rightly or wrongly, preachers and propagandists have in the case of those religions, emphasized the truth of their religion, not merely emphasized the truth of their particular religion, or creed, or denomination, or sect, but somehow, also conveyed the impression that the followers of those other religions are not eligible for salvation, in the religious technical sense of the term.

While that is the case with regard to other religions rightly or wrongly, whether the understanding is right or wrong, whether the scriptures are right or wrong are different matters and I shall presently express my view on that point, but in the meantime, while this state of affairs has actually come into our experience with regard to other religions, our Hindu-Vedic religion has this speciality that it does not claim any monopoly in the path of salvation for followers of the Vedic faith. In fact, we do not claim superiority, we do not claim monopoly, and I would go to the extent of saying, putting it pithily, that the only superiority, the only uniqueness that we claim for Hinduism is that it does not claim any superiority or uniqueness.

Dr. H. Do you feel that there is a basic unity underlying all religions ?

H.H. I feel that there is much more than a basic unity. There is solidarity and practical parallelism in all directions with necessary differences of a very small character which are to be accounted for by unavoidable historical backgrounds and things of that type of the moment, (superficial differences of temporary character appearing) from time to time, and nothing basic, nothing serious, nothing especially worthwhile with regard to questions like peace and war.

Dr. H. What do you feel about our educational system here in the United States, our college program ? As you are lecturing to our most outstanding universities in the United States, I'm sure that you have seen many of our students and our student exchange program. Do you feel that we are lacking in our educational program in teaching these fundamental essentials that you have just referred to ?

H.H. I have the feeling that while the attention of all thinkers in general and educationists in particular has been on this point, by virtue of circumstances, owing to stress and strain of other considerations, political, and so forth, probably the educational side has not had the benefit of the full consideration which it ought to receive. And if there be an earnest and whole-hearted effort for quickening up the educational processes and procedures, the curricula, syllabi, and so forth, with regard to education, it will go far to help us in the objective before us, namely, the achievement of world prosperity through world peace and world cooperation.

Dr. H. We have in many of our Universities, and we trust many more will have it as one of their outstanding course, and that is a course in humanities where we can understand each other. Well, thank you your Holiness.

(End of first night's broadcast)

Dr. H. Do you feel that the people believe in India that the United States or the Americans are too materialistic ?

H. H. I've repeatedly answered this question with regard to the materialistic tendency of the Western World and so forth, but I feel that the very question is the result of a misunderstanding with regard to the real meaning of spirituality and of materialism. The Spirit and matter are inextricably intertwined, and any attempt to divorce the one from the other is bound to mean absolute failure with regard to both. And I've always held, and even in the last press conference here a few days ago I gave expression to the feeling, that the idea that Americans were materialistic by nature and incorrigible and so forth from this standpoint was an absolute delusion, based upon a misunderstanding. The very genesis of America, starting from the Pilgrim Fathers, and coming on to George Washington and down to the present time, the whole history, disproves any such allegation. There is no question of materialism standing in the way of spiritualism. The matter is the medium through which the Spirit manifests itself. The Spirit is the thing which manifests itself through the material which is the medium. There can be no conflict between the two. Any separation of the two, I'm talking of spirituality on the one side and materialism on the other, is based upon wrong conceptions and fanatical or bigoted notions with regard to spirituality.

Dr. H. Yes, well, I thoroughly agree. As there are millions of people listening to this programme of many faiths, many nations, I wonder if you could present to them some suggestions which through experience you have proved to be effective where we can find that which is basic in our lives, and find that which will point the way to an understanding of each other and to world peace.

H. H. There is no kind of antipathy, on the contrary there is a great deal of sympathy towards all such movements and attempts. There can be no doubt about that. At the same time, there may be differences of opinion as to the efficiency of the methods, the quality, the quantity, and so forth. These are matters in which by mutual and internal consultations, things can be brought to a satisfactory level for all persons concerned. I do not believe there is any inherent trouble at all on the intrinsic merits of the case from any standpoint. And I believe that if the state and the people, separately working toward the same interests, toward the attainment of the same goal, unite more actively, the purpose can be much better and much more speedily accomplished.

Dr. H. Do you believe there is any conflict between science and religion ?

H. H. So far as our own Hindu theory, Hindu doctrine is concerned, every science is an integral part of the religious literature. There can be no question of any hostility between religion and science. Unfortunately, it is true that in the Western World for some time there was continuous animosity between the two but, even there, the modern philosophers, the modern theologians and the modern scientists have come to a great deal, a large percentage, of agreement and no one believes there is any inherent contradiction or inconsistency between religion and science. But as for Hinduism, as I have already stated. the Hindu includes every secular subject, as we speak of secular subjects today, as an integral part of religious literature. The first part of our Vedas, the religious scripture, is called the Ṛgveda, and that contains what you call Āyurveda. Āyurveda is the name for a combination of sciences which in modern medical terminology we would describe as anatomy, physiology, hygiene, sanitary science, medicine, surgery, and so on. And this is not intended for the purpose of procuring, promoting the health of persons who have passed into another world. In this material world of ours, in these physical bodies of ours, we need health and strength and the sciences which concern themselves with these subjects are the part of first of our Vedas. Similarly, archery and various military sciences, constitute what we call Dhanurveda. And that Dhanurveda is part of second of our Vedas (Yajurveda). Thirdly, we have the art and science of music. And fourthly, we have what is called Sthāpatya Veda, which includes higher mathematics of every denomination, of every type, engineering, architecture, and all the secular sciences. Then we have what we call the Vedāṅgas, contributory elements, and there we include grammar, prosody, astronomy, and all these subjects. And all these subjects which are in ordinary western terminology supposed to be secular subjects are integral parts, inseparable parts of our religious literature.* So the question of any antagonism between religion and science is absolutely out of place from the standpoint of a believer in the Hindu scriptures.

Dr. H. What role, do you feel, religion can play in reducing the tensions, the strain and the stress of living in this so-called space age ? Do you really feel that it is more than just an idealistic practice, that it can become a workable practice within the hearts of men to find this peace within and share it with their brothers ?

H. H. Religion can make the best contribution possible for the attainment of peace all round, not merely from any academic

* The following table will clarify the relationship of these sciences with the main Vedas.

Main Veda	*Upaveda* (minor Veda)	*Vedāṅga* (auxiliary sciences common to all the four Vedas)
1. Ṛgveda	Āyurveda (medicine etc.)	Śikṣā (Pronunciation)
2. Yajurveda	Dhanurveda (military-sciences)	Jyotiṣa (Astronomy)
		Chandas (Prosody)
3. Sāmaveda	Gāndharva veda (Music)	Nirukta (Lexicography & etymology)
Atharva Veda	Sthāpatyaveda (Architecture etc.)	Kalpa (Ritual rules)
		Vyākaraṇa (Grammar)

or doctrinal standpoint, but from the standpoint of practical realism, for the very simple reason that most of the conflicts between people and people, race and race and nation and nation, are concerned with and are due to misunderstandings of each other and the fanatical, bigoted insistence on exclusiveness and monopoly agencies and things of that type. And a correct reading of religion will necessarily and naturally and still further. most encouragingly. automatically remove all these misunderstandings. With regard to other things, with regard to other means possible for the attainment of this goal, there are inherent possibilities of objections because they are feelings of a personal character perhaps. the individual's personal idiosyncracies coming into play which the next generation may not share. There is nothing of this seed of permanency with regard to opinions, with regard to other subjects. But, with regard to religion, where the followers of each religion believe in their scriptures and try their honest best to act up to the scriptures. the intentions and prohibitions contained therein, well, it automatically follows that religion can be the strongest bulwark against all misunderstandings and these frictions caused by misunderstandings.

IX ROLE OF INDIANS ABROAD

Address to the Hindu Community of Los Angeles assembled in the SRF India Hall at 8 *p.m. on Saturday, February* 15, 1958. *His Holiness was introduced by Sri Sri Sri Daya Mata (then Sister Daya).*

Sr. Daya. I would like to say good evening to all of you who have come this evening. Many of you are known to me, and for the first time some of us are meeting. It is our signal honour to present to you this evening one of India's great spiritual leaders. I tried to think how I might introduce him to you, and in a book that His Holiness gave me to read — one that he had written — I found a news clipping which was written by one of India's news writers.* And it seemed to me that it was a very fitting time to read it, that you might know a little bit about His Holiness:

"Easily the most unforgettable character I have met in a quarter of a century crowded with personalities, His Holiness Śrī Jagadguru Śaṅkarācārya of the ancient and historic maṭh at Puri (Jaggernaut) must rank, I think, the greatest of them all. Five foot nothing, spare of frame and figure, and clear-eyed and courteous with that old-world courtesy which not many generations ago was a distinguished trait of our people, but which the new generation of our free Indian(s) seems to have foresworn, and humble with a transcendent humility of saint and ṛṣi, this Pope of four hundred million Hindus displays a power of mind and soul which in the calm assurance of its knowledge and its complete conquest of doubt marks him a giant in a world of men harried by uncertainty and driven by fear. Versed in the scriptures of the major human religions and the greatest living authority on those of his own, with a mastery of the Vedas unrivaled in centuries, and speaking a dozen modern languages with the fluency of a native, filled with the learning of the past as well as that of the present, Śrī Jagadguru is amply

* This article by "The Rambler," a noted columnist was published by *The Times of India* (Bombay) in its issue of June 7, 1953.

qualified to be what that title means, namely a world teacher. So disarmingly human is his quiet warmth of welcome which makes one instantly intimate, that one can almost miss the greatness of this man. But one does not; one cannot possibly do so. Through the silent chuckling laughter and the gentle irony and understanding criticism, the precise comment and clear analysis, it steals upon one imperceptibly with the full power of a knowledge complete and assured with that maturity of enlightenment which is achieved by a lifetime of observant experience and ripened by contemplation in the solitude of nature, such as the ṛṣis enjoined upon all who would teach their fellow men."

"When we first learned of his Holiness, I thought, 'How shall I greet this holy man?' He arrived at the airport in the midst of rain, and we were rather sad that Los Angeles should greet him, thus, until, as he stood in the rain, he turned and in a quiet voice said to me, "It seems that the rain has come to become a part of this reception today." I liked his quiet humor; I liked the way he accepted the inevitable. And in the few precious moments that we have had, and I have sat listening to his wonderful philosophy — a philosophy that is not Hindu, that cannot be limited to any particular race or nationality but that universality which is the truest philosophy of all. It reminds us that we are all made in the image of the one Divine Father and that by tearing away all the barriers that stand between nationalities, stand between races, we can come to that common understanding and arrive at that common bond which is God, which is love, which is peace, which is wisdom. It gives me the greatest pleasure to introduce to you this evening His Holiness Śrī Jagadguru Śaṅkarācārya.

(Sanskrit chant by Mrs. Trivedi preceded the address by the Jagadguru.)*

His Holiness. Friends, in the course of my discourses here during last few days since my arrival in America, I have been stressing the need for what one might call a federation of religions and the promotion of world peace, and therethrough of

* Such Sanskrit chants by Mrs. Trivedi invariably preceded the addresses of His Holiness in America. The chants and their meaning are given in the introductory portions of this book.

world prosperity. I feel that India has a special part to play in the necessary evolution before we can expect to achieve any sentimental (integration) or other such feeling which would be justifiable on its own merits. But because of the intrinsic merits India has a special message to deliver to the world; and the times are such that maturity, ripeness for the necessary action has already been reached. And the exigencies and the requirements of the present day demand that no time should be lost in starting the work on these lines and towards this purpose. The fulfilment of the purpose of world peace (through) world prosperity depends upon the various factors and facts of the situation, and there is absolutely no doubt whatsoever that any and every person who can possibly contribute to the consummation in question, and to the happiness resultant therefrom should be regarded as a benefactor to the race. And although the times are propitious in that way, for the purpose, and in fact necessitate this kind of activity on the part of all concerned — all religions, all the nations concerned and so forth — yet if we look back to the traditions of the past it cannot be denied that we Indians by birth have a special message to deliver to the world. I have thought it necessary to start with America on this world-wide tour for the simple reason that America's military, political, financial and other positions of advantage in similar respects, carry with them a corresponding, a proportionate responsibility. The facilities being there, responsibilities naturally follow.

Now, I wish to talk to the Indian element assembled here for the simple reason that India has a special part to fulfil if she can do so. And Indians abroad can go a long way, can do a lot for the consummation of this kind. I feel that a study of elementary history of the world will be quite enough for the purpose of making plain to all, the duties, responsibilities of Indians in this matter.

In the first place — not by way of any self-laudation, nor in the spirit of superiority and so forth, but solely on the intrinsic merits, in order that we realize our responsibility and act up to it — I wish to call your attention to the history of other parts of the world in connection with this very subject and the part that India has always played in past history. We have before us in all the books of history that we learn and study in schools and colleges, the picture of internal strife and internal strife not on account of any really compelling exigency or any such thing, but internal conflicts of the various types, supposed to be based on differences in religion. Now here, not as a layman, not as a pacifist who has his own sentimental views on the subject and who has some sort of special feeling toward world peace and world prosperity and so on, but with a full sense of my responsibility as a representative of India, not merely of India in general, but of Indian ecclesiastical profession in particular, I wish to place before you this story of what was the case in the past in other countries and what has been the case with regard to India in respect to the same matter.

Crusades

We have the history of the Western world, the history given to us of the crusades which were supposed to be fought on the basis of religious differences. Peter the Hermit, in the name of Christianity, preached crusades to the people in that way. And then came the Roman Catholic and Protestant quarrels in England, France, Spain, and so on. And instead of discussing matters, even if they were discussible on the merits, they went to the extremes of not merely heartburning but also of body-burning, burning of bodies alive. That kind of history has been placed before us. And from time to time this kind of thing has happened, and history seems to have been fond of repeating itself in this respect much more than in other things. Good things repeated, well, are matters for congratulation, for self-felicitation. But things of an evil character, things of a destructive character, things which can do no good to anybody but can only do harm to everybody, these things have been happening, and history has been repeating itself again and again in these respects.

Now we shall try to analyse the position with regard to the crusades and so on. Each side held that it had complete mastery over the details, and its path was right and all the other paths were wrong. People were not satisfied with finding a passport for themselves to heaven; they were not satisfied until they confined all other people to hell, and that too, an eternal hell.

That kind of mentality was there all the time causing all that heartburning and bloodshed and things of that type.

Uniformity of views not possible

Now, an elementary reflection on the subject — nothing deeply philosophical, metaphysical, moral, spiritual and so forth is necessary at all — a very slight but, careful thinking on the subject will make it clear that there can be no possibilities of oneness, and especially of mechanical uniformity in matters relating to religion. In all countries we have differences not merely with regard to other religions but inside each religion, the various denominations, the subsects and the sub-subsects too have their own differences. And these differences can never be settled except on the basis of faith. We are told again and again by the various preachers and propagandists of each religion, each denomination and sect, that their's is the right path, the right interpretation. Well, it is quite possible that their claim is correct and that the other party is all in the wrong; but that does not give them any justification at all, or even extenuation for fighting and for losing the peace of the world in all matters. The question is one in which no deep analytical thinking is necessary at all. We find differences, for example, even with regard to (things within) the jurisdiction of our physical senses, with regard to the objects of vision, smell, sound, touch and taste, things which are said to be purely objective, material portions of the world. Whatever may be the noumenon behind the phenomenal universe, these things are said to be the common property and within the jurisdiction of the physical senses of each and every human being. Even in these matters we find that inclinations, tastes, capacities differ, and opinions cannot be the same.

With regard to a work of art, for example a beautiful picture, different artists of the highest calibre, all sincere, give different opinions. Similarly with regard to music, with regard to taste and so on. There is no oneness, no uniformity possible even with regard to these matters which are admittedly within the realm of the physical senses, within our physical jurisdiction. Much more, therefore, must it be impossible for us to have any uniformity of opinion, views and so forth, with regard to things relating to life or existence after death and so on. In fact you will find many persons coming and telling you, in the name of philosophy, in the name of science and so forth, that such and such thing will necessarily happen in the after-life as a consequence of belief in such and such faith, and so on. But even with regard to the continuance of the spirit, or the soul, after death, with regard to other worlds, other lives, other existences and so forth, there is tremendous difference of opinion. Philosophers and scientists have not yet agreed upon whether there is such a thing as Soul.

Many believe in it; philosophers and theologians have always insisted upon it. And some modern scientists through the present day, and big people in the forefront, of the topmost rank, have come to acknowledge the existence of God, the existence of the soul after death, and so on. But not all of them. Uniformity is impossible in matters relating to after-death existence and so forth. Whether a person will have salvation after death or will go to hell, that is a matter to be decided not by us, but by the powers that may be in existence at the time and may have the authority for deciding such matter. We certainly cannot claim to have that kind of dictatorial voice in the matter.

Now if we look at it from this standpoint we can understand why in the various penal and criminal codes, in the various civilized countries in the world, there is a chapter on offences relating to religion. Anything that serves to wound the sensibilities, the sentiments, the feelings of people of another faith, is regarded as a criminal offence punishable according to law. The question is not whether the complainant or the defendant has any proof for his views. The law says that it is a criminal offence to wound, to exacerbate the feelings, the sentiments of any community, any religion, any sect, any denomination. The law is perfectly justified for the simple reason that in the ultimate analysis of the matter, there must necessarily be at least a small degree, a small percentage of faith involved. Even a person who claims that he has understood the whole philosophy, the whole science of religion and is a master, is an expert, even he will have to grant that although he has satisfied himself with very rigid proofs, authorities, scriptural and so forth, his own experiences and so on, there is at least one small gap that will be there and which will have to be filled in by the faith of the individual. Faith forms a connecting link between the proved things and the unproved things simply believed to be true.

Even those who speak of faith, speak of it as faith which is based upon understanding. St. Paul, for example, speaks of the faith that is born of understanding. Each person has his own conclusions to draw from the same set of facts. Our inferential powers, our powers of induction and deduction are limited after all; and when it is not a question of proved fact, when it's a question of faith, then it comes to almost a gamble; and as I frequently say, in all lotteries there are more blanks than prizes, and mistakes are more commonly to be expected than would be desirable. Therefore we have to contend with, and, well, somehow bow down to, submit to the inevitable in the shape of inferences of different kinds from the same set of facts.

In this connection I frequently refer to the way in which judges in law-courts are called upon to decide the innocence or the guilt of a certain person in regard to a criminal offence. Two judges — not of two different courts, one of a lower court and the other of a highar court — but two judges sitting on the same bench in the same High Court or Supreme Court, and hearing the same evidence, reading through the same oral and documentary evidence on the matter, hearing the arguments of the same advocates, and guided by the same penal code, come to different conclusions. I am not talking of persons who are corrupt and are likely to give false judgment owing to corrupt motives. Persons who are absolutely sincere, who have a conscientious sense of their duty as judges, as upholders of law and order in society, even they differ in their views and they give not always concurrent but sometimes dissenting judgments.

Well, that means that we can't demand, we can't insist on uniformity of faith. If we ask for liberty to express our opinion and also force it upon others, the other persons will have the same right to do it; and that would mean absolute confusion. That would lead to chaos altogether. So that is the position from the academical standpoint of any person who goes into the subject with even a little thinking, A great deal of struggle and recondite metaphysics is not necessary for the purpose. This is very simple. With regard to the material things outside in the universe we have our differences in tastes and capabilities. And even with regard to judgments the same difficulty comes in; we are limited down by various things. The same record, the same evidence produces different impressions on minds of different judges. So under these circumstances to insist on uniformity is to ask for something which is not justified which is not justifiable by any canon, by any standard of rationality.

In the Western world, in the mediaeval ages, wars after wars were fought in the name of religion. Even with regard to those wars, history tells us that the fighters themselves finally gave up the fighting not because of disgust at the futility of it all, but because they felt that the criterion by which they were judging things, the motives by which they were motivated, were not correct at all. I was just giving the example of Richard I of England, a great warrior; and very famous as a crusader. And he gave up altogether this fighting in the name of religion for the simple reason that apart from the futility of the wars, which continued for centuries without meaning, he felt that the standards by which the opponents were being judged were wrong. Saladin was the hero, the warrior on the other side, on the side of the Muslims. The name of Saladin was a terror to children. The parents were in the habit of frightening the children into obedience by uttering the name of Saladin. Afterwards, however, when Richard was on the actual battle-field and he was suffering from a disease which the doctors could not diagnose, and could do nothing to treat and cure him of, Saladin went in disguise. He was a great man, not merely a great warrior, but a man of great character, a man of humanitarian, benevolent, philanthropic disposition. He could not come into Richard's camp announcing himself as Saladin, because he was an enemy. He was a great physician as well as a great warrior. He cured Richard. And Richard said to himself, "Who is this whom I am fighting ? What kind of relationship have I with him ? What is his character ?" Richard felt that his character was of truly noble and sublime type, and quarreling with him and saying that he was a candidate for hell and was sure to be there eternally and so on, seemed to be irrational. He gave up fighting. Others went through the same experiences. In France, in England, and in Spain the inquisitions and the quarrels of the

Roman Catholics and Protestants tell a similar story. No one can possibly justify that kind of conflict in the name of religion. That is elementary common sense. And the kind of common sense that we are talking about is very often found to be the most uncommon sense in the world. Now I wish just to place before the Indians here the gist of India's attitude towards such questions. Whenever people came here, with a different religion which they wished to practise in peace, there was no difficulty at all. India welcomed the foreigner, the persons of a different religion altogether, with open arms, gave them not merely of shelter and accommodation but every kind of other facilities — monetary and so on. That has been the history of India from the earliest times.

Consecrated to spiritual light

You probably know, — well, I don't suppose there can be anyone that does not know — the original name by which India was known before the name India came upon the historical scene. The name was Bhārata. And the word Bhārata, has a tremendous significance. It has the signification which tells us what India's ideal was, what India's goal was, what India's attitude and approach to these questions was.

Bhārata. Bhā dīptiḥ bhāsi dīptau rataḥ Bhārataḥ.

Dedicated, consecrated to the light — the light of knowledge.

Tamaso mā jyotir gamaya.*

From darkness, lead us to light. Praying for light, and always preferring light to darkness. And light alone can dispel darkness. Darkness was never yet removed, and can never be removed by abusing it, by beating it with a stick or with anything else. The light of knowledge alone can dispel the ignorance of darkness. That was the line that our ancestors took. In the Vedas, and in the scriptures, Śāstras, as we call them, held sacred by the Hindus, this is the attitude all the time.

Tamaso mā jyotir gamaya.

Light, more light wanted. And when the quest is after light, the search after truth, the seeker after knowledge is there with all humility :

* Bṛhadāraṇyaka Upaniṣad I-3-28.

Tad viddhi praṇipātena paripraśnena sevayā.*

Not dictating to others, not forcing upon others, but trying to seek, trying and seeking to learn. And there again we have the teacher described not as a teacher, but as a co-thinker, thinking aloud along with his students, and the students helping the teacher in new ways which the teacher probably never dreamt of before. That kind of attitude is there all the time. Paripraśnena. Inquiry, the spirit of inquiry, the quest after knowledge, is always before us.

Śrotavyaḥ, mantavyaḥ, nididhyāsitavyaḥ.**

These words I translate into English with three phrases: Investigate carefully; decide correctly; and follow faithfully. Follow faithfully. Sincerity is the only thing there.

Indian attitude towards other religions

Ye (a)pyanyadevatā-bhaktā
yajante śraddhayānvitāḥ,
Te (a)pi māmeva Kaunteyà
yajantyavidhi-pūrvakam.†

In the Bhagavad Gītā we have Śrī Kṛṣṇa saying to Arjuna, "Even those that worship other deities with purity of heart and sincerity, they worship Me." There is that open statement in categorical terms. From time to time, from place to place we find this kind of text staring us in the face and telling us that compulsion is absolutely wrong with regard to intellectual matters and with regard to faith.

So that being the case, our course is clear. And the actual traditions that India has placed before us are of the same type. As the result of persecution in their own native land, Iran, the

*Gitā IV-34. Also compare—"Tad vijñānārtham sa gurum evābhigacchet, samitpāṇih śrotriyam brahmaniṣṭham."

[Muṇḍaka Upaniṣad I-2-12]

"For knowing That he should, with sacrificial wood in hand (this signifies, humility) approach a Guru (Master) who is well versed in Vedas and who has realised God."

** Bṛhadāraṇyaka Upaniṣad II-4-5.

†Gita IX-23.

Parsees came to India. They had gone to various countries and sought shelter there and everyone fought shy of harbouring them. The Parsees wanted merely freedom to follow their own faith, to worship their own deities. Just as the Pilgrim Fathers came all the way to America to have freedom of worship, freedom to follow their own path, the Parsees came to India. At first they went in various directions and found no shelter anywhere. They came to the western coast of India, Gujarat, in what is called the Bombay province now. There was Rājā Yādava ruling there. He was told of the huge shiploads of foreigners coming in, strangers who were strange in dress, strange in appearance, strange in talk, strange in everything. And he did not know what his duty was towards them. It so happened that the Śaṅkarācārya of Dvārakā was camping nearby. And Rājā Yādava went to him for advice as to what his duty was toward these strangers at the gate. And the reply that he got was, "Treat the stranger at the gate according to the Indian law of hospitality, according to the eternal duty of hospitality towards the stranger, the stricken, and the suffering ones." And Rājā Yādava accordingly accommodated those people, looked after them and made them prosper in every way. In fact, he gave them every possible encouragement and help; so much so, that the Parsees flourished in India and at the present day, in terms of rupees, anas and pies, the Parsees are the richest community in India.

Then again we may take the example of spread of Christianity into the Western world and its advent into India. Not merely was Christ crucified, his disciples his apostles, his evangelists, St. James, St. John, St. Peter, St. Paul, all had to suffer the same fate as the Master. That was in the Western world. The Christians had to fight their way through. And only when Constantine the emperor became a Christian, things began to become smooth and easy for the Christians. Until then there was enormous persecution. Over against that picture let us consider what is to India's credit in connection with that very subject. St. Thomas came to India. He settled in the west coast of Malabar, the present Kerala. And there the then Rājā Zamorin of Calicut accommodated them, treated them with utmost kindness, and at the present moment the Christian colony there is regarded as a very cultured and advanced one in every way. The first colony, the earliest Christian colony in the whole world, was established in the southern part of south India. We have these things to our credit.

Conflict with Muslims on political grounds, not religious

Well, a question may be asked as to what about Islam. Was there no trouble between the Hindus and the Mussalmans when they came? And the answer is: There was trouble but not of a religious character at all. The Mussalmans did not come into India seeking shelter, seeking a peaceful life as the Parsees did, or as the Christians did. They came as conquerors; they came with their political and military power to subdue India. And the Hindus at the time opposed the invaders purely from the military and political standpoint. The people were not prepared to accept foreign domination; that was all. There was no question there at all of religion—Islam in danger or Hinduism in danger, and so on—but the liberty of India was in danger, and they fought accordingly. We have this kind of history. And both the religious texts themselves and the traditions too concur in the respect. We are told :

Te prāpnuvanti māmeva sarvabhūtahite ratāh.*

those who in earnest and sincere singleness of purpose do good to others reach God. Bhagavān Śrī Kṛṣṇa tells Arjuna that sincerity is the only thing, that even those who worship other gods and goddesses worship the same Lord. A question may arise. "But what about others who do not believe in any religion, any god, goddess let alone worship ?" Well the answer is:

Nahi kalyāṇakṛt kaścit
durgatim tāta gacchati.**

"No one who with purity of heart, with benevolence of disposition, with humanitarian considerations, who does good to others

* Gītā XII-4.
** Gītā VI-40.

can possibly come to an evil fate." So even the atheist, the agnostic is not shut out. We don't consign to an eternal hell with flames of sulphur and brimstone and things of that type those who profess another faith. We are distinctly told that goodness is the criterion.

Te prāpnuvanti māmeva.*

All are entitled not merely to salvation, because salvation may be of different degrees, but they are all entitled to the highest, the topmost rung of the spiritual ladder. And salvation is for all if there is sincerity of heart.

I have studied the writings of various Western authors who are known as atheists and propagandists of atheism, who are described by Christian writers the theologians the exclusive minded people, as limbs of the arch devil and so forth. I have had occasion to study and study carefully, with all modesty as a student seeking the knowledge of the truth, the lives of these great people — Ingersoll, Ernest Hickol, Charles Bradlaw, and others. They were known as atheists, and they fought in the name of atheism against what they regarded as wrong views of theology, philosophy, and so forth. But they were men of character. And when I see a person of that type described as a candidate for hell, I feel like king Richard I of England who felt that if Saladin was a candidate for hell, hell was worth going to. If we err, we err in good company, not in bad. Richard compared himself and his nearest associates and the bigots and fanatics who egged the people on in the warfare, with Saladin and he said, "We are very much inferior."

True religion

The mere fact that a person is an atheist does not disqualify him. The religion of humanity — is the true religion. Other things are the externals; they are rites, rituals, external forms and so on which may and do have their own parts to play as collateral aids for achieving the purpose. But the root of it, the gist of it, the substance, the solid core of it, is purity, sincerity, and humanity. That is what is wanted; and if that is there, there can be no difficulty at all.

* Gītā XII-4.

We fight in the name of religion, and then we fight in the names of various other things, and we use catch words for the purpose of disguising our own partialities and hatreds, Rāga-Dveṣa as we call them in Sanskrit terminology. Partialities on the one hand and hatreds on the other. Prejudices against and prepossessions in favour of this or that side. But that is not the path of justice. We are not here as partisans; we are not here as witnesses or as advocates for one party. We are here to learn the truth and act according to it, to live up to it to the utmost extent of our power, physical, intellectual, moral, spiritual, and so on. And if we do that, I think we have earned our passports to heaven. There need be no worry at all about other matters. Other matters may be helpful, as collateral aids. But this is the chief thing. And this is the teaching upon which we have insisted in the past as laid down in our theoretical, dogmatic, doctrinaire literature on the one hand and as demonstrated in our actual history on the other. I feel, therefore, that in the present condition of the world, with regard to war and peace, conditions in which there is the apprehension that the war drums may be heard at any moment, the cold war may be turned into hot war at any moment, at such a time it is the duty of all persons who have a feeling of responsibility in these matters, to unite and do something to avert this kind of calamity, which, in the name of science and with the help of science may, if unchecked, reduce all knowledge of science and civilization and culture to nothingness, wiping off not only this or that particular enemy, this group of persons or that group of persons, this country or that country, but sweeping off humanity from the history and even the map of the earth. Every person who can possibly contribute in any way whatsoever, should contribute the highest, the utmost that he can in that direction. And I feel that the role of the Indians is much easier than in the case of others, because their traditions are against wars. India and the Indians cannot blame the prejudices or the inheritances from the past. We can't do that. We, at any rate, have this to our credit. I don't put it as a matter of pride or vainglory, but only to remind ourselves what our duty is, what our ancestors believed in, enjoined, and actually acted up to. With this great heritage of ours, it must be quite easy for us, at any rate much easier for us than for others, to walk the path of peace and prosperity. Without peace there can be no prosperity. Students of history will remember about Pyrrhic victory. What is a Pyrrhic victory? The victory in which the enemy has been completely exterminated, but the victor has suffered more in consequence than the vanquished. That kind of result, from the standpoint of economics and so forth, is inevitable. Such is the consequential aftermath of the war. The persons who succeed, actually suffer more than the conquered. So that from the standpoint of practical realism which we pride ourselves on during these days, we ought to tackle the question and take concerted measures carefully devised, for the avoidance of this threatening calamity. It is not an ordinary calamity, but a cataclysmic calamity that may overtake us if we do not gird up our loins and think over and actually take up the necessary steps for bringing about world peace and therethrough world prosperity all around.

Well, I can only conclude by appealing to all in general and to the Indians in particular to contribute whatever they possibly can for the achievement of this felicitous consummation. That is my prayer to almighty God on the one side and my benedictions to Indians here who have their ideas, their conceptions of themselves as Indians. To themselves let them be true. We have it in Shakespeare's "Hamlet," "To thine own self be true; and then it must follow as the night the day, thou canst not be false to any." Let us be loyal to ourselves; let us keep the name of India absolutely uninjured, absolutely unperturbed, undisturbed. Let us keep the ideal that our ancestors placed before us and do whatever we can to prevent any deterioration. If we can improve upon the past, so much the better. If that is not possible, let us at least stay where we are and not go down, slide down the scale, carrying down the flag. That kind of thing is not desirable and will do no credit to India. Here you are in America as practically citizens of America. That is the next point I will take up and conclude within one minute. Because Indian citizenship is a great thing; American citizenship is a great thing, we stand, in all these many respects, for something great, grand, and glorious — both with regard to the doctrine, the dogma, the principle involved and the practice thereof.

But there is something greater than that. Indian citizenship and American citizenship are good enough in their own way, but nothing like world citizenship. Let us come to that. That is India's message to the world — "Vasudhaiva kuṭumbakam"* We emphasise the unity and the solidarity not merely of man and man, but of man and the whole universe. The Divinity within ourselves demands to be given scope for actual manifestation in every way so that we may fulfil the purpose of our lives to the satisfaction not merely of this or that party but of the whole world. Let us have, as philanthropists, as humanitarians, the whole world as our subject, as our jurisdiction. And I can't think of anything greater for people of Bhārata — those who are for light as against darkness. Let us fulfil, let us be true to the ideal of the Bhāratas, of Indians and thereby bring to fruition, bring to perfect perfection all that is within us by way of potentialities. Let us give the potentialities withi ourselves full scope to manifest themselves and work for the uplift, the prosperity and the salvation of the world. Let us work for world peace, for world prosperity, for a federation not merely of religions, but of nations, of countries — all united in the task of making things better in future. That is my prayer and that is my appeal to the Indians and to you in particular, that are settled here in U.S.A.

* Ayam nijaḥ paro veti gaṇanā laghucetasām.
Udāracaritānām tu vasudhaiva kuṭumbakam.

—Pancatantra.

"He belongs to us or he is an outsider," only the low-minded people reckon like this. For the broad-minded people, whole world is their family."

X PRACTICAL METHODS OF WORLD PEACE

Discourse at Los Angeles City College,
February 17, 1958.

Friends !

In the course of my discourses, ever since I reached America, I have been, day after day, at meeting after meeting, referring to, emphasizing and calling attention to the present day exigencies and requirements of the world, not from the standpoint of this or that particular individual, party, nation, continent, sub-continent, and so forth, but from the standpoint of the highest and the lasting interests of the human race itself. Human civilization and human culture are now threatened with the possibility of absolute and final disaster. I am speaking on this subject again and again. I am being asked to speak on this subject for the very simple reason that catastrophic calamities are being apprehended. It is apprehended on every side that the war-drums may be heard at any moment. And people are passing anxious nights, not nights but nightmare-nights. And everywhere, there is panic; there is fear; there is uncertainty and all that these three things mean to the world. Where there is uncertainty, there is no possibility of persons engaging in regular work and going on undisturbed by other thoughts. Where there is no peace, there is no possibility of prosperity, except for a few who may benefit by the war and other activities of war-mongers.

Now, it is the duty of all of us to look into these questions, the facts and factors of the situation as they exactly are, without prejudices and prepossessions of any kinds, without partialities and hatreds, solely actuated by concern for the welfare of the human race as such. It is our duty, it behoves every person amongst us, every thinking intelligent person amongst us, to think of the question from this standpoint, weigh the pros and cons, and arrive at conclusions calculated to lift us all as individuals and as society to higher and higher stages of advancement, of progress, of happiness, and of joy. And as I've been saying, without the foundation of peace, there can be no possibility of joy, Aśāntasya kutaḥ sukham.* The Bhagavad Gītā says : "Where there is no peace, where there is no calmness, no quietness, no certainty, no freedom from anxiety, there is no possibility of our being able to engage ourselves in occupations which, although congenial to ourselves, are at the same time dependent upon the continuance of peace for their existence and continued progress."

This being the state of affairs, I have naturally been stressing this subject and pleading for what you might call a "Comity of world-peace loving nations," a brotherhood of persons who are pledged, not merely to look after themselves and their own welfare, but also the welfare, prosperity, and joy of other human beings.

Instinctive desires

Now, it is elementary to reason that all human beings have certain instinctive desires. These instinctive desires have to be carefully analysed and, on analysis, they will be found to be, on the whole, generally of an exhilarating character. For example, the biological urge to live on. That is what the scientist calls it. The desire to live on, that is there. The desire to know things, that desire is also instinctively in the minds of all sentient beings. The desire for joy unadulterated, not even with the least little modicum of misery. And then, the desire for independence. All these are naturally implanted by nature in our minds. In fact, they're instinctive and there is no doubt, there is no difficulty about them at all. And as a matter of fact, if you analyze the nature of these lower instinctive desires, there is no inherent conflict. On the other hand, there can be cooperation, coordination, harmony, brotherhood, unity and solidarity. There is nothing that stands in the way. But there is another desire, a desire for domination, a desire which is found everywhere, a desire which is the root cause of all the miseries that the world suffers from, from time to time on account of internal and external bickerings, conflicts, and so on, until the stage of actual hot war is reached. Even

* Gītā II-66.

the cold war stage is sufficiently bad. It is bad enough in our conscience. And hot war means something very much worse for the ordinary citizen who has no special interest in war-mongering and profiting in that way.

Now, the fifth desire is one which needs to be looked into. Because if it is an instinctive desire and also a desire which can never possibly be given up, then, it means the position is hopeless. There is no possibility of any success in our attempt for the formation of a brotherhood of nations, for the peace of mankind's culture and other heritage.

Desire to dominate : root cause of conflict

Now the question is to be asked whether conflict between one person and another is inevitable, because of this fifth desire. That desire is an irrepressible desire. It is a desire which can never possibly be remedied, which can never be lessened and so on. If that be not the case, if there is a possibility of harmony between one mind and another, then there is the possibility of success of our activities in this direction of peace, brotherhood of man, all and such ideals. The first desire is, the desire to live on. That doesn't cause any trouble to another person who is living. The desire to know, that also doesn't cause any trouble to another person who desires to know. The desire for joy unmixed with unhappiness, that too does not interfere with any other's desire for joy. The desire for independence, that too similarly is not necessarily in conflict with other people's desires for independence. In fact, others have the same right to have these desires fulfilled as we have. We desire to remain undisturbed, untrammeled by any kind of restriction in respect of these four desires, namely, the desire to live, the desire to know, the desire to enjoy, and the desire to be free. But the fifth desire is one which means a conflict, the desire for domination, the feeling of superiority, the feeling not of differentness, or what you might call dualism, but the desire for monism and monism of a type which doesn't give similar liberty to others to follow their own path independently. Our fifth desire comes into conflict with the fourth desire of other persons. There is no more reason, no more logical or pychological justification for our wishing to rule over another person than that person's right to rule over us.

So, from the standpoint of ethics, from the standpoint of moral justification, this fifth desire is one which stands in the way of peace and progress, of harmony, of a harmonious co-ordinated and cooperating kind of life and mutual relationship. Therefore, we have to look into the question still further.

Is it a desire which is inevitable, which is irrepressible, which is insurmountable, and therefore, which is a hopeless thing for us to try to tackle under the circumstances ? If that kind of idea is right, then all the efforts in that direction are futile, because (if it is inevitable), strife will take place tomorrow, the day after, or the day after that. All our activities of the previous periods, of previous generations, and so forth, are absolutely wasted. There would be the feeling of sheer inutility, nay, positive futility of all our attempts.

Crusades

But is that the case ? Well, we were told centuries ago that different religions meant automatically different viewpoints of an irreconcilably antagonistic character. People who belonged to different religions took it for granted that by virtue of their difference in religion they were bound to fight. Well, the result was that in the name of religion, wars were being continually fought. In the history of Europe we have the story of the Crusades, fought by the Christian kingdoms of the world against the Mussalmāns in occupation of Jerusalem, and other holy places, sacred to Islam, and sacred also in the history of Christianity. They said that that was an inevitable struggle, Peter the Hermit preached to the kings, to the people of Europe, to engage in Crusades, to fight against Islamic control over these places. They wanted that they should have the control, and the persons actually in possession should not be allowed to continue. Well, that kind of war, the Crusades, went on for some centuries, and at the end it was found that there was no possibility of the goal ever being achieved. And they reconciled to the fact that there was no possibility of any useful result arising therefrom. Thousands of people were killed and to serve no purpose whatsoever. It was not in their own defense, or in vindication of any principle of high morality, of high sacrifice, and things of that type, but something much lower, because, they introduced into the motivating factors, elements which were not historically correct. They started with the basis that people professing Christian faith were ipso facto superior and the others were inferior, who ought not merely to be suppressed, they ought to be wiped off the face of the earth. In England, we are told, during those days the name of Saladin was used to quieten a crying child, to stop his turbulence, to stop his disobedience. The very name inspired terror and signified something horrible, something monstrous, not merely gigantic, titanic, but something colossally wicked. That kind of idea was there.

King Richard of England took a leading part in those Crusades. And he was regarded, and praised everywhere as the warrior-king of England who proved his gallantry, his great prowess, his military and other organizational powers, his physical courage in the battlefield. But, he found by actual experience that Saladin, the leader, and the generalissimo on the other side, was not a man of bad character. He was a man of very high sensibility and supreme character. Richard compared himself and his co-partners in the Crusades, other kings and princes who took part in the Crusades against Islam, with Saladin. And his heart told him, his conscience told him, his sense of fair play, his sense of truth told him that Saladin was not inferior in character but was much superior to himself and his allies in those very Crusades. So the question took a different form thereafter, namely, whether a religious label was the necessary requisite for character, for a passport to heaven, or was there something else, something of importance? King Richard felt that he was not justified in warring against Saladin, a man of noble character. King Richard himself was suffering from a serious illness. His doctors could do nothing to alleviate his suffering. And Saladin came in disguise and cured his enemy, King Richard. And from descriptions by others and also from his personal experience, King Richard felt that his enemy, against whom he had been fighting these wars of the Crusades, was of noble and magnanimous character, beneficently inclined, philanthropically minded, and was doing everything in his power to alleviate the condition of those in suffering and in sorrow. King Richard said to himself, "I have neglected my country. The internal sufferings of the people I did not pay heed to because I was concerned with this religious war as I thought it to be. no longer think it to be religious, I have only failed in my duty to look after my people's interests. Instead of working there for the uplift of my people, I'm spending my time elsewhere, and in fighting with a person whom I should feel it an honour to serve and to obey." That kind of feeling came. So the question comes back to the roots of what we call religion.

What is religion ?

What do we mean by religion ? What do the various religions say with regard to religion itself ? What is their own version of it, their own description of it? No doubt, there are descriptions, with regard to the karmakāṇḍa, the bhaktikāṇḍa, and the jñāna-kāṇḍa as we call them. These three are the path of karma or work, the path of devotion, and the path of illumination. In the Bible you have all of these three preached by the Lord Jesus Christ himself. His disciples, according to their own mental temperament perhaps or, may be, on account of their own personal idiosyncracy, or perhaps, according to the needs of those whom they were teaching, whom they were preaching, emphasized one or more of these three paths. St. Peter and St. James repeatedly emphasized the path of works, what has been called Karma Yoga in the Bhagavad Gītā. St. John devoted himself to the propagation of the doctrine of love, a loving devotion of the devotee to the Master, to the Lord and Saviour. And there was a third disciple, St. Paul, who emphasized the path of illumination. An illumined person is one who has transcended all the lower instincts, sadness and anger, grief, love and hate, ideas of profit and loss, desire for victory and this and that and who, having transcended these stages, lives a sedate life of quiet, of peace, of meditation, and of such benevolent activities as his own capacity, physical, intellectual, moral, financial and so forth permits.* That was the way in which the three disciples, the three schools of disciples carried on their preaching, showing thereby, that Christ's religion was not of an external character. It was not ritualistic or ceremonial only. Rituals and ceremonials are there.

* Compare Gītā II-55 to 61, where Lord Kṛṣṇa gives a brief description of persons who have acquired equanimity and control over themselves.

External forms are there. But, these are external things after all. And unless the internal side is illumined, the internal side is sincere, unless the heart is pure, well, all these external forms amount to nothing. On the contrary, they will only brand the person professing the faith, as a liar, a hypocrite, and so on. In the Bible, you have famous passages* in which we find Christ rebuking the Pharisees and the Sadducees for a huge lot of pomp and pageantry, paraphernalia and show of religiosity. I don't call it religiousness, but religiosity, because it was all formal. It was meant for the purpose of show and not for one's own uplift on the spiritual ladder. Well, Christ condemns them. But what do the others do ? The saints, the sages, and the seers, of other religions also do the same thing. In our Vedic scriptures, in India, we have the same principle laid before the people :

Aśraddhayā hutam dattam
tapas taptam kṛtam ca yat,
Asad ity ucyate Pārtha
na ca tat pretya no iha.**

And again and again this question is taken up and discussed. "What is religion? What is pitey? What is religiosity? What is the qualification which one must have as the prerequisite in order to attain salvation after death?" This question is taken up. And the answer given is uniformly the same as Christ gave in the biography that we have of him from St. Mark, St. Matthew, St. John, and St. Luke. The stories, the narratives in the Gospels, the whole life story and the teachings of Christ leave no doubt at all on the matter. Our texts also say again and again, "Even persons who belong to other faiths, to other religions, who worship other deities, with sincerity, they worship Me." That is the teaching of Śrī Kṛṣṇa in the Bhagavad Gītā.† And if a further

* See St. Matthew XVI-3,6,12 and St. Luke XII-1.

** Gita XVII-28 "All sacrifices, charities, penances, or deeds done without sincerity are profane. They are useful neither in this world nor hereafter."

† Ye (a)pi anyadevatā-bhaktā
yajante śraddhayānvitāḥ,
Te (a)pi māmeva Kaunteya
yajantyavidhi-pūrvakam.

[Gītā IX-23.]

question is taken up and posed, as to what about atheists who do not believe in any religion at all, and who do not recognise the existence of any god and who do not adore any deity, what about them? Well, with regard to them, the text says:

"Te prāpnuvanti mām eva
sarvabhūtahite ratāḥ."*

All persons who seek to do good to others and who are benevolently minded, and beneficently activated all the time and who are engaged in thinking of the good of the people instead of doing harm to them for their own personal selfish self-centered interest, all such persons, well, must necessarily be candidates for salvation. None of such a character can possibly come to an evil end. That is what we find Lord Jesus Christ himself saying in his own life story from day to day. That was the kind of life that you see him explaining, expounding, and advocating before the people. Purity of heart. In the beatitudes you have this single beautiful passage sufficient for the whole purpose, "Blessed are the pure in heart, for they shall see God."† It is not (merely) knowing about God, thinking about God, but actual visualisation, what we call "sākṣātkāra" "They shall see God." Who? "The pure in heart." The outside traits, the elements of ritual and ceremonial are there. They are necessary, I grant. And they are necessary as collateral aids for the pursuit of our path to salvation. But by themselves they mean nothing. By themselves they mean that we are pretending to have something within which is not there, trying to cheat other people with show of religiosity. Now, other people can be cheated, but God the All-Knowing, the Omnipresent, the All-Powerful Lord and Creator of the World, who knows what is going on within the heart of the individual, cannot be cheated. And any attempt to cheat God can only end in self-deception of a most disastrous character, with most disastrous consequences. There is no possibility of cheating God. And we have instance after instance mentioned in the Bible as regards Christ's denunciation of people who were pretenders in this way and not

* Gita XII-4.
† St. Matthew V-8.

of the right type. Our scriptures too. say that a person who shows off and doesn't have the actual reality within his heart, well, he is not entitled to salvation. He is a hypocrite, and people should beware of him. Beware of being cheated by such a person. That kind of description is there. So, the taking of the name of religion for the purpose of waging war with one another. well, that is due either to ignorance as in the case of King Richard of England, or due to deliberate misrepresentation.

True religion

Well, neither mistakes nor misrepresentation are desirable for us. We should steer clear of both. If, there be one person who deliberately misrepresents, one thousand persons will be carried away by what he says. It's a common proverb, that there are more fools than knaves in the world. One knave is sufficient to pervert the minds of one thousand fools. Well, we should have a system by which we can have assurance of a fool-proof and a knave-proof character. And that is the religion of humanity. The religion which all religions preach. That's the common religion of all. I don't call it the "basic religion, the basic idea underlying all religions and so on. I don't talk of it as the base. I talk of it as the "inside", the very kernel. The very spirit of religion is in the purity of heart, in the sincerity with which people do what they can to the utmost extent in their power for the benefit of people whom they're in a position to benefit.

A great journalist of England who, during the last years of the nineteenth century and the beginning of the twentieth century was known as a giant amongst journalists, once defined religion. He said "Religion is the service of all who can, in the service of those who need." That was his description of it.

And we find Christ, as well as the scriptures of other religions, telling us again and again that this is the ideal, and the other things that we have along with this central principle of it all, the external things, are by way of collateral aid to expedite the process. If there is sincerity within, the fruition of it, its fructification in the proper direction is to be expected. But if the whole thing is false, there is hypocrisy inside, no amount of external aid can retrieve the position or salvage the man.

Again and again, we have this question discussed in the various scriptures of the world. And peace is considered the foundation of all. Peace, so that all may live in peace, all may have happiness:

> Sarve bhavantu sukhinaḥ
> serve santu nirāmayāḥ.
> Sarve bhadrāṇi paśyantu,
> mā kaścit duḥkam āpnuyāt.

"May all people enjoy happiness; may not even a single person be unhappy." That is the prayer which, according to our scriptures, we are called upon to recite day after day. We pray for others and not for our own individual selves. As regards the individual self, the position may be explained in terms of Euclid's ninth axiom, "The whole is greater than the part." The whole, namely, the family, the interests of the family should be considered as greater, as higher than the part, namely, the petty needs and desires of the individual. Then, from the family you go on expanding your jurisdiction to the locality. From the locality, you go on to district, after district, state, after state, the country, after country, the world. And then, in the same process of further extension which can be carried on infinitely, you come to speak of not the federation of this or that particular kind or race or limited type of people, but of mankind as such. The whole continent, no, even that is not enough, the whole universe.

Faith

In this connection, I repeatedly refer to the fact that this conception of religion to start with, which is an obstacle in the way, must first go. In England you had the trouble between the Roman Catholics and the Protestants. In France, and in Spain, there was not merely heart-burning but also body burning, burning of bodies alive. And, that was supposed to be for pleasing the God. People were cursed, and denounced, and consigned to eternal hell because they differed from us in certain articles of faith. And after all, what were these articles of faith? The articles of faith are after all, articles of faith. And even the person who is most devout in his beliefs of a certain religion, and its rules and regulations, about the existence of God, about the existence of the soul, about future lives and so on, even such a person can only say, "I am morally certain of the existence of God." The existence of God cannot be proved in the way you prove mathematical theorems of scientific theories and so on. Even after a huge lot of ground has been covered, after all the preliminary troubles have been cleared, even then you have one stage, a small percentage of the whole distance perhaps, a small gap in which you have to fill things with the aid of faith. "This is what I believe, so far, I have reached with scientific certainty, with mathematical precision, but here, there is a gap." That gap, each person fills in according to his own personal psychology. The same intellect is not there in the minds of all the people. They have their own different ideas owing to different parentage, different training, and a different everything from childhood. I frequently give the example of judges in courts of law, before whom an accused is brought up and they have to adjudicate on whether he is innocent or guilty. It is not merely the case of two judges of two different courts, a higher and lower, but even two judges sitting on the same bench, in the same court, hearing, reading the same records, guided by the same law codes, and hearing the same arguments by the advocates on both sides come to different conclusions, sincerely and honestly. So the human mind has its own particular contribution, it has its own part, own role to play, in coming to decisions. And it's a matter of faith. "I have the absolute faith that such and such things were historically correct; such and such things were theoretically, doctrinally perfect, but I cannot prove them to the satisfaction of a fellow being of the same type of intelligence, the same acuteness of intellect, and so on." The philosophers and scientists have not yet agreed with regard to all these details. You have the established Church of England, the Middle Church, the Low Church, the High Church, and so on. You have in Scotland, the preachers of Scotland, the Episcopalian, the Presbyterian, the United Free Church, and all because of differences with regard to certain small details. And these differences are not things which can be established by reference to anything in the objective material life of the people around. We cannot see things and say, "This belongs to this group; this belongs to that group." We cannot categorically, dictatorially insist that this is the right thing and the others are wrong. Great scientists and philosophers have disagreed and quietly, in a most peaceful and friendly way, after the friendliest discussions, they say, 'Well, we have no option but to disagree. Let us agree to disagree." And that is all there is to it.

That is how things go on in the affairs of the world. But here, in the name of religion, we have been seeing things of a very different type, which are absolutely wrong. I again and again mention in the course of my discourses, I have no quarrel with any religion, any denomination, any sect or sub-sect. My only quarrel is with quarrelling. And that too in the name of religion. Religion ought to be a unifying factor. Religion means sincerity. It means purity. It means renunciation. It means benevolence. These are common to all. The religion of humanity should be before us. Our own particular religion is a matter of individual temperament and of individual allegiance to God, whom we sincerely believe in, and whom we adore.

So in this way, if we think over the matter from a rationalistic standpoint, it must be clear that wars in the name of religion are not justified at all. Christ comes as the Prince of Peace. In our Vedas we have, step by step, almost after each mantra, "Śānti, Śānti, Śanti*—peace, peace, peace." And greetings to one another in Latin used to be Pax vobiscum—"Peace be with you." Everywhere peace is taught. Men who love peace are praised for their work, doing what good they can to others, and not interfering, not meddling with other things which are not their concern. That kind of attitude is respected by everybody. If someone comes and tells me about a person like St. Francis of Assisi, a man of a most saintly character, that because he was a Christian of this particular type of Roman Catholic faith, therefore, he is not adorable; well, I cannot help feeling that there is something wrong with the person's capacity for assessment of moral values. And if St. Francis of Assisi is not, according to a

*See Footnote on page 46.

certain person, good enough for admission into heaven, well, I should think very few persons would be capable of being included in that category.

The same is true with regard to so many saints and sages and seers all over the world. There can be no question of any quarrel with them.

Word meanings change with time

And now, I take up a question connected with this. I'm talking of world peace and I'm taking up a subject connected with today's discourse here to you with regard to languages, foreign languages and so forth. The languages have their differences on account of historical causes of a momentary character, transitory character, changing from time to time. Things have been named in a particular fashion by the persons who were using those things. From place to place, even in the same region you find words changing their meaning. I shall just give you a small passage from Chaucer's Canterbury Tales. The poets of the Anglo-Saxon period, Chaucer and others of the Middle English period, Shakespeare and others, wrote in a language different from what we know of as the academical English of present day orators, writers, and so on. Chaucer writes "The tyme is come a knave child she beer."* This was English, ordinary English of Chaucer's time. I suppose many people would not have been able to follow it. Even people whose mother tongue at present is English would not be able to follow it, for the simple reason that the language has changed considerably from time to time, and the present English has very little in common with the ancient English of Chaucer or of Gower, and so on. These are the things that we think of. The changes are there. And in this passage that I quoted, there is a mention of a "knave child." "Knave" in Chaucer's time meant, "male." "Male-child." Well, at the present day, any person who finds another described as a knave will regard him as a scoundrel, a rogue. That is not the case at all. It simply meant, "male". How the word "knave," which used to stand for male, has come to mean "rascal," a man of evil character, well, that we cannot now trace. But,

* Canterbury Tales (Man of Law's Tales).

there must have been historical antecedents, some kind of background which were responsible for these differences in the languages of persons living in different times and different climes, and cut off from one another. They speak foreign tongue, but the foreign tongue is due to natural causes and there is no inherent conflict between one and another.

Differences in languages are immaterial

I have been giving passages from Sanskrit and explaining them again and again. I give you a passage by way of variety from Tamil. "Ūrār kuzhandaiyai ūṭṭi valartāl tan kuzhandai tāne valarum." Well, you may say, "Oh, this is some kind of boorish tongue which I can't understand." You may not understand it, but that does not necessarily mean it is boorish, or it has no sense at all. This is a splendid passage which says, "A mother who feeds another person's baby with love and nourishes and looks after the child will not merely go to heaven but her own child will grow and be nourished of itself, and would be looked after." That kind of sentiment is there in a small passage like that. Similarly, in Telugu, in Hindi, and other languages all over my country. India is a big sub-continent. And there are so many languages in the country. But in spite of all these differences of languages, the sentiments are the same; the ideals are the same; the doctrines laid down are the same; the traditions are the same; and it is not correct to divide one person from another on the basis of difference in language. The foreign language week that you are celebrating, is a good thing by itself and is one of the necessary means for bringing about that kind of federation which I am asking for, federation of religions, federation of nations, federation of languages, in fact, federation all through. There is no inherent, innate, and unavoidable conflict between one and another. Human beings are human beings all the world over, made in the image of God Himself. And, making allowance for difference in circumstances, there is nothing specially bad or specially good about this or that person. Shakespeare's critics have stated that his characters are all representative characters, splendid characters. Only three exceptions have been mentioned by Shakespearean scholars which do not fit into his conception of humanity as such, Iago,* Iachimo** and King Richard the Third of England. These three were absolutely unmixed characters of the most unscrupulous and cruel nature. And these characters, we are told, are not natural. Shakespeare always held up nature before us and explained things in the natural way. We are told, he deviated, he erred in this respect with regard to these three persons. He created these three characters which are absolutely characterless, soulless, heartless. That kind of creation is impossible in actual life. We have everything in ourselves. Divinity is within. The all-pervading Divinity is in us. By judicious means we ought to draw out all the potentialities, bring them into play, and thereby benefit ourselves and the world. This is why we speak of education. In English, the word education has a beautifiul relative significance. Education is a process by which you draw out the innate capacity, the potentiality within, and bring it into play for the benefit of the world.

Basic unity

Now, I'll conclude with only one small addition to what I have said. I'm not satisfied with the word brotherhood. Brotherhood still means difference. As a step towards the ideal which I am placing before you, brotherhood is very good. But it is only a preliminary step. Brotherhood of man, from the standpoint of language, from the standpoint of religion, from the standpoint of economics and so forth, well, that brotherhood is very good. But brotherhood by itself does not do away with the differences. There are differences still left. It's most unfortunate, it's a sad thing to remember that according to the Biblical narrative of the creation of humanity by the Lord, the first human child that was ever born into the world was a murderer. And the second child was the victim. And the book on the subject speaks of it. Abel's death was caused by his own elder brother Cain. They were brothers. There was the Fatherhood of God no doubt, and brotherhood of man consequent thereon, but there was no fellowship. There was no unity. There especially was no

* In Othello.
** In Cymbeline.

solidarity. So I wish you to go further. Have the brotherhood as an earlier step, a previous step, but have as your goal, as your final objective, not merely brotherhood, but unity and solidarity, the oneness, just as you have unity of the whole physical body in respect of the various limbs situated in the various places, having different capacities, different functions and so forth. That is the kind of ideal which you should strive to attain. I look forward to continuous co-operation and coordination from every side with regard to this ideal which I have been laying before the people about the world condition, about the need for world peace and the method of achieving peace in a very practical way. Educationists should take care that they don't bring in or emphasize the differences. The differences are all superficial and the oneness is within. The innate oneness being there, that should be drawn attention to. And in your schools and colleges, the students on the one side, and the staff, the professors and others who are in charge of the education and who have the enlightenment of the students committed to their charge, they should all cooperate for a speedy advent of the day in which we'll think not of this or that particular group, that particular nation or tribe and so on, but of humanity as such, because we're members of the same human fraternity. We are all human. And that humanity is fraternal not merely in name but there is absolute unity and solidarity, the differences being absolutely external and nothing further.

I pray to the Almighty for the speedy materializing of this vision of mine and for your earnest, fervent, hearty, cordial, and strenuous cooperation.

XI 'MEET THE PEOPLE' : A T. V. INTERVIEW

Interviewed on KTLA-TV, February 18, 1958.

Question. Your Holiness, you are in the United States on a two-months lecture tour. What is the purpose of this tour?

His Holiness: The purpose of my tour is to remove misunderstandings on the part of people in America and abroad with regard to the attitude of religion in general, and of Hinduism in particular towards peace, war, and so on, and to remove misconceptions with regard to the inevitability of religious wars, conflicts, and so on and also to spread right ideas with regard to the needlessness of wars between nation and nation, tribe and tribe, and so on. There is no sanction for any such wars from the standpoint of the Hindu religion.

Q. What are the basic philosophies or teachings of your religion ?

H.H. Purity of heart, sincerity, meekness, and the various virtues which we describe in ethics as going in to form a good character. These are the principles underlying all the various paths. Philosophies are many technically, but they all come to this point. And there is no question of any difference of opinion at all (regarding basic principles).

Q. How many people are there of this faith throughout the world?

H.H. I can't go into statistics, but I think there are millions and millions of people.

Q. How many in India? Have you any idea?

H. H. I can't give statistical figures for that.

Q. You are also a yogī. Is this part of your religion?

H. H. That is a personal question, more than that a self-laudation, which is forbidden to people of our order.*

Q. Do you feel that world peace is a practical possibility?

* See footnote at the end of this interview, on page 155.

H. H. It is not merely a practical possibility, it is an absolute necessity if people are to survive and to prosper, and to be useful for any positive work and to benefit themselves and other nations.

Q. By what methods or understandings do you feel that it can be achieved in the near future?

H. H. By people's sitting together and talking over matters and finding methods for adjusting differences where disagreement is unavoidable, and not resorting to the arbitrament of war for deciding matters of this type.

Q. Is it true that the Muslims and the Hindus, because of their religious differences have a deepseated hatred for each other?

H. H. The differences are there with regard to formal ceremonial rituals and things of that type. But there is no fundamental and basic difference. The idea of hatred of the Hindus for Mussalmāns is absolutely absurd.

Q. What place do women have in the Hindu religion ? Are they recognized on an equal level with the men of their faith?

H. H. Women are recognized as being on an equal level with men in most points, and superior to them in some.

Q. can't recall what the practice was called, but not too many years ago, there was a practice of Sati where Indian women were dying with their husbands, and it was outlawed. What are the reasons for this?

H. H. It was not according to the scriptures, not according to the dictates of Hinduism, but the practice had started somewhere at sometime. Several people thought it necessary to legislate against it and to ban it and what they did was in concordance with the spirit and the letter of the scriptures.

Q. I understand that many people are starving in India. Do you feel that a strong religious belief can compensate for the lack of food?

H. H. Religious consolation can never be a substitute for physical amelioration and the appeasement of hunger. Any religion which preaches mere endurance on these matters and does not provide for positive, constructive methods for feeding the hungry, the starving people, is pseudo-religion, it is not a true religion at all according to our scriptures.

Q. How long have you been in our country now?

H. H. I reached here on the fourth of February.

Q. And how long will you stay?

H. H. About a month and a half more.

Q. Will you be doing your lectures and meeting people such as you are doing today all during this time that you are here? Is this part of the experience that you came here to have?

H. H. I didn't follow the question.

Q. As long as you're going to be in this country, will you continue making appearances on Television and before public audiences?

H. H. That's the purpose for which I have come.

Q. Where is the next gathering that you will be speaking at? Is it tonight?

H. H. I think there are two functions tomorrow, one in the morning, one in the evening, and again two functions the day after tomorrow, and the whole program is fixed up for about a month and a half.

Q. For month and a half. Where are the meetings held ?

H. H. In different places.

Q. Do you know where the meeting is tonight?

H. H. There is no meeting tonight.

Q. Not tonight, tomorrow?

H. H. Tomorrow, the State College, I believe.

Q. The State College?

H. H. I'm not sure. State College here. The program is, has been made up, already fixed before my arrival, and I'm told from day to day as to where I am expected to speak.

Q. Well, I just enquire that of you because, in case we have some inquiries after the program, we'll be able to tell the people that will call where you will be speaking. I'm sure there are a great number of your followers here in this country who would like to attend one of your meetings. So therefore we'll get that information from you later.

H. H. The persons in charge of the program will be able to tell you about that.

Q. All right, thank you.

Might I advise you and at the same time advise the people that are looking in, that starting on Monday of next week, we are going to have on our program a member of a different religion each and every day. We are going to have another member of the Hindu religion, we are going to have a Jewish rabbi, we are going to have a Catholic priest, and we are going to have another, I don't recall off hand, but there will be a member of a different religion each and every day next week. I think it will be of great interest to you and to a great number of people looking in. I just thought I'd tell you about that.

If it's all right with you sir, I would like to have any questions that we might from the audience. So anyone who is out there who would like to ask a question of His Holiness. Would you please stand up and give us your question?

Q. (from audience): I was wondering if the people who practise Self-Realization in this country take their teachings from you.

Moderator: Did you hear the question, sir? The lady asked if the people who are practising Self-Realization are taking their teachings from you in this country.

H. H. They have already been following the particular course of teaching that has been prescribed for them, which they have been believing in and I find that I have no conflict with them. On the contrary I'm here to help them.

Q. (from audience): Your Holiness, I'ld like to ask, is India developing economically?

H. H. It is developing economically, politically, and otherwise in material respects.

Q. In the Hindu religion, you stated there were cases where women are superior to men. In which way ?

H. H. The mother is given preference and precedence in regard to all matters where reverence and worship are concerned. And a person who enters holy orders continues to venerate his mother, but not his father. Once he takes holy orders he renounces the rest of the world, but not the mother. There are many other details in that way in which the mother gets preference over the father.*

Q. Your Holiness, where were you educated? Your Holiness, pardon me.

Moderator. May I answer that for His Holiness. He has told us before that he does not like, or does not prefer to answer personal questions, although he did receive his education in India.†

(Announcement of lecture appearances given).

* Under the old Hindu Law (based on scriptures) the mother got preference over father in the matter of inheritance. Now after the amendment of the law by the Indian Parliament, both rank together.

† A saṁnyāsī is not allowed to advertise himself or indulge in self-laudation which is an impediment in the path of knowledge as the following texts show :

(i) Khyāpayen naiva sadyatiḥ. A good samnyāsī should not make himself known.

(ii) Śaṅkara commenting on Brahma Sūtra III-4-50 quotes the following passage from the Bṛhadāraṇyaka Upaniṣad III-5-1 :

Tasmād brāhmaṇaḥ pāṇḍityam nirvidya bālyena tiṣṭhāset.

"Therefore the brāhmaṇa (a person desirous of renunciation) having attained erudition in scriptures, should desire to live like a child."

Śaṅkara goes on to say :

Jñānādhyayana-dhārmikatvādibhir ātmānam avikhyāpayan dambha-darpādirahito bhavet. Yathā bālo (a)prarūḍhendriyatayā na pareṣām ātmānam āviṣkartum īhate, tadvat.

"He should not make himself known through a show of his intellectual attainments or religious performances. He should be free from hypocrisy and pride. Just as a child does not, owing to its immaturity, wish to come out before strangers, so also the renunciate (should not make himself known)".

XII VEDIC MATHEMATICS

Introduction and demonstration of the practical application in basic mathematical functions of a long misunderstood Sanskrit-Vedic key to the entire field of mathematics, by His Holiness Jagadguru Śaṅkarācārya Swami Sri Bharati Krishna Tirthaji Maharaja. The talk and demonstration were given to a small group of student mathematicians at the California Institute of Technology, Pasadena, California on February. 19,1958.

Ever since I reached America on this tour of mine, I have been in my discourses, speaking again and again about the goal of human life, the objective which all people have as the result of their activities in various directions, and the paths that would enable them to attain that goal and to benefit by it permanently. And with regard to this question of the goal and the path, I have been pointing out that although the paths may be different, the views with regard to the attainment of happiness may be different, yet the goal is the same. All people desire to attain perfection in the particular direction which they are interested in. Physical health, intellectual efficiency, moral and spiritual progress, all sorts of subjects there are, and in all these, people have their own conceptions of what constitutes happiness and what constitutes unhappiness, and the activities of all are calculated, at any rate intended, to benefit them, to help them to attain the particular goal they are after.

* Among those who witnessed the demonstration were : Mr. Guy Mr. Hartman, Brother Kriyanand, Brother Arna, Brother Donald, Mr Mackey and Mr. Peseux. (This also includes excerpts from a demonstration at California Institute of Technology, Dabney Hall Lounge, attended by students and teachers March 4, 1958.)

His Holiness Sri Jagadguru Shankaracharya
Demonstration of Vedic Mathematics at the California Institute of Technology

Science and religion

In this connection, I have gone further into details and have spoken about the spiritual side of life and the secular side of life because this is a point which many people emphasize. There are those who say that the spiritual, the religious, the moral, the philosophical aspect of life, is more important, and the secular side is practically of no account whatsoever. And there is the reaction from the other side which says, well, spiritual things are things which we don't recognize at all, and material prosperity or secular affluence is what we believe in and what we seek to obtain. There is generally an impression abroad that spirituality and secularity are two mutually inconsistent things. The man of religion, the theologian, the philosopher, the moralist, emphasizes the spiritual side, and if he does not absolutely ignore, at least does not give much importance to the secular side. And the person who insists on the secular side generally shows a disposition to belittle the spiritual side. It has generally been supposed that theology and science are ipso facto, antagonistic to each other. In the Western world, by Western world I mean generally Europe for the simple reason that the United States of America and other countries in this part of the world have come into the picture later and the East and the West meant Asia and Europe — there was not merely ridiculing but actual persecution of science and the scientists in the name of religion. That went on for a long time. The story of Galileo and other scientists is an illustration on point. The general idea was that the person who was for spiritual attainment, for salvation as the technical expression went, should absolutely neglect and throw aside all considerations of a secular nature. In fact, secular things were regarded as something contemptible, not worth while much attending to and so on.

And probably as the result of this, as a natural reaction to that very action on the one side, following the dynamical law of action and reaction being equal and opposite, the opponents went to the other extreme and said that spirituality, other world, salvation, and all these things are absurdities; they are not things at all worth attending to ; the material side, the secular side is all that matters.

So this kind of opposition went on between science and

religion in the past. And there was a time when scientists as such were regarded as anti-religious people, as limbs of the arch-devil and so on. That kind of expression we find in the theological literature of those days.

Secular sciences part of religious literature of Hinduism

With regard to Hindu scriptures however, we have a different story. Over against the picture that I have just been putting before you, we had this great thing, this unique thing that the Hindu scriptures do not merely claim to insure, or to show us the path to salvation, heaven, and so on after death, but the scriptures take into account what we call the physical and other aspects of the secular life and provide the necessary teaching, the necessary instruction in the various sciences themselves. In fact, all the material sciences, or the secular learning as we may call it, will be found to be an integral part of the Vedas, the religious scriptures.

The Vedas have four parts, the Ṛgveda, the Yajurveda, the Sāmaveda, and the Atharvaveda. In the Ṛgveda we have what is called the Āyurveda. Āyurveda is the Sanskrit name for a combination of sciences which in modern terminology we speak of as anatomy, physiology, hygiene, sanitary science, medicine, surgery, and so on. The very name Āyurveda will show that it is a part of our spiritual learning, of our Vedic, our religious learning. In the Yajurveda we have Dhanurveda, that is archery and other military sciences. And then thirdly, in the Sāmaveda, we have what we call Gāndharvaveda, the science and art of music, and along with music other portions of the fine arts as we call them at the present day, drawing, painting, and so on. And then fourthly, in Atharvaveda we have what is called the Sthāpatyaveda which is the Sanskrit term for a combination of sciences starting with mathematics and all its branches without a single exception and going on to applications of mathematics in various other departments, including architecture, engineering, and so forth. These are the four Upavedas connected with the four Vedas : Ṛgveda, Yajurveda, Sāmaveda and Atharvaveda.

So, these subjects are not regarded as secular subjects to be thrown out of the jurisdiction of what we call the religious learning.

And similarly, we have got what are called the vedāṅgas, elements necessary, prerequisite limbs of the Vedas, and they include grammar, prosody, astronomy, and even lexicography. These are regarded as integral parts of the religious learning. So, there is no question of any quarrel between any type of spiritual learning and temporal learning as something inherent in itself. Each person, according to his own taste, his own inclination, his own capacity, and his potentialities for understanding and progressing, can choose his own subjects and thereby, he can attain the kind of satisfaction, the delight, the happiness, which he seeks to attain, and for attaining which he has the necessary congenial constitution and other capacities. That is the position with regard to science and religion in our Indian scriptures.

Religious teachings differ owing to difference in circumstances

Well, I don't suggest that on that account there should be any kind of superiority claimed and so forth, because I hold that from a historical standpoint, from time to time, the exigencies and requirements of the situation are responsible for the actual form which any kind of preaching or teaching takes. It is like two doctors treating two different patients for two different diseases. In the discourse at noon, I referred to this. Suppose there is a person who is suffering from diabetes and the doctor prescribes for him a sugarless diet. And over on the other hand, there is a person suffering from heart trouble on account of which the doctor prescribes a saltless diet. We will not say that the two systems are antagonistic to each other, and there should be a fight to the finish between the two, and each should destroy the other's works and followers and so on. It's not necessary at all. It all depends upon the requirements and the extent of each situation. And if in India, from time to time, whenever a need was felt for progressing on material lines, on secular lines, and that requirement was attended to, that long-felt, acutely-felt need was actually supplied in the shape of the Vedic scriptures themselves, there is nothing to wonder at. I don't claim any kind of superiority, but I claim that the ordinary impression about religion and secular science being antagonistic is also wrong so far as the Bible and scriptures of other religions are concerned.

Well, this kind of historical circumstances may not have been there and we have no right to dogmatize and postulate about the possible historical conditions, environment, background and so forth, which have necessitated each preacher's selecting the particular line which he was going to emphasize. We do not find any of the Masters themselves at any time prefering one and condemning the other. Later on, some traditions grow and persons who are bigoted, fanatical, and exclusive in temperament, come upon the scene as interpreters and according to their own particular mental make up, their own physical constitution and so on, they draw inferences wherever gaps are to be found. The inferences are not always based on the scriptures, but are according to the particular intellectual trend and so forth of the interpreters themselves.

This is how I account for the various religions coming into existence into the world at all. Well, when a certain great teacher has come and preaches his views and shows the right conduct and so forth why should there be another renaissance of religion in which another Master has to come and things of that type have to be done? My explanation is that something which is necessary for the constitution has been dropped and that deficit has to be made good. Or, something which is necessary has been overdone, and then, that surplus has to be dealt with and eliminated. And from time to time, the Masters who come, are cognizant of the exact needs of the situation and emphasize the necessary actions and eliminate unnecessary activities according to the needs of the times, That is the only rational explanation that I can think of. We actually find in historical providence that from time to time the needs of a nation, the needs of a particular community, the needs of a particular country, go on changing, and according to the changing needs, the Master comes with a seemingly new message. But in reality it is not a new message at all. It is a message which was specially required during those peculiar circumstances of the particular country or community concerned. That's my explanation of it.

That is the doctrinal, the theoretical aspect of the matter. In our Indian scriptures, we do not find anywhere a condemnation of what you call the positive or materialistic frame of mind. That is not there at all. In the Bhagavad Gītā, Śrī Kṛṣṇa, whom we regard as an avatār of the Lord gives his advice to Arjuna the disciple. We find Śrī Kṛṣṇa dealing with the subject from every conceivable standpoint, the standpoint of Sānkhya Yoga, of Jñāna-Yoga, of Karma-Yoga, and after the various yogas which have their own technical meanings have been dealt with, there is also the standpoint of pure materialism, what you call pure naturalism, or attention to biological science and everything else in the world :

Asatyam apratiṣṭham te
jagad āhur anīśvaram,
Aparaspara-sambhūtam
kim anyat kāmahaitukam.*

Even from the purely atheistical standpoint, the naturalistic standpoint, consider the question and the conclusion can be the only one which is the right one from the other standpoints. So even there, we do not find the atheistic standpoint condemned (beforehand, without examination).

It is not merely with regard to different religions, different sub-sects, and so on, but even with regard to the negation of all religion that we find an attitude of this type, an approach of this type (examination of opposing views) in the Gītā.

Conflict between religion and science owing to short-sightedness

Although the past history of the western world shows a deep conflict between religion and science, we find now that modern philosophers and scientists have, well, recognized the historical causes which led to this conflict, so much so that at the present moment, among the great scientists of the modern world, you will find people with very high notions of spirituality, persons who have been theists not merely agnostics, but theists and theists of a confirmed, not to say incorrigible, character. That

* Gītā XVI-8.

stage too has been reached now in due course. There has been no quarrel. With the exception of one or two persons, Bertrand Russell and so forth, we find modern scientists, including Sir James Jeans, the great astronomer and physicist, expressing themselves in favour of what we call spiritual philosophy, the Vedānta and not feeling ashamed of it. Sir James Jeans goes so far as to say, "I accept this as the new physics, and in doing so, I don't feel any regret at all. My Physics leaves me no option in the matter." Such language he uses, showing that the conflict between science and religion which people long imagined to be inherent in the situation, that conflict is due to shortsightedness and wrong notions as regards what constitutes religion and what constitutes science, respectively.*

I have been, from my childhood, equally fond of metaphysics on the one side and mathematics on the other. And I've found no difficulty at all. And as a consequence of my interest in what you call the positive sciences on the one side, and what you call theology and religion and philosophy on the other, I have felt from a long time ago, that the Vedas which openly declare that these subjects are integral parts of the Vedic scriptures, should be studied from the standpoint of the scholar, from the standpoint of a person who is absolutely impartial, has no prejudices and no prepossessions, a person who is a seeker after truth and welcomes the truth from whatever direction it may come. So we have to start with open minds, nothing *a priori*, nothing taken for granted. We have had long centuries of traditions extending over a long period of time,

* Compare Max Planck:

"Only those who think by halves become atheists, those who go deep with their thoughts and see the marvellous relationships among universal laws recognise a creating power."

"For religion, the idea of God is at the beginning; for science the idea of God is at the end."

[quoted by Ellen Juhnke in a discussion on Prof. Heisenberg's lecture on 4-9-1958. From "On Modern Physics" by Heisenberg, Born, Schrodinger and Auger.]

not merely various climes. And in all these climes and times we have found a certain attitude taken in the name of religion against science and so forth. There should be no room for such a hesitation or doubtful frame of mind so far as the Indian scriptures are concerned. We don't find any difficulty at all because each science is an integral part of a particular Veda, a particular scriptural portion of our literature.

Guṇita Sūtras

Now, in dealing with various texts which are to be found in the Vedic literature, I found my first difficulty because the translators who translated these books started with certain notions. I felt that these notions were *a priori* conclusions, conclusions with which they started. And when they started with their conclusion all ready, when they had closed minds, there was no possibility of their going further into the matter and actually finding out the exact meaning of the various texts. That was my first difficulty. Professor Colebrooke and other translators of the ancient Indian scriptural and other texts into English, were meek enough, and modest enough, scientifically-minded enough to say that there were certain portions of the Vedas which were not intelligible. One particular portion I am referring to, a particular portion of the Atharva-Veda is called the gaṇita sūtras. The gaṇita sūtras, are also called the Śulba sūtras "the easy mathematical formulae," that's the meaning of the expression. And there are sixteen sūtras, sixteen aphorisms in all, and the general name "gaṇita" mathematics, is given to the subject. And then Colebrooke, in his translations, went as far as that, but at that point he stopped and said, "We are unable to understand what the contents of these sūtras are, and what connection these sūtras have with mathematics." And therefore, there was no possibility of his translating what was absolutely unintelligible to him. But he had the meekness of mind, the scientific frame of mind, to say, "I do not understand. It is unintelligible, it is beyond me." But Horace Hayman Wilson and others of that type, with a superiority complex in which they could not possibly admit that something was unintelligible to them, took another stand altogether.

Coming to the same passage. the same portion of the Atharvaveda, Horace Hayman Wilson said, "This is all nonsense." That was the single word with which the whole thing was dismissed. And R.T. Griffith, the translator of the Rāmāyaṇa and other poetic works in Sanskrit literature, followed the same course. He said it was not merely nonsense but that it was "utter nonsense." So he improved on his predecessor by adding a very significant and a very dogmatically assertive adjective, utterly nonsensical, no sense can be made out of these matters. Well, that put me on the track. I said there must be something. The ideas may be wrong ; the conclusions may be wrong ; the details of all the things considered may be wrong; the facts and the factors of the situation taken into account may have been insufficient, and sometimes, irrelevant factors may have been taken into account. And as the natural result of taking irrelevant factors into account and of excluding relevant factors, well, naturally the vision is distorted and the judgment is bound to become warped. The text may be all wrong; the conclusion, the arguments may be all wrong, and yet there must be something in the subject which was being discussed with so much earnestness and which the commentators were trying to understand but could make nothing out of. So I went on with my simple idea that there was some meaning. The meaning, may be all absolutely wrong but to dismiss something, well, off hand as nonsense because it is not understandable, I felt, was not correct. If for example, I find two Greeks, talking to each other in their Greek language, and I am unable to understand anything of what they are saying, would I be justified in saying that they were talking nonsense? It has no sense for me because I haven't got the sense or the equipment for understanding the sense behind it. But to call it nonsense because I don't understand it, or because a number of people in my community, in my country, do not understand it, well I felt, that was unfair. And, that was the first thing which started me on this line. And going to the forest, seeking the solitude of the forest meditation, I tried to make some meaning out of these sūtras. Sanskrit has a certain peculiarity about it, that the same passage very often deals with a different subject and is capable of yielding different meanings relating to different subjects. For example, there is the hymn of praise addressed to Śrī Kṛṣṇa.* It can be interpreted in such a manner by the various combinations of words, the language itself gives facilities for the purpose, that it may be understood as a hymn of praise to Śaṅkara, or Śiva. In some cases we have texts which bear not merely two meanings but three or four and relate to different subjects altogether. In English we have the figure of speech called pun, when a word having two different meanings is used. And people having a sense of humour write about it, in newspaper columns, "wit and humour", "fun and frolic", and so on. For example, we have a very ordinary example in which a person poses a puzzle. He asks another, "What's the difference between a schoolmaster and an engine driver ?" And the answer is, "The one minds the train, the other trains the mind." The schoolmaster trains the mind of the pupils and the engine driver minds the train, he looks after the train, the railway train. Examples of this type are to be found infinitely in our Sanskrit texts. The grammar the literature and the figures of speech in Sanskrit give great facility of expressing one's own individual dispositions in a number of different subjects but with the same formula (set of words).

I felt that there must be something like that. And with regard to these formulae, I came to this conclusion, that there must be some kind of key. In king Kamsa's reign, famine, pestilence, unsanitary conditions prevailed, that seemed to be the meaning of the text**—apparently nothing to do with mathematics. "Mathematical formulae" is the heading of the subject, and inside we are told that the tyrant king, Kamsa, ruled over the people oppressively. He was collecting taxes from them,

* Gopi bhāgya madhu vrāta
śṛngiśo dadhisandhiga.
Khalajivita khātāva
galahātārasandhara.

This verse also gives the value of $\frac{\pi}{10}$ to 32 decimal places.

.31415926535897932384626433832792 [Vedic Maths. p. 362]

** Kamse kṣāmadāhakhalair malaih'.

This expression also gives the key to the evaluation of $\frac{1}{17}$ (Vedic Maths. p. 210).

and was doing nothing for them in return, with the result that unsanitary conditions and thefts and all sorts of vices prevailed in his kingdom. That seemed to be an historical account of the king Kamsa. But here, the heading is Gaṇita Sūtra, mathematical formulae. So I said there must be something. And after long years and years of meditation in the forest, I took the help of lexicographies, lexicons of earlier times, because as a language develops and comes in contact with other languages words change their meaning. Words get additional meaning, words get deteriorated in meaning. All sorts of things of this type take place even with regard to one language.

There is a tremendous difference for example between Anglo-Saxon or ancient English of the earliest times, the language of Gower, Chaucer, and so on, and the English of the middle ages, Middle-English as you may call it, Shakespeare, Ben Johnson, Fletcher, and so on, and finally, the language of our own time. There is a tremendous difference in various respects. And as the time goes on these historical causatives are responsible for certain changes. In some cases we have lost the clue to the changes. We're unable to say what historical background was responsible for such and such change of meaning, for such and such deterioration or exaltation of meaning and so forth. For example, I give you a passage from Chaucer. Chaucer was not one of the ancient writers, most ancient writers, but of later times, not modern, not even middle, but somewhere between ancient Anglo-Saxon as it is called, and Middle-English. Well, many persons whose mother tongue is English would be unable to recognize it as English at all. I give you a sample. (His Holiness gives an archaic unrecognizable though clearly pronounced recitation of Chaucer). This expression of "knave child", particularly I take as an example from the text.*

Knave child. Knave, in modern English, means rogue, scoundrel, a rascal, a man of bad character, a cheat. And in Chaucer's English, knave simply meant 'male'. Male child. A word which includes the whole male sex gradually came to

* Consider the following passage from Chaucer:
The tyme is come a knave child she beer;
Mauricins at the fontstoon they hym calle.
—Canterbury Tales "Man of Laws Tales"

mean, well, rascals of both sexes. We talk of knaves now, knave-proof, fool-proof, and so on. The word has changed its meaning. So many other words have undergone a change in their meanings.

And if we have access to a lexicon dealing with Chaucerian English, we will be able to understand, otherwise not.

Similarly here I felt that I should ransack all the lexicons available in order to find out other possible meanings of the same words, meanings which were extant in those days, that were actually being used, but which have gone out of fashion altogether.

Now, talking to you in America, I need not say that even with regard to American English and English English, there is a little difference. English English of English people, English speaking people whose mother tongue is English, is not exactly the same as the literary English currrent in England. And even there, there are dialectal differences, the Northern dialect, the Kentish dialect, and this dialect and that dialect, all these differences are there.

So I studied the old lexicons, including Viśva, Amara, Arṇava, Śabdakalpadruma etc. books which are known by name only, and which people see in the libraries, but which are never turned for any useful purpose. Well, with these I was able to find out the meanings. I got the key in that way *in one instance*, and one thing after another helped me in the elucidation of the other sūtras, the other formulae. And I found to my extreme astonish ment and gratification that the sūtras dealt with mathematics, in all its branches. Only sixteen sūtras cover all branches of mathematics, arithmetic, algbera, geometry, trigonometry, physics, plain and spherical geometry, conics, calculus, both differential, and integral, applied mathematics of various kinds, dynamics, hydrostatics, statics, kinematics, and all. And, it was a great surprise and a great gratification to me that after all, I was able to get something out of it, and it was not all nonsense as Professor Horace Hayman Wilson and others had declared.

Simplified operations

Since then, in my discourses, as I am talking of metaphysics, philosophy and religion, and bhakti, and karma, and yoga, and this and that, I also speak summarily about mathematics which I have been able to get from the sūtras of the Atharva Veda. I gave blackboard demonstrations in all the various provinces, the various states in India. I have been going from place to place giving, in the universities and colleges, demonstrations showing how very simple methods are quite sufficient for answering, tackling very difficult problems, arithmetical or algebraical or other problems. Questions requiring twenty thirty steps of working, involving memory power, involving various kinds of difficulties, well, they can be solved in one step answers. I have given demonstrations, I don't call them exhibitions because that is not my idea of the thing at all, I have given demonstrations of the wonderful material that's available here. I have given these in almost all the universities in India. In Nagpur, there was a continuous series, three months of studies there. The students, the little boys in the High School stage and professros in charge of post-graduate research classes and so on, all were attending. The subject was new to all of them. The youngsters, as well as the oldsters, if I can use such an expression, were all surprised. A question is taken from the usual textbooks used in schools and colleges, and is written down on the board. I have taught small boys already the sūtra and how to apply it. And the boys go on dictating the answer, shouting the answer from the back of the hall, and I go on writing down the answer on the board to their dictation. And then the answer page is taken from the book, and the answer is found to be correct, I've always had this experience, when the first demonstrations were being shown to professors in schools, colleges, and universities, they have always. almost invariably asked, "Is this magic or methematics·!" And I have been telling them. "It is magic until you understand it and it is mathematices thereafter." (sincere laughter).

Little boys come dancing forward with joy and professors ask, "Well, how can the answer be written down without any intermediate steps of working at all?" And the answer is, "The sūtra is so, the aphorism is so-framed that each digit automatically yields its predecessor and its successor. You may start from either end and go on, and the answer is there. No separate working at all. This kind of mathematics I was able to discover, I'm afraid it must have been lying dormant for centuries and centuries together. There is no trace of any reference to these sūtras anywhere at all, and therefore naturally, the supposition is that mathematics was not part of the Vedic literature. Other subjects have come in, various other subjects have come in, but mathematics seemed to be lacking in the Vedic lore. But when I was able to find it, well, it was easy sailing. One clue led to another, and that led to a third, and so on.

Well, I would like to give a sample illustration or two for the subject is one which would require regular class study, because the whole subject is different. It is not a condensing of one or two steps here or there into a less number of steps. Suppose you have ten steps of work according to actual modern system taught in the universities, and instead of ten steps, you are able to do it in eight steps, saving two steps. That would be regarded as a mathematical discovery, new light thrown on mathematics. But here, from the starting point to the destination, the paths are different absolutely. The whole thing is different. And the answer comes if you mechanically follow the meaning of the sūtras.

Well, the subject is one into details of which I like to go at every place. At many places, I have been doing it. In Calcutta, in Banaras, in Nagpur, in Bombay, in Madras, in the Punjab, in various other parts of India, I have been giving demonstrations. I don't make any great distinction between metaphysics and mathematics as regards salvation of the soul and so on. Salvation of the soul depends upon personal character, and whether you are fond of mathematics or not, and in Mathematics whether you are fond of trigonometry or fond of geometry, or whether you like acoustics or chemistry or biology, that doesn't come in as a question for determining your eligibility for salvation. That depends on the individual taste, the individual inclination, the individual bent, the individual capacity and so forth. I have been giving these demonstrations and the whole course of the primary schools, the high school stage and the intermediate stage and the graduation and the M.A. degree in mathematics and so on, the course prescribed for all these can be completed. I've actually had experience in some cases of students whom I have trained along these lines, that the course can be completed in about fourteen months.

Not merely the course of ten or twelve or fifteen years for the matriculation, the entrance, and the graduation and so on, but the course of over twenty-five years in all can be completed in that time. And for those who are interested in finding out as to how these sūtras work out and give the answer, in relation to modern mathematics as we know it now in the universities, well, I can give the explanation as to how these results come from the sūtra. But, for the actual working, even that is not necessary. The formulae are quite enough.

To take a very simple example, Pythagoras' theorem. In the Pythagoras' theorem, well, generally the student feels that the proof is very complex, very complicated. The proof of the theorem is very cumbersome, long and so on. But once the purport of the theorem, "the square of the hypotenuse equals the sum of the squares of the other two sides," is understood, any person who knows how to work it and demonstrate its correctness, well, can apply it. People who have practical knowledge of the application of the sūtras, need not go in for the theory side of it at all. The actual work can be done. Tremendous time is saved. It is a saving not merely of time and energy and money, but more than all, I feel, it is saving the child from tears that very often accompany the study of mathematics. I have known students going in for study of mathematics by wrong choice and who have been repenting and regretting and shedding tears over the mistake. They waste one year, and change the subject. I feel very much about that.

All that is saved and children come dancing to the board to write down answers to questions an so on.

Well, I do not propose in one discourse to cover a large ground. It is not possible to do it. The whole subject can be finished in about, fourteen months. Even very slow students take sixteen to eighteen months for completing the whole course. And their fellow students who are brilliant and have developed a lot of superiority complex, have expressed surprise at the way the persons who are supposed to be very much inferior were able to tackle difficult things and in such a short time. Only by way of illustration, I do not know when there wll be an opportunity, an occasion for giving detailed demonstration and diffusion of this knowledge contained in the Atharvaveda sūtras. I do not know about that, because the program for the future is uncertain, but just now, by way of illustration, I may give a few sample specimens. And the specimens will show how tremendous is the saving in time, energy and so on.

Well, there is one handicap which I shall also mention to you immediately, for myself at present, I have just had both of the eyes operated on for removal of cataracts, and while still convalescing just after coming out of the hospital, I've come over here on my tour, and for the first time today, I am making use of the eyes for it.

Demonstration

(Attendant offers to place demonstration board on H. H's lap to write on.)

The audience, they won't be able to see it.

(Attendant speaks, "Sir, would you like to write from sitting position or standing?)

Standing would be much better, but whether I can stand the standing.

I'll take up a very simple thing to start with. Suppose we have to deal with multiplications of numbers. Take something from elementary arithmetic to start with. Well, you have a multiplication table which boys are called upon to get by heart. And they get the multiplication tables by heart. In different places, the number studied in the multiplication tables may be different, sixteen multiplied by sixteen, twenty by twenty, and so on...What's the usual figure here? (twelve by twelve) Twelve by twelve. Yes, well, if you have a student who does no know the multiplication table above five times five, I'll give him to start with the method by which he can himself deduce the necessary answer with regard to higher numbers. He goes on developing in that way. I think a few examples will quite suffice for the purpose.

Multiplication

Now, let us take a very simple example, multiplying eight by nine. Well, a boy who has not studied the multiplication table cannot by memory tell you what eight times nine is. He is given the sūtra by which he will be able to deduce it. He has to get by heart only the multiplication table as far as five times five.

The first power of ten above these (numbers), or near these is taken as the base. That is ten. I'll not explain the sūtra because that is in Sanskrit, and would require more explanation. I'll just give you the application, so that afterwards if you're interested in the matter, you can go into it further.

Well, we take ten (as the base). What is the deficit here from ten (of each of the terms in question, eight and nine), we'll put that here minus two (ten less, eight), and here, we have minus one (10 less, 9), I ask you to observe. From observation in this, you will be able to extend the application indefinitely and infinitely. Now here, we have got a left hand side (the usual way of setting up two figures of multiplication) and a right hand side (made up of the difference between each of the terms of the multiplication and the base, in this case, ten, these difference being written to the right of their corresponding terms):

Base 10		
	9	—1
	× 8	—2

And ordinary multiplications go from left to right. That is another peculiarity. They go from left to right. In reading numbers...they go from left to right. You say seven hundred and eighty three. You don't say three eighty and seven hundred. Even that process may be from the right hand side (in the Vedic method) in multiplication and addition. When you actually arrive at the result you say seven hundred and eighty three, four hundred and forty five, and so on, going from left to right. Here the process of multiplication is itself from left to right.

Well, we take the first digit here. Add these two and subtract the base (nine plus eight minus the base, ten). Seventeen minus ten is seven, or add these two and subtract from ten (minus one plus minus two subracted from ten). That is also seven. Or, cross subtract from here (eight minus one or nine minus two). This is seven and this is seven. That is the left hand side.*

* The left hand side of the answer is obtained by (i) adding the nine and the eight and deducting the base from the result, or (ii) adding the deficits and deducting (algebraic addition) the result from the base or (iii) & (iv) by cross deduction:

[Contd.

Base 10

$$\begin{array}{rr} 9 & -1 \\ \times\ 8 & -2 \\ \hline 7 & \end{array}$$

You have not merely got the answer, but you have got confirming proofs of verifications. In all cases we have this kind of application coming up. We find the actual result by one method and check it up, verify it, by another method.

Multiplication of these two (minus one times minus two) gives the right hand side. Isn't that correct !

Base 10

$$\begin{array}{rr} 9 & -1 \\ \times\ 8 & -2 \\ \hline 7 & 2 \end{array}$$

I have taken a very simple example to start with because it should be easy of assimilation to anybody.

Well, suppose we multiply eight by seven.

(Base 10)

$$\begin{array}{r} 8 \\ \times\ 7 \\ \hline \end{array}$$

Ten minus eight equais two, we put two, and similarly we put three here.

$$\begin{array}{rr} 8 & -2 \\ \times\ 7 & -3 \\ \hline \end{array}$$

Eight minus three is five; seven minus two i sfive (cross subtraction); fifteen (8 plus seven) minus ten (the base) is five; ten minus two minus three (right hand side) is five; so five is the left hand side.

$$\begin{array}{rr} 8 & -2 \\ \times\ 7 & -3 \\ \hline 5 & \end{array}$$

[Contd.]

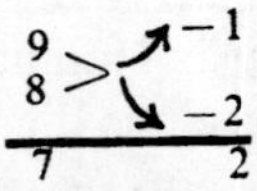

"In fact old historical traditions describe this cross-substration process as having been responsible for the acceptance of X mark as the sign of multiplication". (Vedic Maths. p. 15)

Two times three, six. That is the right hand side.

$$\begin{array}{rr} 8 & -2 \\ \times\ 7 & -3 \\ \hline 5 & 6 \end{array}$$

Now, we take numbers which are above a base taken. Suppose we have twelve multiplied by thirteen.

$$\begin{array}{r} 12 \\ \times\ 13 \\ \hline \end{array}$$

Ten is the base. We put here plus two, and here plus three.

$$\begin{array}{rr} 12 & 2 \\ \times\ 13 & 3 \\ \hline \end{array}$$

It is not deficit but excess and that is put down. And the same methods are followed. Twelve plus three is fifteen; thirteen plus two is fifteen (cross addition this time).

$$\begin{array}{rr} 12 & 2 \\ \times\ 13 & 3 \\ \hline 15 & \end{array}$$

Two times three is six. And that is the answer.

$$\begin{array}{rr} 12 & 2 \\ \times\ 13 & 3 \\ \hline 15 & 6 \end{array}$$

This is the observation to start with.

In the next place, I will show some other cases in which there seems to be a slight difference, but the difference can be easily understood and dealt with.

Suppose we have to multiply seven and six. Ten is the base.

$$\begin{array}{r} 7 \\ \times\ 6 \\ \hline \end{array}$$

We put down minus three here, and minus four here.

$$\begin{array}{rr} 7 & -3 \\ \times\ 6 & -4 \\ \hline \end{array}$$

Seven minus four is three; six minus three is three: three into (times) four is twelve, we get two digits.

$$\begin{array}{rr} 7 & -3 \\ \times\ 6 & -4 \\ \hline 3 & 12 \end{array}$$

But we're entitled to only one digit (for every zero in the base), in this case, because our base is ten. Therefore we put two here.

$$\begin{array}{rr} 3 & 2 \\ +\ 1 & \end{array}$$

And add the one over here, carry it two the left, and there you've got it.

$$\begin{array}{rr} 4 & 2 \end{array}$$

That follows.

We have dealt with cases of numbers, both of which are less than the base, and cases of numbers which are both higher than the actual base taken.

The next thing we should take up is the multiplication of numbers where one yields a deficit and the other a surplus. We take twelve times nine. Ten being the base.

$$\begin{array}{r} 12 \\ \times\ 9 \\ \hline \end{array}$$

The excess is plus two (regarding twelve); deducting nine from the base, this deficit is minus one.

$$\begin{array}{rr} 12 & +2 \\ \times\ 9 & -1 \\ \hline \end{array}$$

Twelve minus one is eleven (cross-subtraction); nine plus two (cross-addition) is also eleven.

$$\begin{array}{rr} 12 & 2 \\ \times\ 9 & -1 \\ \hline 11 & \end{array}$$

Two into (times) minus one is minus two, that should be remembered. We'll put the (minus sign at the side) to show that this is not to be added, it is to be subtracted.

$$\begin{array}{rr} 12 & 2 \\ \times\ 9 & -1 \\ \hline 11 & -2 \end{array}$$

It is not merely eleven minus two, it is one-hundred and ten minus two, that is one-hundred and eight.

$$\begin{array}{rr} 12 & 2 \\ \times\ 9 & -1 \\ \hline 10 & 8 \end{array}$$

So, this time, you have seen, we extend the process to higher digits. This method can be extended infinitely and indefinitely in all directions.

I take up now numbers of two digits. Suppose we have seventy-seven multipled by ninty-seven. Here, our base is one-hundred.

(Base 100)

$$\begin{array}{r} 77 \\ \times\ 97 \\ \hline \end{array}$$

This gives us twenty-three; and this gives us three.

$$\begin{array}{rr} 77 & -23 \\ \times\ 97 & -\ 3 \\ \hline \end{array}$$

Seventyseven minus three is seventy-four (cross subtraction); ninetyseven minus twenty three is also seventy four.

$$\begin{array}{rr} 77 & -23 \\ \times\ 97 & -\ 3 \\ \hline 74 & \end{array}$$

And twenty-three multiplied by three here is sixty-nine.

$$\begin{array}{rr} 77 & -23 \\ \times\ 97 & -\ 3 \\ \hline 74 & 69 \end{array}$$

Another example:

(Base 100)

$$\begin{array}{r} 88 \\ \times\ 88 \\ \hline \end{array}$$

Here I have twelve, and here I have twelve.

$$\begin{array}{rr} 88 & -12 \\ \times\ 88 & -12 \\ \hline \end{array}$$

Eightyeight minus twelve is seventy six, and twelve into (times) twelve gives me one-hundred and fortyfour.

(100)

$$\begin{array}{rr} 88 & -12 \\ \times\ 88 & -12 \\ \hline 76 & 144 \end{array}$$

Now, (with regard to 144) we are entitled only to two digits, hundred being the base. So we put the fortyfour here.

$$\begin{array}{rr} 88 & -12 \\ \times\ 88 & -12 \\ \hline 76 & 44 \\ +1 & \end{array}$$

and increase this six (in 76) to seven.

$$\begin{array}{rr} 88 & -12 \\ \times\ 88 & -12 \\ \hline 77 & 44 \end{array}$$

Now, another kind of case is also possible which should be taken into account, and that is a thing like this : ninety-seven multiplied by ninety-six (changed to ninety-eight). Hundred being the base....

(Base 100)

$$\begin{array}{r} 97 \\ \times\ 98 \\ \hline \end{array}$$

...we put three here, and we put two here.

$$\begin{array}{rr} 97 & -3 \\ \times\ 98 & -2 \\ \hline \end{array}$$

Ninety-seven minus two is ninety-five; ninety-eight minus three is also ninety-five.

$$\begin{array}{rr} 97 & -3 \\ \times\ 98 & -2 \\ \hline 95 & \end{array}$$

Three times two give us six, but six contains only one digit, whereas we are dealing with hundreds (and therefore need two digits on the right); therefore, we put a zero here and the six here.

(100)

$$\begin{array}{rr} 97 & -3 \\ \times\ 98 & -2 \\ \hline 95 & 06 \end{array}$$

Notice, when there are more digits than permissible, we carry the extra digit over to the left. When the number of digits is smaller than permissible, we fill up the gap with zeros, just as we do in multiplications of decimals.

(Another example) One-hundred and two to be multiplied by one-hundred and four.

(Base 100)

$$\begin{array}{r} 102 \\ \times\ 104 \\ \hline \end{array}$$

We'll put two here and four here.

(100)

$$\begin{array}{rr} 102 & 2 \\ \times\ 104 & 4 \\ \hline \end{array}$$

So, one-hundred and six, and zero eight.

(100)

$$\begin{array}{rr} 102 & 2 \\ \times\ 104 & 4 \\ \hline 106 & 08 \end{array}$$

Start with the easiest samples of the easiest kind of work, as we go on we'll be able to tackle bigger things.

Those students who wish to go into detailed study of it, I can give the sūtras and the meaning of the sūtras and how it was applied. But this is the practical application of it.

There is the one sūtra in which we say—

"Nikhilam navataś caramam daśatah."*

Suppose I have a bigger number like this :

$$\begin{array}{r} 888 \\ \times\ 997 \\ \hline \end{array}$$

Now, we'll put here, one-one-two.

(Base is now 1000)

$$\begin{array}{rr} 888 & -112 \\ \times\ 997 & \\ \hline \end{array}$$

(and) zero, zero, three.

$$\begin{array}{rr} 888 & -112 \\ \times\ 997 & -003 \\ \hline \end{array}$$

And the answer is eight hundred eighty eight minus three is eight hundred eighty five on the left hand side.

$$\begin{array}{rr} 888 & -112 \\ \times\ 997 & -003 \\ \hline 885 & 336 \end{array} \quad \text{(or 885,336)}$$

(heavy sighs from pleasure)

The three steps of multiplication and the addition are all over.

(rustle and whispering)

* "All from nine and the last from ten." [Vedic Mathematics p.14]

I'll take only a few examples by way of illustration because subject after subject, chapter after chapter, can be dealt with in detail in this way. And, well, I think it will not be possible for me to give you examples of different subjects if I go into details in everything. But I might mention one part of it before I go to the next point. Of course, a question was asked the other day by a student here I believe. That was with regard to multiplication which I gave examples of at the very outset.

Numbers nearing the base, ten, hundred, thousand, and so forth, could be multiplied in that way, but what about smaller numbers which are not near the base ?

(From the audience, forty-eight and forty-six).

$$\begin{array}{r} 48 \\ \times\ 46 \\ \hline \end{array}$$

Suppose this kind of multiplication is there. Well, the difference from one-hundred (base) will be fifty-two. And the difference here (46) from one hundred will be fifty-four. And (the multiplication) will be very hard. What should be done in this case ? Here also, we adopt the proportion method, Ānurūpyeṇa "according to the ratio." That is, intstead of taking one hundred as our base, we take the nearest submultiple of it as sub-base, our working base, and calculate accordingly. Now it as instead of one hundred, we take fifty as our working base.

(Base 50)

$$\begin{array}{r} 48 \\ \times\ 46 \\ \hline \end{array}$$

This gives minus two; this gives minus four

$$\begin{array}{rr} 48 & -2 \\ \times\ 46 & -4 \\ \hline \end{array}$$

...forty-eight minus four is forty-four, and two into four will be eight, we'll make that zero eight...

$$\begin{array}{rr} 48 & -2 \\ \times\ 46 & -4 \\ \hline 44 & 08 \end{array}$$

...and this forty-four is divided by two because we have taken the sub-base fifty, half of hundred...

$$\begin{array}{rr} 48 & -2 \\ \times\ 46 & -4 \\ \hline 2/\ 44/ & 08 \\ 22 & 08 \end{array}$$

...and the answer is 2,208. Whatever proportion there is between the original base and the sub-base the same will come here so far as the left hand side is concerned. And the right hand, side won't be affected at all.

Now, we will take a particular kind of multiplication. Well, I may say at this point that whatever kind of question there may be, in whatever chapter it may be, simple equations, quadratic equations, cubic, bi-quadratic, and various other subjects of algebra, geometry, plane trigonometry, spherical trigonometry, calculus, and so on, the question *must* come under one of the sixteen rules. All that we have to do is, let me repeat, to recognize and identify the particular type and apply the sūtra relative to that particular type.

Now, here is a special case where we multiply a number by itself. Now, the same thing will follow here if we want to know the value of nine squared independently by this method. Now, this is a corollary to the formula which I've just now been employing. As the formulae are in Sanskrit, it can't be possible for me to explain them. It would require an extensive treatment and algebraical demonstration of the whole work. And that is the kind of work that I have done in the volumes that I have prepared.

Now, nine is to be squared. We are told, Yāvad ūnam tāvaḍ ūnīkṛtya vargam yojayet. That is the corollary to the formula. Well, we are told there, treating the base as ten, whatever the deficit may be (between the number to be squared and the base, in this case nine and ten), well, decrease the number by that much (nine minus one), and put down the square of that difierence (one squared is one).
Nine is to be squared.

$$9^2$$

This (9) is one less (than base 10)
Therefore we will reduce this (9) by one that is 8

$$8$$

and one we add here (on the right hand side of 8)

8 1 (two steps)

Eight squared

8^2

This (8) is two less (than base 10), in other words deduct two (from eight), six

6

and two squared is there (four).

6 4

Seven squared. Three less, therefore, three further less (deducted from seven) or 4 and three squared or 9.

4 9

This is also applicable in all directions. We have, for example eleven squared

1 1

This is one more (than base ten) so add one more (to 11, that is 12)

1 2

and put the square of that 1

1 2 1

Thirteen squared

$1\ 3^2$

This is three more than the base add three more (than 13 is)

1 6

and the three squared here

1 6 9

The method applies to a number of several digits. Suppose we have to square nine-hundred and eighty eight. This is twelve less than the base (1000) and therefore, we reduce it twelve more (988—12 or 976), nine seventy-six; and twelve squared, one four four, 976 144.

In that way, equations are rendered much easier by these formulae. (Spontaneous hearty laughter frome the "class").

And if here we had had only ninety-eight squared, it is two less (than base 100), so we'll put ninety-six; and two squared will give me four, I put zero four, 9604. Under all the cases where we find an excess or a deficit (compared to the number of zeros in the base). The excess is taken over to the left and the deficit is filled up by zeros.

And then there is "Ekādhikena Pūrveṇa". It comes up again and again, in chapter after chapter, in subject after subject, and has a new and fresh application of an astounding character, starting with elementary multiplication of numbers, squares of numbers, ending in five. For example, fifteen squared. Here we are told that the rule is 'by one more than the previous 'one". The last digit here (15) is five, the previous one is one. Multiply the one by one more than itself. It is two. And put the five squared here, 225.

Twenty-five squared. Two times three (one more than the 2 in 25) is six. Five times five is twenty-five, 625, the previous portion multiplied by on more than itself.

Suppose it is ninety-five squared. Nine times ten is ninety; five times five is twenty-five, 9025. In this way, multiplication is rendered easier.

Now, this is called the 'Ekādhika Pūrva' Sūtra, that is, where the multiplication is by one more than the previous digit. The 'previous digit' is the last but one, that is, the last on the right hand side, and the last but one.

Suppose we have one-hundred and ninety-five squared. Nineteen into (times) twenty gives me three hundred and eighty; five into five is twenty-five 38025.

And this is also applicable to multiplications where we have not got five as the last digit of each number, but the sum of the two is ten. This rule applies even there. Suppose I have thirty-seven being multiplied by thirty- three.

$$\begin{array}{r} 37 \\ \times \quad 33 \\ \hline \end{array}$$

Three into (times) four is twelve; seven into three is twenty-one, and that is that, 1221.

(Another example)

$$\begin{array}{r} 122 \\ \times \quad 128 \\ \hline \end{array}$$ (the 'previous one' here is 12)
(add one, giving 13)

Twelve into (times) thirteen is one-hundred and fifty-six; two into eight is sixteen, because two plus eight will be ten (thereby putting this problem into this simplified class), 156 16 or 15616.

This rule applies to multiplication of numbers whose previous parts (left hand side portions) are the same and whose last digits add up to ten, such as five and five together making ten, or three and seven, two and eight, or one and nine. But in the case of one and nine, we have to be careful in the second step. One into (times) nine gives us nine which has one digit we should have two digits. So we put a zero.*

I take the case of division now :

One over nineteen, (1/19), expressed in its full decimal form, will take eighteen recurring decimal places in the answer. And that means eighteen steps of division.

(At this point, His Holiness demonstrated the familiar, laboriously long conventional way of converting fractions to decimals through long division).

Eighteen places. One by nineteen. The sūtra Ekādhikena Pūrveṇa applies here, one more than the previous digit. Now, the last digit is nine ; the previous digit is one, one more than one means two, so we go on muitiplying by two. Or going the other way, in the reverse order from left to right, we'll divide by two and get the same answer.

Now, we start with one on the right hand side (predetermining the eighteenth decimal) as the last digit. I'll explain why we put the one there. Where the fraction has a denominator which has only the factors two and five, it is a non-circulating decimal. Where it is composed of factors that do not contain two or five, it's purely a circulating decimal. In the case of those numbers which contain partly (multiples of) two (and) five, and partly of another type, there the integral is partly circulating and partly non-circulating. Here we have nine, or one (divided) by nineteen. Nineteen does not contain the factors, two and five, and therefore it is purely a circulating decimal, a recurring decimal.

* For example :–

$$\begin{array}{r} 31 \\ \times 39 \\ \hline 1209 \end{array}$$

The relevant Sūtra is "Antyayor daśake (a) pi." [Vedic Maths. p. 34]

And we start there with the digit which when multiplied by nine will give nine as the last digit. So we start with one.

And then, Ekādhikena Pūrveṇa, "By one more than the previous one," that is two (in this case).

...1 (multiply this last figure by 2 and every succeeding result by 2)

...1 One into two is two (put two to the left hand side of 1).

...21

Multiplying 2 by two, four

...421

four into two is eight

...8421

sixteen. I put down six with one to carry,

...68421
   1

(Multiplying six by two gives) twelve plus one is thirteen (put down 3), one to carry,

...368421
   1

(Three into two is) six, six plus one is seven,

...7368421

two into seven is fourteen (that is four) with one to carry,

...47368421
   1

(four into 2 is eight) eight plus one is nine,

947368421

and then two into nine that would be eighteen

   8
947368421

... that way, we go on ...

052631578
947368421 (or .05263157894 7368421)

...until the eighteen steps have been done and the answer is before us.

And the whole process is one of multiplication by only one number, two. If we actually had to divide in the usual process, we would take a trial digit and a quotient, multiply the divisor by that trial digit, and then subtract it from here, and so many processes have to be gone through, eighteen steps to the answer. And if one step goes wrong, the whole thing is ruined. And besides, there is multiplication, there is division, and all this work is of several digits and not necessarily the same digit. In fact, generally, it is a different digit. But here, we go on multiplying by two, starting on the right hand side with one. And if there are more than one digits, we carry the excess portion over to the left.

This can also be done in the reverse process. We take one by nineteen. One more than the last digit is two. Now, if we are going in the reverse direction it will be not multiplication by two, but division by two. That is to say, we start with (dividing one by two). One by two, One is not divisible by two, we put down zero...

.0

...one is the remainder left. As in multiplication, we carry to the left, here in division we carry to the right and affix to the left of the quotient obtained immediately before. That one is here (affixed to the left of zero). Ten (divided by two gives) five...

.05

...five divided by two gives two with one as remainder.

.052

...that one is affixed to the left of two, twelve, so that (divided by two) is six...

.0526

Six divided by two gives three; three divided by two gives one, with one to carry. This makes eleven.

.052631

...eleven gives five with one to carry. Then fifteen gives seven again with one to carry. Seventeen gives eight with one to carry which makes eighteen...

.052631578

...and the eighteen gives nine...

.052631578
9

...and we go on in this same way and we get the same answer,

.052631578
947368421 (or, .052631578947368421)

This is a simple division and...(pointing to a different part of the board containing the result previously obtained)... that is a simple multiplication. And multiplication by two there and division by two here.

I have deliberately put these figures in two lines one over the other, because there is another point to be noticed. Here we got the answer by multiplication by two, here by dividing by two. But, if we observe again, we'll find this peculiarity, that these digits (the completed two rows above) all give nine as the total. Zero plus nine, five plus four, two plus seven, six plus three, three plus six, one plus eight, five plus four, seven plus two, eight plus one, all give nine as the total. So that means that even this method may not be applied to eighteen digits. We do half the work, then simply subtracting these numbers from nine, we get the other numbers automatically.

Now, suppose we have to take one by seven (1/7). To apply the rule above we want to have nine as the last digit of the denominator. So, multiply the numerator and the denominator by 7.

7/49

This is the base which we take for calculating the multiplier or the divisor as the case may be. The last digit is nine; the previous digit is four; one more than four is five. So, we multiply by five.

.... 7*

Five into seven is thirty five, three to carry...

.... 57
3

...twenty-five plus three is twenty-eight, two to carry...

.... 857
2

...forty plus two is forty-two (8 × 5 plus the two carried over) ...four to carry...

.... 2857
4

...ten plus four is fourteen, one to carry...

* In every recurring decimal where the equivalent fraction has one as the numerator, the product of the last digit of the denominator and the last digit of the decimal, has nine in its units place. Here 1/7 is the fraction. Its recurring decimal equivalent therefore ends in seven. See Chapter XXVI Vedic Maths.

.... 42357
1

...twenty plus one is twenty-one. I put one, two to carry.

.... 142857
2

This expression will go on repeating itself (so we get)

.... 142857

Those who witnessed what was shown the other day with regard to number nineteen, must have followed it at once. Five is the number by which we multiply.

Now we can divide also and get the same thing. Divide seven by five. It goes once with two to carry.

.1 (The two to carry is 'affixed to the left' of the figure 1, giving 21 as the next term to be divided by five.)

...dividing twenty-one by five, we get four...

.14

..and then two ...

.142

..eight ...

.1428

...five, seven ...

.142857

In this case also, we find ...

.142
857

...one plus eight in nine, four plus five in nine, two plus seven is nine. So, after you have done half the work,* you can stop using this formula and merely take the complements from nine. You can work it out in that way.

And there are other formulae which can be used with regard to other (problems). Any formula can be used with regard to others also. But, the most economic thing would be to use that particular formula which suits the particular case best.

I'll take one by forty-nine as an example.

1/49

* That is when you get denominator minus numerator as the result. [See Vedic Maths. p. 20]

This contains forty-two recurring decimal places in the answer, and forty-two steps of division will be involved according to the ordinary process, the current process. But according to this method, we take one at the end and go on multiplying back by five. Or, we start from here (at the decimal), and go on dividing one by five, and we get all the forty-two digits in the answer. But even that is not necessary. There is a particular case of a particular type which I wish you to note.

When we start here (at the decimal), dividing one by five

.0204

as soon as we reach this, we can stop the work. This comes under another type, Ānurūpyeṇa. This formula applies here. If and when a certain proportion, or ratio is observed, well, you may apply that proportion throughout and carry on without any further help from any other direction. Human beings have their partialities, their hatreds, and their discriminations in favour of one person against another, and so on. But, numbers and mathematical figures have no such partialities, no such partisanship or taking of sides. They behave uniformly. And, as they behave uniformly, we can rely upon them absolutely.

We have zero two and zero four coming up, and the next would be (following in series) zero eight.

.20408

So, that ratio is kept up. And when that ratio is kept up, we can go on the basis of that ratio. How it works and all that is a subject matter for explanation later when I get the chance for it, another opportunity for it. Meantime, I wish you to note, zero two, zero four, zero eight, Well, keep up that proportion. That is to say, it will now be sixteen.

.02040816

and sixteen gives thirty-two; thirty-two gives me sixty-four...

.020408163264

Here I call a halt, because sixty-four will give me one hundred and twenty-eight. And I'am entitled only to two digits there and therefore sixty-four is turned into sixty five.

.020408163265

The one comes over from there (from 128); and the twenty-eight is to be corrected into thirty because the corrected figure (65) has to be doubled. Sixty-five, thirty,...sixty...

.0204081632653060

one hundred and twenty will come from there. I put down sixty-one...

.0204081632653061

...and twenty-two..forty-four, eighty eight...

.0204081632653061224488

...that will become eighty-nine...

.0204081632653061224489

...hundred and seventy-eight will become seventy-nine...

.020408163265306122448979

...and that gives me fifty-eight: and adding.one, that will be fifty-nine...

.02040816326530612244897959

...and then, eighteen, thirty-six, seventy-two...will become seventy-three...

.0204081632653061224489795918367 3

...and that makes forty-six;

.020408163265306122448979591836734 6

...ninety-two gives me ninety-three...

.020408163265306122448979591836734693

This gives us eighty-six which becomes eighty-seven...

.0204081632653061224489795918367346938 7

...then seventy four which becomes seventy-five....

.020408163265306122448979591836734693877 5

Now seventy-five gives fifty which becomes fifty-one...

·020408163265306122448979591836734693877551.

Fifty one gives 02 and the decimal now repeats itself. We stop here.

That's the answer.

Forty-two places of decimals, recurring decimals, worked out, and by merely writing down the digits, and nothing more.

There's another method also, nay, a series of methods by which these questions can be answered. And any type that you find before you, on being recognized, will give you the clue to the particular formula, the particular aphorism, or sūtra that you use.

Now, we take the case of one by seven (1/7) again. Now, with regard to one by seven, suppose we actually begin division according to this method, mentally...

$$7\overline{)1.0} \quad \underline{.1}$$
$$\frac{7}{3}$$

...you'll get three (as a remainder of the first step). Well, this three gives us a clue to another method, proportionate method. What we do is, if one divided by seven gives me the remainder three, one gives three, three must give me nine. It must be in geometrical progression.* I wish you to follow this. It's very simple. The relationship between this** and this first remainder will be carried on all through.

This being one (first result of division, above), we'll put down the remainders in this way. Three is the first remainder....

$$\begin{array}{r} .1 \\ 7\overline{)1.0} \\ \underline{7} \\ 3 \end{array}$$

We need not work out the divisions and find the remainder. Three into (times) three will give nine. But nine is more than the divisor (seven), So, casting off the seven, you'll get two...

3, 2

...two into three gives six...

3, 2, 6

...six into three eighteen; that gives four...
(after subtracting 7 twice)

3, 2, 6, 4

...and four into three is twelve, that gives me five...
(after subtracting seven) five into three is fifteen...

* $\because \quad \frac{\text{Dividend}}{\text{Divisor}} = \text{Quotient} + \text{Remainder}$

Q R

$\therefore \; 3X \; \frac{\text{Dividend}}{\text{Divisor}} = 3Q + 3R$

In actual division, 3R may further be divisible by the Divisor. So only the reduced remainder is taken into account and the proportion is again applied in the same way to this reduced remainder.

** The first dividend which is 1 in this case, and not the first quotient which is also 1.

3, 2, 6, 4, 5

. . .and that gives me one. . , (after subtracting seven from fifteen twice)

3, 2, 6, 4, 5, 1

These are the correct remainders. Now Śeṣāṇyaṅkāni caramеṇa, that is to say, "We multiply these remainders by this last digit"* and the digits of the quotient are to be found. Seven times three is twenty-one. Put down one digit,. . 1...

.1
3 2 6 4 5 1

Don't mind the two (in 21), the last digit is there. Seven times two is fourteen, put down four...

.1 4
3 2 6 4 5 1

Seven into (times) six is forty-two. Put down two...

.1 4 2
3 2 6 4 5 1

Seven into four is twenty-eight. Put down the eight...

.1 4 2 8
3 2 6 4 5 1

Seven into five is thirty-five. Put down five...

.1 4 2 8 5
3 2 6 4 5 1

Seven into one is seven. Put down seven...

.1 4 2 8 5 7
3 2 6 4 5 1 OR .1 4 2 8 3 7.

...and that's the answer. You can write down all the remainders beforehand by this method of geometrical progression. The proportion is kept up, and after that, multiply each of these remainders by this last digit (7), and put down the last digit there. That is correct.

Harder equations

Now we shall take up an example from algebra. Algebra text-books have a portion devoted to questions relating to what are called, "harder simple equations." The chapter is usually headed, "Harder Equations." I'll take an example of that type which is specially marked in the text-books by the authors themselves as

* Last digit in the denominator.

"hard" and generally the instruction is also found in the books that this chapter may not be taken up at the first reading, and may be reserved for a later reading and so on. I do not know about American examinations in American Universities and Colleges, but in India, in almost all the universities, you invariably find a question of this type figuring in the examination paper, and is regarded as "hard." And, what is regarded as the hardest is the easiest, according to this method.

One by x minus seven plus one by x minus nine is equal to one by x minus three plus one by x minus thirteen.

$$\frac{1}{x-7}+\frac{1}{x-9}=\frac{1}{x-3}+\frac{1}{x-13}$$

This is a particular type. And this type of equation is described as "hard." And it's also recommended to be dropped at the first reading. But, if we observe and try to find out the connections between the figures, we find, the total here (total of denominators on one side) and the total here (total of denominators on the other side) are the same. The ordinary method is to transfer one of these (fractions, such as 1/(x-3) to the left, and one of these (fractions, such as 1/(x-7) to the right, so that there might be a plus and a minus on the left hand side and a plus and a minus on the right hand side, a transposition.

And then, several steps are there, eight or nine steps of working. But here, we can give the answer orally by mere mental exercise. Śūnyam sāmya-samuccaye, that is the formula in Sanskrit. And it simply means, "When the total is the same, the total should be equated to zero."*

The total of these (x-7 and x-9) is 2x-16 (left hand side); and the total of these (x-3 and x-13) (right hand side) is also 2x-16. Therefore, 2x-16 is equal to zero; 2x is equal to 16, and "x is equal to 8" is the answer. The whole work has been reduced to mental arithmetic of this type, not merely with regard to small things like this, but even with regard to big multiplications where a lot of labour has to be put in before the result can be had. I give another example of that type.

* "The Vedic Sūtra tells us that if (other elements being equal) the sub-total of the denominators on the L.H.S. and the total on the R.H.S. be the same, then that total is zero." [Vedic Maths. p. 110]

Suppose you have x minus three upon x minus five, whole cubed, is equal to x minus one upon x minus seven.

$$\frac{x-3^3}{x-5} = \frac{x-1}{x-7}$$

Now here, the usual process is to transpose. That means x minus 3 into x minus 3 into x minus 3 into x minus 7, is equal to x minus 5 into x minus 5 into x minus 5 into x minus 1. And expanding both sides, well, you've got four factors on each side. And the expansion of them by the big formula—

$$(x + a)(x + b)(x + c)(x + d)$$
$$= x^4 + (a + b + c + d)x^3$$
$$+ (ab + ac + ad + bc + bd + cd)x^2$$
$$+ (abc + abd + acd + bcd)x$$
$$+ abcd.$$

That's the formula that has to be used. And after all that is done, you'll get your answer, after the seventh or eighth or tenth step, each involving a rather strenuous hard work.

Now, what we do is, we apply this sūtra, where we say, "If the sum total is the same, that sum total should be equated to zero." Now here x-3 cubed, (x-3 to be considered thrice) that means 3x-9, adding x-7, that is 4x-16. Similarly here (right hand side), x-5 cubed (x-5 to be considered thrice) that is 3x-15, and x-1 is 4x-16.* As we get 4x-16 on both sides in this way, 4x-16 equals zero, therefore, x is equal to 4 is the answer; the whole work is over. And, this is also tested and verified in another way.

We took x-3 thrice and x-7 to get 4x-16...x-5 thrice and x-1 to get 4x-16... Well, I'll add the numerator and the denominator and I'll get the same thing.** This is 2x-8 and this is 2x-8. 2x-8 is equal to zero, therefore, x is equal to 4.

* Designating the numerator and denominator of the L.H.S. by N_1 and D_1 respectively, and similarly those of the R.H.S. by N_2 and D_2, we can explain the application of the sūtra as follows:—

$$N_1 + N_1 + N_1 + D_2 = D_1 + D_1 + D_1 + N_2$$

(N_1 and D_1 have been taken thrice as there are three factors on the L.H.S.)

** Here the relationship can be expressed simply as—

$N_1 + D_1 = N_2 + D_2$ (ignoring the cube on L.H.S.)

[For algebraical proof and fuller discussion, see Vedic Maths. p. 118.]

All the work is of this type. We do things mentally. And, the whole work is merely writing down the step digit after digit, and with no explanation of the steps intermediate. And persons who look at myself or a small school boy writing down the answers on the board, well, three hundred and forty digits if necessary, continually writing and wondering where each digit comes from. In fact, I may mention to you the sad fact that I have come to know about two or three cases of persons who had seen some demonstrations of these things by me, and unable to understand bigger things, taking up one or two small things which they could understand, and having exhibitions with gate money and so on. They told the audiences present that by special psychic and spiritual processes of self-control and self-abnegation and starvation and so on, for years and years together...fifteen years living on ground-nuts and water alone (uproarious laughter from audience), that was prescribed by the guru, the preceptor, they acquired control over a particular ghost, and as soon as the sum was written on the top, well, the ghost whispered digit after digit into their ears, and they went on writing on the board. This kind of pretension has also been made, and people have been exploited in that way. The whole thing is so surprising. Where does the next step come from ? The next step is the answer, with all the digits involved in it. And no intermediate step being intelligible to the onlooker unless the secret of it is explained. And the secret is very simple, easy to apply as I said, and easy to remember.

I take another example. x-77 cubed plus x-47 cubed is equal to two into x-62 cubed.

$$(x-77)^3-(x-47)^3=2(x-62)^3$$

The expansion of these three cubes would require enormous labour, and sooner than undergo that labour the examinees give up the whole thing in disgust. Well, x-77 whole cubed, x-47 whole cubed...But this 'comes under the particular type governed by the above-mentioned sūtra. x-77 and x-47 that is 2x-124; and here is 2(x-62) or 2x-124 And therefore, the formula applies here; x-62 is equal to zero; x is equal to 62.

This kind of work we have all through in all the various departments.

I'll just take an elementary example from analytical geometry and close for today. On another occasion, I will go into more difficult and more advanced portions dealing with hyperbola, conjugate hyperbola, asymptotes, and so on. Just now, I take one example of a simple type from an earlier portion of analytical geometry.

To find the equation of a straight line passing through two points whose coordinates are:—

(9.7) (7.4)

What is the equation of a straight line joining these two.. a straight line upon which these two points lie. Well, the ordinary method is one in which you say, y is equal to mx plus c. That is the general equation of the straight line.

$y = mx + c$

And then, substitute, 7 is equal to 9m plus c . . .

$7 = 9m + c$

and 4 is equal to 7m plus c . . . . .

$4 = 7m + c$

These are simultaneous equations in mx and c. Find out the value of m, find out the value of c, then apply the m and c to the equation $y = mx + c$, and then transpose, remove fractions, do all sorts of gymnastics (ripple of laughter).

Now the way in which we do it is simple. Parâvartya yojayet.* That is this formula. All that we do is, we put it down in the ultimate shape of ax plus by is equal to c. That is to say, we have x with a certain coefficient and y with a certain coefficient, and the sum is equal to the independent term to come on the right hand side. Now, "the product of the means minus the product of the extremes" will be the right value of the independent term c.

The points are (9,7) and (7,4). We'll put down the answer in one step. Fortynine minus thirtysix, that is thirteen.

("means", 7×7)—("extremes", 9×4)

$49 - 36 = 13$

And the coefficient of x is the difference in y coordinates. That

* See Vedic Maths-Chapter XXXIX.

is 3. And the coefficient of y is the difference in the x coordinates-2.*

$3x-2y=13$

And that is the answer.

We check, twentyseven minus fourteen is thirteen. And twentyone minus eight is thirteen. This thirteen is arrived at in three ways, by substituting nine, seven.... substituting seven, four, and also by the product of the means minus the product of the extremes. And we put down the answer immediately.

On another occasion, if it will be convenient to arrange for it, I'll take up other examples from other portions of mathematics, other subjects of mathematics. For the present, we'll stop here today.

> (The transcriber was present at this mathematical discourse. Immediately following the end of the demonstration, one student was heard to ask his friend beside him, "what do you think ?" His friend's reply, "Fantastic !")

* To evaluate the coefficients the deductions have to be made in the following order:—

↑9 , 7 , | Coefficient of X=7—4=3
| 7 , 4 , ↓ Coefficient of Y=7—9=-2.

XIII KARMA AND OTHER PATHS OF YOGA

Discourse in the Humanities Building of University of California at Los Angeles, February 20, 1958.

Universal goal

Friends,

It is a matter of universal experience that although we human beings and all sentient beings have differences of physical capacity, intellectual acumen, and views and ideals and ideologies and so forth, yet we are all, according to our own inner ideas and conceptions, right or wrong, in pursuit of something which we seek as the goal, the objective to be reached at the end of all of our activities. From time to time, we go in for various kinds of activities. And none of these can be without a purpose. It's quite possible that a person does something with a subconscious motive, but the motive is always there, whether he is conscious of it or not. And very little introspective analysis will be quite sufficient for the purpose of determining for ourselves what the objective of human beings like us is. No doubt, there are differences of views with regard to the means for attaining our goal. We have differences of opinion, and not merely differences of opinion, perhaps, positively antagonistic views altogether, as regards what should be done in order to achieve our purpose. But as regards the goal itself, as regards the objective itself, there can be no manner of doubt, and there can be no difference of opinion at all. That goal is the goal of happiness, physical, mental, moral, spiritual, and all round. We desire to avoid misery and we desire to enjoy happiness all through. It may be that owing to differences, defects in our mode of thinking, owing to our negligence in taking into account all the necessary facts and factors of situation, we may commit errors. And as a consequence of these errors, we may, from time to time, increase the misery that we have been deploring, and lessen the choices, the chances of joy and happiness which we have been seeking. That is quite possible. But, so far as the object is concerned, the objective is concerned, there is no doubt whatsoever that we all desire to live on, live for ever if possible, and to live happy lives. That is the goal.

The whole question is with regard to the path.

Even with regard to this goal, we sometimes find exceptions. There are cases of suicide. Some people are unable to bear the sufferings which they are called upon to endure, and think of suicide as an easy way out of their difficulties. But even then, it is because of circumstances beyond their control, and not because of their own instinctive desire, that they commit suicide. And it will be noted that coroners or juries, in the verdict they pass in such cases, whatever the other circumstances may be, they invariably say, committed suicide in a fit of insanity. Not wishing to live on and not wishing to live happily, these are not at all imaginable. There must have been at least a temporary out-break of what you might call, an insane mood that was responsible for the suicide. It is not natural. And therefore, the coroners and juries give this kind of verdict, "committed suicide while of unsound mind." That invariably accompanies the description of the suicide as the cause of the death.

So then, as there is no question of any difference of opinion with regard to our goal, the next thing that we have to consider is the adoption of the right method, considering all the facts and factors of the situation, weighing the pros and cons, and forming conclusions that will be calculated to carry us on as individuals and as members of society to higher and higher reaches, step by step, of happiness. We are on different rungs of the ladder of material prosperity, spiritual advancement. and so forth, and we naturally try to better our position as we go along, and not to worsen it. At any rate, if we can't better our position, we wish at least to retain what we have already obtained. So that is the position with regard to the goal.

Three paths

And as regards the means for the attainment of happiness, here as well as hereafter, well, there are three well-known paths. We speak of them in Indian Vedic literature as Karma Yoga,

Bhakti Yoga and Jñāna Yoga. There are corresponding paths in the Western system, in the Christian system also. The Lord Jesus Christ himself refers to the three paths. And we find that his evangelists, his apostles, who carried out the task of diffusing of Christian knowledge, diffusing of the Christian example, of the Christian teachings and so forth amongst the people, followed one or more of these three paths. Generally we find, in all institutions, in all religious philosophical systems, that the founder himself has not made any distinction of a serious character between one or another of the paths, but in the next generation itself, which is a matter of historical experience, we find that the evangelists who carry on the mission, who carry on the message of the Master, seem to confine themselves to one or more of the alternatives, and do not take all the three of them into consideration as being of equal importance.

For example, in the Bible we have the Lord himself giving his advice on all the three paths. We do not find that the Lord has made any distinction with regard to the emphasis to be laid thereon, any distinction between this or that particular path. All the three paths, in the different contexts, have equal importance. And the exact circumstances in each person's case will have to be considered on the intrinsic merits. And the decision as to which of the three paths would be the prepondering element in a particular person's case, is a question, not of elimination of one or more of the paths, but of harmonizing all of them. And in the harmonizing of the three paths, well, there will be differences of proportion. What you might call, for example, differences of proportion in chemical compounds and so forth. For example, in elementary chemistry, we talk of several oxides of nitrogen, N_2O, NO, N_2O_3, NO_2, N_2O_5, NO_3, nitrous oxide, nitric oxide, nitrous anhydride, nitrogen peroxide, nitric anhydride, and nitrogen trioxide. The component parts, the elements, are the same, nitrogen and oxygen. The proportion varies. And according to the varying proportion, we find differences in the qualities, the consequences, the therapeutic properties so to say, of the different compounds. Similarly here. We find all the three paths emphasized. But as to which one particularly suits us, will be a matter of decision on the intrinsic merits of each case, and there can be no mechanical rule about it. But all the three are necessary. There is no doubt about that either.

We find St. Peter and St. James, stressing the Karma Yoga path, the path of works, more than the other two. And St. John, who is described as a favourite disciple of the Lord himself, pays more attention to the path of faith, devotion, and self-surrender. "The Lord is Love."* In a small verse of only three words, we find him describing God as love. Not as a loving person or full of love and so on, but God is equated with love as such.

And then we have for example St. Paul, who represents the third path, Jñāna Mārga or the Jñāna Kāṇḍa, as we call it, that in which one absolutely transcends all emotions of an exciting and agitated character. A person who transcends all sorrows, anger, prejudices, prepossessions, and so on, and keeps himself absolutely under control, never loses his balance, even under the onslaught of a number of physical, financial, and other troubles, a person of that type is said to be a Jñānī, a jīvanmukta, or a person who has received spiritual illumination, and is incapable of being dragged down or dragged out of that solemn peaceful attitude at all times in all places and under all circumstances.**

Inclination or capacity of the student determines the path for him

Now, when we have these kinds of three paths, and the three paths stressed in different proportions, a question naturally arises for the enquirer as to what is the right path for himself. In the great majority of cases, with regard to worldly people, with regard to persons under worldly limitations of various types, we would say that the emphasis laid on one path more than another by a certain particular teacher must be due to his own personal equation, his personal idiosyncracy and so on. But with regard to persons of the type that we are dealing with here, the saints, the sages, the seers, well, it cannot be said that they had any particular idiosyncracy

* First Epistle General of John IV-8,16.

** See Gītā II-55-58, which describe person who have attained equanimity.

in favour of this or that particular line and any prejudice against the other two and so forth. That cannot be a satisfactory explanation. The explanation in such cases would seem to be, naturally, that the difference of the spiritual level, the intellectual calibre, the physical capacity and so forth of the student himself, was responsible for the difference in the approach of the teacher. I frequently give the example of doctors prescribing for different patients under different conditions. We have, for example, a doctor prescribing a saltless diet for a heart patient, and another doctor prescribing a sugarless diet for a diabetes patient. Now, from this very fact that the two are giving different prescriptions, are giving different medicines, and imposing different diet restrictions and so forth, we will not be justified in arguing that they belong to different schools, to opposite schools of thought, and that they must go on, as if they were heads of two different religions, two different denominations, and must fight out the matter to the finish and so on. In all such cases of difference in the treatment, we say that the difference is not due to anything subjective in the mind of the doctor, but something objective in the condition of the patient. If a certain element in, the physical constitution ought to be there and is found in deficit well, the doctor will see that that defect is remedied; the deficiency is supplied. And where there is something in excess that ought to be eliminated, the doctor will prescribe accordingly.

So, this kind of explanation is the one which we would naturally expect to have. And this is textually, in categorical terms, mentioned in the Vedic and other scriptures of India. We do not find a similar kind of disquisition and discussion of the subject in the New Testament or in any other scripture or any other book, but the inference is the same, namely, that the exigencies and requirements of the particular patient in question, not a physical patient, but an intellectual, moral, and spiritual patient, well, are responsible for the kind of treatment that is prescribed for that particular patient.

Now then, we start with the idea that the three Mārgas, the three paths, are necessary. Sincerity of heart, faith, devotion, are there as the qualifying attributes to start with. And then, secondly, in the actual doing of the various deeds that we decide to perform, that we are enjoined or advised to perform, there should be a clear and balanced judgment. No prejudices and prepossessions, no kind of closed mind should stand in the way of our realization of the right method. That is to say, our vision should not be distorted and our judgment consequently cannot be warped. That should be the starting point of us. In going into any inquiry of this type, we shall have to start with clear minds, with no partialities, hatreds, and so forth, in fact, with open minds. And, whatever direction the light may come from, the right advice may come from, we should welcome it and we should be incapable of bigoted fanatical exclusion of something before hand. *A priori* reasoning is out of the question. It won't help us arrive at correct judgments and take proper decisions.

In this way if we approach the matter, there is no question of any trouble at all or any quarrel. All the differences that cause so much trouble between religion and religion, between denomination and denomination, sect and sect, sub-sect and sub-sect, even in the same sub-sect and so on, all these differences and conflicts arise because people do not pay proper attention to this aspect of the matter. For their own conviction, for their own satisfaction, people go through various textbooks, study various other things, and probably study the historical background and so on, and according to their physical and intellectual capacity, their inclination, their tastes and so on, come to a certain conclusion. But although that kind of conclusion is perhaps justified under those circumstances, there can be no justification for such persons imposing their conclusion upon others and insisting that the others should follow the same path and accept the same position as they have accepted. All persons should give others the same right to think for themselves and decide for themselves according to their own tastes, their own inclinations, their own capacities, and so forth, and should not dictatorially, dogmatically impose any thing on the others, especially in matters relating to faith.

I speak of matters relating to faith for this reason, that even with regard to the external physical world which we can sense with our sense organs, that is, organs through which we can see hear, smell, touch, and taste, even with regard to things which are said to be purely objective, and which do not come from the inside of our brain, and are not connected with temperamental and other idiosyncracies, but have an independent existence of their own on what you may call a positive, materialistic, and scientific basis, even with regard to these things, oneness of opinion, uniformity of opinion, is not to be found at all. Differences are inevitable.

In an art gallery, for example, in an exhibition of art, we find a painting adored, eulogized in superlative terms by a great artist. Another artist of similar authority and prestige in the art world, says, "It's all rubbish; it is not even elementary drawing." That kind of, not mere difference of opinion, but extreme difference of opinion, is possible, even with regard to a matter which we can decide with our eyes. But the eyes do not give the same evidence They do not give us the same assessment of the value, the importance, the beauty or the ugliness and so forth, of the painting before us. Similarly with regard to music, what is most enchanting, fascinating and melodious to me is detested by another person. And the converse is also true. This kind of thing goes on with regard to touch, with regard to smell with regard to taste. Our tastes differ. "bhinnarucir hi lokaḥ."* All the differences arise because of differences of inclination, of tendencies, of bent of mind, of angles of vision, and so on, and not due to any difference within the thing in itself.

Similarly in the courts of law we have very puzzling experience from time to time. Two judges not in two different courts, one a lower court, the other an appellate court, but two judges on the same bench, in the same Supreme Court, listen to the same evidence, go over the same documentary evidence, hear the same arguments, and are guided by the same code of law, and yet they come to dissenting conclusions. They are not always of the same opinion. And then, when there is a dissenting judgment, the case has to be heard by a third judge or has to pass through some other such device, as has been provided in the Constitution, for expediting the processes of judicial decision.

So even with regard to such things where the human intellect and the human sense organs are supposed to be sufficient for the purpose of assessing the value of things before them, there is difference of opinion and personal element is responsible for

* Kālidāsa in Raghuvaṃśa (VI-30)

it. In fact, if I put it into the language of optics, I would say, our eyes, I'm not speaking of only the physical eyes, even the mental eyes, are not all reflecting mirrors. Most of them are refracting lenses. And therefore, the differences arise, not from any objective difference in the thing in itself, but on account of the subjective condition of the eyes with which we see. Similarly, with regard to all matters, we find a tremendous difference and that difference is inevitable. If we grant that, well, that cuts away the whole ground of all possibility of conflict in the name of religion and religion, because when even with regard to these physical objects, which we're sure about from the evidence of our physical senses, there is such tremendous difference of opinion, much more therefore must it be impossible to have oneness, and uniformity, mechanical uniformity of opinion, with regard to things which relate to future worlds, to the life after death and so on.

As regards life after death, well, there are many persons who do not even believe that there is such a thing as continuation of life after death, the immortality of the soul, the continual existence of the soul after the death, after the shuffling of the mortal coil. And, that they do not believe in it is not due to any perversity on their part, but because, with the material before them they have not been able to understand and accept the doctrine. With regard to students in school and college and so forth, the same difficulty comes up. Students who are unable to progress in a certain subject and who go on failing in it, well, turn to some other subjects, and there, they find themselves to be brilliant successes. Well, all persons' brains, all persons' intellects are not capable of going into and mastering every subject. Each one has his own particular inclination and bent, and along with it, his capacity or potentiality for progressing and achieving success in the particular line, also differs.

Harmonious blending of the three paths

So then, we have no real ground for a quarrel in the name of this or that sect, in the name of the karmakāṇḍa, bhaktikāṇḍa, or Jñānakāṇḍa. All that we can say is that there should be a proper harmonizing of the three paths, because all the three are required in every case. The proportion, the ratio of one ingredient or the other, that's a different question. But, all the three are necessary. And that is why, in regard to this question of the Karma Yoga, the Bhakti Yoga, and the Jñāna Yoga, in the very first verse of the seventh chapter of the Gītā,* we have Śrī Kṛṣṇa saying to his disciple Arjuna, "the three paths are to be taken together." Bhakti, that is, faith and devotion, must be there; sincerity and purity of heart are necessary, along with proper judgment, acumen, capacity to rise above possibilities of agitations and excitements which warp our mind and distort our judgment. Well, all these possibilities should be avoided. That is the Jñānakāṇḍa. And then, we are to perform the karma, the duty which is ours according to the various circumstances under which we have been placed. Different circumstances, different combinations of circumstances are responsible for different duties being imposed upon us, not by the scriptures but even by requirements of social order and mutual relationships of friendship, cordiality, and so forth. Society is based upon a proper adjustment of conceptions of duties, and actual performance of duties, and therefore, there should be no question of a quarrel at all.

Now, the question to be taken up first is about the Karma Yoga, and that, in view of its being the subject of the discourse here, is of importance on the intrinsic merits itself, because there is generally a tendency at the present day to emphasize one or other of the other two paths, Bhakti or Jñāna, and to pooh-pooh, ridicule, or at least make light of, if not absolutely ignore what we call the Karma Yoga, that is, the path of works, the path of performance of duty, duty for its own sake, irrespect-

* Mayyāsaktamanāḥ Pārtha yogam yuñjan madāśrayaḥ,
Asamśayam samagram mām yathā jñāsyasi tac chṛṇu.

Gītā VII-1.

"Arjuna now hear the way you can, by attaching your mind to me, by taking refuge in me and by practising yoga, you shall surely and completely know Me".

Here the words 'mayyāsaktamanāḥ' and 'madāśrayaḥ' denote the path of devotion. 'Yogam yuñjan' stand for karma or path of works while "mām jñāsyasi" signify path of knowledge.

In fact sincere adherence to any one of the paths will, in time, lead to the other two.

ive of profit and loss, victory and defeat, and so on. We perform our duty because it is our duty. And as regards the fruits of action, they are for the Giver of the fruits, for God Himself to decide. We perform our duty with all sincerity of heart. That is all that can be demanded of us, all that is possible of us. This is the proposition, with which we have to start. It is the starting point.

Now, a person may be doing enormous work. He does not thereby become a Karma Yogī of the type that our scriptures indicate. Well, if the whole thing is for pomp and paraphernalia, if it is for show, if it is not sincere, if it is not from the heart, then, we find the scriptures of all the religions in the world condemning such a person as a hypocrite, as an imposter, as a cheat, and nothing more. We are told that purity of heart is essential. "Blessed are the pure in heart for they shall see God."* That is Christ's own injunction in the "Sermon on the mount." We find expressions like this coming up again and again, "Blessed are the meek for they shall inherit the earth."** Everywhere you find sincerity portrayed as an essential prerequisite for any Karma, before any action performed by us can be regarded as right.

Well, the temporal masters who are not omniscient, who cannot look within our hearts and see what is going on within them, well, they may really be cheated by all kinds of show, by all kinds of pageantry, all kinds of pomp and paraphernalia, but the All-Knowing, the All-Powerful, the All-Pervading, the All-Permeating Creator and Protector of the universe, cannot be bamboozled in that way. Therefore, any action which savours of hypocrisy, however efficient the action may in itself be, however splendid it may seem to be, is meaningless as a path to salvation, as a means to the obtainment of eternal welfare in the life after death.

Now, when scientists and philosophers are themselves not unanimously agreed with regard to the existence of the soul, the existence of God and lives after death and so forth, it is not possible for us to expect any kind of uniformity with regard to

* St Matthew V-8.

** St Matthew V-5.

religious theological doctrine, dogma, and so forth. All that can be done is that, with sincerity of heart, we should do what we can in obedience to the highest light that we have received. We must be loyal to the light that we already have. And, in a passage, Carlyle says, "know the duty, do the duty, which lies nearest to thy hand; thy next duty will already have become clearer." Similarly, if we are loyal, faithful to the light, the light that we have received, then, the path will clear out for further light, further illumination on the path for the performance of our next higher duty.

Religions do not conflict

So that is the line that is followed, and we find, not merely the scriptures of this or that particular religion but of all the religions, emphasizing this purity of heart, sincerity, as the essential prerequisite before anything else can be considered. We have for example, in the Indian scriptures,

Dharmam yo bādhaṭe dharmaḥ
na sa dharmaḥ kudaharma tat,
Avirodhī tu yo dharmaḥ
sa dharma iti niścayaḥ.

"Any religion which comes into conflict with other religions is not a real religion, it is pseudo-religion. And, a religion which not merely lives alongside of another religion in a merely passive or neutral manner, but in actual, active, strenuous, and whole-hearted cooperation and coordination, that is true religion." There is harmony between religion and religion, the essence being truth and sincerity—not subjective truth, because subjective truth is a matter of individual faith. Great philosophers, and scientists are not agreed upon these questions. And in the ultimate result, in the last analysis, you will find, a Christian, a Hindu, or any person who believes in religion, who believes in the existence of God, who believes in the continual existence of the individual soul, giving explanations as to how he has come to have his faith in these existences, the existence of God, man, soul, and so on. He will give you philosophical and scientific explanations for a lot of things, but, the whole gap cannot be bridged. There is at least one small point left unproved. It may be one in a hundred. It may be one in ten thousand. There will be at least one small point which has to be covered by faith. "That is what I believe." After discussion with ourselves, we reach a certain point upto which we say, "we both agree." And then, as to the particular theory, the particular theorem, the particular dogma, by which we wish to bridge the gap, well, that is a matter of individual faith. And in matters relating to faith, there can be no compulsion at all. So, that's the line that is taken in the Gītā.

And in the Gītā, we find Śrī Kṛṣṇa saying again and again, "Those who believe in and adore other deities with sincerity of heart and absolute purity of mind, well even they worship Me."* There is no question there at all of consigning to eternal hell all persons who belong to a different religion or even a different sub-sect of one's own religion. All that is said is, "with sincerity of heart". A person believes, and acts according to that belief. Then he is eligible for salvation. There is no question of race or tribe or caste or nationality and so forth, on account of which one person is eligible and another person has no chance of entry and so on. We do not find any such thing at all countenanced anywhere in the Indian scriptures.

Similarly, in the Bible, you will find the same point emphasized again and again. This is true not only of the New Testament portion of the Bible, but even of the Old Testament where people will generally admit, a harsher line has been adopted with regard to punishments and we find, "Vengeance is mine, saith the Lord"** or words to that effect. God punishing severely and soon, that kind of idea is to be found constantly in the Old Testament. Even there, you find the four major prophets and twelve minor prophets of Israel thundering their denunciations against people leading hypocritical lives. Even there, you will find that the question is not one of what particular belief the person has, but what his particular conduct is in terms of sincerity, in terms of purity, in terms of loyalty to the

* Ye (a) pyanya-devatā-bhaktā
yajante śraddhayānvitāḥ
te (a) pi māmeva Kaunteya
yajanty-avidhi-pūrvakam.
Gītā IX-23.

** See Deuteronomy--XXXII-35.

truth as he understands it, as he himself believes it. A person who is ignorant, of course, finds extenuation because of ignorance, because of defective intellectual power and so forth. He has been unable to understand something. He is not punished for the ignorance, for the incapacity to understand. But if, knowing the facts, he deliberately, suppresses the facts, deliberately proves himself disloyal to the truth as he himself knows it, then he is condemned and is eligible for punishment. That is the kind of attitude you find taken by all. So the bhakti portion, the śraddhā portion, the faith portion, is there all the time as the prerequisite of right action.

Path of Knowledge

And then, in the second place, we have to go into the other part, namely, the Jñānakāṇḍa part of it. Karmakāṇḍa goes with Bhaktikāṇḍa and Jñānakāṇḍa. The Jñānakāṇḍa portion tells us that without prejudices and prepossessions of any type, without being excited or agitated because of personal relationships and so forth, as a result of calm and cool thinking, we should arrive at conclusions, and follow them. That is the right attitude, and a proper description of a person who has attained illumination, who has transcended all the defects of a personal character, defects which are responsible for warping our judgment, for exciting us, and making us do things on the spur of the moment, in the heat of the moment as it is called, and doing things which we afterwards deplore with bitter tears when it is too late. That is the next prerequisite. That is to say, with sincerity and purity of heart, but using all our capacity, intellectual, educational, and so forth, we should arrive at right conclusions. There should be no partisanship about it, no kind of taking sides with this or that party, but absolutely being amenable to the truth, welcoming the truth from whatever corner, from whatever direction it may come.

We have a beautiful couplet in Sanskrit which says,

Yuktiyuktam vaco grāhyam
bālād api śukād api,
Yuktihīnam vacas tyājyam
vṛddhād api Śukād api.

Here there is a pun on the word, "Śuka." Śuka on the one hand means a parrot; on the other hand, it means a famous saint who was known as Śuka Deva. He was a great seer, a sage of the same type as St. Francis of Assisi in the history of Christianity. Well, we are told, with regard to the way in which we should deal with such matters, keeping open minds and not closed ones, not being impervious to the truth on account of partisanship, but welcoming the truth from all sides. This beautiful śloka means "What is consistent with right reasoning ought to be accepted, even though proceeding from a small boy or from a parrot. And what is inconsistent with right reasoning ought to be rejected. even though it emanates from an old man or from the saint, Śuka Deva himself." Truth is the criterion. And that truth is not accessible to all. We are not able to arrive at the truth. As I was saying, judges spending lots of time and energy in trying to find out the actual facts as regards the guilt or innocence of an accused person, arrive at different conclusions. I'm not talking of corrupt persons who abuse their positions as magistrates, judges, and so on, bowing to subterranean influences of various kinds. I'm talking of sincere people. earnest, conscientious in the performance of their duty. They feel compelled to arrive at dissenting judgments. And that is unavoidable. But so far as sincerity is concerned, there is no excuse; no extenuation. If in sincerity we lag behind what we profess to be, all the show that we make of our religion is useless. And that is why we find Christ again and again condemning the Sadducees and Pharisees. They had lots of outer imposing rituals and ceremonials, like praying in the street corners loudly and with all sorts of paraphernalia to show off their religiousness, not religiousness, but religiosity. They were not religious people, but religiose people showing off their religiousness. Christ condemns them. In the Bhagavad Gītā too, we have,

Aśraddhayā hutam dattam
tapas taptam kṛtam ca yat,
Asad ity ucyate Pārtha
na ca tat pretya no iha.*

* Gītā XVII-28. (Also see Footnote 2, p. 141)

The same kind of expression is there. So then, this is the second part of it.

Why Karma?

And with these two on hand, sincerity of heart on the one side, and dispassionate judgment, dispassionate contemplation, meditation, cogitation, all the things that are necessary for arriving at the truth.

Śrotavyo mantavyo nididhyāsitavaḥ.*

We are told again and again that there are three steps for the attainment of truth, for the visualization of God, self-realization, and so on. And those three are translated by me into simple English, with three phrases, each phrase having an adverb and a predicate — "Investigate carefully ; decide correctly; and follow faithfully." That is laid down. And that means that with the aid of these two, the bhaktikāṇḍa and the jñānakāṇḍa, we go in for the karmakāṇḍa. Here, the first question that crops up from the hostile critic is, "Why should there be any performance of this or that duty ? There is purity of heart and there's an earnest attempt to find out things for ourselves. Well, that is sufficient. Why should there be any karmakāṇḍa at all ?" The answer is very simple. With all the sincerity in the world with all the Jñāna, the transcendent calmness and coolness, the wise man, the illumined soul, has still a great deal of practical responsibility from the realistic standpoint in regard to the karmakāṇḍa. The law of cause and effect, which is the root-foundation for the theory of karma, of Karma Yoga that we have, is one in which there are two aspects, one a moral aspect, and another a mechanical aspect. If a person, ignorantly touches a leaking wire, while standing on the floor, and is electrocuted, well, it will not do for us to say, "What sin did he commit ? He was a man of good character. He did not commit theft; he did not commit adultery; he did not tell even a lie. He was a very good man, a very sincere man, a man of purity of heart, and earnestness, and conscientiousness, and so on. Why should he have been punished in this way ?" With regard to all these things there are two aspects. We speak of a result as punishment in certain cases, we

* Bṛhadāraṇyaka Upaniṣad II-4-5.

don't speak of it as punishment in certain other cases at all. The scientist tells us that Nature is as relentless in the case of a deliberate sin as in the case of an ignorant blunder. It doesn't make any difference so far as the mechanical consequences go. In the criminal courts, a judge is often called upon to decide whether a certain accused person has actually committed the murder or not. The evidence makes it clear, the documentary or rather oral evidence makes it clear that the accused person had done a cold-blooded, premeditated murder of the most agonizing and torturing kind. And the man is sentenced to the highest possible sentence available according to the law. There is a second case of another person who did not premeditate the murder, there was no such idea at all, but who, on the spur of the moment, in the excitement of the moment, forgot himself altogether and attacked the other man in such a way as to cause his death. And the judgment is that it is not cold-blooded premeditated murder but only culpable homicide not amounting to murder. Of course it is homicide. It is culpable. It is an offense punishable, but not amounting to direct murder. So, there is the second kind of judgment. And a third kind in which a person in self-defense, defense of property, and so on, attacks the attacker and kills him, the attacker in the process. There we get a third kind of judgment. "That was a case of justifiable murder in self-defense." There are the three different kinds of homicide because of the different motives. The moral side is different in the three cases. But so far as the mechanical result is concerned, the dead man is equally dead in all the three cases. There is no question of any smaller proportion of death in the case where it was not premeditated, and absolutely no death at all where it was in self-defense. So, there are two aspects of the matter. And if a person, calling himself a holy person, calling himself a man of Bhakti and of Jñāna, neglects the interests of society, neglects his responsibility in this way, well, that means that he is causing society to go into chaos. There can be no possibility of an ordered life within the community. Within the society things go on already haphazard owing to several conflicting factors and if persons who claim to be bhaktas and jñānis, devotees and illumined souls, if they are irresponsible and if they don't perform their duties properly, well, the natural result falls upon the community as such. Therefore, the karmakāṇḍa is necessary. It comes there because of the law of cause and effect. We are responsible for whatever we do. There is no tree which comes into existence without the seed of which it is the tree. The seed gets the necessary soil, the manure, the ploughing, and all the other various things necessary, the rain, artificial or natural irrigation and grows into a tree. If all the circumstances necessary are there in proper combination, we have the result. Suppose a person wanting to plant a fruit garden plants, sows various other seeds, but does not deliberately sow a mango seed. If he finds mango tree growing in his garden, he will not be justified in saying, "I planted no mango seed; no one else planted mango seed; and yet, the tree has arisen." That would be false. That would be wrong, botanically wrong, scientifically wrong. Well, all that he can say is, "I'm not aware of any person having done it; I did not myself consciously do it; well, the seed may have fallen from perhaps the mouth of a passing bird and found the proper soil, the proper manure; the proper water, and so on, and sprouted into this shape." That's the inference. So, all actions have their consequences. And all inactions, too, have their consequences. And therefore, the Karma Yogi has to perform his duty as a member of the society, and as an individual also. He has duties to perform for his own sake. If a person is not concerned about his duties, it augurs a deficiency, a deficiency of a serious nature, a blot upon his character. And to that extent, his progress upon his spiritual ladder is bound to be retarded. And even apart from his own progress, his own welfare here and hereafter, there is this other consideration I've already mentioned, namely, his duty to society. Society is bound by certain regulations and these regulations are not definite. And if from time to time the question of motive will have to come in, the moral question will also have to be taken into account in every case, well, that would lead to chaos. Judges find it difficult to find out the motive. And even with regard to cases where the judge is morally certain of his decision, sometimes he is doubtful whether some other explanation might not suit the particular case, and then, the benefit of the doubt is given to the accused. The judge is morally convinced about the guilt of the man and yet he lets him go free because of a little element of doubt. The responsibility comes in. And we can't shirk responsibility by saying that we are pure in heart, our motive is sincere, and therefore, whatever wrong we do, we shall escape the consequences. No. That doesn't count. That is not logical. Well, the Karma Yoga comes in that way.

Sukhaduḥkhe same kṛtvā lābhālābhau jayājayau.*

Essence of karmayoga

"Irrespective of considerations of conquest and defeat, profit and loss," and so on, we perform our duty because it is our duty. In that way lies, not merely the uplift of the individual, but also the welfare of society. We enable ourselves to become instruments of world welfare. And there can be no better purpose than that. But if a person does not take that high view, does not think of the matter from that sublime standpoint, if he says, "I'm not concerned with the welfare of others. I'm concerned with myself and my own welfare and nothing further matters to me, even then, it is necessary for him as a member of society to do things in the right way, because otherwise, the society suffers. And if the society suffers, he too suffers along with the rest of them. If we make others happy, we make ourselves happy in that very process by a natural reaction. And from every standpoint, not merely the philanthropists', that's the highest of course, even from the selfish standpoint of one's own gain, it is desirable that we should have benevolent ideas, and carry out those benevolent ideas as far into actual practice as we possibly can.

There is an English proverb which says "Honesty is the best policy." From the view point of the intrinsic merits on the moral plane, honesty of course is the only thing possible. There is no question of "best policy," and so on. But even from the standpoint of policy, the lower angle of vision of mere policy for profit's sake and so forth, we are told, honesty pays in the long run, and therefore, honesty is the best policy. But, of course, I would add a corollary that a man who is not honest at heart, but honest merely for the sake of policy, is not an honest man.

Now, that is the relationship between the three. We have to perform the various karmas leading to the various results which

* Gītā II-38.

we wish to have as individuals and as members of society. But that Karma Yoga is useless unless there is purity of heart behind it. And, it will not merely be useless, it will be positively injurious to society if proper judgment is not exercised, if the brains, such as we have, are not used in the proper way, and conclusions are not drawn of the right character. We will be doing harm to society. This is the relationship between the three paths. And Karma Yoga, in combination with Bhakti Yoga and Jñāna Yoga, is the ideal. There is no question of harmonizing the three. People come and ask, "How can we harmonize the three paths?" The answer is, the harmony is already there. All that we have got to do is to recognize that harmony and profit by it.

I want to conclude by praying to the All-Mighty for the necessary light to all persons, in matters of this type. And I also appeal to all of you to think of questions from the standpoint that I have been placing before you today, so that your own welfare may be ensured, and you may also become instrumental in bringing about the welfare of other persons.

World welfare through world peace, and so on, that is the noblest of ideal which can motivate any person. And that is the kind of ideal, that is the kind of ideology which I would recommend to all of you. In the light of this, think on questions, and act accordingly in your daily life from moment to moment.

XIV T.V. INTERVIEW

Interview by Mr. Hank Weaver on "The Hank Weaver Show", February 21, 1958. KABC Television, Los Angeles, 11 p.m. to midnight.

Mr. Weaver : This is National Brotherhood week and I think perhaps this is as good a time as any to go over and talk to this gentleman. Now, tonight we have with us, the privilege of conversing with one of the most important but least known personages in the world today. His actions and words dictate the thinking of millions of Hindus. But because he preaches only peace and cooperation, he is seldom heard in our Western world. This week has been set aside as National Brotherhood Week, and certainly no personage exemplifies the feeling of oneness than our guest His Holiness Jagadguru Śaṅkarācārya. Your Holiness, do you mind if I sit down for a few moments to talk to you ?

First of all, I might explain that he is eighty-two years of age.* The robes he wears are three shades of orange called ochre** in India and signify that he has renounced the world. Is that true Sir ?

His Holiness : It's not a question of renouncing of the world, but enlarging our world, and having the whole world as our own family whose interest we should look after.

H.W. Your Holiness, I would like to ask you something now, you've had a little difficulty with your eyes. Do you find the light uncomfortable ? Are you comfortable ?

* Dates of events in the pre-samnyāsa life of His Holiness are not correctly known. The samnyāsa rules prohibit discussion of personal life specially pre-samnyāsa life. His Holiness used to regard the date of taking samnyāsa as the date of his birth (new birth). From the information given in the article 'My Beloved Gurudeva' (by Smt. Manjulā Devī Trivedī one of the closest disciples of His Holiness, who also accompanied him on his American tour) given in the introductory portions of the book, it is seen that His Holiness was 74 when he visited America in 1958.

**Kāṣāya or Gairika (red chalk).

H.H. Fairly.

H.W. Fairly. May I ask you how long the Śaṅkarācārya religious order has been in existence ?

H.H. There is no separate Śaṅkarācārya religious order. The origin of the order is from the Vedas themselves. Śaṅkarācārya was only a reviver who came and reestablished the religion.

H.W. What was the reason for founding this order when there are already established sects ?

H.H. There was a decadence in the followers of the Vedic Religion and the Lord Buddha came to restore Hinduism to its original purity. Buddhism was not antagonistic to Hinduism, but was a revival of Hinduism. And in course of time when the followers of the Buddhist faith, well, went off the track, then Śaṅkarācārya came to revive the old religious faith of the Vedas and the Buddha.

H.W. I understand that you're the first leader of your religious order ever to visit our country.

H.H. That's correct.

H.W. Is there any reason for your choosing this particular time to come to these United States ?

H.H. World conditions, with regard to war and peace are such that I felt it most opportune and necessary for me to bring India's message, the Vedic message, of peace and good will and, as far as possibie, contribute toward the prevention of war.

H.W. What part do you feel India can play in a preventive move against war ?

H.H. In explaining to the people concerned that there is no antagonism inherent between religion and religion, that all religions have a basic and fundamental oneness and solidarity which covers almost all points of differences, and only unimportant external rituals and things of that type need differ.

H.W. We've read much about conflict between the Moslems and the Hindus in your country. Is this because of any basic differences in their religious beliefs ? And what is being done to alleviate this situation ?

H.H. People of other religions came to India. They came to settle down as peaceful citizens of India, and were welcomed, accommodated, and looked after. For example, the Parsees and the Christians had their earliest colony there in India. But the

Mussalmans came, not as peaceful citizens, with the desire to follow their own method of worship in India. They came as conquerors and all the conflict between the Hindus and the Mussalmans was of a political nature and had never anything to do with religious differences.

H.W. Extreme poverty of the masses has always been a major problem in India. Is there anything being done in the concepts of your philosophy to raise the standard of living for your people ?

H.H. Well, we regard religion as a practical utility in so far as it is full of beneficent intentions and philanthropic activities for the benefit of humanity as such. And where there is neglect of any such rules and principles of the religion and its traditions, attempts are being now made to restore the balance by bringing the people to the right point of view and to understand their duties in this direction.

H.W. I understand that you are the founder-president of the World Reconstruction Association. Could you tell us what the principles and aims of this organization are ?

H.H. The principles and aims are the same as I've indicated just now, namely, the uplifting of humanity all round in all respects, physical, material, moral, spiritual, economic, and in all respects.

H.W. Can the World Reconstruction Association be compatible with Communism ?

H.H. They have nothing in common.

H. W. Well, today one hears nothing but satellites, rockets, H-Bombs. What are your thoughts about our deep concern about such materialistic projects?

H. H. We don't make much distinction at all. In fact, any distinction, whatsoever between the spiritual life and the material life is uncalled for. The material and spiritual aspects of life are inter-twisted together, they are combined, and inextricably intertwined. And all that is necessary for the uplift of human beings as such is included. In fact, according to our scriptures, all the various branches of science are integral parts of the Vedic culture, of the Vedic religious study.

H. W. Do you think we Americans devote too much thought and attention to "things that money can buy" and money itself ?

H. H. I can say nothing about individuals but so far as Americans as such are concerned, the statement cannot find support from historical facts. The Pilgrim Fathers, Washington, and so on, and the whole history of the United States does suffice to refute such an imputation.

H. W. Speaking of Washington, tomorrow's Washington's birthday. As a student, do you believe Washington would have found himself a great man, a big man today such as he found himself in his niche in history, some few hundred years ago?

H. H. I should like the question to be repeated.

H. W. Do you think Washington could have attained the greatness and the prominence in history today, that he received and accomplished so many years ago?

H. H. He continues to have the same kind of historical importance, and should have greater and greater importance in future as ideas become more and more clarified in the minds of people, without any kind of prejudices, political and so forth.

H. W. I understand that His Holiness is an outstanding mathematician. And from your years of study of ancient scriptures, I believe you've formulated several new mathematical concepts. May I ask whether these discoveries of yours are in practical use yet?

H. H. They are of the utmost importance, for four hundred, five hundred steps of working necessary at the present time according to the present method are saved, and answers for big mathematical problems can be had in a line or two of working alone, and it was only yesterday, I began giving my blackboard demonstrations here, by way of specimen samples and illustrations of the way the mathematical sūtras, aphorisms, of the Vedas, help us to solve these problems.

H. W. I believe that was at Cal Tech?

H. H. Yes. It was in the California Technological Institute.

H. W. Your Holiness pardon me, Sir, were you going to say something?

H. H. It was a select audience of specialists in mathematics and the physical sciences, and the first demonstration was a very impressive one. And they expressed tremendous wonder at the ease with which difficult problems involving a huge number of steps of working can be condensed into one-line answers.

H. W. How can mathematics be applied to the future? Do you feel that we are just arriving at a mathematical age?

H. H. All the sciences are of importance. And mathematical computations become necessary, not only with regard to the study of astronomy, but with regard to ordinary agricultural and other productions also. Mathematics is of all-round utility.

H. W. Do you feel that all religions are basically the same?

H. H. I believe they're not merely basically the same, but even with regard to, well, plenty of details there is not merely basic unity, but a basic oneness and solidarity which is most astonishing in view of the fact that people have been always thinking that they're antagonistic inherently.

H. W. Many of our Western religions believe firmly in converting members of other faiths by use of missionaries. Do you advocate this procedure with your own group?

H. H. I've always been against the idea of proselytizing people by methods of this type. Differences of opinion there may be. And these differences are inevitable so long as it is a matter of faith. And in matters of faith, the individual's personal equation, or personal idiosyncracy will be responsible for the particular line which he prefers, because it is more congenial to him than the others. And, there can only be a change of heart in the direction of cooperation and coordination between people of different religions and there can be no possibility of having a complete uniformity of opinion on any question whatsoever in the name of religion, denomination, sect, or sub-sect.

H. W. Do you feel that there's any conflict between religion and science?

H. H. Religion and science, so far as we are concerned, have never been in conflict. Every branch of science is an integral part of our Vedic lore. If you want, I can give fuller details of that also.

H. W. Would you please?

H.H. Yes. In the first Veda, the Ṛg Veda, that we call the first part of the Vedas, the sacred scriptures, we have anatomy, physiology, hygiene, sanitary science, medicine and surgery, as the component parts, the ingredients of the system which we call the Āyurveda. In the second part, we have Dhanur Veda which means archery and other military sciences. And in the third part is included Gāndharva Veda, which is the science and art of music. And the fourth part, includes what is called Sthâpatya Veda, which covers all branches of mathematics, astronomy, engineering, architecture and so forth. These subjects, which are supposed to be purely secular, are integral parts of our spiritual education. There is no conflict between religion and science in any respect whatsoever.

H. W. Your Holiness, as a student, philosopher, historian, mathematician, what do you think is the immediate future of the world from a general political and economic sense, with the conflict between what has been established as East and West, on the political basis, not so much from geographical?

H. H. I do not believe in any distinction of "East" and "West". East and West are terms which we use in an ordinary common parlance, when a place can be described as west of what is east of it, and conversely. There is no such thing as "East" and "West" because the earth is globular and the sun travels from the east to the west, or from "west" to "east". This makes the position clear, that there is no such thing as West at all. We don't believe in that difference even on political basis.

H. W. Well, do you believe that in the next few decades to come we can avert a war?

H. H. It depends upon ourselves, and the earnestness with which we pursue our path of peace. There is nothing difficult about it. And if there is the willingness to do it, I think the way can be very easily found. People will have to make it their chief purpose, to see that war is averted and peace is preserved. There can be no question at all of the necessity, the actual utility, and so forth. It is absolutely necessary for the survival of the human race that there should be peace. Especially with present day conditions, when science has equipped us with lethal weapons of a much more dangerous character than in the past. It is absolutely necessary and not merely desirable, that there should be absolute peace between country and country, and matters of difference could be settled by cordial, internal cooperation and consultation, and not with arbitrament of war.

H. W. Do you feel that science should be diverted into more peaceful measures immediately, or do you think that it's right for us to continue to experiment with nuclear weapons?

H. H. Well, nuclear weapons are there, and the facts of nature are there to be taken into account. But, the more and more we use the nuclear power for the constructive purposes of nation-building, the better it will be for humanity. And the less and less we use these instruments for mutual destruction, the better it will be for the world all round.

H. W. One closing question, your Holiness, do you feel that people the world over should revert back to religion more than we do today, and study it more seriously than we have in the past, and are doing, regardless of faith? Do you feel that the salvation of the world lies within religion, or just a philosophy between men?

H. H. Religion, in a technical sense, is not what we are after. The spiritual Spirit behind, is the chief thing. And fundamental principles behind the spiritual Spirit, as I have called it, is the feeling of oneness and solidarity. No question arises of excluding any person or persons, any tribe, any race, any nation, and so forth, from the possibility of salvation. And there is no question of deciding these matters except on the merits of an ethical consideration.

H. W. I would, before thanking you sir, just point out that His Holiness will be giving lectures in this area, and as a matter of fact, in the near future, at the Wilshire Ebell Theatre, at 8 p. m., Sunday, February 23, this coming Sunday at the Wilshire Ebell Theatre. If I don't pronounce your name correctly, please forgive me, Jagadguru Śaṅkarācārya. And His Holiness will be speaking at the Wilshire Ebell Theatre at 8 p. m., Sunday, February 23rd. And what is the subject Sir?

H. H. "Basic Unity of All Religions."

H. W. I thank you, Your Holiness, for coming out on a cold night to share your thinking with us. Thank you, sir.

XV VEDIC METAPHYSICS AND ADVAITA

Discourse at Stanford University before a gathering of the Students of Professor Spiegelberg, Associate Professor of India Civilizations — students of Philosophy & Comparative Religion — February 16, 1958.

Friends,

It is the common and universal experience of all of us, whether intellectually great, philosophically learned or not, and irrespective of the factors which might be taken into consideration with regard to the outlook, the angle of vision, and so forth, of individual thinkers, that we all have felt, in fact there can be no person who at some time or another has not felt within his own mind, within his own intellect, these questions coming up and pressing for an answer, "What am I ? Where have I come from ? Whither shall I go ? What are these other beings that I am seeing ? And what is the nature of the phenomenal world which I am seeing around me ?"

Well, every person does not have the necessary inclination, taste, and capacity for going into these questions at great length and arriving at a satisfactory decision on the matter. Very few people can actually do that, and do actually do that. But that does not mean that the questions don't arise in the minds of others. These questions, this series of questions, are such which every mind asks itself. The learned man, the philosopher is the person who tackles the question all through, goes through it, analyses every aspect, every conceivable part of it, and is not satisfied until he gets a satisfactory answer. And the man in the street, the common man, hasn't got the time or the capacity for it, and soon gives up the attempt. That's all the difference. The questions are those which are unshirkable, which naturally come to every mind.

Metaphysics is not difficult

Well, our attitude towards these questions is of great importance because the approach itself makes a tremendous difference. Somehow or the other, rightly or wrongly, and in my view wrongly, the impression is abroad that philosophy and especially metaphysics is a difficult subject. We approach the subject with this preconceived notion; that the subject is very difficult, it is beyond the ordinary intellects of the ordinary common mass of humanity. And therefore, with this prejudice in our mind beforehand, with our minds closed as it were, against receptivity and investigation and so forth, well, we find ourselves handicapped. The subject itself has got the label, "Difficult." And it is a splendid example of what the English proverb means when it says, "Give a dog a bad name and hang him" for having a bad name. We start with the idea that philosophy and metaphysics are too abstruse, too recondite for us, and therefore, we shirk their study.

External Information not necessary for Metaphysical discussion

As a matter of fact, I have to start by saying, that whole question is the easiest possible one and it ought to be so for all minds, even for minds with very poor erudition and things of that type as their equipment. As a matter of fact, from my standpoint, philosophy should be the easiest, the pleasantest, and the smoothest of all studies, for the simple reason that in philosophy we are not dependent upon information from outside. Information from outside may help us in our study but that is not the basis on which the whole thing is built up. And that is not the foundation. In fact, our study does not depend upon anything from outside.

By way of comparison, in order to make the position clear as I have just explained it, I would give you the examples of other subjects. Take up any subject you like whatsoever. History, geography, physics, chemistry, biology, botany, zoology, anatomy, physiology, any subject whatsoever, and compare the position with regard to the study of metaphysics. Let us for example start with the case of history.

We are told in our books, the school and college text books of history, that William the Conqueror, invaded England in 1066 A.D., and by winning the Battle of Hastings, became the king of England in succession to Harold the Second. Now, I ask you a simple question which probably you have not been asking yourself. I wish you to consider that question as the starting point of this enquiry. Is there anything in the world by which one can know independently that William the Conqueror came to England in 1066, and not in 1433 ? In 1485, Henry the Tudor, Henry the VII, the first of the Tudor Kings, won the battle of Bosworth Field and became the King of England. Well, the only information that I get is from my teacher or from my textbook of history. Have I anything by way of evidence, by way of convincing proof, that the statement made there is the correct one ? Is there any method by which I can get at that answer without taking on trust things that people have told us ? It is bad enough that in matters of non-controversial character there is this difficulty, that there is no independent method by which I can arrive at a certain decision with regard to the correctness or inaccuracy of the statement made to me, and taken in trust by me. It is bad enough. But where controversial matters come up, you find even the so-called books of authentic history confusing. They are misleading. For example, the war between England and France, the fighting between Protestants and Roman Catholics and so on. In all these matters you will find, the representation as claimed to be historical, well, suffers from the handicap that other considerations come in, that irrevelant factors as I regard them, come in to distort our vision and warp our judgment.

Take the case of Queen Mary who was known as Bloody Mary amongst the Protestants, and Queen Elizabeth. The trouble was between Roman Catholics and the Protestants. There was the Spanish Inquisition. In all these cases the books of History differ. The accounts given are very different. And in most places you will find that the result (of war) is the thing that determines the whole approach, not the intrinsic merits.

Now, let us take the example of William Wallace and Robert Bruce. They were Scottish heroes who fought for the independence of Scotland. William Wallace was a Scot, and he was beheaded as a traitor to England. His head was hung up as a warning to all those who were treacherous to England, who would oppose England. And William Wallace passed away. His spiritual and political successor, Robert Bruce, won the battle of Bannockburn, made Scotland free, and he is today recognized as the liberator of Scotland.

The same thing is with regard to George Washington here. You know the story of George Washington very well. As citizens of America, you know about the historical background and so forth. If, like William Wallace, Washington had been captured, he would have gone the same way that William Wallace did. He would have been described as a traitor to the British crown, and he would therefore have been hanged. But he succeeded, And nothing succeeds like success. That is what goes on in the world. We judge by results. Not on the intrinsic merits, or the rightness or wrongness of a cause. The cause that has survived is supposed to be, ipso facto, the right thing. That is the short and simple method, by which we assess spiritual and other values. That is how things go on in the world.

Now what I mean is that the histories of the different nations are before us and we take things for granted. But the histories themselves are written from different standpoints. And there is a lot of admixture of, I would not say falsehoods, but inaccuracies, or in Churchill's language, "terminological inexactitudes" where we expect accurate records of history. That kind of thing is there.

Similarly, with regard to geography. Well, is there any reason why that particular country should have been named this or that ? What about Serbia, Montenegro* and other countries which used to figure in our maps in the past ? I suppose there are few people here who would be able to recognize those old names. Things go on changing. And therefore, there is no intellectual process, no process of head or heart of any kind whatsoever by which we can assure ourselves that we have the actual historical record before us, that we are believing what actually happened and that we are not misled by what we have heard from others, or read from others. That position is there.

The same is true with regard even to chemistry and other such positive sciences. Zinc and sulphuric acid produce zinc sulphate and hydrogen. Hydrogen is released. We take that from the textbook and from actual experience. But even that actual experience

* Serbia and Montenegro both are since 1919 part of Yugoslavia.

is not one which has any independent authority of its own. If the next time trouble arises, a difficulty arises, well, we either have to remember what we got by heart, what we crammed to put it bluntly, in the past. And perhaps, if we have not remembered the thing, we go again and do it. Upon full investigation again the experiment gives us results which we tabulate and which we rely upon. This is the kind of thing that happens with regard to every study in the world. But the study of metaphysics, the study of philosophy including metaphysics as its chief part, as its chief ingredient, is a study in which we don't depend upon external material at all. It is not because so and so said it. It is not because so and so wrote it. But because, in answer to our own questions, our own head and heart give us the reply.

Metaphysics examines internal information

We ask ourselves, we ask our hearts, our minds, our intellects, "O heart, O mind, O intellect, what is it you want ? What is it you seek ? What is the objective, the goal you are after ? In all the things that you are doing, so actively and so strenuously in the worldly life, what is the purpose, what is the goal to be reached ? And the answer is not by consulting Professor Roscoe or Professor Chalmers or this or that author. The answer is, "I seek to be happy."

Well, that doesn't need any kind of corroboration, any kind of external evidence from others. What is it you want ? I wish to be happy. And I wish to avoid all sorts of unhappiness. And the answer is based on what our own inner experience tells us from moment to moment. There is no question of any alteration. "We have gone so far and then we'll have to make further experimental researches into the matter to find out what is the truth." That's not the case at all. From moment to moment we get the same answer. And not merely I or you or this or that particular individual, but every individual can ask himself that question, and the answer comes. The quest is for happiness, and for the means which will help to attain happiness, joy.

In the Vedānta, in our Indian metaphysics, we speak of Sat, Cit, Ānanda. These are words that are not merely learned by us parrot-like from outside, but words which convey to us the confirmation of the feelings within ourselves, the aspirations within ourselves. And when we are talking about the Vedānta, about the goal of life and the path to that goal and so on, we have, as the givers of evidence, as the deciding factors, what our own minds, our own intellects, our own hearts tell us.

So from this standpoint, that we can rely upon the evidence, the relevant facts and factors of the situation that we have before us, that is a tremendous advantage in our study of philosophy and metaphysics, and which is not to be found in the case of the study of any other subject whatsoever.

Internal evidence sufficient

So, this is the first point that I would like to stress; namely that the philosophical study which we generally shun as being too high, metaphysical, transcendental, and this and that, that philosophical study is the most natural study for ourselves. We are going on with it unconsciously. A person who has not analyzed his feelings and does not know what exactly he wishes to obtain, well, even he will acknowledge, if he did not himself originally of his own initiative feel it, he will at least recognize, the correctness of the statement that his own internal evidence is all that is necessary. And that is how philosophy, comes in. And when we begin to study philosophy, well. if there is anything which goes against our own heart's and head's views on the matter, we at once say, "Oh, this is ridiculous. This may have been all right in connection with that particular saint or that other particular author, that lecturer, this preacher, and so on, but that does not fit in with what I myself feel on the matter." So, you have got this standard, this touch-stone, this criterion, by which you can judge for yourself whether you are on the right track or not. Some new material is placed before you, and that material appeals to you, to your intellect independently, (and) not because someone has said it. Of course, the case of those who believe and who have faith in that particular author and so forth, is a different one. But for the person who is an inquirer, who wants to find out the truth for himself, and is unwilling to take things on trust, for such a person, well, metaphysics has a kind of unique feature which you will not find in any other subject whatsoever.

Indian Philosophy and Religion, not in Conflict

So this is the first thing we start with. And the second thing is that our theology and our philosophy, I'm talking about India, and Vedic, Sanātana dharma, Vedanta philosophy. Well, that philosophy and our religion have no kind of possible conflict or clash. That's the second point which I would like to place before you in your consideration of Indian philosophy, or Hindu philosophy if you like to put it that way. The point is simply this. With regard to other religions, you do not find the theology and the philosophy going together. The philosophical side is for a few persons and can be found in a few books, but not in the regular literature of the religion itself. In the theological literature itself you will not find much of philosophy. Well, I can understand the explanation and I believe the explanation that that state of affairs is due to historical circumstances of an inevitable character which rendered such a case absolutely unavoidable. The results of the theological discussions and philosophical introspection have been given by the founders of religions to their disciples as rules to be followed, as formulae to be acted upon. And therefore, in the texts themselves, in the sacred liturgy itself, you will not find much philosophy, and in some cases you will find no philosophy at all. The philosophers are different and the theologians are different. And very often they have been at loggerheads. Theologians and philosophers were at loggerheads with each other and philosophers and theologians were at loggerheads with scientists. Friction of this sort continued in the name of religion. There was a time when, in the Western world, science was being persecuted. The case of Galileo and others is in point. You will find that in the history of the relationship between the Church and science in the Western world, there was continual clash, and the natural result was that the scientists when they came into power, when they began to be recognized as authorities in intellectual matters, turned the tables on religion, but of course, did not persecute the religionists in the same way that the scientists had been previously persecuted in the name of religion. But pooh-poohing and ridiculing the elementary ideas about the existence of God, the existence of the soul, and so on, that was a natural result which actually ensued.

Reason, the sole arbiter

But here, in the Indian philosophical system, we have this other unique feature, namely, that there is no question of a closed mind. There is no question of formulae which have decided the matter once and for all, and never to be reopened.

Yuktiyuktam vaco grāhyam
bālād api śukād api,
Yuktihīnam vacas tyājyam
vṛddhād api Śukād api.

Here is a pun on the word, "Śuka". On the one hand, the word śuka in Sanskrit means a parrot. And it is also the name of a great sage, Śuka the son of Veda-Vyāsa. And the text says—"What is consistent with right reasoning, ought to be accepted, even though proceeding from a small boy or even from a parrot (śuka) and what is inconsistent with right reasoning ought to be rejected even though emanating from an old man or the saint Śuka-Deva himself."

There is no question of any barrier to investigation. Investigation is encouraged everywhere. Our philosophy is an integral part of the religious literature. The Vedas, the general name given to the sacred literature, include the Vedānta, the Upaniṣads. The portion relating to metaphysics is an integral part of our sacred literature. It is not a separate entity by itself at all. And in the Vedānta, we are told the methods by which we should arrive at correct knowledge, or the facts relating to God's existence, to our individual souls, and to the universe around us. Paramātmā, Jīvātmā, and Jagat, these are the three technical terms we use in Sanskrit. Well, with regard to this our position is very simple and clear. "Accept the truth." And in the Vedānta, in the Upaniṣads, we are told of three steps for the attainment of correct knowledge, Brahma Jñāna, Ātma Jñāna where we are told, "Śrotavyo mantavyo nididhyāsitavyaḥ.* I translate these three Sanskrit words into English with three phrases, each containing an adverb and a verb. "Investigate carefully, decide correctly, and follow faithfully." These are the three steps be-

* Bṛhadāraṇyaka Upaniṣad II-4-5.

fore us for the attainment of the goal, for the acquiring of that knowledge which leads to mokṣa. Mokṣa means emancipation from all bondage. There is no conflict between one branch of education, one branch of learning and any other branch whatsoever.

Secular sciences and Vedas

Not merely is this the case with regard to theology and philosophy. It is the case also with regard to philosophy and theology as against what we call the modern positive sciences. Even there we have this great advantage, namely, that there is no quarrel between the two. On the contrary, every branch of material science, what we would call secular knowledge — in the present day terminology in English we speak of secular knowledge. "This is purely spiritual and this is purely secular" — well, what we call secular knowledge, every branch thereof, is an integral part of the Vedic learning. Such is not the case with regard to the sciences and the religious literature of the various peoples of the Western world. That has been the trouble all the time. We have never had a quarrel. We have what are called the Upavedas; the Ṛg Veda, the first Veda, has what we call the Āyurveda. The name (Veda) itself will show that it is part of religious literature, Vedic literature. And what is Āyurveda? Āyurveda is a complete harmonized combination of anatomy, physiology, hygiene, sanitory science, medical science, surgery, and all other branches relating to the cure of minds and bodies. The second Veda, Yajurveda has what is called the Dhanur Veda, archery and other military sciences. And the third, the Sāma Veda has what is called the Gāndharva Veda. In the Gāndharva Veda we have the science and art of music. And in the Atharva Veda, the fourth, we have what is called Sthāpatya-Veda. And that Sthāpatya-Veda includes all branches of mathematical learning, engineering, architecture, and so on. I have myself had the privilege of studying some of the Atharva Veda sutras in connection with astronomy, finding therein sixteen sutras which apply to and cover every branch of mathematics. And the sixteen sutras are sufficient for the purpose of getting the answer readily to any mathematical problem in any line whatsoever, problems requiring twentyeight, forty, or nine hundred and forty-two steps of working according to the present system, can be readily solved in one line, the answers being written down continually without any intermediate steps whatsoever. I've done it for years now in India. And I've begun doing it here already. And people are surprised, not surprized, amazed at the whole thing, because little children, whom I've taught these formulae, they look at a question written on the blackboard before them, and from the body of the hall they shout out the answers. And if we take the answer page from the book from which the question was taken, the answer is correct, four hundred and forty-five decimal places, recurring decimal places, and the answer exactly correct.

Well, when I mention this, it will necessarily be difficult for the hearers to believe it, but the actual experience will convince people in that way. We have got that material also. I'm only mentioning it by way of illustration.

Common sense and scriptural authority

Similar is the case with regard to chemistry, with regard to biology, with regard to all the various positive sciences as we call them, the modern sciences, as we call them, speaking of them as purely secular knowledge. Well, with regard to all of these, we have this position, that, the Vedas, our religious scriptures, include these as integral parts of their own. The spirit of inquiry, the Jijñāsā, "investigate carefully, decide correctly, and follow faithfully," that injunction is there, easy for us to follow because any independent thinking is not at all banned as being sacrilegious, blasphemous, and so forth, as indicating want of faith in the saints, in the authors of the scriptures, and so on, as is the case with regard to other systems. Our philosophy has this great advantage, that it marches side by side with theology and with science. And anything which is not testable by scientific illustrative examples and experience, goes out of court altogether. We find Śaṅkara himself saying that if any text came into conflict with common sense reasoning based on actual experience, it automatically goes out of court, so far as that particular thing is concerned.*

* Following passages convey this idea:-
(i) Jñānam tu pramāṇajanyam. Pramāṇam ca yathābhūta-vastuviṣayam.

Well, I'm not aware of a similar statement with regard to any other system of thought. Not with a view to criticism, to finding fault, or picking holes, but as a student of religion, as an earnest seeker after the truth, I have been trying to find out for myself what is the actual teaching in the various scriptures of the world, and I have always found that this attitude of receptivity to the truth is not there. We don't accept something merely because some such authority, as we hold unquestionable, has told us that. Well, that such an authority, with such vast experience, and such capabilities, and potentialities for intellectual disquisition has mentioned it, is not proof of the correctness of the view. Well, it is something favourable no doubt, it means simply that the balance of probability is on the side of the authority. But that itself does not prove the statement of the authority. The authority has to justify itself before, well, what I might call the Supreme Court of Reason. Reason is there—'Yukti yuktam vaco grāhyam'. In all places you will find that. Two passages may seem to be of a conflicting character, and both are from the Vedas; -- I use the word 'seem' very guardedly, I'll explain why. If two passages from the same Veda, equally

Ato jñānam kartum akartum anyathā vā kartum aśakyam. Kevalam vastutantram, na codanātantram.

[Śankara's commentary on Brahma Sūtra I-1-4.]

"Knowledge is born of evidence, and evidence depends on the things as they actually are. Therefore, knowledge cannot be artificially created, destroyed or varied. It only depends on facts and not on injunctions of scriptures."

(ii) Pratyakṣādi-pramāṇānupalabdhe hi viṣaye agnihotrādi-sādhyasādhana sambandhe śruteḥ prāmāṇyam na pratyakṣādiviṣaye. Adṛṣṭadarśanārthatvāt prāmāṇyasya.

[Śankara's commentary on Gita XVIII-66]

"The scope of scriptural testimony is restricted to subjects not covered by direct perception etc, like sacrifices, their means and objects. The purpose of scriptural testimony is to explain subjects not open to perception etc."

(iii) nahi śrutiśatam api śītaḥ agniḥ aprakāśo vā bruvat prāmāṇyam upaiti. [Ibid.]

"Not even a hundred scriptures, declaring fire to be cold or not shining, can give valid knowledge."

authoritative, are before us, and one is consistent with the common sense experience that we have, and the other is not, the former is accepted and the latter is to be rejected so far as that particular point is concerned. Now, the Vedānta will tell you that there is no such passage, in which on account of inherent, hostile purpose or inner antagonism and so forth something will have to be rejected.* It will only mean that there has been misrepresentation of it, a misunderstanding of its application, some principle which was all right but which has been wrongly applied, misapplied or not properly applied. Anyhow, that should be the explanation for it. And we always say, as between these two passages, although the formal external superficial meanings seem to be of a hostile character mutually, yet, such and such passage will necessarily have to be subordinated to the other one and its meaning will have to be interpreted in a different way. That kind of criterion for arriving at decisions is also there.†

We have this system. And with this preliminary, I believe I can go now freely into the next subject which I wish to take up as regards the Vedānta itself, and Śankara's Vedānta in particular.

Śāṅkara Vedānta

With regard to Śaṅkara's Vedānta, well, we have been told again and again that Śankara's Vedānta represents a school of thought which doesn't agree with our own experience. That is the first objection many people take. And with regard to the character of the individual soul, they say, the features, the pro-

* First of the four parts of the Brahma Sūtra is named 'Samanvayādhyāya' and is devoted to bringing out complete harmony of seemingly divergent passages from Upaniṣads.

† Yadi brūyat sītaḥ agniḥ aprakāśo vā iti athāpi arthāntaram śruteh vivaksitam kalpyam prāmāṇyānyathānupapatteḥ. Na tu pramāṇāntaraviruddham svavacanviruddham vā.

[From Commentary of Śaṅkara on Gitā 18-66.]

"If the scriptures say, "Fire is cold or not shining," it should be assumed that a different meaning is intended because it cannot be validated otherwise. The interpretation should not contradict other sources of knowledge or another passage of the scriptures."

perties of the individual soul as depicted in the Vedānta do not agree with our own experience. Well if this were true, well, it would be a paramount consideration for me, and it would mean my rejection of Śaṅkara's doctrine. But as a matter of fact, that is not the case. Superficial thinking, want of deep thinking, has been responsible for that feeling about the Advaita system. The system of Absolute Monism, as inculcated by the Lord Śaṅkara as the right interpretation of the Vedas, well has not been properly understood and all the trouble has arisen because of that. Let me take a simple example. In the Advaita Vedānta, we are told again and again that Ātman, the individual soul, is—Saccidānada-svarūpa — Sat svarūpa, Cit svarūpa, Ānanda svarūpa.* And these words have been carefully defined. In our system, we define each particular object or term correctly so that there will be no misunderstanding of the meaning; the talkers, the discussers, the debaters, use it in the same sense. Quarrel arises owing to misunderstanding of what the other man is saying. And at the end of the fight we find that our views were the same all the time. And because of difference of language, we were misunderstanding each other and fighting with each other. As with a person who did not know that a dozen meant twelve, and said, "No, I have not received twelve copies of this book, I've received only a dozen or I've not received a dozen copies, I've received only twelve." That kind of thing is ridiculous, but it very often happens in life.

Now we have another instance of a still more ridiculous character which I can place before you. Suppose there are two people fighting about a certain bottle, one saying, "This bottle is half full," and the other saying, "It is half empty." Should they fight, saying that they're making statements of exactly an antagonistic character, when the meaning is the same? Well, with regard to Vedānta, with regard to all metaphysics of all countries and all climes and times, there is this difficulty, that words of a technical character have been used without a proper definition.

Now I take up merely by way of illustration the nature of the individual soul in respect of happiness and misery.

* Sat means being; Cit, sentience; and ānanda, peace or joy.

Joy

The texts* tell us, "Ānanda svarūpa". The Ātman, the individual soul is of the nature of joy. Note ssentially joy or a large percentage of joy, but absolute joy, without the least little admixture of any kind of unhappiness. That is Ānandasvarūpa. Not enjoyer of happiness but Happiness itself. For example, as we have in St. John's Epistle, with regard to God, "God is love."† Not God loves, or should be loved, but God is love. Similarly, we are told here, Sat svarūpa, is continual existence. That is to say, past, present, and future have no meaning, have no difference at all with regard to what is eternally existing, what was, is, and will ever be. And then Cit svarūpa, that is absolute illumination, Jñāna svarūpa. And thirdly we have what we call the Ānanda svarūpa, that is, absolute joy.

Now, this third statement, well, all statements in general, and this third statement in particular, would seem, from a superficial look, from an outside look, to go, against our own actual experience. In the actual experience, we say we are going through so many sorrows and sufferings all the time. And what little of happiness we get is only a small percentage out of all of our experiences, and therefore, people say in general, Paramātman, that is God, is Ānanda svarūpa, is endless ineffable immeasurable unapproachable joy, whereas, the Jivātman, the individnal ātmā, or the individual soul within each particular body, is not Ānanda svarūpa. It is duḥkha-svarūpa, duhkḥamaya. And all the grammatical explanations** are there to show that it is not absolute joy, but greater percentage of unhappiness than joy that we have in our actual experience. How can these two be reconciled? The question comes up. And, as I was mentioning earlier, our not clarifying our words, defining them properly, is the cause of the trouble.

Meaning of inherent property

When we speak of the ānanda as the inherent property, the natural, inevitable, unchangeable inside of the quality, which you

*"Ātmānandamayaḥ"...Taittiriya Upaniṣad [II-5]
"Raso vai saḥ etc.".. Taittirīya Upaniṣad [II-7]
"Vijñānam ānandam" Brahma"...Bṛhadāraṇyaka Upaniṣad [III-9-28]
†First Epistle General of John IV-8, 16.
** Tat prakṛtavacane mayat (Aṣṭādhyāyī V-4-21]

associate with a thing, we should make our definition clear. The definition is clear by taking the example, for instance, of a quantity of hot water. A question is asked, "Which is the natural property of water, heat or cold?" Śaityam hi yat sā prakṛtir jalasya.* The text tells us that not heat, but cold is the natural property of water. How do you say that ? We have in our experience, the experience of hot water as well as cold water, and both these qualities are associated with water, and therefore, we may say, both properties are properties of water. Occasionally, both come to the surface and are experienced and both are equally the properties of water. That would be the ordinary, normal, superficial objection to it. But if we go a little deeper down into the question as to what we mean by properties, the thing is cleared up at once. What do we mean by properties? With regard to properties of solids, liquids, and gases, in physics and chemistry, properties of sulphuric acid, of hydrocyanic acid, and so on, colour, taste, this and that, all are mentioned. And finally we are told, such and such are the properties of such and such chemical substance. Well, let us take the case of water and consider it carefully.

If a person comes across for the first time some sulphur springs, hot springs, where the water in a tank or a river is hot, he asks the question, "Why is this water so hot?" That very question, "Why?" shows that water does not have the normal property of heat. Hot water requires an explanation. And the explanation is always forthcoming—the sun's rays, fire underneath, sulphur springs and so on. There is some reason or the other why the water is hot. And secondly, there is another part also to be considered, and that is, if you keep a quantity of highly boiled water, and carefully try to preserve the warmth by thermo-flasks and so on, well, you find that gradually the heat goes on decreasing until at last it dies out altogether. Now, this is what we should not call a property of water. It comes from an external cause. And for going away it does not need an external cause, the

The suffix "maya" is also used to denote abundance. Grammatically 'duḥkhamaya' will, thus, mean 'abounding in misery'.

* A passage from Kālidāsa's Raghuvaṁśa (V-14) which has become almost a proverb in Sanskrit.

mere flux of time is sufficient to throw out the outsider that has come in for the moment, for a short time, and owing to external causes of the moment. Similarly, with regard to various other things in life. We see for example, gilt, brass rod, or electrical gold, chemical gold, Canadian Gold. All sorts of imitation gold are there. And you make it, the seeming gold, shine like burnished gold, and you keep it carefully away from dust and dirt. Even then it naturally reverts to its original dirty colour. Why? Because that burnished lustre that you saw was not its own property, it was something which came from outside owing to external causes of the moment.

Now, this distinction between what is a real property and what is merely a passing feature, a feature caused by something temporary from outside, and bound to go of itself in due course, this distinction must be carefully studied before we can arrive at a right conclusion.

Now take the case of fire and of heat. If the heat has gone on diminishing and diminishing until at last it has gone out altogether, you say the fire has gone out. You don't say the heat has gone out, but the fire still remains. But with regard to the water, the matter is different. When the heat went out, you did not say the water has gone out, you said the heat has gone out. You are distinguishing between the passing feature, heat, and the actual substance, namely, water. The two are different. Similarly, here. This method of judging things, I think, will be quite sufficient for us to answer most of the problems relating to Advaita, that is, Monism and self-realization.

In the case of the heat of the hot water, the question arises, "Why is this water hot?" And there is always an answer. Similarly here with regard to sorrow, the question always arises in the same way. We see a person coming in front of us weeping. Well, we ask him "Why?" "What is the matter?" If it were his normal property, internal property, what we call 'lakṣaṇa' in Sanskrit, then the question would not arise at all. There would be no surprise and no question would be asked. But the question is actually asked, "Why are you crying?" And there always is an answer — headache, toothache, "somebody hit me," "I lost money," "some person died." All these possibilities are there. Something happened on account of which the sorrow began.

That is all. That is not the normal condition. And here too, the second part applies equally. The sorrow may have been caused by a blow, a shock, a loss, which you thought you would be incapable of enduring, and yet, what you find is that on the second day, the agony, the torture, the sorrow is not so keen as it was on the first day. Like the heat of the hot water, the sorrow goes on diminishing and diminishing until, at last, a time comes when you have forgotten the person for whom you mourned and mourned so bitterly. That means again that sorrow is not an inherent property of the individual. It comes through external causes of the moment and it departs by mere efflux of time.

Well, this is only by way of illustration. We jump to conclusions based upon insufficient data and still more insufficient argumentation. Superficiality is responsible for that. But when we have gone into the analysis from every possible standpoint and the result has been reached, you will find that there is absolutely no possibility of any mistake on the matter. Judging matters in this way is a very simple method. And this method can be applied even with regard to the first quality, sat-svarupatā, that we mentioned, "Immortality."

Life, not death inherent property

Well, with regard to immortality also, the same principle applies. We see in the newspapers or hear from somebody the news about some person's death. And the immediate question that rises to our lips, "why, what happened ?" The very question "Why" shows that death needs an explanation. There is an explanation always. It may be one of one thousand four hundred and forty different causes. It may be cholera, it may be plague, it may be a motor car accident, it may be a cobra bite, it may be anything in the world, but there is something. Death is caused by something and when the doctors are unable to diagnose the nature of the disease, then, they at once tell you, "He must have had heart disease." Why that must if death is normal ? The "must" shows that without cause, death does not happen. There is a cause; and very often suspicion of poison and so forth comes in, with regard to a person who is healthy and strong and then you say, "He died suddenly and no explanation is forthcoming, perhaps he was poisoned."

Well, there is examination of the body, a post-mortem, and if no conclusion is reached, even then the doctors, the diagnosing experts, do not say, "He died because it was natural to die. Death is a natural property." No. What they say is that it needs a cause. The cause may be visible or invisible, may be traceable or not, but it is always there, showing thereby that not merely misery but even death comes from external causes. This kind of argumentation is of a very simple type which you need not refer to any author for deciding. You need not go to any great or highly evolved saintly soul and so forth. Your own knowledge of the small things within your experience will be quite sufficient to show you that this kind of principle can be applied infinitely and indefinitely. We arrive at the same conclusion. Thing after thing is taken up in the Vedānta from the standpoint of yukti, as it is called.

What is yukti ? Yukti is reasoning. Whatever is there which is given to us from the śāstras, from the scriptures, that is for our benefit by those who have gone through these experiences and want us to benefit by their experiences. They have left records in the shape of the scriptures, in the shape of oral teachings and so on. And we try to benefit by them. But the mere fact that someone has left something on record or has given us some oral teaching does not prove the correctness of the view. The correctness has to be tested on its own independent merits. Yukti yuktam vaco grāhyam. That kind of attitude is here. And from this standpoint we discuss all questions.

Mithyā, the principle of illusion

Now with this, I'll take up Śaṅkara's doctrine with regard to the world. Śaṅkara's doctrine with regard to the world is very often, well, ridiculed by critics who don't understand what Śaṅkara's teaching was, with regard to the illusory character of the world and so on. Mithyā is the expression we find used in the advaita literature. "Brahma satyam jagan mithyā"* Mithyā

* "Brahma is the ultimate reality and the world is Mithyā (not ultimately real)".

The expression is from Vivekacūḍāmaṇi (stanza 20) of Śaṅkara and occurs in his other writings also.

is always translated by the translators as illusory, false and so on. The world is false. The world is illusory. And therefore, we are told that Śankara's philosophy involves a negation of the existence of the world in any way whatsoever.

Well, we have to go into a very detailed study of this subject for grasping the main points in detail. But, at present, I just simply propose to place before you what is the correct interpretation of the word mithyā, and then the whole trouble is removed.

We have, not two categories, true and false, satya and asatya, but three categories taken into account in the vedānta. Very few people take this into the reckoning. Satya is, "that which is always existent, that which is eternal, that which never changes, never ceases to exist." That is called Sat. Then, there is the other one which is called asat, or asatya. Well, the asat or asatya is that which never comes into the experience at all, which, if a person reports that he saw it, well, he is giving a false narrative. What is called falsehood in ordinary English is what is meant by 'asat.' And, there is a third category which people have not taken into account. There is a third category of things which can be described neither as satya nor as asatya.* What is mithyā? Mithyā is that which has no independent eternal existence of its own, but at the same time is a matter within our experiential knowledge. We experience it. We feel it. We see it. We sense it in other ways. And therefore, we cannot say, 'a person who sees the world is telling you a lie.' For the first time, when a child sees a mirror, and sees his own reflection in it, he finds, or he seems to find a child at the same distance inside, as he himself is in front of the mirror. And wishing to make the acquaintance of the child inside, he goes to the mirror, but does not find the child. The mirror has not much thickness as to allow a person to be inside there at that distance. Now, will you say 'the child is telling a falsehood'? Even after verifying that the child that he saw was not actually there, he comes back to look

*... tattvānyatvābhyām anirvacanīye nāmarūpe avyākṛte..." (Śankara's commentary on Brahma SūtraI -1-5).

...(the world of) names and forms is not describable (or cannot be thought of) as real or other than real.

into the mirror. Not a little child, even we grown up people, when we come in front of the mirror and look into it, well, we see the reflection there. What will we say with regard to the reflection ? With regard to the object ? Will we say that the statement about seeing a child is false ? For that is doing injustice to the person who sees and reports that he has seen something. At the same time, has the reflection any independent existence of its own ? No. Apart from the object of which it is the reflection, it has no independent existence of its own. That cannot be held as absolutely true, "Trikāla-satya" eternally existing. Therefore, we say, it is not satya. At the same time it is a matter within our actual experience. So we say, it is not asatya. We are having both these qualities at the same time and therefore, we call it mithyā. We have this position, if two things are so related to each other that the existence of one depends upon the existence of the other, and not vice versa, that with an independent existence of its own is real and the other is called unreal. In optics, the image seen at a point through which the light rays actually pass, is called real image. The image seen at a point through which light rays only appear to pass, but do not pass, and which image cannot be received on a screen, is called virtual image or unreal image. Not real and false, but real and unreal. Asatya and mithyā are translations, or rather, the real and the unreal are translations of satya and mithyā. False is different. When you report to have seen something which you have not experienced, that is telling a lie, that is falsehood. But when you are reporting what you actually felt, not departing from it in any way whatsoever, well, you can't be blamed, you can't be accused of having told a lie. So there are these three categories, real, unreal, and false. And mithyā corresponds to unreal.*

*Citsukhācārya understands "mithyā" as 'indescribable' or anirvācya—

Pratyekam sadasattvābhyām vicārapadavīm na yat
Gāhate tad anirvācyam āhur vedāntavedinaḥ.

—Citsukhi-I-13.

"That which cannot be thought of either as "existent' or 'not existent', is called anirvācya by knowers of Vedānta".

We see the phenomenal world around us, and notice that it is not eternally in existence. That everybody knows. Things come and go. They don't last forever. All the things that we see in the phenomenal world, are transitory. And these phenomena are described as not being 'satya' on that account. And yet we see them. We actually experience them. Now we can't say that they are therefore 'asatya'. They are neither 'satya' nor 'asatya' but in between, into the third category, the middle category. You will have the 'mithyā' coming in.

Well, if the word mithyā is understood in this way, there is no difficulty in understanding Śaṅkara's system of mithyātva. And then again, if we look at it from the standpoint of physics and chemistry, we can come to the same conclusion. The same conclusion namely, that nothing which was not in existence comes into existence and nothing which is in existence goes out of existence. In the second chapter of the Gītā we have Lord Kṛṣṇa saying to Arjuna — Nāsato vidyate bhāvo nābhāvo vidyate sataḥ* — that which is not in existence, cannot come into existence; that which is in existence cannot go out of existence." Then what happens? Change of place, change of shape, change of name, change of functions, change of combinations, all sorts of changes are there. But no transmogrification from existent to non-existent and non-existent to existent.

Let us, for example, take the case of the wooden chair. We say the carpenter made the chair. What did he make? Did he create anything which was not in existence before? He took the God-made, or nature-made wood if you prefer the word nature, he brought it into different position, put it in a different shape, and gave it a different name. Stool and table and desk and cot and all these are things not newly created in the sense that they were brought into existence by him without having had existence before. And then again, you say you will burn a thing out, burn the wood, the cot. Well, what can you possibly do when you burn it out ? You have not brought into non-existence what was existing. Instead of being in the shape of wood, now it is in the shape of ashes, coal, charcoal, this and that. Lots of things there are. Combinations change. Positions change.

* Gita II-16.

Shapes change. Names change. 'Vācārambhaṇam vikāro nāmadheyam...'* That's all that happens.

In Chemistry, you read that zinc and sulphuric acid, give zinc sulphate and hydrogen. $ZnO+H_2SO_4=ZnSO_4+H_2O$. What has happened ? Only a transposition of the combinations and nothing brought into existence, nothing gone out of existence. That is what the text says. And that is what we mean when we talk in our physics and chemistry about the uncreatability of matter, the indestructibility of matter, the conservation of energy, and so on. These ideas which we think of as the regulations in physics and chemistry and so on, these are the very things taught in the Gītā in that ślokārdha or hemistich, 'Nāsato vidyate bhāvo nābhāvo vidyate sataḥ' "That which is not, cannot come into existence. That which is, cannot go out of existence." And the very word which we have, the words which we have for all these purposes show that a thing is of this nature and not of a different character at all. The words that we use for all these, for birth, for creation, and so on, in Sanskrit, themselves contain this meaning. 'Janī prādurbhāve.'** As the audience is not a Sanskrit-knowing audience, on the whole, I don't go into details of Sanskrit grammar and literature and derivations of words, but I would just place before you the idea that whatever comes into existence, has not been created. It has merely changed position, shape, combination, function, and so forth. And nāśa, meaning death or destruction—"ṇaśa adarśane"*** that is, going not out of existence, but out of sight. What was in front of us has gone behind us. What was above has gone below. That which was outside has gone inside. And that is called nāśa, that is destruction. That is all that takes place. Nothing else takes place. That is what we have in the teaching of the Gītā, in the teaching of the Upaniṣad, and in Bhagavān Śaṅkara's own rendering of it, interpretation of it. All that he did was to make the right meaning clear. Owing to

* Chāndogya Upaniṣad. VI-1-4.
"The change is only in name, which has origin in speech."

** The root "Janī" (Jan=to be born) is used in the sense of manifestation. [Dhātupāṭha IV Conjugation]

*** The root 'ṇaśa' (=naś) means 'not seen.'
[Dhātupāṭha IV Conjugation]

superficial thinking, lots of people misinterpreted the texts with consequences injurious to the people as such, and therefore, that work (Śaṅkara's commentary on Gītā etc.) came in.

And then again, the question is often asked as to how could Śaṅkara, regarding the world as an illusion, as an optical illusion, how could he consistently have carried on such tremendous activities during his life time ? Travelling from place to place, established Imbalaka Temple, and wrote hundreds of volumes, and went on propagating the doctrine of Advaita, Monism, in the world. How did he do it ? This question is asked. Well, the Advaita system does not condemn action at all. Even when we say something is illusory, that illusion too has some principle, while it is working. For example, when you treat, or deal with lunatics, absolutely mad people, we say, "Psychological examination will show what the real root of the trouble is. At present, we are not able to diagnose the nature of the trouble that has brought about this kind of affliction." But, at the same time, we say, "There is a method behind the madness." And that method has to be discovered. But of course, with regard to "jagan mithyā"* it is not absolute illusion or hallucination in that sense. I've explained what we mean by mithyā: "That which has no independent and eternal existence of its own, but becomes the subject matter of experience." Just as in the dream state, we see in a dream lots of things which we afterwards acknowledge were merely illusory. The waking state is no more vivid than the dreaming state. The things that we see in the dream are as vivid as we see in the waking state. And in Māṇḍūkya Kārikā, in the very first śloka, the very first verse, starting on this subject, we are told,

> Vaitathyam sarvabhāvānām
> svapna āhur manīṣiṇah,
> Antaḥsthānāt tu bhāvānam
> samvṛtatvena hetunā.**

* "The world is unreal."

** Māndūkya Kārikā. II-1.

"Logicians say that all dream objects are unreal, as they are (seen) within the body and in insufficient space."

A person goes to sleep in a small room where he has not sufficient room for stretching himself comfortably, and he begins to dream. And straightaway in the dream, he sees a procession of ten thousand elephants. Where did he see the elephants ? In that small room which could not accommodate him ? Even if that small room was there, the ten thousand elephants could not be there. Where does he actually see ? He sees with eyes closed. He himself says, "I slept with my eyes closed." And the onlookers also say, "He slept with his eyes closed." And yet, he saw. So where did he see the ten thousand elephants ? Between the eyes and the eyelids ? And is that sufficient space for ten thousand elephants ? After coming into the waking state, you say, "I dreamt." The vividity of the experience is no proof of its correctness, of its truth. So with regard to the waking world also. The things that we see, we can merely say we seem to see them.

Inadequacy of language

Here's another point which I would like to emphasize for the correct philosophical standpoint. We generally make use of predicates and active voice and passive voice according to grammar and so on in various ways, but it has come in by usage, by mere custom, by mere thoughtless custom. And, the sentences that we use in such connections, in such context, are incorrect, from the standpoint of real philosophical thinking. For example, when we say, "I see" such and such a thing, "I" is the subject and "see" is the predicate. What is the action ? Is there any positive action like "seeing?" Well, people will generally say, "I see." The sentence may be given for grammatical exercise. "I" is the subject of the sentence. "See" is the predicate. And the object is such and such thing. Similarly, "I hear." What is it that I hear ? All that can be said is, "the sound comes into the ear." I can't say, "I hear." There is no such action as hearing, no such action as seeing. If the obstacle to vision is removed, then automatically the seeing begins. And who is the seer ? No one can say. Because, there is no action which I have, as an active agent or subject of the predicate, actually performed. "I see the cloud," "I see" this, "I do" this. And in language, well, we use the passive voice also sometimes, and the passive voice is very often ridiculous. For purposes of grammatical exercise, in converting from active to passive voice, and passive to active voice, and so forth, we have these examples given. But nobody actually makes use of them because they're too ridiculous. For example, suppose I say, "I drank a cup of milk this morning." Now, render it into the passive voice. The grammatical textbook gives it. And I say, "A glass of milk was drunk by me this morning." Nobody ever dreams of saying that. It's too ridiculous. "I have had a cup of milk," "A cup of milk has been had by me." Nobody dreams of saying that. That is clearly ridiculous. But even with regard to the ordinary things that we do say in our common language, in accordance with grammar, and without feeling any kind of oddity or absurdity about it, even there, there are lots of things which we take for granted because it has become the usage. And in the usage we have not used our brains to see how far the usage correctly interprets the real philosophical action, quality, and so forth.

I take the example of the verb, "see". With regard to seeing there is no such action as "seeing." 'Being seen,' even that is not there, because the active portion is not there. All that can be said is : "Something has come into view." I am not the actor. I am not the active performer of any deed. How can I say, 'I see,' 'I hear', I smell,' 'I taste.' The sound comes into the ear, and I claim the credit for having heard something. What have I done ? If there is anything preventing my hearing, if there is cotton wool that has been placed into the ear, and I remove it, even then I am not doing an active action of "hearing." All that I have done is, I have removed the obstruction in the way of sound coming into the ear. That's all that takes place.

Some more instances may be taken which show how we have the tendency to claim to do things.

Prakṛteḥ kṛiyamāṇāni
guṇaiḥ karmāṇi sarvaśah,
Ahaṅkāra vimūḍhātmā
kartā (a) ham iti manyate.*

* Gītā III-27.

"All actions are done wholly by properties of Nature. But the person whose intellect is clouded by ego, thinks that he is the doer."

We claim to have done things. And lots of the things that we claim are false claims. The ego, the personal vanity, seems to be unconsciously fed by this kind of use. When a person says, "I have got fever" did he go out of his way to get something ? It is no question of "I have *got* fever." Still worse, "I have caught cold." That's the ordinary expression that we use in English. "I have caught cold," as if the cold was running away, refusing to come in, I pursued it, overtook it, and caught it. "I have caught the infection." Lots and lots of words are used in this way automatically, without careful thinking, without analysis of the actual process involved. In most of these cases you will find that the whole thing is of this type. We take credit for actions in which we have done nothing. And the most that can be claimed is that we have removed obstacles. That's a positive action. We remove the obstacles.

Now, if there is a cloud which veils the sun from our vision, the passing away of the cloud reveals the sun to us. There is nothing which we do as active performers of an action. Similarly with regard to various things. We judge by superficial, external appearances and commit blunder. But if we, with our own experience, look into these things carefully, there will be no difficulty at all. I give the example very often of the way in which we use the first person plural. The first person plural is "We." But what is we ? We always use the word "we". I am just now using the word, "we". We use the word "we" but what is "we ?" "We" is the plural of "I". That is wrong. What is a plural ? Plural is the singular taken more than once, twice, thrice, and so on. That is plural. Boxes. A box plus another box will make two boxes. Similarly with regard to all the things there. With regard to the third person pronouns, "he, she, it", we see that "he," and "he", together make "they." "She" and "she", "it" and "it", "he" and "she" all make "they." The plural "they" is all right. And similarly with regard to the second person, "you". "You" and "you", make "you two." I say to two persons "Go away !" Who? "You" and "you." "Let *him* go away," "Let *her* go away," "Let *it* go away." After the "he", "she" or "it", there can be repetition of the phrase "go away." Similarly with regard to the second person. But the first person plural, is a false plural. When I say, "Let us go," who ?

"I" and "I" ? Never. "I" and "you" "I" and "he". 'We' a false plural. "He, she, it" in plural can become "they" independently, because after using the word "he" you can use the word "he" again. After using the word "you" you can use the word "you" again. "You should go; you should also go; you shall also go." But after "I"? "I shall go tomorrow," and then there is no other "I" left at all. "I" plus "I"? No. "I" plus "he", "I" plus "she", "I" plus "you" will make the "we". "We" is not really a plural at all. But these are matters of rather subtle analytical character. And even though a little explanation will be sufficient to bring the matter within the experience of everybody, well, the usual usage is there. And according to the usage, we go on using the words.

Bible supports Vedānta

Now, I just simply want to state that from various standpoints that I have studied the philosophy, from the standpoint of other religions, from the standpoint of science, physics, chemistry, and so forth, I believe that the Advaita system, the monistic doctrine, is one which fits in with the facts. Similar is the case with regard to other religions. We find Christ himself saying — I am mentioning by way of illustration, we find Christ himself saying — "I and my Father are one."* And again, you have a passage in which Christ says to those who expressed surprise when he calls himself the Son of God, "Are you offended because I have called myself the Son of God ? Have not your forefathers said unto you, 'Ye are gods.'"** These passages are there. And in St. John's gospel, in the very first chapter of the very first Para we have, what we might call an exact parallel, or practically the translation of what in our scriptures is known as Para-Brahma, Nāda-Brahma, Śabda-Brahma, and so on. "In the beginning there was the Word, the Word was with God, and the Word was God." Logos of the Greeks, we call Śabda-Brahma, or Nāda-Brahma here. Even in details, we find a tremendous degree of close parallelism which can't be explained away in any way whatsoever.

* St. John—X-30.
** See also St. John—X-34.

Then again, we go into other passages. We find no difficulty at all. If you start with the Bible itself, in the very first verse of the very first book, Genesis, the creation of the world is described, "In the beginning, God created the heaven and the earth."* And if the enquirer puts the question to himself, he can find the answer for himself. The world, according to the physical theory that I've already explained, namely, uncreatability of matter and indestructability of matter, can only be a continuous change of place, shape, combination, name and so on. There can be nothing new brought into existence, and nothing can go out of existence. So that is from one standpoint. From the standpoint of the Bible, "In the beginning, God created the heaven and the earth." That is all right. He was the Creator. But what was the material out of which He created the world ?

God is the efficient and the material cause of the world

Now, a potter has the clay with which he makes the pot. A goldsmith has the gold with which he makes the gold ornament, bangle, necklace, and so forth. But at the time of creation as presented in the Bible, "In the beginning, God created the heaven and the earth," it means that the world did not exist when God brought it into existence. After that, God brought it into existence. Well, what was the material like the clay of the potter and the gold of the goldsmith, out of which God created the whole heaven and earth ? And the only answer can be that He created it out of the only existing material, namely, Himself. He was not merely the Creator of the universe, but He was himself the substance, the subject matter, the Material of which the universe was made. Anything and everything that comes into existence in the due course, starting from that early start, from the very origin, comes merely as the same thing in another form. Nāmarūpavikārah. Take the example of a tree that grows from the earth. It is only a thing which has been contributed to by the various factors necessary, the seed, the manure, the soil, and then, the timely rains, and so on. All these things are

* Genesis I-1.

there. And you have got only the result of these things coming up, and nothing further. Nothing new is created in the sense of being brought into existence. And all that we mean by Advaita is the recognition of this fact, that God is only one though appearing as many.*

God is one

We do not call ourselves polytheists. We recognise one God behind a multiplicity of gods, a trinity, a unity, behind trinity. We recognise — Eko devaḥ sarvabhūteṣu gūḍhaḥ sarvavyāpī sarvabhūtāntarātmā.** "One God pervading and permeating the

* In an article published long ago His Holiness wrote :—

"All theists believe, too, that God is omnipresent, i.e. that He pervades and permeates the whole Universe. Most of us, however, fail to realise the real connotation and the inescapable implications of this belief, to wit, that His very Omnipresence, too, proves our oneness with him.

Now it is everybody's common-place experience that, when a potter makes a pot of clay, a weaver a piece of cloth, a goldsmith manufactures an ornament of gold and so forth, it is only the clay, the yarn, the gold, etc.—and not the potter, the weaver, the goldsmith, etc.—that pervade and permeate the entire material of the pot, the cloth, the ornament, etc., respectively. In other words, it is not the maker but the material which pervades and permeates the particular creation in question.

Similarly, although it is perfectly true that God Himself has actually created the Universe, yet it is not as its Creator, but only in His capacity as the material thereof that He can pervade and permeate it. Such in brief is the philosophy of Shri Śaṅkarācārya, who argues that, whatever its outer form, shape, functions, value, etc., may be, every ornament emanating from pure gold must itself be pure gold in its actual substance and everything emanating from God must necessarily itself be God."

** Śvetāśvatara Upaniṣad. VI-11.

Some other texts conveying the same idea of monism are given below:—

(1) Vāyur yathaiko bhuvanam praviṣṭo
rūpam rūpam pratirūpo babhūva,
Ekas tathā sarvabhūtāntarātmā
rūpam rūpam pratirūpo bahiś ca.

(Kathopaniṣad II-2-10)

Just as air fills the world and takes the shapes of different objects it fills, similarly the one God who is the soul of all beings, has assumed different shapes, but He also transcends them.

whole universe," pervading not merely this trinity or that trinity, but the whole universe. Not a multiplicity, but an infinity of manifestations. And the manifestations are different. And these manifestations have different functions, different qualities, size. shape, and so on, as the various limbs of a tree, as the various limbs of the body. There are differences in position, in size, shape, colour, function, therapeutical qualities, and so on, but that does not mean that they are all separate. There is unity underlying all these things. Similarly, with regard to the limbs of the same body. With all their differences, which are of position, of an external character, and after all, of a trivial character, they are manifestations of the same thing from within. Nothing new is imported, nothing is taken out. That kind of feeling of oneness that we have with regard to our own bodies, can be expanded logically so as to cover not merely our own family, our society, our community, our country, our nation, and so on, but the whole universe. The universe is so called because it is '*uni*' that is only one. That is Advaita. That is the monotheism that we have, the monism that we have. And if we achieve this knowledge, it has its own reflection upon the political, social, and other public fields also. The question of peace and war

(2) "Īśāvāsyam idam sarvam...".
(Iśopaniṣad—1)

All this (universe) is pervaded by God ....

(3) Puruṣa eva idam yad bhūtam yac ca bhavyam.
(Ṛgveda—X-90-2)

All this and whatever is past or future is God only.

(4) Om ity etad akṣaram idam sarvam tasya
upavyākhyānam bhūtam bhavad bhaviṣyad iti
(Māṇḍukyopaniṣad—1)

All this is Om (God signified by the Word Om) and past, present and future are its elaboration only.

(5) "Mayi sarvam idam protam..."
(Gītā VII-7)

All this (universe) is embedded in Me.

(6) ..."sarvam khalv idam Brahma..."
(Chāndogyopaniṣad III-14-1)

All this is Brahman (God) indeed.

agitate the peoples' minds everywhere, causing tremendous apprehension as regards the future, not of this or that nation, but of the whole human race itself, with all its culture, civilization, and so on. All these questions are easily solved if this idea of the oneness and the solidarity of the whole universe behind the Paramātman, the universal all-pervading Divinity, is recognized. I have taken more time than was intended to be taken by this discourse, and yet, there is no possibility of my doing justice to any part of it. I have tried with these incoherent perhaps disconnected talks to go into various aspects of the matter, which ought to receive consideration from us as students, earnestly seeking the truth. Not with any axes of our own to grind, not with any partiality, hatred, prejudice, prepossession and so forth, but as jijñāsus, seekers after the truth, if we apply our minds to this question of the metaphysics, of the universe, God, the individual soul, and the universe, from this standpoint without any other kind of adulteration of it with lower motives and things of that type, then we should be able to achieve not merely the soul's freedom, mokṣa, as described in the Vedānta in so many terms, but we shall be able also to contribute our mite, to the utmost extent of our power, for the elevation of humanity as such, in fact, for the preservation of humanity, the human race, and all the culture and civilization, and all the past achievements of the human race. This is the massage which as a representative of India and India's Vedantic religion, I bring to you. I bring this message to you, to persons who believe in independence of thought, who with Pilgrim Fathers to start with, came and settled down here for the purpose of carrying on their own worship, having their own form of ceremony, their own ritual and their own way in all matters. The idea of the ndependence of judgment in all matters including religious, is nothing new to you. You already have it here. And we have categorical statements to this extent, "Yukti yuktam vaco grāhyam." That has been not merely our theoretical, academical doctrine. That is the historical tradition behind us in India. And that is why I have come over here at this stage of my life for the purpose of enlisting the support of all of you here towards the cause of universal peace, universal prosperity. "The Prince of Peace," as Christ is called, can be reached in this way. This is the message I would have you carry home in your hearts, ponder over it, and as far as humanly possible, and consistently with your own reasoning, carry it out in practice for the benefit of humanity and for the benefit of yourselves too at the same time. This is the message which I will ask you to think over and make the working principle of your daily life from moment to moment.

QUESTION AND ANSWER PERIOD FOLLOWING STANFORD DISCOURSE

Q. Is it necessary to keep to the doctrine of reincarnation?

H. H. The question of reincarnation is a separate subject by itself. I have no difficulty about it. Well, the question of reincarnation, can be considered both from the standpoint of religious, theological creeds on the one side, and from the standpoint of what you might call ordinary scientific commonsense argument on the other. It can be considered from both points of view. It is generally assumed, and constantly asserted, that Jainism, Buddhism, and Hinduism are the only religions which recognize the law of karma, and the law of reincarnation in accordance with karma, and that Islam, Judaism, and Christianity do not countenance it. I'm afraid this is a wrong reading of the scriptures of those religions. We have nowhere any statement to that effect at all. The general argument is that according to the scriptures of Judaism, Christianity, and Islam, there is a last Day of Judgment when final Judgment is pronounced on all souls that in the meantime remain within their graves. And it is a question of eternal punishment or eternal reward in heaven. That is the idea that most people ask us to accept as the teaching of the Bible. Well, there is no such categorical statement anywhere. There is constant reference to the day of Judgment. When the Judgment comes, when the day of Judgment comes, there'll be grinding of teeth on the part of people who had led an evil life, on the part of hypocrites, and so on, all these things are there. But that the Judgment Day for all is the same day and that all people have to wait until the end of time, until the end of the universe for having Judgment pronounced upon them, and their admission into heaven or hell, finds no kind of categorical statement anywhere in the Bible. On the contrary, it looks quite clear that according to Christ, that was not the case. Well, we do not find Christ taking up this question and dealing with it in so many terms. But we actually find that with regard to a person blind from birth, the question is taken up as regards what sin he committed in order to be born blind. The question of sin as the cause of all sufferings, and merit as the cause for all enjoyment and so on, that idea is there. And if that idea is there, where could the man blind from birth, have committed whatever particular sin it was that had been responsible for the blindness? Well, it must have been in a previous birth. He certainly could not have been born blind because of anything that he did later on, nor when he was in his mother's womb. It should have been sometime before. That is the inference from it. And there is a categorical passage in which we find Christ saying. that he whom your forefathers knew as Elias the Prophet, the same has now come as John the Baptist. Venerate him.* That is clearly reincarnation. And besides that, there is another passage in which, at the very last time in his earthly life, during the very last moments, he said, "I shall sup with father Abraham in Paradise tonight." And the question that I pose is, as a student of the Bible, as a believer in the Bible, as a believer in and an admirer of the Lord Jesus Christ, that this can only mean that, according to Christ, Abraham had already reached heaven or would reach there by the time Christ himself would reach there. And how did Abraham manage to get into heaven? He knew nothing about the existence of Christ, the coming of the future Messiah. And even those who believed in the Messiah expected him to establish a kingdom, a human earthly kingdom in which the Jews, the Hebrews were to have the supreme power. They were looking forward to an earthly kingdom in that way being established by the Messiah. But as actual history proved, it was not an earthly kingdom that he established in that way, but the kingdom of God. Christ said "The Kingdom of God is within you." "...seek ye first the kingdom of God and his righteousness and all these things will be added unto you,"** and so on. That is the kind of thought that we find him expressing. But as he had always been talking of the kingdom of Heaven, the people ridiculed him. They crowned him with a crown of thorns and jeered at him as king of the Jews. As a matter of fact, nothing happened towards the realisation of the kingship they were looking forward to from the Messiah. All that happened

* See St. Mathew XI—13, 14.

** Matthew VI-33.

was that the Messiah wore the crown of thorns and bore the cross of shame. That was what happened. And yet, what do you find? You find that Abraham, who did not know about the Messiah at all and had no kind of conception of the future Saviour of Humanity, is declared, not by any other theologian, but by Christ himself in so many categorical terms, to be already in heaven. And the question I ask is, "How did he manage to get in?" And the answer that any person can give, and every person actually does give, is "It's perfectly true that Abraham was not a worshipper of Christ, and did not even dream about the coming of Christ, but because he was pure-hearted, and had a noble mind, a benevolent heart, and had ethical virtues, he was entitled to go to heaven. We have the same thing again and again in our scriptures. We are told,

> Ye (a) pyanyadevatābhaktā
> yajante śraddhayānvitāh,
> Te (a) pi māmeva Kaunteya
> yajanty avidhi-pūrvakam.*

Sri Krishna says in the Bhagavad Gītā in so many cotegorical terms, "Even those who believe in and worship other deities with sincerity of heart, they too worship Me." And the next question as to what about atheists and agnostics who do not believe in any deity at all, who do not adore and worship any kind of god or goddess, what about them?

> Te prāpnuvanti mām eva
> sarvabhūtahiteratāḥ.**

is the Lord's reply. He says, "anyone who does good, who has pure motives, who has a beneficient heart, and who seeks the welfare of others, who is moral in fact, he is entitled to the highest bliss, and there can be no question of his ever going to an evil fate and so on.

* Gitā IX-23.
** Gitā XII-4.

Nahi kalyāṇa kṛt kaścit
dūrgatim tâta gacchati.*

So far as the question of reincarnation is concerned, I do not accept the interpretation, that the Bible preaches the last Day of Judgment as the one day for all. It's like arresting persons on charges of murder or some other such offences and keeping them in custody until the end of the world, and then calling upon them to account for their actions. All the persons are then sent either to heaven or to hell at the same time. I do not find the least justification for such an idea in the Bible anywhere. And if Abraham could reach heaven by virtue of his qualities, in spite of all his imperfections and so forth, well I think the principle should be applied to all. A chance should be given for repentance and for reformation; and that is the view that is taken by everybody. And Christ himself, during his very last moment, prays to God, saying, "Father, forgive them, for they do not know what they are doing." Even for those who brought about his crucifixion, with all the agony and the physical torture he prayed in this way. That shows the kind of system which Christ sponsored as his religion. There can be no question of eternal punishment with no chance of reprieve, no opportunity of repentance, no scope of correction. Well, the two don't seem to be consistent with each other. Christ's teaching and his own example on the one side, and this kind of eternal punishment idea, they don't seem to go together.

* Gītā VI-40.

XVI BHAKTI YOGA & DIVINE MOTHER

Discourse at Mount Washington Centre on March 20, 1958.

Friends :

Ever since I arrived here, I have been giving my discourses at different places on various subjects. But I have been feeling that the most important of all the subjects from the standpoint of the sādhaka, the aspirant on the spiritual ladder, has not evoked sufficient recognition from the various persons who have been hearing the discourses. And I have been feeling that that is a deficit which ought to be made up as soon as possible and to the maximum extent possible. But owing to the pre-arrangement of the programmes in different places and the desire of the various audiences it has not been possible to arrange in that way, and as I am to leave, for the present, on the day after tomorrow by the morning's plane and tomorrow is heavily loaded with other work, I myself decided that at this meeting here in the ashram, I would speak on this subject. And requests to this effect having come from others also, I'am going into that subject immediately, and within the short time at my disposal today, I shall try and say something which may be described as the gist of the whole subject.

Three paths of Yoga

There are the famous three paths of Karma Yoga, Bhakti Yoga, and Jñāna Yoga which are described in the scriptures of all the religions, as paths leading the spiritual aspirant to his goal of self-realization. We have this in our Vedic and other scriptures of Hinduism, and we find the same characteristic in the scriptures of other religions also. In the Bible too, we have Karma Yoga, Bhakti Yoga, and Jñāna Yoga, all similarly dealt with. We find St. Peter and St. James emphasizing Karma Yoga, the path of works, good work for the attainment of the goal of oneness with the Divine. We have St. John emphasizing love, or what we call Bhakti Yoga, with, Śraddhá, that is, faith, and other ingredients of the Bhakti Yoga. And thirdly, we have St. Paul laying the utmost stress on Jñāna Yoga. As I 've explained on previous occasions in connection with other subjects, there may be two explanations for this difference in the kind of emphasis laid on the three paths by the three kinds of evangelists. Their own particular temperamental personal equation may be held accountable for it. But much more than that, I feel that the difference is due to the difference, not in the temperamental predilections of the evangelists themselves, but in the background, the exigencies, the circumstances and the needs of the audiences whom they had to address, and of the disciples for whom they were laying down their instructions.

Anyhow, whatever the reasons may be, there are the three paths. And it is also clear that from the standpoint of Christ himself, and of the evangelists themselves, as in our scriptures of the Vedic religion, there is no conflict between the three paths or between any one of them and the other two, and so on. The emphasis is laid more on one particular aspect by a particular evangelist, and that is all. But we find that later on as generations passed by, people took up only one particular aspect which was congenial to them, and which pleased them intellectually and otherwise. They not merely emphasized that particular line, but began talking in objectionable terms as regards the other paths, ignoring the fact that different mentalities, different temperamental indiosyncracies, in fact, the personal equation, as one may call it, should be held responsible for these divisions, and that there can be no mechanical rule by which all people can be fitted harmoniously into the same path. We need not go into that controversial point for the present, but I would like first to give an outline description of, a skeleton-like description of what exactly the three paths denote, and where exactly the Bhakti Yoga fits into the scheme for the great majority of the people of the present day.

Handicaps of Karma Yoga

Karma Yoga is the path in which we are told to go on doing the various things prescribed for us in the Sāstras, enjoined in the scriptures, with regard to rituals, ceremonials, and things of that type, things which you might call the external actions, the outer rules and regulations for people to follow. That is the path of works. That is to say, there are lots of things which we do from time to time for expressing our feelings or sentiments on the one hand, and for gradual ascent on the spiritual ladder on the other. That is Karma Yoga. We may say at the very outset that the path of Karma Yoga is necessarily bound to have one great disadvantage, one great handicap for the great majority of people, that the Karma Yoga does not prescribe one path for everybody. There are various subdivisions and sub-sub-subdivisions in each subdivision. We are told that such and such thing should be done, and when we go into details, we may find one text saying that a certain act or ritual or ceremonial should be performed before sunrise, and other text saying that it should be performed after sunrise. We have texts like that here also in our scriptures, in the Vedānta and so on, "Udite juhoti," "anudite juhoti.* "Offer oblations after sunrise"; "offer oblations before sunrise", and so on. What the effects would be in case of performance before sunrise, and what the effects would be if the ritual is performed after sunrise, these details are not gone into extensively. And even if there were an extensive description, it would be difficult for every person to decide for himself or herself, the best path in that particular case. As I have been mentioning at other places, it is like a doctor prescribing medicines, diets and so on for different kinds of patients suffering from different kinds of complaints, and the same rule would not apply, either with regard to medicines, or even with regard to diet. Each case has to be taken on its own intrinsic merits. In a heart disease salt-free diet is prescribed. In a case of another type where diabetes is the trouble, sugar-free diet is prescribed and so on. And generally it is not possible for the patient himself who is not a specialist, or an expert, and who does not know the exact diagnosis and things of that type, to find out for himself what exactly ails him, and even there, it is impossible for him not only to know the general name of the disease, but what particular subdivision of that particular disease he is suffering from, and to prescribe for himself.

* See Commentary of Śaṅkara on Brahma Sūtra I-1-2.

And there too, it is not a question of absolute prohibition of an act or absolute enforcement of a rule. It's a question very often of proportion that comes in. And when that comes in, the mathematics of it will make it more complicated, and the patient himself will not be able to decide what exactly he should have of this particular diet, that particular medicine, and so on. So in all these cases, the expert is necessary. And, even the experts very often fail in their diagnosis. All are not the evangelists themselves. Even the evangelists' own immediate disciples of the first generation made mistakes. Infallibility cannot be claimed by anybody in respect of any kind of scientific question. And here the result is a matter of very serious consequence. It is not merely a matter of life and death in the present life, it's also a more serious matter involving the happiness in the present, and also having a bearing on what we might call the future life, the life after this existence when this physical body of ours has come to an end.

So, owing to our not being all-knowing — God alone is omniscient — we cannot claim infallibility. All that we can say is, "Such-and-such is my inference." And even with regard to that, you will find in actual experience, as the English proverb says, "Doctors differ." In fact, we may go to the extent of saying, "No two doctors ever agree." That kind of position is reached. Even when experts are on the scene, you can't rely on their being unanimous in their opinion on a subject whatsoever.

So, that is the first handicap with regard to what you might call the Karma Yoga sādhanā portion, where particular rules are laid down for us as being paths to the achievement of physical, mental, and all round peace and happiness, and so on.

And even when we know what exactly ails us and what exactly the proper treatment is for that ailment, the next trouble is that the things prescribed are not available to us. Very often it happens that a particular medicine that is the proper cure for a certain disease is not available within a short time when the critical juncture has been reached. Owing to the delay in obtaining the necessary medicine, well, the life becomes extinct. And by the time the medicine arrives, it is found that the patient has himself left the world. It is not merely the disease that is gone, he is himself gone too. So that kind of two-fold trouble is there because on the one hand we are not all-knowing, and on the other we are not all-powerful. All things are not available to us. So with the best of intentions, and with the best of knowledge of the physical or the material things needed by us, we fail in the performance of Karma Yoga in proper terms.

Well, on account of this double handicap, the Karma Yoga, however splendidly performed, has this inherent defect in itself, and cannot by itself be relied upon altogether. And this is why, in the Indian scriptures, we have at the end of every ritual, of every ceremonial prescribed for any purpose whatsoever, a prayer to God. "Mantrahīnam Kriyāhīnam. Vidhihīnam Janārdana, Yat pūjitam mayā Deva paripūrṇam tadastū me."* The prayer is from the performer of the various karmas, rituals. He says, that there has been deficiency, not deficiency of heart, but deficiency of the material needed for the proper performance of the particular ritual or ceremonial or function prescribed. Well, the All-knowing One, knows the hearts of people and can always judge. He is the Karma-phaladātā, the giver of the fruits of action. He knows that the heart has not been lacking. And taking the heart into consideration, He will excuse all deficiencies with regard to other things. The heart must be taken into account and I surrender with all my heart. But with regard to other things, I am not powerful enough; I am not knowing enough, and therefore, all defects arising from these two causes should be pardoned. So that kind of prayer comes at the end of every ceremonial and every ritual in the Karmakāṇḍa, according to the Vedas, the śrutis, the purāṇas, and other scriptures.

The śraddhā portion, the devotion portion, the Bhaktiyoga portion comes into the Karma Yoga when we say, "God the knower of the feelings, the sentiments, and the desires, should take these facts into consideration and take the intention for the actual action." The Karma Yoga by itself is not sufficient.

* O God, the ceremonies performed by me are deficient in texts rituals, and procedure. May the deficiency be made good by Your grace.

Jñāna Yoga

And then, we take up at the other extreme the Jñāna Yoga portion, in which we are told that continuous study, continuous meditation, logical and psychological and other thinking, introspection, and all these things which come under the heading of vicāra as we call it in Sanskrit, should be so calculated, so mastered, that a person never loses his balance. Things of the outside world, physical, mental, and so forth, should not get us off our balance. We should be able to control our mind and heart and emotions in such a manner that whatever may happen, we remain unaffected, unperturbed, unruffled.* Well, that means the eternal peace that we all speak of, which is the final goal, has been achieved already. The self-control is to such an extent that nothing can possibly have any effect at all upon the mind.

Yas tv ātmaratir eva syād
ātmatṛptaś ca mānavaḥ,
Ātmany eva ca santuṣṭas
tasya kāryam na vidyate.**

"For such a person who has attained that stage there is nothing further that is needed to be done." It is not a question of a sādhaka asking what he should do. It is a person who has attained the loftiest level possible, and there is nothing further left for him to do. There is nothing required of him any

* The same idea is conveyed in the following verses from Gītā [II-56,57.] :—

Duḥkheṣv anudvignamanāḥ
sukheṣu vigataspṛhaḥ,
Vītarāgabhayakrodhaḥ
sthitadhīr munir ucyate.

"Steady-minded sage is one whose mind is not agitated in distress, who has no longing for comforts, and who is free from desire, fear or anger."

Yaḥ sarvatrānabhisnehaḥ
tat tat prāpya śubhāśubham,
Na prahṛṣyati na dveṣṭi
tasya prajñā pratiṣṭhitā.

"One who is detached from all and has no love or hate for good or bad things, has attained equilibrium of mind."

** Gītā III-16.

further in order to enable him to reach the goal. He has already reached the goal. The Jñānakāṇḍa, the more and more we go into it, well, takes it for granted that we have passed stage after stage, ladder after ladder on our ascent to the goal, that is oneness, absolute identity with the Divinity inside which we for a long time past have not been actually experiencing. That experience comes from regular practice. That is to say, when we have transcended the stage in which things can affect us, we are no longer in the category of sādhakas, of persons who are trying to attain something higher. We have already reached there. So that means that the number of persons that can be counted as on this path must necessarily be very small. And therefore, without going into further details, I may say that Jñāna Yoga is what we aim at. It is not so much a means as the goal itself. A person who has mastered the Jñāna Yoga is incapable of being shaken off his moorings. Well, that person is no longer to be regarded as a person who is trying to do something. So there too, we may say that the Jñāna Yoga. although being of the highest type of sādhanā and so forth, really means that the sādhakas have already transcended the stage in which remedies are necessary.

Fight with the passions in all possible ways. Control your emotions. And whatever suffering there may be, you go on bearing it. Endurance is to be practised, until at last, the things cease to affect you at all.

The number of candidates for Jñāna Yoga must necessarily be small. In the Karma Yoga, candidates may be many. People willing and able to perform things may be many in number, but owing to want of correct knowledge, the exact condition, the proper remedy, and so forth, and the lack of power to have these remedies at hand make any use of them, the double-handicap which I have already referred to, is there.

Bhakti Yoga

So, the third path the Bhakti Yoga, an intermediate path, is the one to which most people have to take resort. From the standpoint of absolute self-surrender; the heart being pure, all the mistakes and things of that type that happen, are excusable because the heart is not there with the mistakes. It is in spite of the heart, owing to lack of omniscience and omnipotence and so on that there is any deficiency. If there is anything in excess of proportion, the proper ratio, that too means suffering. There are various kinds of things that go to compose our physical body, and if anything is found in excess, that means suffering. And if anything is found deficient, that again means suffering, physical ailment. And the remedy is the supply of what is deficient and the reduction of what is in excess.

So this is the physical side of Karma Yoga. And therefore, the Bhakti Yoga is the one that is suitable for most persons. And the texts are all quite clear as to how the Bhakti Yoga will help us through.

Let God be your guide

It is like handing over the driving of our car so to say, or a carriage, or a railway train, and so on, into the hands of an expert driver. We have a certain goal to reach. And that goal is in our minds. And that too is vaguely outlined in most uncertain terms, in terms which we cannot ourselves consciously analyze properly and describe. And we cannot decide properly for ourselves, owing to our weakness in respect of omniscience. The trouble comes in that way. We need happiness. We all seek happiness. And we want not partial happiness, fractional happiness, we want complete happiness. Sampūrṇa ānanda, "complete, all around, perfect perfection" is what we seek. And we do not know where it is to be found, the path which will lead to that goal. And under such circumstances, handing over the reins into the hands of a person who knows the goal, well, that is the first thing to do, and we do it when we make the Lord Himself the charioteer.

Well, when we do not know and He alone knows the path to it because it is He Himself that we are trying to reach. It is the Divinity within that we wish to attain and continually experience. And therefore, there is no question of a possibility of His not knowing where our goal is and where we should reach. He knows our destination. That destination is Himself. And that being the case, well, the first requisite is that the driver should be an expert driver who knows our goal, and the Lord knows.

it much better than we ourselves know. So that first element that is necessary in the driver is to be found in the Lord.

In the Gītā for example, we have the relationship of Arjuna and Śrī Kṛṣṇa. Arjuna represents man as such.

Eṣa Nārāyaṇaḥ Kṛṣṇaḥ
Phālgunaś ca naraḥ smṛtaḥ.*

These are the expressions used. Nara means man, humanity as such, without excluding any person at all from the scope of its operation. And Nārāyaṇa is the Lord. What is the relationship between Arjuna and Śrī Kṛṣṇa, between nara and Nārāyaṇa ? We have Śrī Kṛṣṇa, the charioteer, who drives the chariot, and the person who is being driven to his goal is Arjuna, that is nara. Nara-Arjuna was not asking for himself alone, he was our spokesman, our representative, humanity's delegation, in fact.** And, he places before the Lord all the difficulties and sufferings that he has been passing through, all his mental troubles, and his other worries. The questions he asks are the very questions which we ourselves feel impelled to ask from time to time. So, he is there in the position of the person in the chariot who is being driven along to his destination. And the Lord is the driver of the chariot. As the Lord is omniscient, there can be no question at all as to whether he knows our goal or not. We ourselves don't know it. In worldly affairs day by day, we "know" where we have to go, and we tell the driver where to drive. But here, we don't know, the Driver knows. So, that's the first point gained.

But is it sufficient that the driver knows where we should be taken ? Has he the capacity to take us (to the goal) ? Yes. Being all powerful, the Lord can do that. He is All-knowing.

* "The Lord Kṛṣṇa is Nārāyana (God) and Arjuna is Nara (man).
Mahābhārata—Udyoga. XLIX-20.

**—sarvalokānugrahārtham Arjunam nimittīkṛtya
āha Bhagavān Vāsudevaḥ.
[Saṅkara's Commentary on Gītā—Introduction.]

"On the pretext of instructing Arjuna, Lord Krishna, son of Vāsudev, taught (Gītā) for the benefit of the whole world.

Many people know the theories, the dogmas, the creeds, and so on. In my own days, when I was teaching my students, I was talking to them about physics, the development of the steam-engine, Watt's model, Stephenson's model, etc., I was teaching them a number of theoretical matters with regard to the way the steam worked, the boiler and the engine and the safety in the shape of brakes, rear brake and front brake and all sorts of things. I was talking to my students about steam engines, but if a railway train had been entrusted to me for driving, it would have meant an immediate danger to all the persons. The theoretical side is quite easy enough and cheap enough for anybody to talk about.

Well, it is not sufficient for a person to know where he has to go. He must be able to take the carriage, the car, or other transport along to that place. And who is the driver that we have selected for the purpose ? Not merely the All-knowing, but the Omnipotent, the All-powerful One. He knows how to drive. He is the best driver. In fact, He is the only driver who can do it. He is not merely the best, He is the only one. But, is that sufficient either ?

With this combination of the two essential qualities in the driver, is our success assured ? The question is posed because in a great number of cases in the worldly professions, both these qualifications are found, but are not beneficial to us. Take for example a lawyer, or a doctor. In these cases, if the question is asked, "Does the man know law ?" Oh yes ! He knows it very well, "Can he do it ?" Yes, he does it, he does it day after day, that is his profession. Yes, but, if he will not do it, if he does not care to do it, what happens ? His knowing the law, and his practising of it day after day is of no avail. Similarly with regard to the doctor. His knowing of the medical science, and his doing that medical work day after day, will not benefit us unless he is willing to do it, and he actually does it. Suppose the fees he demands are beyond our means to pay. Well, all his knowledge, and all his experience, his omniscience and omnipotence in his subject will not save us at all. So, the third thing wanted is the willingness, not merely the knowledge and the capacity, but willingness. This third factor is the most important factor of all, because without it, everything is absolutely wasted. And here, what have we ? In the Arjuna and Kṛṣṇa relationship of devotee and the object of devotion, of the person driven along to his destination and the driver, what is the speciality ? Here comes the most important point of all. The Lord is not merely All-knowing and Omnipotent. He has not merely the will, or the inclination to be of help to the devotee, He is Himself the devotee's devotee. He cannot go against the wishes of the devotee. That is the relationship. And that, St. John summarizes in "God is love." Not merely is He a loving person, not merely is he the subject of the predicate, 'love', He is of the Nature of love, abounding love, unlimited, illimitable love, love to all those who have faith in him, who strive to make use of whatever knowledge they have by surrendering it in the service of the Lord. And once we hand over as Arjuna did, the reins into the hands of the Master, who is all-knowing and all-powerful, and at the same time is a devotee's devotee, we are safe. We say he is not merely bhaktavatsala, he is bhakta-ādhina.* That is his attitude. He cannot let you down. It is not a question of his prestige. His temperamental position itself, his mental constitution itself so to say, if you like to put it that way, is one of absolute love. And you find this verified in the experiences described by the seers in the various scriptures of the world. At critical times, when it is beyond man's ingenuity to get over a certain trouble, well, the Lord is there to save you. And, He does so not at all with any kind of commercial or mercenary interest as we have in the affairs of the world. That is because it is His Nature. God is Love. And, such is the driver that we have got. And when we reach that stage, it means all the necessary qualifications are there, and there is nothing to worry about.

Absolute trust in God

Well, if you employ an expert driver who knows where to drive you, who knows how to drive you, and who has the will, not merely the will but the eagerness to do anything possible for your speedy attainment of your goal, you shouldn't be inter-

* He is not merely affectionate towards His devotees, He is subservient to them.

fering and trying to catch hold of the wheel and drive the car according to your own wishes. That would mean danger to yourself and nothing else. The driving has to be given, the wheel has to be handed over into the hands of the person having these three qualifications. In those cases in which we know the goal better, we are more authoritative, no doubt, or where we can drive better, well, the professional driver may be asked to sit aside for a moment and we can take the wheel in our own hands. But, here is a case in which there is no question of such a comparison at all. The All-knowing One, the All-powerful One, and the Loving One, whose very nature is Love, He is there. The relationship between ourselves and the Lord, should be one like that which obtained between Arjuna and Śrī Kṛṣṇa. We hand over everything. That is the meaning of self-surrender — self-surrender, not with any commercial, any mercenary kind of interest at all, but with absolute faith. And there should be nothing that can possibly detract from the feeling of confidence and devotion.

I frequently give the simile of a small child who is seated on a high level somewhere. The father, the mother, the elder brothers, come and stand in front of him, stretch out their hands and ask him to jump into their hands, and the child does it, does it immediately. On what strength ? On the strength of his own legs ! No He is aware of two things. He's sure of two things, namely, that the father and the mother are his well-wishers on the one hand and are capable of protecting him on the other. If he has the least doubt on either of these two points, well, he will hesitate, he will refuse to come down. He may feel that the mother and others are well disposed enough, loving enough, but suppose they're not able to hold him, to sustain his weight, he will come to the ground, and break his legs, or something of that type may happen. He will be afraid to come down. But if he knows that the person who stretches out the arms and asks the child to jump is strong enough to hold him, to sustain him, but hasn't got the necessary love, the child will think, "Suppose I get down now, and after my jumping off from here, that person withdraws his arms, what will become of me ?" But, in the case of the mother and so forth, the child is completely and absolutely sure on both the points that there will be no cheating afterwards, and that there is strength enough to catch hold of him and to sustain and to support him. He comes down.

Similar is the case with regard to Bhakti Yoga. We have the awareness that He is capable of supporting us, He is all-powerful. And secondly, as regards his love towards us, we are absolutely certain. And therefore, there is no reason for any kind of anxiety, any kind of fear of danger, and apprehensions of that type.

So in this path we have these two things, namely, certainty of the devotee with regard to the Lord's capacity on the one hand and his mentality on the other.

Now, in this path when you have once come into it, there can be no difficulties at all. The difficulties of the kind that I outlined in regard to Karma Yoga and Jñāna Yoga are not applicable in this case. In the case of Karma Yoga, it is a question of my being ignorant of the necessary remedies, and my being powerless to get them and get them in time and so on. But here, the All-knowing and All-powerful One being there, there is no question of that type arising. There can be no deficiency at all. Everything is absolutely perfect and absolutely reliable. If there is any deficiency, it may be on our side. It cannot be on His side. It is like a radio station transmitting messages and another station receiving them. Generally, we say, if one of them goes wrong, there will be no communication. But, here is a case in which the transmitting station cannot possibly go wrong. And if there is any deficiency, it must be in the receiving station. And the receiving station ought to correct itself, and there is nothing further to worry about.

Maxim of the bee and the insect

And here we are told of three further sub-divisions, or three paths. And these paths are also connected with the main paths of Karma, Bhakti, and Jñāna. We may start with what is called — Bhramarakīṭanyāya.* Owing to shortness of time, I'll

* Sati sakto naro yāti sadbhāvam hy ekaniṣṭhayā,
Kīṭako bhramaram dhyāyan bhramaratvāya kalpate.

[Vivekacūḍāmaṇi—117]

"With singleminded attachment to Sat (Reality-Brahman or God) man have to condense, I do not know when there will be an opportunity of going into a more detailed disposition of these subjects, but in the meantime, I will condense the argument, and give all that we have to consider and make up our minds about. We have the — Bhramara-kīṭanyāya where we are told that insects and worms, out of mere terror, go on contemplating, meditating on the form and the buzzing sound of the bee or wasp which has caught hold of them, and they gradually, by that constant meditation, get transformed into the bee or the wasp. Constant reflection, constant meditation on a particular form gives us even that physical form. That is one of the elementary things with which our Jñāna Yoga starts. The same philosophy is explained in the scriptures of Christianity, of Islam, of Buddhism, of Zoroastrianism, in fact, of all the religions in the world. Contemplate. And the contemplation, the meditation has to be made more and more concentrated. And if we immerse ourselves in that transformation inside, well, the physical transformation outside also mechanically follows. But, that is the path of Jñāna in which there is absolute self-abnegation, absolute self-surrender, and absolute sinking of the self, merging of the self into the God, and there is no further action necessary on the part of the sādhaka, for the purpose of sādhanā. So, that is there. And very few persons can be candidates for that path.

Maxim of the child monkey

And then, there's the alternative path, for those who can't do that, who can't concentrate absolutely and one hundred per cent on the Lord. The Bhakti Yoga comes in there with what we call, the Markaṭa-kiśoranyāya, or the maxim of the child-monkey. That example is given as an illustration of how Nature makes provision for all the needs of life. Well, what the zoologist, or naturalist, or scientist, who is an agnostic or atheist will call Nature, we speak of as God. God has provided already for all

attains oneness with It, (just as) the insect, contemplating on the bee becomes a bee."

Actually the transformation of larvae and pupae into full grown bees is a purely biological process. These maxims are based on popular beliefs and are used for elaborating a point.

contingencies, for all requirements. Everything is there already. Before the need arises, the needed thing is created and provided for. That is the law of nature. That is the law of God. And that is why we speak of God in the terms of providence and so on, providing beforehand for all needs. And here is an example. When the new-born monkey-child is there, and the mother jumps from one tree to another at a considerable distance, what can the child do? The child cannot jump similarly soon after birth, but there is a provision already made by Nature. The monkey-child grips the mother and in such a way that there is no possibility of loosening of the hold at all. And when the mother monkey jumps from one tree to another, the child-monkey is carried along with it. And no effort is needed on the part of the little monkey. Everything is done by the mother until a stage is reached when the child-monkey can fend for himself. And that is the provision made by Nature, made by God, in advance for that kind of species. That's the second sub-division.

Maxim of the cat and the kitten

And a third kind too has been provided for. That is the Wisdom of the Omnipotent God. God's Providence is to be found in this respect. The third example illustrates the variety we find in our experience of Nature around. And the example is called the Mārjāra-śiśu-nyāya, or the maxim of the cat and the kitten. In connection with the monkey, we find that the child-monkey could cacth hold of and cling to the mother. Well, the new born kitten hasn't got any such capacity at all. And in the case of such animals, we find that the mother does everything. The mother grips the little child with her teeth and carries it from place to place and looks after everything necessary until the kitten is able to look after himself, to fend for himself. So, that kind of arrangement is there.

The great mass of us is of the second variety. Not of course all, there are a few exceptions who are to be classed under the Jñāna Yoga category, but the great majority of people who are aspirants on the spiritual ladder come under the second variety. Well, there are some who are absolutely paralyzed, are incapable of doing things for themselves, and for whom all the thinking has to be done by others, and all the actual work has to be done by others. That is the kitten variety. But the great majority are not of that type. The great majority are of the middle type, and for them Bhakti Yoga is the only path.

Reliance on God

We saw the example of Arjuna and Śrī Kṛṣṇa as the owner of the chariot and the driver of it. The same thing is here. We rely on the Lord. And we have not got strength of our own to move about by ourselves, to discuss things for ourselves, to decide things for ourselves, and to do things for ourselves. We haven't the capacity for all this. We rely on the Lord. And whatever we can do, if we have the physical, mental and other capacities to do, in accordance with the instructions given to us by the Lord, well, that we do. And, the other things, well, we leave them to Him. He looks after things. He need not be reminded by us of His duty in the matter at all. He knows everything. He does everything, and we leave it to Him. But where we have the orders, and those orders are such as we can carry out, then we cannot pretend that we are in the kitten stage, or in the monkey stage, the monkey-child stage. Pretence will not prevail. But in the great majority of cases, as we actually are, with our mind intent on reaching the goal in this way, and with absolute loyalty, with no attempts to cheat, etc., well, there is no need for further anxiety in the matter. We rely on God like the child, in the example I gave, standing somewhere above and jumping down into our arms. The child can't support himself. He leaves the whole thing in our hands with absolute sincerity of faith. And no mother, father, or other such persons ever cheat him. But these people may, owing to want of omnipotence, fail. That possibility is not there in the case of the Lord, when we entrust ourselves unto him. That is the essence of the doctrine of Bhakti Yoga.

Śaktis

And when we come to the Bhakti Yoga, well, it is not one or two, but a large number of things, a large number of forces around us that we may look to. These are called the various mūrtis or śaktis in our scriptures.

Mūrtis means shapes, and the shapes are different. But it does not mean that there is any difference in the principles underlying all these activities in nature around us. Forces are innumerable. You may call them angels if you like, following the Hebrew terminology. Or you may call them devatās, śaktis, and so on, but the principle is the same. They are all forces of Nature. And forces work in the directions of prevention of evil, and protection of the good from the evil. These forces are controlled by the master Śakti. It is unfortunate that I have to use Sanskrit terminology, because the English language is deficient in this respect. Somehow, unfortunately, deplorably, in the scriptures of Christianity, from time to time, there were meddlings by way of additions and by way of subtractions also. Portions were added from the wrong point of view of prestige of the Lord. Things were attributed to Him which could not possibly be reconciled with His qualities. But the people had a wrong notion as to what constituted prestige and they added a lot of things in order to make things conform to their conception of fitness. And a number of things which they did not understand they eliminated, and our scriptures of Christianity have suffered in consequence enormously. One of the greatest things which I deplore is that while we have the conception of the Fatherhood of God given to us from the beginning to the end, we will not find any kind of reference, even of the remotest possible conception of the Motherhood of God. This is evidently due to artificial causes. There can be no question at all of the Mother being ignored. In our system even in the Vedas, we have Puruṣa and Prakṛti from the very beginning, and all the time when we talk of the Divine Father, the Divine Mother is also there. The two are in combination. Pārvatī-Parameśvarau. The Lord and the Devī, the goddess as we call her. What is the relationship between the two? The relationship is like the obverse and the reverse of the shield. The two are inextricably intertwined. *

* This idea is beautifully expressed by Kālidāsa in the first verse of his epic poem Raghuvaṁśa.

Vāgarthāviva sampṛktau
Vāgarthapratipattaye,
Jagataḥ pitarau vande
Pārvatī-Parameśvarau.

There can be no kind of separation of the one from the other. They are like a red object and its redness, the quality, the abstract noun. In English grammar we speak of redness. We never get redness without the red object. We see the red flower, a red cloth, and so on, and by a process of mental abstraction we separate the quality of redness for analysis with the view to re-synthesi ing. There can be no separation of the two. Goodness, kindness, and all these qualities and actions, are inseparably connected with and inseparably bound together to each other. That kind of position is there. And our scriptures have gone into very great details with regard to this question.

God as mother

We have the Motherhood of God, the Divine Mother described. The two are together. The Divinity is the same. It is not that one is of this sex and the other of that sex. God is one. But, God contains within Himself, both the aspects. The word God itself is unsatisfactory to us, for the simple reason that it is of the masculine gender. But there is no getting over the trouble, the language itself does not provide for any other gender for the word. We talk all the time of the Fatherhood of God and the consequent Brotherhood of Man and so on. As between the Fatherhood of God and the Motherhood of God, we are told again and again that the mother is the medium, and the easier to deal with. And the sādhakas are told that without the Mother, the meditation on the Father will not be satisfactory. Of course, there is no statement to the effect that it is useless or is not capable of producing good. That kind of exclusiveness, or fanaticism is not there, but we are told the exact relationship between the two. We have again and again passages coming up in which it is made clear that the two should go together. And in Sanskrit grammar, rules are laid down, that when the two are taken together, the Mother comes first, like Sītā-Rāma, and Rādhā-Kṛṣṇa and so on. In all these cases, even the grammar lays down the order, "Mātā ca pitā ca pitarau" and so on.

"For acquiring right knowledge of the words and their meaning, I pay homage to Pārvatī and Parameśvara, the parents of the Universe who are inseparably blended together like the word and its meaning."

"Mātṛdevo bhava, Pitṛdevo bhava."* "Reverence and obey your parents," that's a common term. The Mother is named first and then the father, because in all matters of this kind, it is the Mother that has the actual work of looking after the child. Regarding the human relationship of Mother and child, we have our own experience as to how the Mother is the nurse. The Mother is the protectress. The Mother is the person to whom the child instinctively turns under all circumstances. A child goes about playing, absolutely ignorant of where the parents provide his food from. He knows nothing about these things, and keeps on playing. He feels hungry, and runs at once to the Mother. It is the Mother that protects the Mother that looks after him. Kṣudhā-tṛṣārtā jananīm smaranti.** "When children are afflicted by hunger, thirst, or other difficulties, they run to the Mother, and the Mother looks after the needs of the child." That is the position. And the Mother makes the natural nurse. Of course there are cases of exceptions on both sides. Exceptions of Mothers who are unwomanly and men who are excessively gentle and so on. But in the great majority of cases, in fact in the normality of cases, you will find that woman's touch as nurse is much gentler and it needs no further expansion. It meets all the needs of the situation from time to time. I do not want to go into details on this subject because it is one which everybody, with a little reflection, can easily understand for himself.

Pre-eminence of mother

And in all these matters, you will find that the preference or the priority that is given to woman in our scriptures, the Vedas and other texts, is explained in this way. There is no partiality at all. There is no question of why the Mother has been given that priority. The Mother has been given priority even in regard to worship. On rising from bed in the morning, the child is asked first to prostrate himself before the Mother and then the Father and so on. But that is nothing. We are samnyāsīs, and are supposed to have abandoned the world,

* Taittirīya Upaniṣad I-11-2.

** From Devyaparādhakṣamāpaṇastotram.

but in fact, have not abandoned the world. We have not renounced anything, but have only expanded our jurisdiction of loving care and consideration, and have made up now a bigger family than before.* Even the sanyāsī is called upon to prostrate himself before his mother even after becoming a samnyasī. But that does not happen in the case of the father. Why ? Is there any partiality in the matter ? Generally, everywhere the complaint is that man has been antagonizing woman and he has been taking a greater share of authority and power into his hands in all matters. Well, as a matter of fact, individuals may be responsible for doing things of that type. But, so far as the Vedic scriptures, the religious trend, and the doctrine and dogma are concerned, the mother gets that priority. And, the reason is also explained. The first reason is based on the physical law of Nature, that as between the father and the mother, the mother is called upon to bear a greater burden. Motherhood means much more in the shape of self-abnegation from day to day than what the father is called upon to bear. In all matters you have that kind of position. A proud father may be fond of his child. He may pat and fondle the child. But so long as the child has had his food and is playing, smiling, and laughing and so forth, the father will show his love for the child taking him up for a few minutes. But the moment the child begins to cry, the trouble starts. He will call upon the mother to take over the child. It is the natural law by which the work had to be divided and the greater burden has fallen upon the woman's shoulders. That is the actual position. The child falls ill, abandons food, and milk, and sleep. The mother looks after the child. Hers is a selfless love, love for its own sake because the mother is the mother and the child is the child. Selfless love is symbolised by the mother. Our scriptures say again and again that the mother having been already dealt with in this raw manner by nature, should have no further burden placed upon her by way of earning her livelihood. She has to be looked after so far as her material needs are concerned by

* Cf Paramahansa Yogananda's concluding remarks in his '*Autobiography of a Yogi* :—"Lord, Thou hast given this monk a large family."

the father in her childhood, by the husband after marriage and by the sons in her old age.

Maternal love is seen in the animals also. When a person comes near a basket where the cat has lodged the kittens, well, the cat rushes upon the stranger to prevent him from stealing or doing any harm to the kittens. Mother's love, that is the natural thing there. The forces in nature, are present in allegorical, metaphorical, and symbolical shapes in the upāsanākāṇḍa of our scriptures. We are told again and again that the mother herself leads us. We rely on her. And, gradually, even when we have transcended the stage of absolute physical dependence and helplessness, we have the mother looking after us. It is through the mother that we feel connected with the father. And therefore, our scriptures say that from the point of view of self-abnegation a samnyāsī, the person who is supposed to have renounced the world is adorable. He is worshipped by all because of his self-abnegation. But the self-abnegation of the mother started long before. That is why the Mother is not called upon to go and prostrate herself before her own son who has become a samnyāsī. Even if she continues in the family life, she is the embodiment of self-abnegation, and selfless service. And if the son has now renounced the world, in the technical ordinary usage of the term, and if he has gone in for a life of absolute self-abnegation for the benefit of others, well, it is a new story for him. But it is nothing new for the mother. From the time of his conception, her responsibility, her self-abnegation began. She had to be very careful during the pregnancy, lest the child in the womb be affected. And then she had the trouble of child birth. Then again in the early years the child had to be very carefully looked after because of his physical helplessness. All these things were there. And this kind of demand is made by nature on the woman. I may give you one small example as to how this kind of thing actually acts in practice within the experience of us all.

A mother with a girl of seven or eight years of age, and a boy who is fifteen or twenty or twenty-five years of age, has a new child. Well, in looking after that child, she will get more help from seven years old girl than from the fifteen or twenty year boy. And therefore in our scriptures we are told, that we should regard all women as embodiments of the mother.* A very unique feature in India is that in our meetings, in our public discourses, we don't address the women in the same way as we address the others. We begin by saying 'mātāo'** 'Mothers,' That's the form of address. Even the little children in the audience, not only the girls but the little female children in the audience also, are regarded as embodiments of the mother. The worship of the mother has been regarded as not a preliminary to, but an integral part of the worship of the father. In fact, the two go together. That is our conception of motherhood, even with regard to our own physical selves, within the limitations of intellect, of character, of thinking and so forth, that we have in this human body of ours.

Divine Mother, Durgā

Much more sublime, therefore, is the feeling with regard to the Divine Mother. The Divine Mother is the all powerful Śakti, or Force in Nature, or Durgā. We have the eighteen-armed Durgā, eight-armed, ten armed, and with four arms, or two arms, and so on. All these idols have various instruments, various weapons in their hands. Well, tomorrow, we are having the first day of what we call the Caitra Navarātra.*** Just like the big Devīpūja festival in October, we have a smaller and briefer pūjā time, starting from tomorrow. Well, there, the motif will be found to be of different type, with a different number of arms with weapons etc. But in all these cases you will find that the objective is the destruction of the evil forces and the protection of the children, the protection of the good people from the ravages caused by wicked, evil-minded persons. The forces at work, are all symbolized in the Divine Mother.

* "Vidyāḥ samastās tava Devi bhedāḥ
striyaḥ samastāḥ sakalā jagatsu."
Durgāsaptaśati XI-6.

"O Mother Goddess, all sciences are your variations, and all the women in the world are your embodiments."

** Plural of Mātā (=mother) in Hindi.

*** The first nine days of the second (bright) half of the lunar months Caitra and Āśvina are devoted to worship of Divine Mother, and are known as Navarātra.

Where we go into details of things, well, naturally the number of things will be greater. I'll not go into detailed description just now of the eighteen arms and the instruments they bear, not even of the two, but the following example will give you the gist of it all. Suppose a student is studying the history of England. He also reads another book on the history of America; another on the history of Greece; a fourth, on the history of Rome; and the fifth on the history of India. Well, you will say there are five books that he has brought to study. Now, if the five books can be stitched together into one volume, and he studies the five books, he will still say, "I am a student of History, and I have to study this book. Going into details, you will find a larger number of books. And with regard to the history of America for example, if you go into further subdivisions, you will have histories of North America, South America, and Mexico. And in South America, you will have histories of so many other states coming up. In North America you have Canada. In the United States itself, you've got so many states. If you go into the details of the symbolism of the instruments the idol wields naturally you have a larger number. But if you bring them under one category or one group, then you will have not eighteen arms but ten. With still further reduction it comes to eight, then four, and finally to two hands. And two hands mean the positive and the negative sides, the protection of the good, the destruction of the evil, the evil powers.* That is the symbolical, the allegorical meaning of the Devī, the Durgā, that we worship according to the rules laid down in the scriptures of Hinduism, that is Veda and so on.

But in all these cases you will find that the attitude is one of children looking lovingly forward to the mother, the Divine Mother, coming to their rescue against all evil forces, all evil powers that attack them, and ensuring their protection. This, in the Bhakti Yoga, is the particular path which is regarded as most efficacious. The efficacy is not because of any individual difference between various gods and goddesses. They are the manifestations of the same God and Śakti. But the manifesta-

*"Vadhāya duṣṭadaityānām. . . rakṣaṇāya ca lokānām. , . ".
Durgāsaptaśatī-IV-41, 42.

tions differ on account of differences in function, differences in details.

For example, we are told that after Durgā had her victory over the demons, Sarasvatī and Lakṣmī came on the scene. Who is Sarasvatī ? Sarasvatī is the goddess of learning. And Lakṣmī is the goddess of wealth. No learning is possible as long as there are enemies for us to be protected from, enemies in the shape of men and women who do evil, who cause harm to us, and in the shape of diseases and things of that type. So long as this kind of obstruction is there, so long as this obstruction is not removed, that is to say, so long as Durgā has not performed her divine duty as Mother, well, the other things are not possible at all, and there cannot be any scope for learning. That is, the goddess of learning, Sarasvatī, comes into the picture only after all these troubles have been removed. A person in serious illness, a person attacked by enemies, can't concentrate on his studies. He needs this preliminary help. And similarly, you can't enjoy your wealth in peace and in happiness until all these enemies are destroyed. That is why we're always given along with Durgā, the pictures of Sarasvatī and Lakṣmī as subsidiary factors. None is subsidiary in importance. They are all one and there is no particular purpose in separating one from another and claiming superiority for one over the other. It is one picture. But, in the picture, there is the question of sequence coming up. One makes it possible for the others to function, to perform different duties which are theirs. Similarly with regard to Gaṇeśa and Kārttikeya. The other forces are there. How the senses cheat us sometimes — our own senses, the sense organs with which we perceive things, shapes, sounds, smells. tastes, and so on. These mislead us, and to that extent, as misleaders, they're our enemies, and they have to be controlled, and brought under rule of intellect. The whole thing is in a picture which, from the standpoint of the ordinary human being, is easy to understand. The worship of the Mother, the Divine Mother, is the easiest of all, because it comes naturally to every child. He has to be told about the others, and the relationship afterwords. The person with whom he is related in the world is his mother. He turns to the mother naturally, and everything is carried on through the mother. And he knows his father and others through the mother. And therefore, we are told that the worship of the mother, being the preliminary thing, needs no explanation. No persuasion is needed for the child to go into that particular path and benefit thereby. So that is worship of the Divine Mother that we have. The Fatherhood of God is of course all right as a doctrine. We have no quarrel with it. We ourselves take it, and we have Durgā as the consort of Bhagavān Śiva, or the Lord. Bhavānī, Rudrāṇī are the names of Durgā. These themselves show the relationship, but, the worship of the mother is the one which comes naturally to us in the very first stage by the instinct implanted in us by Nature herself. And therefore, any process which takes advantage of this natural, instinctive procedure in life is bound to be easier than one which has to be labored about, which has to be explained, and which has to be accepted after a lot of questioning and understanding.

So, this is the cult of the Bhakti Yoga in general, and of Devī Bhakti, Devī Pūjā in particular. Here again, we have this peculiarity, this uniqueness in our scriptures, and in actual ordinary language also. We speak of the ladies all as devīs, forces of nature, goddesses. The popular names for the ladies are Draupadī devī, Pārvatī devī, Lakṣmī devī, Ramā devī, devī meaning goddess. Not only the names of deities but even the names of the ordinary women in our families the girls around, next door neighbours, and others, always end in "devī" that is, goddess. It is like saying Goddess Athena, Goddess Minerva, Goddess Juno, and so on, of the Greek and the Roman worship. Here also the same kind of principle is indicated. As regards the men, they are not uniformly called devas. Those who are devas are taken into account as devas and provided for. We have no quarrel with them. But at the same time, it does not automatically follow that every male person is a deva. But, this devītva, as we call it, the goddessness with regard to all, is instinctive. And as I have said, even little girls look after the little babies much better than their bigger brothers. Natural nursing, natural maternity is there. It is there instinctively, potentially in all female children too. This is the reason for the priority that is actually enjoined in the scriptures with regard to women.

I need not go into further details. I hope I've been able to say something, and to throw some little light at least on the subject, that is, the point of view from which we look at the three Yogas, the Karma Yoga, the Bhakti Yoga, and the Jñāna Yoga, the difficulties of the Karma Yoga on the one side, the Jñāna Yoga on the other, and the consequent need for emphasis on the Bhakti Yoga for the great majority of the human race. And then going further into it, the markaṭakiśoranyāya, the maxim of "Child-monkey" clinging to the mother, not letting her go, and therefore, saving himself in that way. We surrender to the Lord. We cling to the Lord. And it is His burden; it is His work; and He needs no advice from us as to how he should carry it on. And then, the various detailed portions of the Bhakti Yoga, we have "Jaganmātā"—the Mother predominating in our scriptures, and I have explained the reason why that is done. There is no question of partiality in the matter. It's a question of what you might call the economy of Nature in modern terminology.

Well, I shall close here with the prayer that this spiritual centre which has been functioning in this way, for the quest after God, Self-realization being the object, will pursue the paths of investigation of truth with open mind, which is the equipment necessary for the purpose, and carry on the work amongst all the people of the world and illustrate that no questions of denomination and sect and so forth, doctrinal, or other differences, should divide one from another. I hope this centre will act as a powerful force. It has been doing so in the past, and I hope it will continue to do it in future and in greater and greater measure as time passes by.

Well, I close with my prayers to the Almighty for the success and the progress of this institution. I hope, in later days, as soon as I can possibly manage, I shall have further opportunity of mixing with you,* and of contributing what I can towards your mission of helping people, the various adepts, even those who are not adepts, and those who are students on the earliest stages and so forth, in attaining self-realization by the attainment of correct knowledge and the path of correct conduct. This is my prayer to the Almighty, and this is my own personal benediction to you all.

* Alas ! no further opportunity did ever come. His Holiness shed his mortal frame on February 2, 1960 and attained Mahāsamādhi.

XVII WORLD PEACE

Discussion on "World Peace" between Dr. Arnold Toynbee & His Holiness at Washington and Lee University, March 26, 1958.

Dr. Toynbee : Your Holiness, Dr. Hayner, ladies and gentlemen, as we've been listening these last two evenings to His Holiness, a number of questions would have been rising in our minds. Certainly, they've been rising in mine. And I'm going to put forward some of the things that have been in my mind. They're not controversial questions, because there's nothing in what His Holiness has said that I disagree with.........what I want to try and do now is to get further light on what is in His Holiness' mind and what is in my own mind with regard to some of the points which he has already put before us, especially points at the meeting place between his two themes, the unity of the world religions and world peace.

Now, one of the fundamental points that His Holiness made in the first of his addresses was that in each of the great religions we are offered the same choice of several authentic approaches, each approach first being suited to some particular type of human nature, some particular kind of human character. The question I want to raise here is, are these different sects, as His Holiness calls them, in each of the religions, or the different religions themselves, agreed with each other on the question of the use of force in the service of religion ? I think, for instance, in the Koran, there is some authority given for the thing called Islamic holy war, the use of military force to further the cause of the Islamic religion. I don't know that in the doctrine of either Judaism or Christianity there is any explicit condemnation of the use of force in the service of religion, but, in the Old Testament, there are a good many, rather evident precedents, which have sometimes been called upon by those Christians and Jews to justify that use of force, as in the Crusades.

But, when you pass from this Western group of religions, Islam, Judaism, and Christianity, closely akin to each other, to the other great group in the world, the Indian group of religions and philosophies one sees, that Buddhism for instance has spread over half the world, perhaps half the human race are in some degree adherents of the Buddha's doctrine and practise today, and as far as I know, Buddhism has never used war to propogate itself. Of course, there have been states and governments which have been officially Buddhist in religion, and such states have opened up war with each other, for instance, Thailand and Burma, two Buddhist states which have often gone to war with each other. But I don't know of any evidence that the Buddhist religion has ever propagated itself by the use of war.

Towards the end of his address yesterday, His Holiness talked about the remaining possibility that there might be legitimate cases for war and resistance. And he cited the case of the American Revolutionary War. Which brings up, this is a question I would like to raise with him, the official Christian doctrine about so called just wars. I believe it was an accepted Christian doctrine in the past that cases might arise in which war would be legitimate, where war was likely to prove to be the lesser of two evils, and also, where by going to war, the party that made war could have a reasonable expectation of remedying the alternative evil. I suppose the American Revolutionary War would be admitted without much controversy as being a war of that kind. And I think if today you would put that question to say the descendants of the united imperialists of Canada, or myself and people of my generation in Britain, you would not find there was much dispute. All consider that the American Revolutionary War had been a just war and a tradition was set. Then you come to a later time, and think, not about the decisions that George Washington and the other founding fathers had to make but about the decision that Robert E. Lee had to make when he was first offered the command of the Union Army and then the command of the Confederate Army. This question of the just war again arises. Was the Confederacy justified in taking up arms in order to secede ? Was the north justified in taking up arms in order to reverse that secession and force the confederate states back into the Union ? Here we have the question, "was a war just or unjust ?" "Which side was just ?" "Which side was unjust ?" Though the war was fought seventy or eighty years ago, more than that now, it is still a very living question of controversy, which makes the point that this concept of just war can be open to controversy, though the Revolutionary War as distinct from the war between the States is one of a rather non-controversial kind.

Then another question has come up into my mind. What military risks ought one to expose oneself to for the sake of a good cause. The good cause I'm thinking of is the liberation of the East European countries, at present under Russian domination. We've decided that we will not go to war with Russia in order to try to liberate them. I think that's been said by responsible statesmen on the Western side, and we didn't go to war at the time of the repression in Hungary in 1956 for the very good reason that H-war over that issue would destroy Russia, but at the same time, it would destroy ourselves and the East European countries, and therefore would not be effective for producing the aim desired — the liberation of those countries, not destruction, Russia's destruction or our destruction. But there are possibilities (of steps) other than war for their liberation or of getting Russia to relax her control. One of those possibilities is disengagement, an idea that has been brought up by the government of Poland, one of these countries at odds with the consent of the Russian government. Now, disengagement in Europe would undoubtedly mean that the East European countries had a better prospect of liberation than they have now, because if there was disengagement in Europe, they would become of less importance strategically to Russia, and therefore, presumably, she would be more inclined to relax her control over them. So disengagement would be a big step towards their ultimate liberation, I believe, there's no doubt about that. At the same time, military experts on the Western side, point out that disengagement might put us at a strategical disadvantage, because obviously, the Russians being human, won't relax their hold on the East European countries, unless America withdraws her advance force in Western Europe. We shouldn't, if we were in Russia's position, forego an advantage except for a greater advantage. And experts point out that this might leave the West at a relative disadvantage to Russia and would not be a step toward the liberation of the East European Countries. How much of a risk ought we to take to help towards their liberation, how much risk at our own expense ? We sincerely desire their liberation. Does sharing our sincerity call upon us to take a risk ?

Then, finally, let me raise the much bigger question of what is and is not legitimate risk, which is being raised at this moment in my own country, and you've read about it in the paper. Should one take the great risk of unilateral disarmament for the sake of insuring the survival of the human race ? It is obvious I think that if atomic military power were in the hands exclusively of one government or one central power in the world, that would pretty well secure the survival of the human race, because there would be no future atomic war. Now we don't know the fatal effects of an atomic war, but we do know that even at present, it would probably destroy, perhaps, should we say, a third of the human race, two-thirds, and at the rate which armaments are progressing, we can foresee in no distant time when it would literally make the whole earth uninhabitable. The survival of the human race is obviously the supreme interest of all human beings, and I can't think of any more overriding duty than to provide for the survival of the human race, even at what seemed in the past a prohibitive sacrifice. You've seen the movement which Lord Russell, Bertrand Russell, has been heading in Britain, in which he advocates the unilateral disarmament of the West, or anyway, of Britain, at least disarmament in the atomic field. But, even if that led to the domination or perhaps the conquest of the West by Russia, that would be a lesser evil than an atomic war involving the destruction of the human race. And I think it's clear it would be a lesser evil. It puts quite a new problem, moral problem as well as physical problem before us. I'm today interested to know what His Holiness thinks on this point.

I feel myself, that if I were told that the price of peace would mean my country being occupied by the Russians and people like myself, who have perhaps said things very obnoxious to the Russian regime, being at best muzzled, and at worst, liquidated, but that I knew that at that price, I could be sure that everybody's grandchildren would have grandchildren, including the Russians and myself and people in this country and everywhere, I think that would be a very good bargain. This is something that we shall have to weigh and discuss, I think, in the coming months and years, with very much heart-searching.

I have one more question. By far, the most striking, I'd say, marvellous example of achieving great results by non-violence in our lifetime, has of course been the Mahatma Gandhi policy of non-violent non-cooperation with the British Government in India, which produced true results. It made it quite impossible for the British to go on ruling there, and it also made it impossible for them to depart with bloodshed, because you cannot fight somebody by force who is abstaining from using force against you. Now, in that I think, all English people, looking back on that episode of Indian and British history, feel that great as the service was that Gandhi did for his own countrymen, his service to us British was hardly less, because whereas we went out of the thirteen colonies, with defeat, and a good deal of dishonour, we went out of India with the friendship of the Indian people and I think with honour. And I think we owe that very largely to Mahatma Gandhi and to the spirit of the Indian people and the spirit of our own people who were able to conduct the final separation between the British and the Indians in a non-violent way. The question I want to raise is whether the forces which were successful in bringing independence to India and promoting goodwill between the Indian people and the British people, could in His Holiness' opinion, be applied outside India and in other cases, if not why not. Were there special favourable circumstances which gave the policy of non-violent non-cooperation this remarkably happy ending in this case ? Or, is it something with universal application ? If it is, I think it has a very great bearing on the question of how to secure peace in the atomic age, and on this question I was raising just now, what are the legitimate or necessary risks that we ought to take ?

But now, I've raised a number of questions, I've taken quite a lot of time, and I'd like to hear His Holiness speak.

Moderator : Thank you very much, Dr. Toynbee. I think it appropriate to ask His Holiness first the question which I think Dr. Toynbee raised first, with respect to the religious basis for a just war. Does His Holiness believe that there is any religious justification for what is sometimes called a just war ?

His Holiness: The first question is as regards the possibility of a just war. That is to say, in the light of what I was saying the day before yesterday and yesterday here, is all war ruled out under all circumstances ? That is to say, war is not justified at any time, any place, or under any circumstance. Is that the position that I take up in the name of religious prohibition that I was speaking of on these two days ?

I believe I have answered the question already although not in this particular form. Yesterday, I was referring to the possibility of a person being so obtuse and obstinate as to be incapable of hearing anything reasonable, listening to reasonable arguments and so forth, and, under such circumstances, I said, that there would be no possibility of our saying that peace is sacrosanct under all circumstancer, and was is never justified. I said "peace with honour" is what we want. And if we have reached a stage in which that is impossible, war is justified. War can be a just war as well as an unjust war, and the whole question is whether the war we are fighting is just or unjust. But long before that stage is reached, we have to see whether it is an avoidable war or absolutely inevitable. The idea that according to religious faiths war was inevitable between people of different countries, different faiths, and so forth, that idea, being a wrong one, fundamentally, radically wrong, I began the series here with my objections to war supposed to be motivated by religious sanctions, religious injunctions of the founders for the destruction, for the extermination of pepole of other faiths and so forth. That is what led me to speak on the religious aspect of the matter on the first day and, to some extent, yesterday also.

But there are cases, there have been cases, and there must be cases in which there is no possibility of justice unless the arbitrament of war is sought. I referred in general terms to this aspect of the question yesterday, and I said, that in case we have reached a stage when war becomes inevitable, then we prepare for the "deluge" the final destruction of the universe. I mentioned especially St. John's Revelation, wherein, there is a prediction of the world coming to an end as the result of what we might call the biggest of "deluges" possible, fire and rain and everything. And the whole world is bound to be destroyed. If and when that stage is reached, well, we bow down to the inevitable and accept it as being unavoidable. I have said that yesterday. And incidentally also, I spoke of the American war of Independence. I mentioned George Washington's name in that connection. I said that the Pilgrim fathers had to leave England and to come over to America for the purpose of obtaining freedom of religious worship and belief. With that to start with, as the genesis of the present American government, the present American states, the United States of America, Washington had, as I mentioned later on, to oppose and stand up before the might and the persecuting fire of the British Empire of those days. And from the way I talked about it, it must have been clear that I regarded the war of Independence under George Washington in the time of King George the Third of England, a just war, a righteous war, and I have absolutely no objection to such a war. I did not go into details of it because I thought this would be sufficient for the purpose.

And then the question came up of the Civil War, the trouble about the Negroes and so on. Even there, I have always held, and I still repeat, that I regard that war as having been a just war and an unavoidable war. And when war comes down upon us as duty, in the interests of righteousness, in the interests of peace "with honour," then, well, there is no backing out of it, there is no shirking of it, no shinking from it. The duty has to be performed. There is no doubt about that. There is no difficulty about that question at all. It is only where war is unavoidable and war is inevitable, because the unjust party is absolutely unamenable to reason, it is there that war is justified. If and when there is the possibility of avoiding war and there are avenues unexplored for bringing about peace "with honour," it is then that I wish to say, and wish to repeat again and again, that as a pacifist, well, I am for pacific measures, but not under all circumstances, not with dishonour as the price of peace.

I think I have made the question clear.

Moderator : Would you like to comment on His Holiness reply, Dr. Toynbee?

Dr. Toynbee : Really, I have nothing to say, because he's explained the point.

His Holiness : There is the possibility of our own religious principles being involved. By religious principles I mean fundamental, ethical principles which found the basis of all religions, not something in the shape of ritual, ceremonial, and things of external nature. Where fundamental, basic principles of an ethical character are involved, there is no getting away from war. Well, war is justified because that is a "just" war.

And I think I may take up also along with this question what I thought was indicated in Dr. Toynbee's preliminary talk, with regard to non-vidence, with which we were able to achieve Indian independence without having trouble with the British government, any kind of bitterness and so forth.

I think I was right in my understanding, of Dr. Toynbee's words to that extent. Well, even there, I always took up the position, all I still repeat that non-violent non-cooperation at all times, at all places, and under all circumstances, is not merely an impossibility, but, is by itself, well, a weak surrender to unrighteous might. It so happened, and we are glad it so happened, that without any such trouble we were able to achieve independence for India, from the political standpoint, on pacific lines, on non-violent lines. And perhaps, to be honest with ourselves, we may feel justified in admitting that even that success of non-violent non-cooperation in India was perhaps due to the big world war that was going on at the time. It may be not consciously, not intentionally, but as a by-product, that we achieved that independence with the aid of non-cooperation measures. Perhaps it would not have been so easy but for the war that was going on at that time on a huge scale, on a global scale. So I was never an advocate of that kind of peace. But at the same time, I have to repeat that if it is possible, 'with honour', to achieve that kind of peace by non-violent methods of non-cooperation and so forth, well, that is the best. And if that is not possible, then, I will have to repeat that we will have to bow down before the inevitable 'deluge' that seems to be in preparation for mankind. I said 'risk' involved. The danger remaining before us is the wiping out of the civilization, not merely the civilization or culture, but, the whole human race itself. And, that being the risk before us, it's all the more necessary that before we come to a conclusion that a certain war is not merely just but absolutely unavoidable, we should do all that is humanly possible for the human intellect for bringing about that 'peace with honour' which I have been talking about.

Moderator : Would you like to raise further questions along this line, Dr. Toynbee?

Dr. Toynbee : This question of 'peace with honour' is connected with the traditional view that there are certain situations in which war is certainly the lesser evil. But, the question is whether between 'peace with dishonour' in the traditional sense, and the ending of the human race, ought we to choose 'peace with dishonour' or ought we to choose the ending of the human race? That may be the kind of choice with which we may be faced. That's why I think the question of non-violent non-co-operation is rather important looking towards the future. If Mr. Gandhi's method were generally applicable, I think it could be applied against the Russians, in case of their conquering the world, as was the count against the British in India. Then we can look forward to a pacifist approach to the Russians with much greater hope, I think, and consideration. But if it were a special case which happened to succeed through a fortunate combination of circumstances, and isn't something to be taken as a general possibility pointing to the future, then I think our prospect is more gloomy. I myself think that however autocratic a government may be, there are always limits to its powers over human beings. And I don't know of any government, however strong that hasn't in some form sooner or later been successfully resisted and frustrated. But that's an arguable point. Opinions can be brought up against me in that. But my point is that this question of pacifism, which has been rather an academic or extremist point of view in the past, has now become a very practical and urgent question which we are going to be forced to consider in the near future.

Moderator : Would His Holiness perhaps like to comment on the question that I think is implied in Dr. Toynbee's remarks: "Is pacifism a practical policy for large numbers of people?"

Dr. Toynbee : In view of the new character of war.

Moderator : In view of the war situation which we now face, would pacifism on a large scale be a practical policy for nations or people?

His Holiness : It's a difficult problem no doubt. And one may say that the difficulty will be in proportion to the number of people called upon to play their parts in non-violent non-cooperation and things of that type. The lesser the number of persons involved, the lesser the difficulty will be. But where we have a huge mass of people involved in the matter and all are called upon to participate in the action from their own standpoint, the actual action, will necessarily be difficult and a great deal of heart searching and things of that type are called for. And that is why active propagandist work is necessary for the diffusion of the right knowledge so that there may not be the possibility of what you might call a 'mass inundation.' In a huge mass, involving lots of people, and when excitement comes, when passions are excited to a very great extent, in the ordinary affairs of war, there is very often the possibility, not always but very often, the possibility of the sensational, the excited condition of affairs, taking people off their feet altogether. Sometimes the excitement goes to the extent of sweeping the politicians off their feet. Or even if they're not intellectually, metaphorically speaking, "swept off their feet," there is the possibility of their being not able to resist what you might call a mass-flood on a huge scale like that. And therefore, the positive constructive side is being constantly emphasized, and I lay great stress on it in schools and colleges everywhere and also on the possibility of doing work, not merely the possibility, but the need, the desirability of doing their work with the consent of the people concerned. And that's always very difficult. I know that. There is what you may call a political stampede. The party in power may not be able to resist, and it may affect their chances of success in the next elections. Lots of complications come in. Factors which are really irrelevant to the subject on hand will come and interpose themselves, distort our vision, and warp our judgment. That kind of thing is possible. And therefore mass education is necessary on these lines. That unless and until the point of absolute tension, the point of absolute break-down has been reached, there should be no nursing of war. The Humanities should be subjects for instruction in schools and colleges and as far as possible, there should be an organized attempt to bring about a change in the angle of vision, a change of heart, and we should not lightheartedly go in for anything which would bring the deluge to us sooner than would otherwise be the case. And then again, when we talk of a just war and things of that type, who is the person to decide what is a just war and what is not ? That again is a problem which requires a solution. And people who have got their minds absolutely unbiased can deal with each issue as it arises on its own intrinsic merits and not be carried away by partisanship, prejudices, prepossessions, and so forth. Well, that is a very difficult thing no doubt. As a practical question from the realistic standpoint, it has to be considered. And that is why I said even with regard to the economic standpoint yesterday, that people concerned should gather together and put their heads together and deal with questions as they arise from the standpoint of the ultimate welfare and progress of the race itself as such. Not that we can step in and prevent colossal disasters, catastrophic calamities which threaten. Sometimes things take their own way and are taken out of our hands altogether and we are unable to do anything in spite of all our wishes, our best intentions, and so forth. But, it is our honest duty to do the utmost in the matter in this direction and if, after we have done everything possible in this way, we fail, well, we should be glad to acknowledge failure; as I said, we bow down to the inevitable. That's the only possible position. Whether it is possible or not, well, that question is one which will depend upon the intrinsic merits of the situation at each moment as it arrives. There can be no mechanical rule laid down beforehand that such a thing is avoidable under all circumstances, or it is to be regarded as abominable under all circumstances. There can be no such mechanical formula at all. Each case will have to be taken on its own intrinsic merits and dealt with in that way, without prejudice, without prepossession, even in favour of pacifism. While we are pacifists, we should not at the same time become bigots and fanatics with an exclusive frame of mind, well, with a closed mind, and refuse to listen to reason, and the dictates of reason. So the whole question has to be weighed and considered from this standpoint, that war is avoidable. In many cases we have to consider the question from the standpoint of persons looking on now. On looking back on ancient history, in very many instances we will say that such and such war was fought under circumstances of a compelling nature as they were believed to be at the time, but they were not really so. That is our feeling with regard to many wars connected with history of the various countries in the world. But then, at the time of crisis the passions run high, and reason hasn't much chance of getting a hearing. That kind of thing comes. And therefore we should take every possible precaution to prevent that possibility. That is all that can be said. I cannot, even as a pacifist, as I said yesterday, support the idea of peace at any price, of peace with dishonour. Where the honour, justice, truth, and the welfare of the people are concerned, there can be no other considerations at all in the matter. We can't have our own ideas, however keenly and eagerly felt by us imposed on others. Our ideas cannot change the situation for the better. And we have to deal with these matters as they actually come.

With regard to non-violent non-cooperation in India, I took the view, and I expressed my views openly, that that was the best thing if we could possibly do it. And putting it in a blunt form, I used to say that if we wished to achieve the independence of India, from the political stand-point, that was perfectly right. But, the independence was to be achieved by non-violent means if possible, and by violent ones if absolutety necessary. Well, it can't be put more clearly than that.

Moderator : Would you like to comment on His Holiness' remarks, Dr. Toynbee ?

Dr. Toynbee: Yes. My own impression, is looking back on the years since the end of the second World War, that there has been quite considerable change of heart on both sides of the Iron Curtain as a result of the invention of atomic weapons. I think we've seen a number of situations since the end of the second World War in which, in times past, with the weapons people then had, and with the attitude towards war which they then had, one or other of the sides would have gone to war. And in the present circumstances, they haven't gone to war. I don't think there is any great danger that any government including the Russian Government will go to war lightheartedly or irresponsibly in the world as it is today. I think the danger of the situation is rather that we have these terrific arms on either side. They are geared to go off at a touch. And war might be started by accident. Certainly, in my country, that is what people are afraid of. They don't think either America or Russia would deliberately make an atomic world war, but they think that it might be started by some mistake of some rather irresponsible individual. Then the thing might go off automatically.

Now, that raises this further question, ought we therefore, for the sake of peace, to take much greater risks to our own national interests, even national independence than we have thought reasonable in the past ? Because disarmament always involves risk. You can't get anywhere in disarmament unless each side in its own way takes considerable risks. How big are the risks that we are going to be willing to take in these times just ahead of us for the sake of insuring the continuance of the human race ? That's the way I see it. Therefore, I think it would be clear that if we still say that there are some situations that would be intolerable, we will, as in the past, make war rather than face that situation. But the alternative may be, there may be no situations. May be the end of mankind. And I think that is something new which we haven't been compelled to face before. And I think it does ultimately make our choice a more serious one, and perhpas alters its character and puts the question of pacifism versus just war in a new light.

Moderator : Dr. Toynbee, would you allow me to ask you a question ? Do I understand you to say that you favour a policy such as that which I think is associated with the name of Bertrand Russell, of total unilateral disarmament, such that a given nation might voluntarily give up all armaments for the sake of peace and survival of the human race ? Would you want to come in favour of that ?

Dr. Toynbee : I don't know whether I favour it. But I feel that it's up to all of us to think about it very seriously. We dismissed it before the invention of atomic weapons, as not practical and also probably as not reasonable or right.

But I think we have to reconsider it. I don't know what my final view would be. But I do feel as far as I'm concerned that the question I am having to decide — we each have to decide this question in our own minds — is a new question and a different one from what it was before the invention of atomic weapons. I wouldn't go further than that. I don't think one can give an immediate yes or no answer. I think it will be stretched out. It will be at least months and years in all our minds.

Moderator : I wonder if His Holiness would care to speak on this point. The question is, would His Holiness favour a national policy of total disarmament ? A voluntary laying aside of all armament for the sake of the survival of the human race in the atomic age, a policy which conceivably might be pursued by one of the great powers such as Great Britain or the United States or even Russia. Do you understand my question, sir ? Would you care to speak to that point ?

His Holiness : The question of disarmament is one which requires careful consideration and which the people concerned can alone take responsibility for. We, giving advice as well-wishers, and even as armchair politicians, can't take the responsibility for taking positions on these matters. And that again brings us into a vicious circle. The whole trouble arises in that way. There is mutual apprehension, mutual fear. Each side seeks justification for its policies before the bar of public opinion, world opinion, stating that there is no aggressive intention on the part of this nation towards others, but there's a possibility of the other side going in for aggression, and in sheer self-defence, this nation has no option but to keep on at full strength and prevent all possibility of any such catastrophe actually materializing. And each side blames the other for it. And this kind of thing goes on all the time. I'm not going into any particular question, any particular detailed issue with regard to any person, any group, any party, any government, any country, and so forth, because in all these matters, the individual personal equation comes in again, as I was mentioning yesterday and the day before. You cannot take it for granted that every Russian is necessarily procommunist. You cannot take it for granted that every American is anticommunist.

These are personal differences. People who have power in their hands, who have the destinies not merely of their own country but of other countries in their hands, have to decide matters. And when they have to decide matters there is every possibility of their personal predilections, prejudices, prepossessions, and if you like to add, bigotry, fanaticism, exclusiveness, and all these having their own repercussion, and, well, tending to sway the judgment of the people. And it is because of this possibility that, as pacifists interested in the salvation, the salvage of the world, we feel that all that we can do is to appeal to all parties concerned that before any exciting situation of that type comes in and prevents cool reasoning, prevents all possibility of cool and calm thinking, they should sit together and devise positive constructive measures for mutual consultations and so forth. And it is by this kind of previous work that there can be less and less argument and we can even hope to reach the stage of practical absolute disarmament. Otherwise, of course, each person will naturally feel that if he gives up his armaments from the standpoint of the moralist, from the standpoint of the one who is interested in culture and wants to prevent the destruction of the world and so forth, then the other side may take advantage of it. The whole thing breaks up because it is this vicious circle that is going on all the time. And therefore, we must do something before any kind of 'incident' happens, that's the technical expression they always use, for a border incident somewhere in a small corner of the globe, that sets a whole big huge conflagration up for the world to look after later on. Long before that stage is reached, when things are still what you might call in an incipient stage, or in a preparatory stage with possibilities in the wrong direction, if there can be arrangements for politicians, diplomats, and others, religious heads, pacifists, and the students and professors in colleges, universities. and so forth, and politicians and others who are in power, to gather together and see that things are not worsened from any hasty action of ours. All along the history of the world, we have been seeing that the people of the country involved in a particular war some centuries ago are themselves now convinced that their ancestors fought that war without sufficient justification. They themselves feel it. The troubles we had between

England and France, England and Scotland, England and Ireland and various other places are of this nature. Futility of such wars could have been realised much earlier; only the mind, the willingness was not there. Their decisions were not sufficiently supported by valid reasoning or even by rational thinking as regards the future. People lost their balance of mind, their sense of proportion, and did unreasonable things. Later on, the descendants of those very people felt in their own heart of hearts, and very often they actually said in their public writings and speeches, and even when they did not say it, they felt, that such and such a war was fought unnecessarily and needless bloodshed was caused by it, and much harm resulted to the human race as a whole. That kind of after-thought comes in. Instead of having to go through this experience of repentance, we should have the arrangements for previously discussing matters and preventing awkward incidents. You have a saying with regard to medical science, "prevention is better than cure." The same thing will have its proper application here.

And with regard to the question of armaments, as things stand at the present moment, there can of course be no kind of advice given by armchair politicians and armchair critics, and especially people who are not likely to be directly involved in the actual operations of the war and who will not be personally affected in any manner. For such armchair critics and armchair advisors it would be cheap to give advice, but, difficult for others to carry it out. The principle would be all right, but the advice has to be supported by positive and constructive work of a steady character for the purpose of bringing about the uplift, of not one nation but of the very world which is to be regarded as one state, one government similar to the United States of America, which is a federation of all the various states. There is local autonomy for purposes of a local character. And the interests of the whole nation, the whole state, as such, are looked after by the federal government. This kind of arrangement is there. The same things should be possible for other countries, other portions of the world, the whole of Europe, for example. As I was mentioning the other day, we start with our own personal idiosyncracies, needs, fads and so forth, and then we extend our region of love or jurisdiction, to the members of the family, and we go on from stage to stage until we cover the whole globe within that jurisdiction. That is the kind of feeling that I have. Unless and until that stage is reached, there will be sorrow and suffering and, avoidable sorrow and suffering, that is what makes it worse. Things which are being brought about pacifically in various ways, even at the present day, could have been similarly dealt with in the past. We learn from past mistakes. But now, I think, the time for learning, the time for novitiate, has long expired, and there should be no further need for that kind of training by constant suffering and by repentance and turning back when it is too late. Even when a person cannot but feel that his people were in the wrong in the past, he cannot say so. Prestige stands in the way. And lots of other things come in. Lots of irrelevant factors come in which should not guide us, which should not, well, warp our judgment. And if we make necessary preparation in this way from a positive and constructive standpoint, I think in due course, even the question of disarmament will prove easy to solve. That is the line I would adopt for the purpose. I don't ask the United States or England or any country to go in for disarmament immediately because I realize the difficulties that stand in the way of that kind of easy and quick solution. A solution that is easy and quick is not necessarily practical and is not necessarily the best under the circumstances. I suggest that a positive and constructive method for promoting of peace, is to bring about one world-state, with the various states, the present countries in the world taking their positions as autonomous units with sufficient autonomy to look after local affairs for themselves. The world affairs should be looked after by a world body, a world government, one State, one Tribe, one Nation, One Brotherhood. And even more than that, as I have said, it is not only universal brotherhood, but Universal Solidarity, not merely amongst human beings, but also amongst all sentient beings. That is the line that I would advise. There is no mechanical formula which I can place before anybody for consideration from the standpoint of the desirability of reducing armaments and achieving disarmament itself if possible.

Moderator : Thank you. Would you care to comment on His Holiness' remarks, Dr. Toynbee ?

Dr. Toynbee : Yes. One point. In a future war, do you think, your Holiness, that there would be anyone who would not be involved ? Wouldn't the whole human race be involved ? At the time of the Revolutionary War, only men, and men in uniform were involved. The civil population, male and female was out of it. At the time of the war between the states, a far larger part of the total population was already involved. I think in a future atomic world war the whole human race would be involved; the whole of it would be in danger of destruction. And that, I think is one of the new features. I agree of course, that we should press our governments to come together and never grow tired of trying to look for agreement by negotiation between each other, however disappointing the results may be, however slow, and laborious the work may be. And it will be laborious and disappointing, I think. But, then there is the vicious circle which His Holiness talked about which we've had unhappy experience of, especially over the question of negotiations between governments about disarmament. We've seen how difficult it is then to agree that such and such concessions on one side are exactly equivalent to such and such concessions on the other. And, as a result of that, we've seen between the wars a lot of very serious well-prepared and well-intended disarmament conferences come to nothing and we've seen, I'm afraid, a good deal of the same thing since this second war. And I think it is probably in the light of this that Lord Russell has started his movement. I've seen no more of this movement in Britain than what we've been reading in this country about it, but I think probably Lord Russell's movement is, the idea behind it is, that we have to break this vicious circle, break this deadlock, and do it by some rather revolutionary act, even at a great risk to the people. But that risk which might have seemed Quixotic or foolish or anyway unreasonable in the past may be reasonable in view of what the alternative is, on the principle of the just war, you have to weigh the two alternatives. Is war the lesser evil ? Will war, if you decide that it is a lesser evil, bring about the results for which you fight ? If it's not a greater will, it is not the lesser. And if it is not going to bring about the results for which you are fighting, then, according to the traditional doctrine about the just war, war is not justified.

Well I think I can't imagine a future world war which would bring about results intended by either belligerent, effectively. And I can't imagine a greater evil than even partial destruction of the human race. No tyrannical regime lasting for even many generations could be as bad as that. That's why without giving a 'yes' or 'no' answer to this tremendous question, I say that we have to consider this question. And I think probably that the movement led by Lord Russell has perhaps done a service in raising it in this rather revolutionary and dramatic form. I think probably the feeling in Britain, is very serious. It has to be taken seriously, on this subject of atomic warfare. It seems to be shared in Western Germany to some extent.

Moderator : Would His Holiness care to make any further comment on the remarks of Dr. Toynbee ?

His Holiness : I would reemphasize the point with regard to practical points to be taken for disarming, not mere disarmament, but disarming opposition and hostility from people's minds. I would like to give by way of illustration the examples of eloquent character in the history of England, Scotland, America, and so on which go far to support the view that I have been placing before you.

Between England and Scotland there was continuous warfare going on. Similarly between England and France. When at the time of King Henry the Fourth of England, there was fighting with France, and Henry the Fifth carried it on, well, the people of England were convinced that the French people were in the wrong and Britain was in the right. I don't suppose at the present time any Englishman would make that claim. Even students of Shakespeare's King Henry the Fourth, King Henry the Fifth, and so on, will agree that it was not a just war on the part of England. Historians definitely record that it was not a justifiable war. According to the law which prevailed in France at that time, such and such things were rightly done and such and such things were wrongly done and so on. The students agree about it. And present day English Historians, agreeing about this question of war with France in those years, well, that is a pointer. With regard to Scotland, William Wallace, one of the greatest Scottish patriots, fought continuously but he failed and was captured and, as an example to all would-be traitors, traitors to England, his head was stuck up at Tyburn. And soon afterwards, his own political and spiritual disciple, Robert Bruce, carried on the war, and he succeeded. The battle of Bannockburn resulted in the liberation of Scotland from England. And people talk of Robert Bruce to the present day as the liberator of Scotland. As for William Wallace, he was not talked of as a liberator. He was talked of as a traitor. And if Robert Bruce had been similarly captured, he would have been hanged too as a traitor. The same thing is with regard to Washington here. If, during the time of King George the Third of England, the ministers and others had had the good sense to look at things from the standpoint of justice, I don't suppose there would have been any trouble at all. And, on various occasions, such things happen and are amicably adjusted. Things go on like that. But if, like William Wallace, Washington had been captured, he would have met same fate at the hands of his English captors, as William Wallace had. And at the present day, year after year, when you have your Independence Day celebrations here, Washington's Birthday celebrations and so on, you find similar celebrations of the same events in England by English people. It was inconceivable in earlier days. I remember that in *The Tale of Two Cities*, Charles Dickens with his usual humour, makes fun of the position taken by the big Englishmen of those days. To think of Washington as being on the same terms of equality, on a level with King George the Third of England, was resented as an act of the utmost treason to England. And any person who suggested any thing like that, who took the name of King George the Third and George Washington together in the same breath was regarded as an enemy and a traitor to England. At the present time, we have reached the stage when English people even celebrate Washington's birthday. But such change of heart is gradual. Any attempt to expedite the process, is bound to end in failure. All the difficulties in the way, mostly of a psychological character, have to be dealt with, have to be removed, before we can expect to have the success we desire. In the meantime, if we are not reckless about things, if we take sufficient care to devote our utmost attention from the standpoint of unbiased truth and justice, we shall be going a long way to avert disaster that I've been talking about. I don't suppose that there is anything more that can be done. When people come into that kind of excitement, it is difficult to control them. It becomes too late to attempt to control them. Any kind of preventive measures like damming of rivers and so forth have to be taken before the big floods begin. The same principle has to be applied here. And from my standpoint, it is the positive and constructive work of a nation-building character, and subsequently, world-reconstruction character, that I am interested in academically and practically. And this is the only appeal that can be made to any body of intelligent persons, and no mechanical formula will solve the problem. We have to gird our loins; we have to put our minds together and achieve whatever we possibly can in the direction of preventing that kind of thoughtlessness, of excitability, and swimming down the stream, which has become very common with us. We float down the stream, and sometimes, we find persons justifying it in the name of the *Zeitgeist*, the Time-Spirit. People say, at such time, when the atmosphere is so full, so surcharged with emotion of this type, excitement of this type, it is not possible to do anything else, well, we'll have to float with the current. Now, this kind of argument is a false argument and is calculated to mislead and misguide the people. To those who talk of the Time-Spirit, as leaving us no option in the matter, I would simply say that in any flood, even where there is a huge, big flood, well, floating down the stream is not a healthy sign at all. The trees on both the banks stand in their own places, and they float down the stream, only after they have been uprooted or felled. Similarly the animals, the human beings as well as cattle, struggle to follow their own path, to reach their own objectives so long as they're alive. But when death has intervened, when they have lost in the struggle they float down only as carcasses and corpses. With persistent work, it is possible to achieve a change of heart, a change of psychology, a change of ideology. It is possible to achieve the federation of all the states of the world as one State, with local autonomy, prevention of crime and so forth. It is not merely desirable, it is not merely possible, I'm afraid it is the only thing that can possibly be done which will help us to let modern civilization and even our race, the human race itself to survive. That is all I can say on the matter by way of, well, the message of peace — peace, not under all circumstances, but graduated and pliant, contributing to the ultimate objective by means of the various peaceful methods and policies possible, without betraying the cause of justice and of honour.

Moderator : Thank you, Your Holiness and Dr. Toynbee. I am sure that we are all most grateful to both participants in this discussion for a most enjoyable and most enlightening evening. We want to thank His Holiness for his extended visit, and certainly Dr. Toynbee for his willingness to take part in the meeting. Thank you both.

XVIII THE SPIRITUAL APPROACH TO WORLD PEACE

This article is based on the lecture delivered by His Holiness at Teacher's College, Connecticut. Lady Chester Bowels presided.

Even the meekest and most unegotistical human being regards man as the crown of creation. It is taken for granted, whether consciously or unconsciously, that we are superior to all other sentient creatures.

Now, having come to birth as a human being, it behooves each of us to think over this matter and to ask himself : "What is the truth about it ? Is the belief well-founded or is it prompted merely by vanity ?" If it is true that man is God's noblest handiwork, he should endeavour fully to express his uniqueness. If man's assertion of pre-eminence is false, he should cease to make it and should regard himself as being on the same level as the brutes.

Persons having the question put before them at once rebel against the idea that the belief is false and that man is no more than an animal. If their attitude is correct, it is based not on conceit but on a real, historical, and psychological truth. What is the quality in which man's greatness, his superiority, resides ?

Even with regard to small things of a worldly type, of a material character, when we come across something that has a special value, that possesses some important superiority, we try to put it to its utmost use and to take the highest advantage of it. Similarly, if there is an element of greatness within us that really makes us the crest-jewel of creation, we ought to realize it and determine to utilize it in all conceivable directions.

Considering merely the physical side of man, the belief that he is the greatest in the universe cannot be supported. Elephants, rhinoceroses, and a number of other animals surpass man in hugeness of body and in physical strength. In regard to numerous other considerations, we could take up one point after another and would have to admit that in these respects, also, man is not superior to other parts of creation.

Finally we would have to say that the one and only way in which man transcends other creatures is in his spiritual and intellectual qualities. Intellect not in the sense of acuteness or cunning but intellect motivated in all its activities by a spiritual urge is the high privilege and the special qualification of mankind, as such.

How far have we been able to employ our unique gifts for the benefit of all — not merely for ourselves as individuals but for the races, nations, communities, and groups of the world ? In what way have we rendered our intellect and our spirit of use to ourselves and humanity ?

If we go into this question we will have to admit with sadness (and not merely with sadness but with a sense of shame; with our heads bowed down) that we have not done justice to ourselves as human beings.

Quoting a few words of my own from another context, I will say : "Strange and stirring, critical and epoch-making are the times." The transition period in which our lot is cast has brought us tremendous conflicts between ideologies, frames of mind, and modes of life. We have come to a point of imminent nightmare, of apprehension that war drums may be heard at any moment. There is trouble everywhere. And man, with all his intellect, with all his ingenuity, has not yet been able to face the actual historical fact of the situation.

Things are going in a direction that all people, desiring the welfare of the human race, are deploring. Leaders of different schools of thought, of different systems of religion and culture, agree on this point. It may be that the details are different, that we have our differences of opinion as regards the path to the goal; but that the aim of humanity is the attainment of peace and joy is admitted by all. Our religions may be different, our denominations, our sects, our subsects, and our sub-subsects are there in plenty, with great differences marking one group of humanity from another. All these contradistinctions being present, we cannot hesitate to say that on such and such points we differ. But so far as the goal is concerned, there is no difference at all.

What is the goal ? If we put it in philosophical terms, as found in the Upaniṣads (the Vedānta of the Hindu scriptures), the goal of mankind is perfection. Physical perfection ? Yes. Material ? Yes. Political, educational, intellectual, and spiritual ? Yes. All-round perfection is what man seeks.

Every person desires a strong, healthy physical body and is unwilling to have it tainted by any weakness or disease. Man craves perfect health and strength not merely for the body but for the mind also. No one wants any kind of lopsided development. The word perfection does not admit of any qualifying, any limiting adjective at all. We want complete, all-round perfection.

This is the goal we are after. That we are unable to fulfil our aspirations and to attain perfection in physical strength, intellectual power, and spiritual insight is a matter deplored by all of us.

What have we done, what are we doing, to justify our nature with its unique endowment of reason and spirituality ? Physically, mentally, educationally, artistically, culturally, and so on, we have got many of the various things we desire. But at the end of it all, as the resultant, the consequence of it all, what a world situation we see before us!

From time to time we have the urgent feeling that something should be done to avert the threatened calamity. World peace is desired by all because prosperity is dependent on peace. We talk about prosperity in various senses. There may be physical health, there may be economic strength, there may be military power. All sorts of resources may be available to us, at our disposal. And yet so long as there is no peace we cannot derive true satisfaction from these advantages and facilities.

This being the case, we have to think of the matter from the standpoint of spirituality, coordinating all the various parts that go to make up what you might call our physical, intellectual and spiritual "build". The body is there; the intellect is there; and the motivating spirit behind them. We possess these gifts; and what use are we putting them to?

If there be an honest, introspective study of this particular point, we should be able to arrive at conclusions of benefit to humanity. It behooves every thinking person to take all the facts and factors of the situation into account, to weigh the pros and cons, and to offer solutions calculated to lead humanity on farther and farther in the direction of real progress, with no "ifs" or "buts" to spoil the whole meaning of all that we have been acknowledging as not merely man's rights but man's duty. Man's prerogative is there; and at the same time man's responsibility is there.

We can look at this matter from the standpoint of religious study, the examination of various religions. We are told, for example, in the first book of the Old Testament that man is God's noblest creation, that God created man in His own image. Other texts in the Bible say the same thing.

In the Indian scriptures we find similar passages. "Man is the highest in creation." Verses after verses, chapters after chapters in the Vedas describe Man's superiority and consequent responsibility. He has facilities and advantages that none else in creation has. And responsibility naturally follows facility. Every advantage we possess is, *ipso facto*, a reason for our further responsibility. And insofar as we are loyal to the performance of our duty we justify the greatness that the scriptures ascribe to us.

When we go into this question the first thing to do, as in the case of treatment of an illness by a doctor, is to diagnose the disease. There is something ailing humanity. All persons from the most religious to the most atheistic, from different schools of thought, admit that something is wrong with the world and that conditions require rectification.

Reconstruction is necessary. Not that we propose to construct something superior to that which God created; that's not the idea. But when a house that has been splendidly built becomes dilapidated, we repair or rebuild it. We rectify matters and try to bring them to their proper state. Anything in our life that is an aberration, a deviation from normalcy, may be regarded, in doctors' language, as a disease.

In diagnosing man's ailment, we have first to consider the factor that distinguishes him from the other parts of creation. That is his Divinity within, his potentiality for the highest development possible. Such a potentiality is there. And that potentiality has to be brought out, to be manifested, to be given full scope so that the world may benefit by it. And we ourselves, as individuals, automatically benefit by whatever helps society on to further and further progress.

Diagnostic discussion is first necessary because in most cases one must know the root cause of the trouble before he can take steps to eradicate it; the cure automatically follows. In certain cases some additional treatment must be given, but generally the removal of the root cause of the disease is sufficient to restore one to health. That is why careful diagnosis is given such a prominent place in medical science.

One of the gravest factors in the present world situation is a lack of true religious understanding. How many wars have been fought in the name of religion ! During the 11th to 13th centuries Europeans conducted the Crusades. People imagined, they were told by interested parties, by bigots, by fanatics with exclusive notions of all sorts, that loyalty to one's own Lord was incompatible with permitting other people with different ideas to thrive, nay, to live. So for centuries, in the name of God, the Crusades continued.

In the history of England we are told about King Richard I and the great part he played in the Crusades. It was taken for granted by him, as by thousands of other persons, that it was a religious duty to exterminate the Saracens, not to let them live under the same sun, and so on. That kind of idea was there. It was not based upon anything intrinsic to spirituality nor to anything basic and fundamental in the moral law. It was an attitude adopted merely from the standpoint of exclusiveness, of self-laudation, as I have called it, and of the superiority complex that causes men to say : "We are entitled to passports for heaven. We are not satisfied with assigning ourselves to heaven; we cannot rest until we have consigned the people of all other religions to hell."

Peter the Hermit preached the "Holy War," and the kings and the people of various parts of Europe followed his advice and carried on the Crusades. But two things gradually became clear. One : that the war was a waste of effort. The mere inutility of it, from the standpoint of success, and the utter futility of it impressed itself upon the people concerned. They came to the conclusion that it was not possible for them to achieve victory within any length of time whatsoever. That was the first thing. And the second thing was that they — not merely saying we cannot redress matters, we are unable to change things, we must bow to the inevitable — came to know a real change of heart.

That change of heart was exemplified in the case of King Richard I as a personal experience. He knew that in England and other countries the name of Saladin was uttered by parents to troublesome children as a threat to enforce obedience. Saladin was regarded as a monster of cruelty, an embodiment of everything evil. That was the idea which King Richard himself entertained about the personal character of Saladin.

During his campaign King Richard suffered from a malady that his own physicians were unsuccessful in treating and that they regarded as incurable. Saladin, who besides being a great warrior was also a great physician, learned about the condition of the enemy. He went in disguise into the camp of King Richard, treated him, and cured him of the disease. The impression produced on the King's mind was naturally one that we would expect from a person of Richard the Lion-Hearted's noble character.

He said : "Is this the person who is considered a fiend, whose name is sufficient to make little children fearful lest he come and take them away, spirit them away, and eat their raw flesh, not waiting even to boil it ? Is Saladin this kind of person ? He enters the enemy camp. He does not seek to injure me in any way. And he treats my illness. He comes disguised because in his own personal role as Saladin there was no possibility of his being allowed to enter and treat the enemy king. He must be a man of extraordinarily philanthropic instincts and benevolent activities. If hell is the only destination for such a person, I'll have to change my views as to where I myself would like to go."

Richard revised his ideas to that extent, because he knew his own foibles, his own weaknesses, his own vanities; and was aware of the defects of his associates in the Crusades — the Duke of Austria and others whose characters could not be described as morally edifying. When Richard came to realize what kind of enemy he was dealing with, he did not feel justified in continuing the war.

After the Crusades, troubles arose between Roman Catholicism and Protestantism. During the Spanish Inquisition there was not merely heart-burning, there was body-burning, burning of living persons. That too was regarded as man's duty to his Lord, Master, and Saviour. Bigots said : "If we do not fight heretics to the death, fight to the finish, then we are disloyal to God." And what was all the trouble, the conflict, about ? About things which few on either side properly understood.

For example, amongst the doctrines and the dogmas that were in dispute was the theory of transubstantiation. What is transubstantiation ? Most of the people arrayed in battle on the two sides knew nothing about the subject. Yet thousands of them were dragged into the war to defend or attack this or that interpretation of transubstantiation. They fought on account of difference in faith, difference in intellectual grasp, difference in the inclination, the taste, and the capacities of persons of various backgrounds.

As time went on, people began to think about the matter further, and concluded that it is not wise, it is revolting to common sense to go to war over articles of faith, creeds, dogmas and doctrines. Even in the secular world, where man deals with objective facts—shapes, sounds, smells, and so on — even with regard to these, unanimity of opinion is not to be found.

For example, if you go to an art gallery and see the various paintings that are newly come for exhibition, you may find that your taste inclines you to admire only certain particular pictures. An eminent art critic may describe a certain new canvas as beautiful, splendid, angelic, perfect, and so on; while another person, equally renowned as an authority on art, may express a different opinion : "It is utter rubbish." This kind of extreme language is often used by both sides. Similary, with regard to music, what attracts and fascinates me, what captivates me, may be detestable to another.

Such differences in opinion are present even with regard to purely physical matters, in which one may justly say : "It is not a subjective affair, coloured by my mind and my emotions; it is something connected with objective Nature around us." The values of material things can be assessed by means of our five senses of perception : sight, hearing, taste, smell, and touch.

But, even there, wide differences of opinion exist among people, even with regard to matters that many men take for granted as being incontrovertible.

Leaving aside questions of this type and going into something more intellectual, let us consider courts of law, in which fundamental principles of jurisprudence and justice are discussed. Even there the same trouble is found. For example, in a case of a person accused of murder, two judges sit to review the evidence. Not a judge of a lower court and a judge of an appellate court, but two judges sitting on the same bench, in the same Supreme Court. They hear the same evidence, the same arguments; they read the same documents; and they are guided by the same principles of jurisprudence, so far as textbooks on law can advise them.

Yet often the two judges will give dissenting opinions. Sometimes they agree, and sometimes they totally disagree. One may say that it was a cold-blooded, premeditated murder; and the other judge may hold that legally it should not be considered a murder at all.

There are such tremendous differences in men's capacity to understand things and to decide wisely. I am not talking of persons of corrupt character, men who take bribes and render wrong judgements for that reason, but of sincere, earnest judges who desire to see justice served, who wish to fulfil the responsibilities of their high office with the utmost conscientiousness. Even in persons of such honourable intent, we find differences of opinion.

Therefore it is unwise to make differences of opinion a ground for conflict, especially a conflict in which the risks involved, the consequences involved, are not of a temporary character, are not of a trifling nature, but are serious things relating to matters of life and death in this world and to punishment or reward in hell or heaven after the departure of the soul from the physical body.

Unanimity of opinion is unobtainable even with regard to secular things; let alone in matters relating to the world beyond, about which there is no possibility of agreement. Yet that demand is often made in the name of religion.

Religious feuds, denominational feuds, sectarian feuds, and so on are not justified from the standpoint of common sense. But the persons who encourage such conflicts allege that they have no option in the matter, that their sense of loyalty to the Lord and to the particular religion they believe in demands of them that intolerant attitude. Yet, in my opinion, no scripture supports any such view.

In the sacred texts of all the various religions in the world, the fundamental and basic principles are of an ethical character. The foundation is moral. The stress is on personal goodness, purity of heart, and so on. These are the things emphasized.

Other matters, where differences are to be found, concern ritual, ceremonial, and other externals. And these externals vary. They are bound to vary so long as human minds are differently constituted. And that will be the case until the very end of the world. There are different inclinations, different tastes, different capacities; therefore differences of opinion are inevitable. Any attempt to rule, to dictate, on matters where faith is the chief element involved is unreasonable.

I am not putting myself in the position of a critic who studies texts in order to pick holes here and there; I am a student of religion. As a reader of the scriptures of the various religions in the world, I have been noting from time to time not merely the clear parallelism, the close harmony between the teachings of one religion and another so far as fundamental ideas go, but much more than that. It is practically perfect identity, with regard to basic matters. The principles are the same; the foundation is the same. The whole groundwork is ethical.

For example, Christ said : "Blessed are the pure in heart : for they shall see God." In another context he told us : "In my Father's house are many mansions" —an informative rather than an ethical statement. One may interpret the latter passage as meaning there are different kinds and gradations and degrees and intermediate degrees and sub-degrees of level in regard to the various heavens. But in the passage : "Blessed are the pure in heart : for they shall see God," there is no qualification, no implication that non-Christians are unable to see God or that they are consigned to an inferior heaven—one that might be supposed to be the proper place for an inferior kind of candidate for heaven.

Jesus tells us that "seeing" God, that is to say, the actual experiencing of God's presence and not merely faith in His existence, is possible for all men who are pure in heart.

Christ thunders forth his fulminations against the Sadducees and the Pharisees because they had no sincerity of faith, no purity of heart, but engaged in religious pomp and ceremony merely for the purpose of "showing off".

Similar texts against hypocrisy are found in all other scriptures. The Bhagavad Gitā speaks of the religious impostor, one whose profession of belief is high but whose personal life is low — an insult to the Deity within him.

Nowadays men use the words "religious toleration" constantly in their talks, in an effort to show that they are superior to the medieval bigots. "We are not like those who fought the Crusades or who permitted the Spanish Inquisition," they say. But I feel that the idea of religious toleration is not of a satisfactory character.

When we talk of religious toleration, what do we mean by it ? We are not burning living bodies, as people did centuries ago. Are we therefore superior ? Well, that may be granted. We have to be thankful even for small mercies, when they come. And from the standpoint we may say that the present attitude of religious toleration is better than the fanatical spirit of the past.

But is not the word 'toleration' itself an insult to people of all religions not our own ? What do we generally "tolerate" ? It is what is evil, what is injurious; we don't say we tolerate a good thing. And when we speak of religious toleration as the proper description of our feelings towards adherents of other faiths, we offhand and beforehand condemn their religions as inferior to our own. We like to think that we are broad-minded enough, civilized enough, and cultured enough to 'tolerate' other religions.

The Hindu Vedas state that it is not passive neutrality, it is not toleration, that is wanted; it is something more. What is that something more ? Positive coordination and cooperation with people of other religions and denominations.

I frequently say, in my discourses and writings: "I have no quarrel with any religion, any denomination, any sect, or any sub-sect. My only quarrel is with quarrelling, and quarreling in the name of religion." Religion, which ought to be a unifying force, has so often in history acted just to the contrary : as a disintegrating force, causing bloodshed and so on. Our texts say that a religion which comes into conflict with other religions in the name of faith is not a true religion; it is a pseudo religion.

Just as each of us claims the right to follow his own path, to have freedom of worship and freedom of thought in religious matters, so we should grant to others a similar liberty. Matters of discussion are on a different plane. If we find that a person is thinking along wrong lines, there is nothing objectionable about our attempting to persuade and convince him by means of argument and exposition. But to insist that what I have come to as the right decision in a certain matter must be accepted by all, at my dictation, is tyranny, is a denial of liberty to others.

The greatest philosophers and the greatest scientists in the world today are not yet agreed even about the continuance of the soul after its departure from the physical body. As regards the existence of God, the existence of the soul, the existence of heaven and hell, and future rewards and punishments, there are vast differences of opinion. Even a person who has the highest moral conviction, who is completely satisfied that he is in the right in such and such a respect, will have to tell you that at the last moment there is at least one little step or perhaps a series of steps to be got over; a gulf to be bridged. And that bridge must be supplied by faith.

Often a sacred text admits of two or more interpretations. Each person, according to his own intellectual calibre, his own tendencies, trends and associations, forms his own opinion. If I am asked whether that is the right one or this is the right one, I may say that both seem to be quite consistent with the central doctrine of the scripture in question. Both views appear to be equally permissible; but I may prefer or believe in one interpretation rather than the other. This is the undogmatic attitude the philosopher and the scientist take.

The philosopher and the scientist, convinced as they may be

of the rightness of their views, will not tell you that there is no element of faith required at all. The element of faith is required. And when that element of faith comes into the picture, it automatically means that differences of opinion are bound to arise.

It is not as between one religion and another, but as between different sects of one religion and different sects of another religion. For example, in the Hindu scriptures, we have three paths given for spiritual aspirants. Each man follows a particular path, one that is most suitable to himself. The individual bias, the personal temperamental idiosyncrasy, is taken into consideration. We call these paths Karma Yoga, Bhakti Yoga and Jñāna Yoga.

Westerners may have the idea that these three paths are peculiar to Hinduism, characteristic of the Vedic religion only. But, as a matter of fact, we find that counterparts of these three paths are found in the New Testament. Christ's own evangelists, St. James and St. Peter, were exponents of what we call the Karma Marga or the Law of Karma — the path of works, the performance of this and that duty, religious rituals, and so on.

St. John emphasized Bhakti Yoga, the path of faith, devotion, and love. "God is love." That is how John described the Creator.

St. Paul stressed Jñāna Yoga, the path of wisdom and illumination, in which the devotee transcends the small joys and sorrows of ordinary life and is conscious only of God. In this path all actions are done with quietness and calmness, as duties that have fallen upon the devotee, and are performed without passion, excitement, dislike, partiality, and so on.

The Lord's own apostles make use of different kinds of arguments; sometimes it seems as if the evangelists differed in their views. But that is a wrong notion. I will tell you how I have explained to myself the differences in the teachings of St. James and St. Peter on the one side, St. John on the second side, and St. Paul on the third. The differences are called for by the varying needs of the persons to whom the evangelists are addressing themselves.

The preacher has to prescribe for his flock just as the doctor prescribes for his patients. Conditions have to be taken into account; the exigencies and requirements of the situation may be different in various places, with different groups of people, and so on; and such conditions have to be catered to by the evangelist. Just as a doctor prescribes certain medicines and a certain diet for a heart-disease patient, and a different regimen for a man afflicted with diabetes, so each evangelist takes into account the diagnosis he has made of the condition of his pupils. He considers all the factors and decides his plan of treatment accordingly. There is no question of antagonism between one and another spiritual regimen; each is prescribed for a different condition.

The case is similar with science and religion. Nowadays we hear much about a supposed division between them. There is no reasonable ground for any quarrel. A person who, in the name of theology or philosophy, tries to ignore the values of science automatically dubs his own religious thought as unscientific and therefore unacceptable to thinking people. The greatest disservice one can do to religion is to divorce it from the secular side of life.

The Hindu scriptures state that every branch of knowledge, including the positive sciences, is an integral part of a religious education. The Vedas instruct us in anatomy, physiology, hygiene, sanitation, medicine, surgery, engineering, military science, music, art, architecture, law, physics, astronomy, the highest branches of mathematics, and so on. All these come in under the name of religious education. There is no opposition between science and religion; all knowledge is one.

Similarly, with regard to tribe and tribe, race and race, East and West, and so on — all differences between them can be adjusted by wisdom. Sometimes Christian missionaries, talking in the name of Jesus, denounce the peoples of China, Japan, India, and other Eastern countries, and an expression often used is the "Wily Oriental". The preachers evidently forget the historical fact that Christ, their Lord and Master and Saviour, was an Oriental. Sweeping generalizations about races and religions are responsible for much of the misunderstanding on earth today.

So, when we think of attaining world peace and world prosperity, we should remember that there is no inherent conflict between one religion and another religion, between science and religion, or between East and West. All men are component parts of the same whole; there is no possibility of divorcing one from another.

We find that the spiritual and the temporal are inextricably intertwined. The temporal, that, is, matter, is the medium through which Spirit manifests itself, and Spirit is that which manifests itself through the medium of matter. There can be no quarrel between the two; they are interconnected.

It is for us to think carefully, to avoid prejudices and prepossessions, all kinds of partialities and hatreds, and to attune ourselves to the Infinite Lord of the Universe, He who is both transcendent and immanent. If we make our approach on spiritual lines like this, the difficulties that are brought forward from other standpoints will be easy to overcome. The obstacles will be quickly surmounted. We will sit together with the determination to achieve peace. Where there's a will there's a way, and we can find that way. It is our duty to find it.

If we do not succeed, the responsibility is not ours. If we perform our duty, and fail, we will still have the satisfaction that we did the best we could under the circumstances there would be no reason for any kind of regret, self-accusation, and so on. Such are the comforts of a spiritual approach.

I frequently give the example of a tree and of the human body to indicate how we should coordinate and cooperate with one another. In the seed are found all the various portions relating to the tree : the trunk, the branches, the leaves, the flowers, and the fruit. Each is different in size, in position, in shape, in colour, in functions, in therapeutical qualities, and so on. And yet, behind all the diversity is this unity : they are parts of the same tree. Similarly with regard to the human body; it possesses many parts, many limbs and organs, having different locations, sizes, shapes, colours, and functions. But they are not, therefore, antagonistic to one another. They form one beautiful and harmonious whole.

If human beings recognize their essential harmony and interdependence, the chiei source of trouble on earth will be eliminated. By such recognition of the truth, men will awaken within themselves the fount of wisdom that will dissolve all their difficulties.

The message of the sages of India is '(Om) Śāntiḥ, Śāntiḥ Śāntiḥ (peace)'. Christ also said : "Blessed are the peacemakers: For they shall be called the children of God."* The world will have peace only when peoples of all faiths work together for the same purpose: each contributing its quota, its own quality and distinctive genius, according to its highest capacity, for the enduring welfare of the world.

We have reached a state just now, with regard to nuclear weapons, in which it is not a question of this or that particular race or nationality or tribe or country : it is a question of humanity itself. Man, with all his past achievements, his present glories, and his future potentialities, is in imminent danger of being wiped off the face of the earth.

That is the state of affairs to which we have come. If our intellect, which gives us our superiority over other sentient beings, can take us no farther than our present situation, it is a shameful admission, one that will leave us responsible for an utter catastrophe.

We should make up our minds that we are going to achieve peace. If we are determined to do it, God will surely bless our efforts and crown them with success. This is the message that I would have you carry home in your hearts, ponder over, and, as far as humanly possible, make the working principle of your lives from moment to moment.

Once again, I pray to the Almighty; I appeal to all concerned—students, professors, persons in authority—to put themselves in this frame of mind. There is no question of harmonizing; the harmony is already there, for all men are children of the One Father. What is necessary is to realize that harmony and bring it into manifestation in the best manner possible, a manner worthy of the human race.

Once again, I appeal to the individual as such. With my prayers to God, I conclude with this thought:

OM ŚĀNTIḤ ŚĀNTIḤ ŚĀNTIḤ

* St Matthew (The Sermon on the Mount)

Appendix I

RELEVANT SANSKRIT TEXTS

(Conveying ideas discussed on p. 73 ff.)

It is difficult to say which particular Vedānta texts His Holiness had in mind. The identity of Brahman (God) and Ātmā (Self) is the central theme of the Upaniṣads and other Vedānta literature. Almost every Vedānta text can be taken to convey the identity of Brahman and Ātmā. Some Vedānta texts propounding divinity of Self and the need and mode of Self-realization are given here.

1.* Paricchinnam ivājñānāt tannāśe sati kevalaḥ,
Svayam prakāśate hy ātmā meghāpāye 'ṁśumān iva.

Ātmabodha, 41 of Śaṅkara

* Vinoba Bhave has preferred 'avicchinnam' in place of this word.

The self appears divided (many) owing to ignorance. On removal of ignorance, the Self shines by itself, alone, like the sun after the clouds have dispersed.

2. Yadi deham pṛthakkṛtya citi viśrāmya tiṣṭhasi,
Adhunaiva sukhī śānto bandhamukto bhaviṣyasi.

Aṣṭāvakra Gītā I-4

If you detach yourself from the body and rest in intelligence, you will at once be happy, peaceful and free from bondage.

3. Praṇavo dhanuḥ śaro hy ātmā Brahma tallakṣyam ucyate,
Apramattena veddhavyam śaravat tanmayo bhavet.

Muṇḍakopaniṣad II-2-4

'Om' is the bow, Self the arrow, and Brahman (God) the target. With utmost concentration one should aim and become one with Him (God), just as the arrow becomes imbedded in the target.

4. "Ya ātmāpahatapāpmā vijaro vimṛtyur viśoko vijighatso 'pipāsaḥ satyakāmaḥ satyasaṅkalpaḥ so 'nveṣṭavyaḥ sa vijijñāsitavyaḥ—

Chāndogyopaniṣad VIII-7-1

The Self which is sinless, ageless, free from death and sorrow, not subject to hunger and thirst, (which has) pure desires and intentions, that (self) is to be fought for and realized.

5. "...ātmā vā are draṣṭavyaḥ śrotavyo mantavyo nididhyāsitavyo Maitreyi..."

Bṛhadāraṇyakopaniṣad II-4-5

O Maitreyi, the Self is to be seen (realised), investigated (with the aid of guru and the scriptures), (its existence and nature) tested (decided on) with the aid of reason and with conviction meditated upon..."

See "three steps of spiritual inquiry" in the index and the interpretation by His Holiness of this passage in the body of the book.

6. Iha ced avedīd atha satyam asti,
na ced ihāvedīn mahatī vinaṣṭih.

Kenopaniṣad II-5

If man realizes Self in this life, his life becomes fruitful otherwise a great calamity (unending cycle of birth, old age and death) is in store for him.

7. Yathā somyaikena mṛtpiṇḍena sarvam mṛṇmayam vijñātam syād vācārambhaṇam vikāro nāmadheyam mṛttiketyeva satyam.

Chāndogyopaniṣad VI-1-4

O dear, by knowing one lump of clay, all things made of clay are known, the modification is in name only which has origin in speech. Only the clay is real. [Similarly all this is Brahman (= Ātman) only, and the apparent modification of Brahman into things of the world is unreal. This idea is conveyed in several texts that follow (not quoted here).]

8. Aṅguṣṭhamātraḥ puruso 'ntarātmā
sadā janānām hṛdaye sanniviṣṭaḥ,
Tam svāc charīrāt pravṛhen
muñjādiveṣīkām dhairyeṇa,
Tam vidyāc chukram amṛtam
tam vidyāc chukram amṛtam iti.

Kaṭhopaniṣad II-3-17

The Self (when treated as covered by nescience) is thumbsized and always resides in the heart of man. One should, with perseverance, extricate it from his body like the stalk of grass from the outer sheaths and should know it as the effulgent Brahman (God).

9. Jñānena tu tadajñānam yeṣām nāśitamātmanaḥ,
Teṣām ādityavaj jñānam prakāśayati tat param.

Gitā V-16

For those who have removed their ignorance (which is responsible for infatuation with the worldly objects) with the aid of (discerning) knowledge, the knowledge illumines the ultimate reality (Self or Brahma) as the sun (lights up the world).

10. Dantini dāruvikāre
dāru tirobhavati so 'pi tatraiva,
Jagati tathā Paramātmā
Paramātmanyapi jagat tirodhatte.

Svātmanirūpaṇam by Śaṅkara

In an elephant made of wood, the wood is not noticed but is still there. So also in the world the God (is there though unnoticed) and the world also disappears in God.

Appendix II

HIGHLIGHTS OF THE AMERICAN TOUR

(February 4—April 29, 1958)

* indicate Lecture included in this book

1. February 4	Guruji arrived in New York alongwith Shri C.M. Trivedi and Smt. Manjula Trivedi. He was received by Mr. T.A. Raman, Director of Information United Nations and a Welcoming Committee of New Yorkers. After resting for few hours his party emplaned for Los Angeles, arriving there at 10-17 p.m. the same day.
2. February 4	At Los Angeles Guruji was received by Shri Shri Shri Daya Mata and a party of Monks and sisters of the S.R.F. order.
*3. February 6	Guruji received newsmen at a press conference in the hall of the S.R.F. Centre at Mt. Washington, California, and also gave a radio-interview.
*4. February 7	Guruji addressed students and faculty at Pepperdine College, Los Angeles, on 'World Peace.'
*5. February 8	At 5.0 p.m. Guruji gave a talk on "Spiritual Inquiry" to the Monks of the S.R.F. Mt. Washington, India Centre and Lake Shrine.
*6. February 9	Guruji spoke at S.R.F. Church of all Religions in Hollywood on "Light from Ancient India" (Extracts from this lecture appeared in the S.R.F. Magazine, March-April, 1958).
*7. February 9	In the evening Guruji spoke on 'Karma Yoga' at Community Methodist Church, West Wood.
*8. February 10	Guruji gave an interview to Dr. William Hornaday, Minister of Church of Religious Science at the radio station K.F.I. The interview was broadcast in two parts in the 10 p.m. programme "This thing called life", on

	11th and 13th February. The broadcast was also picked up for rebroadcast to U.S. Armed Forces in Europe and in the Far East.
*9. February 11	Guruji spoke at St. Monica College on "India's Role in the Modern World."
10. February 12	Guruji spoke on "Practical Methods of World Peace" at Santa Barbara College, University of California.
11. February 13	Guruji visited Encinitas and was received by the Vice President, the members of the S.R.F. World Brotherhood Colony in Encinitas.
12. February 13	He went to San Diego where he lectured on "Practical Methods of World Peace" at the San Diego State College.
13. February 14	Guruji spoke on "Basic Unity of All Religions" at the San Diego State College. The lecture was broadcast on the evening of Sunday the 16th February.
14. February 15	Guruji visited the Vedanta Society in Hollywood on Saturday and gave a discourse on the "Meaning of Vedānta."
*15. February 15	In the evening he attended a reception sponsored by the S.R.F, at S.R.F. India Hall, Hollywood, and addressed the Hindu Community assembled there.
16. February 16	Guruji spoke at the Church of Religious Science on "Practical Methods of World Peace."
*17. February 17	He gave another discourse on "Practical Methods of World Peace" at the Los Angeles City College.
*18. February 18	Guruji appeared in a T.V. Programme "Greet the People" over K.T.L.A.—T.V., Los Angeles.
19. February 19	He gave a discourse on "Karma Yoga" at a Faculty Club Luncheon at California Institute of Technology in Pasadena.

*20.	February 19	In the afternoon Guruji gave a demonstration of Vedic Mathematics at the California Institute of Technology.
21.	February 20	Guruji spoke on "World Peace" at the Los Angeles State College.
*22.	February 20	Same evening he gave a public lecture at the University of California in Los Angeles.
23.	February 21	Guruji spoke on "World Peace" at the Pasadena City College.
*24.	February 21	Same evening Guruji appeared in a T.V. programme called "Hank Weaver News" on KABC—TV, Los Angeles.
25.	February 22	Guruji attended a reception in the home of Mrs. Leiland Atherton Irish, and gave an informal talk on "Practical Methods of World Peace" and on "George Washington."
26.	February 23	In the evening he appeared in a public lecture at Wilshire Ebell Theater in Los Angeles and spoke on "Basic Unity of All Religions."
27.	February 24	Guruji left Los Angeles for Fresno, California.
28.	February 25	Guruji spoke at Fresno State College.
29.	February 25	He gave another lecture on "World Fellowship" in the college auditorium.
30.	February 26	Guruji spoke on "Religious approach to World Peace" at Mills College, Oakland, California.
*31.	February 26	Guruji went to Palo Alto. At the Stanford University he gave a talk on "Indian Philosophy."
32.	February 28	Guruji appeared in public lecture at the American Academy of Asian Studies, San Fransisco. He gave a discourse on "Vedānta Philosophy".
33.	March 1	Guruji cancelled his intended Lecture Tour across U.S.A. on account of the illness of Shri C.M. Trivedi, his aide.
*34.	March 4,	Guruji gave another lecture and demonstration on "Vedic Mathematics" at the California Institute of Technology, Pasadena.

35. March 10 — He gave another lecture at Cal Tech demonstrating the application of the rules of Vedic Mathematics to Calculus.

36. March 18 — Guruji visited Ananda Ashrama in La Cresenta and spoke on "Vedānta Philosophy."

37. March 13 — Guruji gave a discourse at the East West Culture Centre, Los Angeles on "The Upaniṣads."

38. March 20 — Bhakti Yoga was the topic of a discourse given by Guruji in the S.R.F. Chapel of Mt. Washington.

39. March 22 — Guruji left Los Angeles for Washington.

40. March 22 — Guruji was interviewed in the plane at Amon Carter Field, Fort Worth, Texas by Ed. Johnson who wrote a report of the interview in the *Star-Telegram*.

41. March 23 — After an overnight stay in Washington Guruji flew to Roanoke (Virginia) en route to the Washington and Lee University, Lexington (Virginia). He gave an interview for W.S.L.S.-T.V. (Dr. Toynbee was visiting lecturer at Washington and Lee University during spring semester. . Dr. Paul Hayner, Asst. Professor of Philosophy at the University had arranged for Guruji's lectures and a discussion with Dr. Toynbee).

42. March 24 — In the Lee Memorial Chapel Guruji spoke on "Basic Unity of All Religions."

43. March 25 — Guruji spoke on "World Peace" in the same institution.

44. March 26 — Guruji had a discussion with Dr. Arnold Toynbee. Some highlights of the discussion appeared in the May, 1958 issue of the S.R.F. Magazine.

45. March 28 — At the Rutger's University New Brunswick, New Jersey, Guruji's lectures were sponsored by the International Students Club, the Graduate Student's Council, the International Relations Club, and the Philosophean Society.

In the evening of 28th March, Guruji spoke on "The Basic Unity of All Religions."

46. March 28 Guruji was interviewed by Staff Correspondent of *Newark Evening News.*

47. March 30 Guruji visited the U.S. Naval Academy at Annapolis, Maryland and gave a discourse on "A Comparision between the Hindu and Christian Faiths."

48. March 31 Guruji and his party arrived at New York. He was welcomed by Shri T.A. Raman, Director of Public Information United Nations. Guruji stayed in 'Cambridge House', New York.

49. April 1 In the morning Guruji met Overseas Press Club Members at a Press conference.

50. April 2 Guruji attended another Press Conference and appealed for world peace, a write up about which appeared in *New York Times* on 3rd April.

51. April 2 Guruji spoke at the Theosophical Society in Warren Austin Auditorium, World Affairs Centre — Carnegie Building. The subject was "The Wisdom of the Vedas."

52. April 7 Guruji spoke on "Buddhism" at the American Buddhist Academy, New York.

53. April 8 Guruji addressed the students of Fairleigh Dickinson University, Teaneck, New Jersey. The theme of his address was 'Universal peace and understanding.'

54. April 10 Guruji spoke on "Man's Fateful Choice at Mid-Twentieth Century" in Casa Italiana Hall of Columbia University, New York.

55. April 11 Guruji was interviewed by the V.O.A. The interview was also broadcast on the All India Radio.

56. April 14 Guruji was earlier interviewed by *Newsweek.* A write up of the interview appeared in the 14th April issue of the *Newsweek.*

57. April 15	Guruji visited Teachers' College of Connecticut Berlin, New Britain and at 10-30 a.m. spoke on "Spiritual Approach to World Peace."
58. April 15	At a Luncheon meeting at 12-15 p.m. he spoke on "Basic Unity of All Religions".
59. April 15	He also gave two T.V. interviews and one Radio interview.
60. April 17	Guruji met U.N. Correspondents from several countries.
61. April 18	Guruji visited Rama Krishna Vivekananda Centre, New York, and gave a discourse on the "Essentials of Vedānta."
62. April 19	Guruji spoke on "One Race One World" at the Y.W.C.A.—Harlem.
63. April 20	Guruji gave a demonstration of Vedic Maths for the N.B.C.—T.V.
64. April 20	At the Community Church, New York Guruji spoke on "The Spiritual Nature of Man in the Modern World."
65. April 24	At the U.N. Building, Guruji had an interview with Canadian Broadcasting Company.
66. April 27	Guruji was interviewed by the Correspondent of the Columbia Broadcasting System.
67. April 29	Guruji left for India.

BIBLIOGRAPHY

1. *Aṣṭādhyāyī (with Śikṣā, Paribhāṣā-pāṭha, Gaṇapāṭha, Dhātupāṭha and Liṅgānuśāsana-pāṭha* Khemraj Sri Krishnadas, Bombay 1897.
2. *Aṣṭāvakragītā* Ed. by Swami Nityaswarupananda, Advaita Ashrama, Almora 1953.
3. *Ātmabodha* by Śaṅkara. See reference Nos. 8 and 18.
4. *Autobiography of a Yogi* by Paramahansa Yogananda, Self Realization Fellowship, Los Angeles. 1946. JAICO, 5th Edn. 1972.
5. *Brahma-sūtra-śāṅkara-bhāṣyam* Ed. by Narayana Ram Acarya, Nirnaya Sagar Press, Bombay 1948.
6. *Brahma Sūtra : The Philosophy of Spiritual Life* by S. Radhakrishnan. George Allen & Unwin Ltd. London 1960.
7. *Bṛhadāraṇyakopaniṣad* with Śāṅkarabhāṣya and translation in Hindi. Gita Press, Gorakhpur 1942.
8. *Bṛhatstotra Ratnākara*, Venkateshwar Steam Press, Bombay.
9. *Browning, Poetry and Prose* selected by Simen Nowell Smith, Rupert Hart Davis, London 1967.
10. *Canterbury Tales* by Chaucer see reference no. 12.
11. *Chāndogyopaniṣad* with Śānkarabhāṣya and Hindi translation, Gita Press, Gorakhpur 1954.
12. *Chaucer*, Complete Works Ed. by Walter W. Skeats, Oxford University Press 1973.
13. *Cymbeline* by William Shakespeare, see reference no. 39.
14. *Devyaparādhakṣamāpaṇastotram* by Śaṅkara, see reference no. 30.
15. *Dhātupāṭha*. See reference no. 1
16. *Durgāsaptaśatī* Gita Press, Gorakhpur 1951.
17. *Gītā* (*Śrimad-Bhagavad-Gītā*) with Śānkarabhāṣya and Hindi translation Gita Press, Gorakhpur 1941.
18. *Gurubodha* (selections from poems of Śaṅkara) by Vinoba Bhave, Parandhama Vidyapitha Prakasana, Pavnar 1957 (Maharastra) India.

19. *Iśopaniṣad* with Śānkarabhāṣya and Hindi translation, Gītā Press, Gorakhpur 1951.
20. *Kaṭhopaniṣad* with Śāṅkarabhāṣya and Hindi translation, Gita Press, Gorakhpur 1951.
21. *Kenopaniṣad* with Śāṅkarabhāsya and Hindi translation, Gita Press, Gorakhpur 1951.
22. *Kissa-i-Sanjan* Ed by Rustam Barjorjee Paymaster, The Fort Printing Press, Bombay 1915.
23. *Mahābhārata*. Gita Press, Gorakhpur, October 1956.
24. *Māṇḍūkyopaniṣad* (*and Māṇḍūkyakārikā*), with Śānkarabhāṣya and Hindi translation, Gita Press. Gorakhpur 1942.
25. *Manu-Smṛti* with commentary of Kulluka Bhaṭṭa (10th Edn) Ed. by Narayana Rama Acarya, Nirnaya Sagar Press, Bombay 1946.
26. *A Manual of Buddhism for advanced students* by Mrs Rhys Davids D. Litt., M. A., The Sheldon Press 1932.
27. *Muṇḍakopaniṣad* with Śānkarabhāṣya and Hindi translation, Gita Press, Gorakhpur 1952.
28. *Othello* by William Shakespeare, see reference no. 39.
29. *Raghuvaṁśa* of Kālidāsa Ed. by Narayana Rama Acarya Nirnaya Sagar Press, Bombay 1948.
30. *Ṛgveda-Saṁhitā*, Ed. by Śripāda Dāmodara Sātavalekar, Svādhyāya Maṇḍal, Aundh (Maharastra) 1940.
31. *Śri Śaṅkarācārya* by Baladeva Upādhyāya (Second Edition) Hindustānī Academy Nagari Press 1963. (Mahānuśāsana by Śaṅkara is given at 238-239 of this book).
32. *Stotra-Bhāratī-kaṇṭhahāra* Vol. I By Jagadguru Śaṅkarācārya Srī Bhāratī Kṛṣṇa Tīrtha, Bharatiya Vidya Bhawan, Bombay 1966.
33. *Stotra-Ratnāvalī* Gita Press, Gorakhpur 1971.
34. *Svātmanirūpaṇam* by Śaṅkara, see reference no. 18.
35. *Śvetāśvataropaniṣad* with Śāṅkarabhāṣya and Hindi translation, Gita Press, Gorakhpur.
36. *Taittiriyopaniṣad* with Śāṅkarabhāṣya and Hindi translation, Gita Press, Gorakhpur 1943.
37. *Tattvadipikā* (*Citsukhī*) Udāśīna Sanskṛta Vidyālaya, Banaras 1956.

38. *The Holy Bible* (in three volumes), The Nonesuch Press, London 1963.

39. *The Works of William Shakespeare* with introduction by Sir Ernest Barker, George Newnes Ltd. London.

40. *Vedic Mathematics*
by Jagadguru Swāmi Śrī Bhāratī Kṛṣṇa Tīrthaji Mahāraj, Benaras Hindu University Press, 1965. Motilal Banarsidass, Delhi 1975.

41. *Vivekacūḍāmaṇi* of Śaṅkara, Gita Press, Gorakhpur 1963.

GLOSSARY

adhikāribheda difference in capacities of students or devotees (which determines the type of instruction or the path of God-realization prescribed for a student or devotee).

ādhina subservient to

advaita monism; absolutist creed; the philosophical system (expounded by Śaṅkara) which holds that there is only one reality that is Self (Ātmā which is identical with Brahman or God).

ānanda joy, pure bliss; one of the attributes of Self and God.

aṅga (s) books on pronunciation, astronomy, prosody, etymology, grammar and rules for ceremonial acts used as aid in the study of Vedas.

asat non-being; non-existence; unreal; is not.

asatya falsehood; false.

ātmajñāna knowledge of self; self-realization.

āyurveda science of life; science of medicine, surgery etc.

bhakta devotee

bhakta-adhīna One who is subservient to his devotees.

bhakta-vatsala One who loves his devotees.

bhakti devotion

bhaktikāṇḍa portion of Hindu scriptures dealing with devotion to God.

bhaktimārga path of love or devotion to God

bhaktiyoga same as bhaktimārga, considered as a kind of yoga.

bhramarakīṭanyāya maxim of the bee (and the insect), a maxim based on the belief that the larva continuously thinks of the bee and becomes a bee. The maxim is used to bring home the point that contemplation of God leads to God-realization.

Brahman the ultimate reality transcending the universe (identical with mā Self in Vedānta).

brahmajñāna knowledge of Brahman; God-realization; Self-realization.

Caitra lunar month of the Hindu Calendar in which the full moon appears near the star Citrā (Spica in Virgo). It falls in March-April of the Gregorian calendar.

cit pure consciousness; perfect knowledge; one of the attributes of Self and God.

deva (s) shining, gods in Hindu Mythology.

devatās gods in Hindu mythology.

devī (s) goddesses in Hindu Mythology.

devītva goddesshood, divine quality in women.

dhanurveda science of archery; military science.

dharma duty, duties enjoined by scriptures; religion.

dharmaśāstra Smṛti; Hindu scriptures dealing with law, ethics, social codes and rules of expiation.

duḥkha misery.

dveṣa hatred, prejudice against (a person or view).

gāndharva Veda science of music

gaṇita mathematics.

guru destroyer of ignorance (of the disciple); master, teacher.

jagat universe.

jijñāsā desire to know.

jīvātmā individual soul.

jñāna knowledge, illumination.

jñānakāṇḍa portion of Hindu scriptures dealing with knowledge or absolute illumination as the way to God-realization.

jñānamārga path of illumination.

jñānayoga same as jñānaṃārga considered as a yoga.

jñānī One who has attained knowledge (realization of God or Self) or absolute illumination.

karma deeds; works; a theory which says that a man has to enjoy or suffer the results of his past and present good or bad deeds in this and future life.

karmakāṇḍa the portion of Hindu scriptures enjoining performance of rituals and other duties; rituals and duties enjoined in scriptures.

karmamārga path of works or sincere performance of duty as a way to God-realization.

karmayoga sincere performance of duty without any attachment to the fruits of action which are surrendered to God.

lakṣaṇa characteristic.

mahāpralaya Doomsday. End of the universe according to Hindus when it dissolves into the ultimate reality.

mārga path, road.

mārjāraśiśunyāya maxim of the cat and kitten exemplifying absolute trust of the devotee in God like helpless kitten's absolute reliance on the mother cat.

markaṭakiśoranyāya maxim illustrating devotee's total reliance on God and the role of his own weak effort, like that of the child monkey clinging to its mother.

maṭhāmnāya Texts handed down by tradition containing rules for conduct of work in monasteries.

mithyā unreal; not ultimately real; delusion.

mithyātva the principle of delusion.

mokṣa liberation from the cycle of births and death; Nirvāṇa.

mūrti icons, shapes.

Nādabrahma God as Sound; Om.

nāmarūpavikāra modification in name and appearance.

nāśa destruction, become invisible.

Navarātra nine nights, first nine days of the bright half of the lunar months Āśvina (Sept-Oct) and Caitra (March-April).

pāpa sin

Paramātmā God, the transcendental Self.

phala fruit, fruit of action.

prabhutva domination, an attribute of Self and God.

Prakṛti Nature

pūjā worship

puṇya merit

pūrṇa perfect.

pūrṇatā perfection.

Puruṣa The Conscious Principle in the Universe (in contradistinction to the inanimate nature—Prakṛti).

rāga attachment, love or partiality in favour of (a person or view).

Ṛtam inviolable order of things; ethical law governing the universe which produces results of good and bad action.

Śabdabrahma God as Word; Om.

sādhaka One who pursues spiritual discipline leading to Self-realization.

sādhanā self-discipline practised as a means for attaining goal (of Self-realization).

sākṣātkāra realization, to come face to face with.

śakti potent power, energy, manifestations deified in Hindu Mythology.

Śakti Consort of Śiva; She represents the active principle of Paramātmā (God).

sampūrṇatā all round perfection.

Sanātana Dharma Eternal law; orthodox Hinduism.

Śaṅkarācārya pontifical head of monastery established by Śaṅkara.

Śāṅkara Vedānta the system of monism taught by Śaṅkara.

Sāṅkhya path of knowledge.

śānti peace.

śāstra (*s*) scriptures (of Hindus), Works by ancient sages on Hindu law, ethics and philosophy, grammar, prosody, poetics, drama, etc. are also known as Śāstra.

sat eternal existence; an attribute of Self and the God.

satī the custom (not prevalent today) of self immolation by the wife ascending the funeral pyre of the dead husband.

śraddhā reverence, faith

sthāpatyaveda science of Civil Engineering.

śuka parrot

sūtra (literally) thread; aphorism.

svarūpa of the nature of.

svātantrya freedom.

tanmātrā (*s*) infinitesimal substances, immediately preceding causes of gross elements; potentials of gross elements which enable the perception of the physical world to take place.

trikālasatya existing in all the the three times—past, present and future; eternally existing.

upalakṣaṇa temporary attribute, passing quality.

Upaniṣad literally secret instructions; the name given to that part of Vedic literature which deals with speculations on the cause of the world, nature of the Self and God etc.

upāsanā devotion, worship.

upāsanā-kāṇḍa portion of Hindu scriptures dealing with devotion and worship.

upāsanāmārga path of devotion.

upavedas subsidiary sciences attached to various Vedas.

Vedāṅga see 'aṅga'

Vedānta literally end of Vedas, Upaniṣads, system of philosophy based on Upaniṣads.

vicāra consideration of the pros and cons; thinking; thought.

yoga discipline of meditation leading to Self-realization.

yukti valid reasoning.

INDEX